Secret Lives of the Dalai Lama

The Untold Story of the Holy Men Who Shaped Tibet, From Pre-History to the Present Day

Alexander Norman

Foreword by

HIS HOLINESS THE DALAI LAMA

DOUBLEDAY

New York • London • Toronto • Sydney • Auckland

⬭D

DOUBLEDAY

Copyright © 2008 by Alexander Norman
Foreword Copyright © 2008 by Tenzin Gyatzo,
the Fourteenth Dalai Lama of Tibet

Originally published in hardcover in Great Britain
as *Holder of the White Lotus* by Little, Brown, London, in 2008.
This edition published by arrangement with Little, Brown.

Published in the United States by Doubleday Religion,
an imprint of the Crown Publishing Group,
a division of Random House, Inc., New York.
www.crownpublishing.com
www.doubledayreligion.com

DOUBLEDAY and the DD colophon are registered trademarks
of Random House, Inc.

Library of Congress Cataloging-in-Publication Data
Norman, Alexander.
[Holder of the white lotus]
Secret lives of the Dalai Lama : the untold story of the holy men
who shaped Tibet, from pre-history to the present day /
Alexander Norman ; foreword by the Dalai Lama.
p. cm.
Originally published: Holder of the
White Lotus. London : Little, Brown, 2008.
Includes bibliographical references and index.
1. Dalai lamas—Biography. 2. Dalai lamas—History.
3. Buddhism—China—Tibet—History. I. Title.
BQ7930.N67 2010
294.3'9230922—dc22
[B]   2009035046

ISBN 978-0-385-53070-5

PRINTED IN THE UNITED STATES OF AMERICA

2 4 6 8 10 9 7 5 3 1

First U.S. Edition

For
L. M. N.
with love

Contents

Foreword by His Holiness the Dalai Lama

In this book, Alex Norman, an old personal friend, offers a distinctive "outsider's" view of the history and culture of Tibet. In particular, he brings out the human element in telling the story of the institution of the Dalai Lamas. He has gone to a great deal of trouble to explain how this lineage, commonly associated with Avalokitesvara or Chenrezig, the Bodhisattva embodying compassion, is traditionally traced back to an ancient Indian origin and then how it later developed in Tibet. He shows too how it evolved from being a purely spiritual institution into one that also became deeply involved with the political and cultural life of the country.

While Alex looks unflinchingly at the relative turmoil that characterizes important episodes in Tibetan history, his narrative also shows how Tibetan religious culture developed into a system that faithfully preserves the most complete form of the Indo-Buddhist tradition extant in the world today. It is a tradition derived principally from the great Indian university of Nalanda. At the same time, he shows how Tibet's relationship with her formidable neighbor, China, has existed for well over a thousand years. In

the beginning, during the time of the T'ang dynasty, this relationship was one of equality. A relationship of personal equality also
obtained between the Dalai Lamas and both the Mongol and later
the Manchu Emperors of China.

The fourteen individuals who have carried the title of Dalai
Lama naturally display quite a range of difference between their
personalities. From the gentle and compassionate Gendun Drub,
the first Dalai Lama, through the great scholar and teacher,
Gendun Gyatso, his successor, to the visionary Great Fifth in
the seventeenth century right up to my immediate predecessor
the Great Thirteenth, who worked so hard for the cause of
Tibetan independence, and then to my own case, each has quite
clearly exhibited different personal characteristics. Nevertheless,
in the Tibetan mind, there is also a close association between
Chenrezig and the Dalai Lamas, which reflects a longstanding
special relationship between the Tibetan people and Chenrezig.
Tibetans have a special admiration and faith in Chenrezig
because his unfathomable compassion naturally extends to all
sentient beings without limit or partiality. He shows by example
that qualities such as love, compassion, and the altruistic mind
of enlightenment are like a jewel that overcomes the poverty
and difficulties of cyclic existence, while at the same time
fulfilling the wishes of all sentient beings. When Chenrezig is
referred to as "Holder of the White Lotus," the lotus denotes
wisdom, and while there are various kinds of wisdom, such as
an appreciation of impermanence and a lack of self-sufficient
existence, the main one is the wisdom realizing emptiness.

This book narrates the life story of each of the Dalai Lamas,
situating them in the context of their time. In so doing, it tackles
many difficult and sensitive issues within Tibetan history, many
of which raise important questions. While I do not necessarily
agree with every opinion the author has expressed, I very much
appreciate the frankness he brings to bear in his analysis of these
matters.

Alex Norman is an English gentleman, who, despite our different backgrounds, has been a good friend to me and has helped me in several ways for which I remain grateful. I commend this book to anyone wishing to deepen their knowledge of Tibetan history and culture. It contains insights which, I am sure, will be illuminating even to experts in the field.

March 2008

Acknowledgments

It is my privilege first to thank Tenzin Gyatso, Fourteenth Dalai Lama of Tibet, for lending his support to this project from the outset. He did so in spite of my warning that I intended to tackle several of the most delicate and controversial aspects of Tibetan history. I take it that, by placing his confidence in me in this way, the Dalai Lama was honoring an association and—dare I say it—a friendship that began more than twenty years ago. In the intervening period, it has been my good fortune to work closely with him on two of his more important books as well as to collaborate with the Dalai Lama on several other projects, both spiritual and secular. I desire, therefore, to thank His Holiness for the extraordinary level of trust he has shown me.

Ippolito Desideri, the great Jesuit missionary in Tibet, records the hospitality he was shown by a people he found "clever, kindly, and courteous by nature." I cannot improve on those remarks. I would like, however, to mention a number of people who have offered me the same great courtesy and kindness as was Father Desideri almost three centuries ago. These are Mr. Tendzin Choegyal and his wife Mrs. Rindchen Khandro, Kasur Tenzin Geyche

Tethong, and Dr. Thupten Jinpa Langri, academic adviser to His Holiness and his principal translator into English. Each in their different ways has contributed enormously to my understanding of Tibetan history and culture. I am especially grateful to Dr. Langri, not only for his friendship over all these years but also for his scholarly advice during the research of this book and for his unflagging readiness to help during its writing and editing. He was, furthermore, a most attentive and perceptive reader of the final manuscript. I doubt that I would have undertaken the work had I not been able to rely on his encyclopedic knowledge of Tibetan literature and his deep familiarity with both Tibetan Buddhist and Western philosophical thought. All this is not to mention his personal generosity.

Among the community of Tibetan scholars, I have been kindly assisted by Mr. Tsering Dhondup Gongkatsang of Oxford University, especially in the matter of translation. Professor Samten Karmay responded readily to several requests for assistance. Geshe Lobsang Jhorden [Lhakdor-la] has, over the years, favored me with a great deal of his time. In the UK, Dr. Charles Ramble, university lecturer in the Department of Tibetan and Himalayan Studies at Oxford University, not only made available to me the full resources of his department but also put me in touch with several of the scholars I mention here. And in connection with Oxford's Bodleian Library, I would like to thank Ralf Kramer who, as Librarian of the Indian Institute's Tibetan collection, responded enthusiastically to literally hundreds of requests for assistance.

I was most fortunate to have Professor Don Lopez read the final draft of my manuscript. Not only did he make many useful suggestions, he also saved me from a number of embarrassing mistakes. Those that remain are mine alone. I would also like to acknowledge with gratitude the answers given to specific questions by Professor Paul Williams, Dr. John Peacock, E. Gene Smith, Professor Morris Rossabi and Dr. Susan Whitfield. For his translation from the Russian of Petr Kozlov, I would like to thank Mark Belcher. I have also received much patient assistance from

Mike Gilmour of Wisdom Books; also from David Chilton of Taikoo Books, who enabled me to track down many elusive titles. I am fortunate to be able to count among my friends and acquaintance the following four distinguished writers: Patrick French (author of the matchless *Younghusband*), John F. Burns of the *New York Times*, Professor Charles Taylor of McGill University and Stephen Priest, senior research fellow in philosophy at Blackfriars Hall in Oxford University. My conversations with each of them helped greatly to clarify a number of important issues. I would also like to thank Jane Perkins, who first encouraged me to visit Dharamsala, for her many kindnesses over the years. For her friendship, her efficiency and her reliability in her role as my part-time secretary (I blush at the word), I am hugely indebted to Jane Rasch. There are three others whom I would also like to mention, for their encouragement and faith in me when I first began to work with the Dalai Lama. These are Michael Trend, the late John Curtis and the late Tsewang Topgyal. And for his anonymous but insistent presence in the back of my mind in all my writings about Tibet, I wish to acknowledge the ex-St Paul's (Darjeeling) student whom I met in a hotel in Southern Tibet during the spring of 1988. It was from a brief conversation with him that I came to appreciate the suffering of a whole people.

Finally, I would like to thank several members of my family. My parents, both of whom died during the writing of this book, were both enthusiastic advocates of my literary efforts. David Jenks and Bo Norman contributed importantly in their different ways. My uncle, Sir Torquil Norman, kindly provided the solace of his DH82a, while my brother, Henry Norman, was frequently helpful and always an inspiration. My children Rosie, Edward, and Theo kept me happy. My wife Linda Madeleine kept me sane and gave me all the support in this endeavor that I could have dreamed of.

Blackfriars Hall
Oxford

A *Note on Spelling and Pronunciation*

Tibetan is a language that defies straightforward transliteration, let alone easy pronunciation. As a result, scholars have long puzzled how to render it in the Roman alphabet in a way that shows clearly what the Tibetan word is without sending the reader running for cover. Simply substituting the letters produces terrifying results. Who would ever guess that the words *bstan 'dzin rgya mtsho* are pronounced "Tenzin Gyatso," the name of the present Dalai Lama? Or that *sprul-sku* is to be pronounced "tulkü"? On the other hand, as in most languages, there are many Tibetan words which, though pronounced the same, or very nearly the same, have different spellings and different meanings. Notoriously, the words for *ice*, *shit* and *fat* can all possibly be rendered phonetically as *gyak'ba*. The distinction between them orally is rendered entirely by tone, a distinction impossible to represent in any non-tonal language.

Faced with this difficulty, I have decided to do my best by the non-specialist reader and hazard my own phonetics. For the benefit of those with some familiarity with the language, I have

put, in square brackets, either the generally accepted transliteration or, where it seems desirable, a strict transliteration.

As to pronunciation, where the transliteration does not make
this clear, and where the word appears for the first time, I give
directions by way of footnote.

One other point to which I would like to draw the reader's
attention concerns my use of the word "sect," "school," and "tradition." I use these more or less interchangeably to denote the
various religious groupings within Tibetan Buddhism.

Introduction

As anyone who has done so will testify, to meet the Dalai Lama is to be caught up in a romance it is almost impossible to resist. Granted an audience at his private office, you must first be frisked and vetted by the guards at the gate, your passport surrendered, its details noted. "Purpose of visit?" "Address in Dharamsala?" "Yes, yes, His Holiness will see you on time." Glancing back, you note, perhaps to your sneaking satisfaction, the half-curious, half-envious faces of one or two onlookers. But once inside, registering the air of unhurried order, of discipline and high purpose, you dismiss your feelings of triumph as unworthy. Ushered into a waiting room just inside the gate, you have some time to collect yourself.

In the distance stand the flashing peaks of the Dhauladhar mountain range, heralds of the mighty Himalayas and of the great Tibetan Plateau itself. In the foreground, beyond the lower courtyard, lies a well-tended garden surrounded by a rhododendron grove. And the air—jasmine and orange, apple and rose jostle for your attention, together with a wisp of juniper burned in offering to the gods in a nearby shrine room. A few minutes later, a young official, dapper in traditional Tibetan *chuba* worn over gray flannels and well-polished shoes, leads you across the courtyard and up a flight of steps. To your right, you notice a neat group of buildings on a lower level, forming three sides of a square around an area of lawn. In the middle, a monk official stands conversing with a lay colleague. You then climb a second short flight leading to a well-proportioned building of colonial pattern. This, you gather, is the location of His Holiness's audience chamber.

You now enter what is obviously an anteroom, the windows of which look on to a verandah festooned with baskets of perennial pinks. Looking around, you become aware of an array of display cabinets crowded variously with Tibetan religious statuary and a collection of awards and citations honoring the Dalai Lama, including his Nobel Prize. Next, you notice the silence. It seems so studied as somehow to drown the exuberant chatter of birds outside. Suddenly it is broken by the crash and flurry of an ape bursting along the branches of a tree to land on top of a building. A call goes up from one of the bodyguards and you hear a stone skittering across a corrugated-iron roof. Another flurry; then a pause; then the birds again. But once more their song is caught up in the silence.

A door opens. An Indian family, showily dressed, passes through the room on its way out, the children chattering excitedly. Now it is your turn to meet the earthly manifestation of the god of compassion! The Precious Protector! Holder of the White Lotus!

Few are untouched. Many emerge giddily proclaiming the great man's wisdom, his insight, his compassion—this paragon from Tibet, Land of Snows. As for his Tibetan visitors—why, more than once have I struggled to contain my own feelings seeing the tears of supplicants rendered speechless at the immensity of this dream fulfilled: men and women and children sustained in the perilous journey on foot from Chinese-held

Tibet over vertiginous mountain passes and across snowy wastes at the prospect of a meeting with *Yeshin Norbu*—their Precious Jewel. All too often they have the most pitiful tales to tell—of family and friends who perished from cold and sickness, or who were shot at and killed, wounded or captured on the way.

No one who has witnessed the devotion of the Dalai Lama's fellow countrymen and women can doubt the profundity of the emotion that he is capable of evoking in people's hearts. Nor could anyone who has witnessed it doubt the sincerity and unaffected humanity of the man himself. The pronouncements of the Chinese government—that the Dalai Lama is a "splittist," a "liar," a "wolf in monk's robes"—seem inept to the point of hilarity. Is he not known everywhere for his tireless advocacy of peace? And is not Buddhism itself universally acknowledged for its gentleness, its care for all sentient beings, and for the absence of stridency among its followers? As for Tibetan society, we have it on apparently good authority that it was "ordered for individuals' attainment of evolutionary perfection in Buddhahood." The country itself was "one huge school for enlightenment," its civilization was a "living wisdom tradition." Even now Tibet's emptiness is "sacred space," constituting the "wisdom heart of the world," its people are the "guardians of a storehouse of spiritual treasures," its religion is an "inner science" comprised of the "highest insights" whose practitioners are exponents of "sacred technology." In this view, is not the Dalai Lama a "genius," the earthly embodiment of compassion?[1]

For many years, years during which it was my pride and privilege to collaborate with the Dalai Lama on a number of literary projects (together these occasioned more than two hundred and fifty hours of private interviews), it never occurred to me to question either the integrity of the Dalai Lama or the justice of his cause. I could see for myself that, whatever his doctrinal commitments may be, Tenzin Gyatso is, to paraphrase St. Paul, quite clearly someone who would sooner bless than curse his enemies; who, to the utmost of his ability, seeks to be at peace with everyone; someone who is patient; who is kind; who is neither boastful nor conceited; who is neither rude nor seeks his own advantage; who is always ready to make allowances, to trust, to hope, and, in adversity, to endure whatever trials may come his way.

Of course I was soon aware of a tension between the popular image of the Dalai Lama and the man I came to know. For example, not a few of his Western devotees take seriously the popular epithet used by Tibetans of the Dalai Lama—Thamché Khyenpa [*thamas ched mkhyen pa*]—"all-knowing one," believing that any apparent limitation of his mental faculties is mere show. In connection with this, I once ventured that not a few of his admirers would take it entirely at face value if the Dalai Lama were to say that the moon was made of green cheese. He seemed a little taken aback at this (of course, I was exaggerating to make the point) but replied that if there was any truth in the suggestion, it was precisely because he made no such claims! Nonetheless, the credulity, especially among Westerners, with regard to the Dalai Lama's alleged powers was something I encountered on a regular basis, even though it quickly became apparent to me that, though encyclopedic in many respects, the Dalai Lama's knowledge was reassuringly circumscribed in others.

But still, it took me a long time to recognize that if there is a tension between the popular image of the Dalai Lama and the man I had come to know, there is an even greater tension between the Tibet of popular imagination and that of historical record. But then something happened—an event so astonishing and unexpected that I was forced—at first almost unwillingly—to reassess everything I believed about Tibet and its history, an event that eventually led me to see that, in both cases, the reality is vastly more compelling than the romance.

1

The Tragedy of Lobsang Gyatso

Dharamsala winters are not what they were, but the night they came for Lobsang Gyatso was as bright and bitter cold as anyone could remember. It was four days before Losar, the Tibetan New Year—that of the Fire Ox—or February 4, 1997, according to the Western calendar. Some see significance in the timing. By tradition, it is just before New Year that all the evils and spiritual defilements of the old year are ritually banished.

They came for him—at least half a dozen of them—sometime between six o'clock, when a servant took him a meal, and eight o'clock, when the same man returned, as requested, with tea. The exact time could not be ascertained because, although Lobsang Gyatso had two students with him that evening, no one heard a sound. No one heard a sound even though the monk-professor's room was in an accommodation block shared with more than fifty other students and their teachers—an accommodation block which is, moreover, situated among the most important buildings of the Tibetan refugee community. It is here that the School of Dialectics stands, of which Lobsang Gyatso was principal. It is here that the Tsuglhakhang, the great temple, stands.

It is here that Namgyal, the Dalai Lama's own monastery, stands. And it is here, not a hundred yards from where Lobsang Gyatso was murdered, that the Dalai Lama's private compound stands: the offices of his secretariat, his audience chamber, his own office, his staff quarters, his guard (consisting of both Tibetan and Indian troops) and, at the top of the hill, perhaps another hundred yards away, the Dalai Lama's residence itself. Ordinarily, you would expect a human voice, especially one at the highest pitch of alarm, to carry that far and further. Yet no one heard a sound.

The attack was bestial. Much blood was shed: not just on the bed, where the old man lay dead (Lobsang Gyatso was seventy that year), not just on the floor, where the two younger men were sprawled, but splattered all up the walls as well. There was bound to have been a struggle. They must have known that Lobsang Gyatso was renowned as a fighter in his youth, before he became a monk, and indeed he snatched a bag from one of them. He was still clutching it when he was found. They stabbed him in the eye, they slashed his throat, they plunged a blade deep into his heart. He had almost twenty wounds, any one of which might have been fatal. But he kept hold of that bag.

The two youngsters fared no better. Like their teacher, they received between fifteen and twenty wounds apiece, though when the servant found them, they were both still groaning their lives away into the chill night air. One of them even made it to the hospital, half a mile down the hill; but he only lasted another twenty minutes.

Word of the disaster spread quickly. The police were called, and in their wake followed the local press. Rumors, faithfully reported, abounded. There was talk of a drunken brawl in the basement of the building flaring up out of control. Somehow, Lobsang Gyatso and his students were supposed to have been caught in the crossfire. Or it was the work of the Chinese government, widely known at the time to have been seething at the forthcoming visit of the Dalai Lama to Taiwan. In the opinion of a local Indian businessman, a travel agent, it was all to do with money. The old monk was well known to have recently returned from a trip to Hong Kong. He must have had a lot of cash—donations from the faithful he was so good at persuading to stump up for the school.

The story was reported around the world, but then weeks went by with little being added to it. Famously outspoken, Lobsang Gyatso was known to have both a fiercely loyal following and a significant number of enemies. In the past, he had courted unpopularity for his scathing criticism of learned monks and lamas who, during the 1959 uprising against the Chinese in Tibet, had sanctioned violence. He also had a reputation for being hard on his students—not so much from being strictly disciplinarian but from his own modesty. By convention, novice monks may not furnish their rooms better than their teacher's, and Lobsang Gyatso's room was barely furnished at all. The only negative characteristic that anybody within the Tibetan community would acknowledge was Lobsang Gyatso's public opposition to the cult of a popular deity within the Tibetan pantheon, Dorje Shugden.

Three months later, the Indian police claimed a breakthrough. Besides a pair of gloves, a handkerchief and a torch, the bag grabbed by Lobsang Gyatso had contained "explosive documents" conclusively linking the murders to a Delhi-based organization, described as the Dorje Shugden Supporters Society. These had enabled them to identify two of the assailants. However, the police commissioner was convinced that they had by now certainly fled the country. Of the other attackers, nothing could be determined: to this day, the case remains open.[1]

The story was soon dropped from the international news pages. But then an article appeared in *Newsweek* linking the tragedy to a British-based Buddhist organization, the New Kadampa Tradition (NKT). Its leader, a Tibetan monk named Kelsang Gyatso, turned out to be one of the few of the Dalai Lama's countrymen to be openly critical of him. Yet, in common with those members of the Dorje Shugden Supporters Society who had been interviewed by the police, he denounced the murders, admitting only to disagreement with those who called for a ban on the worship of their favored deity. The result was that, apart from identifying these two organizations, neither the Indian nor the American press revealed much in the way of a motive for the atrocity. The Shugden Supporters appeared perhaps to have some reason to be upset with Lobsang Gyatso, but hardly for murdering him, still less for the frenzy that brought violent death to the precincts of the School of Dialectics.

As for the deity itself, the press portrayed Dorje Shugden as a minor being, invoked principally for its supposed ability to confer worldly goods on its supplicants. If Shugden had a sinister aspect, this lay in its status as a *dharmapala*, or protector of the faith. These are held to be wrathful spirits whose mission is to keep the Buddhist religion and its followers from harm. And, in particular, Dorje Shugden is considered by many of its most ardent devotees to be responsible for protecting the doctrinal purity of the Gelug sect (the largest and most important within Tibetan Buddhism, of which Lobsang Gyatso was, and the Dalai Lama remains, a member)—a sort of heavenly Grand Inquisitor. Yet, given the avowedly peaceful nature of the religion, this did little to explain what the deity's followers could possibly gain from Lobsang Gyatso's death. Had not the Dalai Lama himself also spoken out against the cult?

If there was a conclusion to be drawn from the press coverage of the day, it was that Dorje Shugden's followers represented, on the one hand, a narrowly sectarian spirituality and, on the other, that they were politically reactionary, opposed to reform and unwilling, whatever might be gained, to compromise with China on the issue of Tibetan independence. By way of contrast, the Dalai Lama—supported by Lobsang Gyatso and others— could be seen to be arguing for a more catholic form of Buddhism and a more liberal political agenda.

Yet herein lay the key—a fact overlooked by most commentators at the time, though not by the 120,000-strong community of Tibetan refugees. They were as stunned as the outside world by the outrage committed in their midst, but many had their suspicions as to the perpetrators of the crime and their motives, even if the exact identity of the killers remained unknown. Above all, they were clear who was the real target on that night in February 1997: the Dalai Lama himself.

Not that the Tibetan leader was the intended victim of the murderers. This was, to use the Tibetan expression, a case of hitting the goat to scare the sheep. A handwritten letter sent to the Dalai Lama's private office, dated March 31, 1997 but not published until the following year, is unequivocal: "Alas, divisionist Da* . . . Did you enjoy eating the three carcasses at the time of the Happy Fire Ox Losar this year? You will be treated to many more carcasses if you continue." In other words, not merely were the murders aimed at the Dalai Lama, but they were in direct response to something he had done.

In the years that have passed since that cruel winter's night, the damage to the Dalai Lama's reputation that some of his supporters feared has not materialized. His popularity in the West, and latterly in China too, continues to grow. Yet this was the most extraordinary development. In common with most of his friends, it seemed almost inconceivable to me that the Dalai Lama was even capable of doing anything to provoke such overwhelming outrage as that to which the murder of Lobsang Gyatso testified—least of all from within his own community. Now, however, I felt compelled at least to entertain the possibility that there could be something that needed to be taken seriously in what his enemies were claiming—that beneath the ever-present smile, there lurks a deceiver who, in his quest for absolute power over his people, is personally responsible for the humiliation

* Generally taken to be a disrespectful diminutive of "Dalai."

of thousands, the beating of dozens, even the deaths of several of his countrymen and women. This, they alleged, was the treatment that had been meted out to those who had the audacity freely to follow their own religious beliefs. Could it be true that I had swallowed a lie—that in reality there is a malaise lying at the heart of Tibetan religion and culture?

The short answer is no, but to see how the question—and the allegations—could arise, we need to place the Dalai Lama in context, and we can only do this by knowing something of the history of Tibet and of the institution of the Dalai Lamas itself. This was a subject which, until then, I had largely ignored. Indeed, because I saw it as my job precisely to communicate the Dalai Lama's own point of view, I had deliberately avoided any serious investigation of anything but his own life story—and that entirely from his own perspective. Accordingly, I now began a study of the subject that surprised me at almost every turn.

For example, like most people, I had not realized that the Dalai Lama enjoys far less power over his fellow Buddhists than does the Pope over Catholics. Whereas the pontiff claims the Apostolic Succession, and the right to appoint every bishop in Christendom, the Dalai Lama makes no such claim and enjoys no such authority. He neither appoints nor controls other lamas. Technically, he has only the status of an ordinary monk in a monastery of which he is not even abbot. So far as doctrine is concerned, his opinion may be sought, it may be influential, but it is neither final nor binding.

Again, for all the support that the notion of a free Tibet has won in the West, it had scarcely occurred to me that Tibet was never formally a state in the modern sense of the word (but then, nor was the country we now know as the People's Republic of China until comparatively recently). And while individuals certainly thought of themselves in terms of their Tibetan ethnicity, they did not see themselves as "citizens" of Tibet, nor even as subjects of the Dalai Lama. Their fiercest commitment was to Buddhism itself. As to individual Tibetans' relationship with the Dalai Lama, the earthly manifestation of Chenrezig, Bodhisattva of Compassion, traditionally this has been a spiritual relationship, transcending notions of mere fealty. But as far as most Tibetans' earthly allegiance was concerned, this was primarily to a clan or tribe, which would in turn be allied to a local monastery, which might—or might not—be loyal to the Dalai Lama. Moreover, because the monasteries were not merely centers of piety and learning but also of political influence, many with their own armies of fighting monks, they were often caught up in regional power struggles. There have even been occasions when the hatred of fellow monastics toward one another has been no less intense than any between Protestant and Catholic.

Yet if it is important to acknowledge that the Tibet of historical record undermines the image of Tibet as "hidden wonderland," I do not mean that China's rhetoric, for which the Dalai Lama is, at best, a "monk in wolf's clothing," is true. Quite the reverse. But, in order to see why, we need to establish what Buddhists call the *madhyama*, the "middle way,"* between the competing claims of those for whom Tibet was a prelapsarian paradise and those for whom it was a "hell for the laboring people." To this end, we need to pay proper attention to the real achievements of Tibetan civilization, achievements that are all too frequently overlooked by the extremists of both persuasions. When we do so, we see that there are far better reasons to admire Tibetan culture than any vague ideas about hidden mysteries. Its literature alone—so hard to translate, so subtle its poetics—testifies to a creativity rendered all the more remarkable for the tiny numbers involved in its composition. The population of Tibet has prob-

---

* Strictly, *madhyama* means simply "middle"; "middle ground" or "middle way" is *madhyamaka*.

ably never exceeded a few million, yet its handful of lettered men produced written works of a beauty and profundity which, it may be argued, rival that of any society in history.* And the Tibetan genius for philosophical reflection is such that its greatest exponents may rightfully claim a place alongside the most exalted minds of humanity's intellectual tradition. There can be no doubt that the highest attainments of Tibetan civilization testify to the genius of a unique and remarkable people.

It is also necessary to give due weight to Tibet's extraordinarily rich folk culture, which, for millennia, has sustained—and to some extent continues to sustain—a way of life long since vanished from the modern world. This is a culture of fierce loyalties and passionate devotion, of extravagant rituals and solemn pageant, of cheerful endurance in the face of the most extreme conditions, of a faith as powerful as it is simply and deeply held.

It is this folk culture which, in collision with Buddhism, provides many of the most colorful aspects of Tibetan tradition. For Tibetans, there was no Big Bang, no single moment of creation, only infinite regression, and in place of a single creator, there are whole legions of gods and demons, of wrathful protector deities, of hells both flame-licked and frozen, of hungry ghosts and walking dead, of earth spirits and oracles. It is a worldview that gave rise to the (still current) practice of divination by the Dalai Lama on behalf of the Tibetan government and, for similar purposes, his use of mediums to consult oracular deities. It is one that underpins Tibet's minutely detailed astrological system and its highly developed—and (especially in the West) increasingly popular—traditional medical system. It even provides for the occasional use of officially sanctioned black magic. The central government responded to the Chinese invasion of 1949–50 by ordering monasteries in the borderlands to manufacture

---

* Admittedly few, if any, women produced important literary works during Tibet's classical period.

demon-laden tantric bombs which were to be tossed in the direction of the advancing enemy. But if there is one aspect of the folk-religious tradition that is central to the office of the Dalai Lamas themselves, it is that of the *dharmapalas*, or protector deities, of which Dorje Shugden is an example. These have occupied a central position in Tibetan thought since the advent of Buddhism and continue to have an impact—not always benign—on Tibetan politics to this day. And it is this aspect which is reflected in the tragedy of Lobsang Gyatso.

Yet while it is true that, from a modern perspective, the Tibetan folk-religious tradition can seem by turns ludicrous and outrageous, it clearly provides an entirely valid way of being in the world, with benefits that are unavailable to modern society. It is also clear that it is this tradition which partly explains our fascination for Tibet. We catch, in Tibetan culture, a glimpse of the universe enchanted, of how our world must have looked before the West's own folk-religious tradition was obliterated by modernity, and it enables us to identify some of the losses that went with it.

Tibetan society prior to the Chinese invasion of 1949–50 had its shortcomings, but the evidence shows it to have been broadly peaceful, that the people were generally contented, and the virtue of compassion was genuinely prized above any material goods. So if it comes as a shock to some to discover that this same society—in which killing so much as an insect is considered something of an atrocity—has also been one in which individuals could be as cruel to one another as any in history, it is important to remember that the misdeeds of a few should not be taken as representative of the many.

In writing this book, I have taken as a guiding principle the present Dalai Lama's frequent assertion that he is "just an ordinary human being." I take it that, if this is true, it is also true that each of his predecessor Dalai Lamas must have been ordinary human beings. It is rather the institution of the Dalai Lamas that is extraordinary, and it is the origin and history of this institution that this book will narrate. Yet although I take an unsentimental view of the Dalai Lamas and their predecessors, I do not deny that the world itself is an extraordinary place. The modern presumption that metaphysics is meaningless, or that it has in any sense been overcome, is, in my view, simply wrong. For this reason, I have tried to validate the Tibetan understanding of the way things are by deliberately leaving blurred the boundaries between what Tibetan tradition holds to be true and what a contemporary, broadly empiricist outlook would assume to have been the case. In so doing and in setting out the religious, cultural and political milieu from which the Dalai Lamas emerged, I have aimed to navigate a course between the competing claims of Tibet as Shangri-La and China's description of Tibet as feudal anachronism, between the popular image of the Dalai Lama as new age icon and the claim that he is a "very political old monk shuffling round in Gucci loafers," as media tycoon Rupert Murdoch once described him.[2] This, I trust, will give a fair picture of Tibetan history and culture, and a portrait which gives a true measure of the man.

2

Chenrezig:
The One Who Looks Down in Compassion

To begin at the beginning—it turns out that there are both several beginnings and no beginning. Strictly, the origins of the Dalai Lamas lie in the fourteenth century—the First Dalai Lama was born in 1391—yet the institution did not take its present form until the time of the Great Fifth, whose dates are 1617–1682. The first to have been recognized during his lifetime was in fact the Third. On top of all this, the First is himself considered by Tibetans to be forty-third in an unbroken succession of incarnations stretching back into the mists of pre-history. According to this way of reckoning, the present Dalai Lama's spiritual lineage spans fifty-seven generations, beginning with a royal prince, who lived some 990 eons ago.* These are the so-called secret lives of the Dalai Lama. And it

* A disciple is said once to have asked the Buddha how long an eon lasts. He replied with an analogy: "Suppose there was a great mountain of rock, seven miles across and seven miles high, a solid mass without any cracks. At the end of every hundred years a man might brush it with a fine Benares cloth. That great mountain of rock would decay and come to an end sooner than ever [an] eon."

is to this spiritual lineage that we must turn for a deeper understanding of the Dalai Lama institution. The first thing to
appreciate is that the fundamental premise underlying it is the
notion that Chenrezig, Bodhisattva of Compassion, together
with his female consort Tara, takes a personal interest in the
Tibetan people and their country and, on account of this, deigns
to manifest in human history through the words, thoughts and
deeds of his spiritual heirs. Preeminent among these heirs are
the Dalai Lamas.

The prince who inaugurates the lineage went by the name
of Lokesvaraja. As a young man, Lokesvaraja was distinguished
for his remarkable generosity. He gave away everything in his
possession—including, finally, to a rival king, his family's wish-
fulfilling jewel. When his father discovered this, he agreed with
his outraged ministers that the boy should be banished for
twenty-five years to the land of headless demons. Yet for all
his impetuosity, the people retained fond memories of
Lokesvaraja. His sentence up, he returned home to a rapturous welcome. The rival king even apologized for having asked
for the wish-fulfilling jewel (knowing that Lokesvaraja would
not refuse). Soon after, Lokesvaraja took a wife and was crowned
king. He then meditated on the Mahayana Buddhist teachings—possible because, even though this was long before they
were expounded here on earth, they already existed on the
spiritual plane—and attained enlightenment. Thereupon he
prophesied his future lives up to that of (the historical) King
Songtsen Gampo of Tibet.

Lokesvaraja went on to become arguably the preeminent
spiritual being in the Buddhist universe after the Buddha
Shakyamuni himself. Known to Tibetans as Chenrezig, roughly,
"the one who looks down in compassion,"* it was he who, in a
short and enigmatic scripture, provided the foundation for the

---

* In Sanskrit, Avalokitesvara, pronounced "Avalokiteeshvra."

uniquely Buddhist concept of dependent origination: "Form is emptiness, emptiness is form; emptiness is not other than form, form too is not other than emptiness . . ."[1] This crystallizes the notion that all phenomena are without intrinsic existence. Yet emptiness in this Buddhist sense is not a void. It is better construed in terms of potential: things exist precisely because they are empty of intrinsic existence.

As the originator of the doctrine of emptiness, or dependent origination, Chenrezig is central to Buddhist philosophy. This is not, however, what he is best known for, either by Mahayana Buddhists in general, or by Tibetans in particular. Foremost in the mind of most devotees is his reputation as the Bodhisattva of Compassion. According to the Lotus sutra, out of compassion for sentient beings, Chenrezig comes to the aid of all who pray to him. He saves supplicants from fire, from flood, from storms, and from the depredations of thieves, murderers, ghosts, and demons.[2] Famously, he saved the seventh-century Chinese pilgrim Xuanzang from certain death on numerous occasions. One night, Xuanzang's young guide came toward him brandishing a knife, but when the Chinese called on Chenrezig, the would-be assailant "went back and slept." Crossing the great Taklamakan desert by following the piles of bones and horse dung that were the only traces of life among its pitiless wastes, Xuanzang was able to drive away "all sorts of demon shapes and strange goblins" by calling on the Compassionate One. Then, as he traversed Tibet's northern reaches, he was attacked by tribesmen. An arrow grazed his knee but again he survived, thanks to the merciful intervention of Chenrezig.

As a Bodhisattva, Chenrezig is held to be the personification, in the form of a fully enlightened being, of a Buddha's activity—in his case that of the Buddha Amitabha, the Buddha of Boundless Light.* As such, he is capable of manifesting when-

* According to the Mahayana Buddhism practiced in Tibet, there is not just one but instead innumerable Buddhas.

ever and wherever he perceives an opportunity to be of assistance to those who remain within the realms of suffering. He has been known, on occasion, to manifest as a bridge emerging from the mist to weary travelers looking for the means to cross a river.* And not only is he able to adapt his form endlessly, he is able to appear in countless different places simultaneously.

Bodhisattvas in general manifest in different ways according to the mental capacity of those to whom they appear. In the Heart sutra, where he expounds the doctrine of emptiness, Chenrezig addresses those of higher ability. But on one occasion, at Benares, he manifests as a bee in order to hum the dharma for the benefit of some worms; and in one delightful Tibetan text, *The Dharma among the Birds*, he appears as a cuckoo who preaches to his fellow fowl, somewhat in the manner of Ecclesiastes: "the trivial joys of this, our life on earth, are like a conjuration, like a dream, like a rainbow in the sky, the echo of a voice shouting into a deserted valley."[3]

Chenrezig is also believed to have a special connection with Tibet, a connection that preceded his own enlightenment. It is said, in the Tibetan White Lotus sutra, that looking toward the "barbaric snowy realms filled with multitudes of demons and ogres," he made a vow to lead to liberation "all sentient beings in this barbaric land, a place untrodden by the Buddhas."

In other texts Chenrezig is described as the father of the Tibetan people. According to this tradition, the lake under which Tibet is said to have lain submerged dried up approximately a hundred years after the death of the Buddha Shakyamuni.[4] In its place grew a forest of juniper, which covered the whole country. Shortly thereafter, Chenrezig manifested as a monkey, which made its home in this great forest. Meditating quietly on the blessings of compassion, he was approached one day by a rock ogress who, full of carnal desire and spurred on

* But once they are over the river the bridge vanishes.

by the fact that all her children had died, importuned the mystic primate. Eventually, out of compassion for her, the monkey accepted the ogress (whom pious Tibetans identify with the goddess Tara) as his mate.

According to popular wisdom, this unusual ancestry can still clearly be seen. From the original union of the monkey and the rock ogress sprang six children and two distinct lineages:

> As to the monkey father's lineage, they are those who are patient, faithful, compassionate, diligent, those who delight in virtue, and those who are eloquent . . . As to the rock ogress mother's lineage, they are those who are lusty, angry, mercenary, profit-seeking, greedy, competitive, garrulous, strong, courageous, active, restless, scatter-brained, daring, those whose minds suffer from an excess of the Five Poisons,* those who enjoy hearing about the faults of others, and those who are tempestuous.[5]

So powerful is this origin myth among Tibetans that it is as much as most have known about themselves and about their history prior to the arrival of Buddhism in Tibet during the seventh century. And so strong is popular devotion to Chenrezig that the literal authenticity of the monkey myth was not seriously questioned until toward the end of the twentieth century, even though many Tibetans had by then long known of the modern worldview. For some of the devout, Darwinian theory actually seems to substantiate the story, despite the vastly different timescales proposed. Just as there are those in the West who continue to accept the Creationist doctrine, so there is no shortage of traditionally minded Tibetans who maintain that, in the less than thousand years between Buddha Shakyamuni's death and the political

---

* These are: greed, hatred, jealousy, willful ignorance, and pride.

unification of Tibet, their race was indeed begotten by a divine
monkey and a rock ogress.*

   There is, however, a parallel tradition. This speaks of thirty-
six successive incarnations of Chenrezig in India leading up to
his first Tibetan incarnation as King Songtsen Gampo during the
seventh century. That this tradition seems to be logically incon-
sistent with the monkey myth does not deter the believer. For
Tibetans, the fact that an event may not be verifiable according
to modern historical-critical methods does not mean that it did
not "actually happen." It may simply mean that it happened on
another—a spiritual—plane. In that case it can be assumed to
have happened no less surely than if it had taken place in accordance with mundane reality. According to this tradition, after
Lokesvaraja, Chenrezig's next earthly incarnation appeared
during the present eon when ". . . in the city of Kapilavastu,
during the time of . . . Prince Siddhartha, I was a Brahmin boy
called Nan'Ba . . . I was shy."[6] Here on earth, at the city gate—
the traditional spot for the town's delinquents—he meets the
future Buddha who urges him not to be idle but to work unfail-
ingly for the good of others.

   The subsequent thirty-four incarnations prior to Songtsen
Gampo comprise, variously, six kings, four princes, seven more
boys, Raja the Single Man, a hare, a bird, a herdsman, and sundry
others (though no women), several of whom change their form
from human to animal and back again. Many of their life stories
also recount dealings with demons and such mythical creatures
as the garuda.† The eighth incarnation, Depa Tenpa, literally
"Steadfast Faith," has a magical horse, which arrives instantly at

---

* The difference between creationists and Tibetan traditionalists is that the
former hold their views in spite of modern science, but the latter hold theirs
while, for the most part, quite ignorant of modern scientific claims.
† This is a sort of bird, with an eagle's head and the beak of an owl, but the
torso and arms of a human being. Perhaps he is a relative of the European griffin, though while the griffin eats humans and horses, the garuda is the eternal
enemy of the snake.

whatever destination its rider thinks of. On this beast Depa Tenpa goes to visit the eleven-headed king of the demons, who is reported to sit on a soft throne of tanned human hide.

Within this tradition, Chenrezig in human form is usually indistinguishable from the common mass. But Ratnadasa, the sixth incarnation, reveals his true nature by having a body which, from the waist up, is "like refined gold," while his lower body is "the color of turquoise." He was, moreover, born with a set of forty teeth.[*] Though each of these unusual attributes has a significance to those versed in the Buddhist tradition, the life stories of the thirty-six are, from a modern perspective, clearly unacceptable as history, even leaving aside the appearances as animals or birds. In Chenrezig's eleventh incarnation, for example, as Prince Mativardhana, he is reported to have been seated next to a leper woman when a black snake appears from one of her earholes. Seizing his sword, he cuts the snake into thirty pieces, at which she regains her true form as a beautiful young woman and the two become husband and wife. In another incarnation, he hacks off pieces of his own flesh (which is immediately restored) to feed a hungry jackal. And in one lifetime, Chenrezig appears as the Yogi of the Burning Ground who, disconcertingly, has a fondness for charnel grounds and for meditating while lying on top of corpses.

A few of the lives convey clearly recognisable spiritual teachings. Prince Asanga, "a peaceful, disciplined, contented, and soft-spoken youth," manages to persuade his father to stop hunting. He does so by pointing out that the animals he is pursuing are in fact reincarnations of the king's own parents. This is a variation of a traditional Buddhist teaching which states that, at some point during the endless rounds of cyclic existence, all other sentient beings have been our father and mother. Taking this to heart we learn to treat all others, whether human, animal

---

[*] The orthodox number is thirty-two, including wisdom teeth.

or supernatural being, with the same degree of respect as our own parents. As the King of a Small Country, Chenrezig imparts a more mundane lesson when he releases the barbarian chieftain who tries to kill him. "If I had had him executed, his people would have become angry and sought only to avenge his death."[7] There is, however, only one life that would seem to convey a universally recognisable spiritual message, that of Rin'chen Chö, twenty-ninth in the list.

> Once, in a certain town, there was a Brahmin called Rin'chen Chö, pure and versed in the Vedas. In the town center, there was a leper woman, without food and so racked by her disease she could not even stand. Rin'chen Chö saw her and took pity on her. Although he himself was ritually clean, he carried the woman to his hermitage, fed her, washed the pus from her sores, and healed them with medicine, covering her hairless skin with soft clothes.[8]

But if most of the lives recounted in the tradition seem just too extravagant to the modern eye, it is important to realize that the claims made for Chenrezig's earthly incarnations are entirely consonant with claims made for Buddha Shakyamuni himself. To think of Buddhism as a quietist spiritual path with, perhaps, a rather flexible approach to ethics is quite wrong. On this view, Buddha Shakyamuni is little more than an unworldly spiritual teacher and philosopher. It was only his overzealous followers who turned him into a supernatural being. Either that or the creation of the Buddhist religion was politically motivated as a means to discipline and control the masses who accepted his teaching. But this is misguided. The earliest stories we have make it very clear that the Buddha was no ordinary human being. These unquestionably reflect a long tradition, according to which he was a miracle worker who not only believed in, but was master of, the numerous gods that populate the universe. He certainly was not merely an inspired teacher, any more than Jesus Christ was merely a political activist with some unusual ideas about love. But, whereas Christ was arguably somewhat reticent about displaying his miraculous powers, the Buddha was completely open about his. The one, challenged to give a sign that he really was the Son of God, retorted with a jibe: "It is only an evil and faithless generation that asks for a sign." The other, faced with a similar challenge, not only accepted but publicly announced the time and the place he would do so. When the day came, he ascended his "road into the sky" and displayed himself:

> The signs which he showed were in the following order . . . First, he caused a great fire to ascend from his head, and a stream of water from his feet; he then mixed the fire and the water above and below him. Then he sent forth fire from his back, and water before him; then a flame of fire from his right eye and water from his left; then the reverse; then fire from his right nostril, and water from his left, and the reverse; then fire from his right ear, and water from his left, and the reverse; and in the same manner, fire and water from his shoulders, hands, sides, legs, feet, thumbs, and great toes, all marvelous to behold. Then flowed from one hair water, and from another, fire. He then sent forth his six glories, and walked to and fro in the air.[9]

So while the biographies of the Thirty-six may not seem particularly meaningful from a modern perspective, they are, of course, entirely so from the perspective of the Dalai Lama institution. They reflect some of the different attributes of the one who incarnates as the Dalai Lamas. For this reason, it is especially important that we understand the significance of the last two incarnations prior to that of King Songtsen Gampo. The first of them, King Tsug'la Dzin, is described as an enemy of Buddhism. And not only that, he attempts to murder, by burning in a fire fueled with a mixture of palm oil and sesame oil, an enlightened being. For Buddhists this is the most serious crime it is possible to commit. As it turns out, no harm is done. The king repents and becomes an adherent of the doctrine. Yet for a manifestation of Chenrezig actually to attempt to kill seems scarcely credible. How could one enlightened being contemplate doing such a thing, let alone to another enlightened being?

This question brings us to the conundrum that lies at the heart of the Dalai Lama institution. It is said that each of the Dalai Lamas is the reincarnation of his predecessor. And the first Dalai Lama is said in turn to be the reincarnation of, among others, a series of historical beings whose lineage can be traced back through nineteen other Tibetans and through the thirty-six Indian incarnations. But what it actually means to say that they are successive reincarnations—or emanations, or manifestations—of Chenrezig in fact varies according to the individual making the statement. From a simple folk perspective, Chenrezig himself is successively embodied, or ensouled, in each of these different people. From a more refined Buddhist perspective the link is altogether more subtle. One might speak of a spiritual association between them. Each is karmically connected with Chenrezig through their acts of compassion. Thus, in the case of the would-be Buddha-slayer, the idea is not that he actually *is* Chenrezig from birth, but rather that Chenrezig, with whom we may assume he is connected through his (the king's) compassionate activity in former lives, is made manifest when he repents and, motivated by compassion, dedicates himself to serving others. In other words, the lineage is both defined and characterized by compassion. But the term compassion must also be understood correctly. Not only does it connote fellow feeling toward the suffering of others, but also the actions taken in response to that feeling. Preaching, or offering, the dharma is itself considered a compassionate act, given that it is a fundamental precept only to preach the dharma in response to a request. Indeed, any action that furthers the practice of Buddhism, or that increases its prestige, will also generally be construed as an act of kindness. It is for this reason that King Gewa Pal, the final incarnation of the pre-historical lineage, is important. He is portrayed—though, chronologically, this seems implausible—as the father of Atisha, the great missionary and propagator of the faith in Tibet. His immense compassion is attested by the fact that he fathered a saint.

To the outsider, this idea, that whatever furthers the practice of the *buddhadharma* can be construed in terms of compassion, is not easy to accept. The same logic can be applied to protecting the doctrine. The danger here is that any action taken in its defense is justified. Poor Lobsang Gyatso's murder seems to have been motivated by just such a desire to protect the purity of the Gelug tradition.

3

Of Silk, Spice, and the Way of the Buddha

Chenrezig's first incarnation in Tibet was as King Songtsen Gampo, whose likely dates are around 613 to 650. It was he who first united Tibet's disparate tribes and clans, forging his people into a fighting machine which came to dominate eastern Inner Asia for almost two hundred years. At the height of its power, the empire he founded stretched from modern-day Kabul in the west to the gates of Chang'an, then capital of China, in the east, and from India's Spiti Valley in the south to Qocho in the north. Yet in spite of this imperial achievement, Songtsen Gampo is chiefly remembered—and revered—by Tibetans for having been the person who introduced Buddhism into the country. According to popular mythology, he was so holy that, at his death, he was absorbed into a statue of Chenrezig. Yet Songtsen Gampo is also an historical figure, and good records enable us to build a picture both of the man and of the early Tibetan world.

Before we turn to this seminal figure in Tibetan history, however, it is essential to know something about the state of central and eastern Inner Asia during the early centuries of the Common Era. Tibet's location at the heart of this region means that it was subject to, and shaped by, a multitude of different influences sweeping back and forth from east to west and from south to north.

Unquestionably the most important development of this period was the gradual rise of Buddhism. For the first hundred years after the historical Buddha's death, or *parinirvana* (probably toward the end of the fourth century BCE), the community he founded remained a local phenomenon. But when the third Mauryan emperor, Ashoka (269–232 BCE), turned to the religion, it gained the patronage to enable it to become an international movement. A series of imperial edicts inscribed on pillars of finely polished sandstone, most of which remain standing to this day, testify to Ashoka's remarkable conversion. The most famous of them describes "His Sacred Majesty's remorse" at the conquest of "a country hitherto unsubdued" because it involved "the slaughter, death, and carrying away captive of the people." Thenceforward, it announces, he will adopt the law of piety, renounce violence and rule according to the debt he owed all living creatures.*

Ashoka came to be recognized by his Buddhist subjects as a *cakravartin*,† and under his protection, Buddhism spread throughout much of India, as well as into Central Asia. It was there, in Bactria (and Gandhara), which together incorporated the greater part of northern modern-day Afghanistan and Pakistan, that Buddhism first came into contact with a non-Indian culture. Bactria having been the easternmost reach of Alexander's great Greek Empire (Alexander conquered the region in 328 BCE), its predominant culture was Hellenic. One outstanding consequence of this was an extraordinary hybrid art form, which, even today, has lost none of its power to move the first-time viewer. Toga-clad Bodhisattvas, Buddhas with European features—one famously modeled on Herakles and wearing a lion skin—vine

---

* Yet, curiously, though he was undoubtedly referring to the way of the Buddha, or something very like it, the Buddha's name is mentioned nowhere in either this or any of the other edicts.
† Literally, a "universal monarch."

scroll motifs, garland-bearing cherubs, centaurs and tritons all
testify to a remarkable synthesis of European and Asian cultures.
Under the Bactrian philosopher king Menander (115–90 BCE),
Buddhism made a further advance in Central Asia. It is said that
this king welcomed teachers and philosophers of all persuasions
to his court. According to legend, he finally became a Buddhist
as the result of his discussions with the Buddhist monk Nagasena.
A famous scripture, *The Questions of King Menander*, charts his spiritual and intellectual odyssey, though Menander's conversion was
perhaps less complete than Ashoka's. He was killed in battle.

The Buddhist cause in Central Asia was taken up next by the
Kushanas, an Indo-European people whose vast empire
dominated Inner Asia for the first four centuries CE. Stretching
westward to within six hundred miles of the border of the Roman
Empire, to the east, Kushan territory included the southwestern
reaches of Tibet and part of eastern and central India.[1] So when
their king, Kanishka—who sent an embassy to Trajan in Rome—
declared himself for Buddhism, the faith secured patronage on
a scale hitherto unprecedented. This in turn provided the foundation for the religion's most creative period. It was within
Kushan's Central Asian territories, particularly Bactria, that
Mahayana Buddhism itself began to emerge. This is the form of
Buddhism that the Tibetans were to adopt.

The Kushan Empire is important to a study of the Dalai Lamas
for reasons other than its status as the cradle of Mahayana
Buddhism, however. The stability it brought to central and eastern Inner Asia was of enormous consequence to the history of
this period. It enabled the development of regular commerce
between China and the Roman Empire along the trade routes
we now know as the Silk Road.*

---

* We owe the name to the German traveler Baron Ferdinand von Richthofen, a
forebear of the First World War fighter ace Manfred von Richthofen, alias the
Red Baron. The term is actually somewhat misleading since there was more than
one route linking east to west, and there were also routes linking north to south.

This commerce was much more extensive than is generally imagined. From China to the West came first and in large quantities: silk, but also satin, spice, precious stones, musk, and medicines.* A lot of goods also went in the opposite direction: Western jade, coral, pearls, glass, linen, and, from the steppes of Central Asia, fine horses. Among the most highly valued imports to China was fruit: in particular the so-called "golden peaches" of Samarkand, and grapes. Testifying to the sophistication of the trade, these were packed in ice and sealed in lead containers to keep them fresh during the long journey from Central Asia, along the northern fringes of Tibet and then down into China.

Given the scope of the Silk Road trade, it was inevitable that control over its routes should be heavily contested. Given, too, that one of these routes ran adjacent to the Tibetan border, it was also inevitable that Tibetans would one day join the fray.†

Although Buddhism was the dominant religion in Central Asia for the best part of this time, the early Middle Ages saw a plethora of spiritual movements join battle with one another in the quest for souls. In so doing, each was to some extent influenced by the others. Iran's Zoroastrianism did not become the national religion of any other country, but converts helped spread its influence far beyond the confines of its homeland. There were Zoroastrian temples in China during the T'ang Dynasty (618–907), probably built by Persian refugees. And there is little doubt that Mahayana Buddhism owes something to Zoroastrian ideas. A striking parallel concerns the future Buddha, Maitreya, who is to be welcomed on earth by one Kasyapa. In the Zoroastrian

---

* An important remedy in pre-modern times was rhubarb, prized for its emetic properties and a Chinese export eagerly sought after in the West. During the Opium Wars, a senior Chinese official threatened Queen Victoria with a ban on the sale of rhubarb, assuming that Britain would soon be rendered prostrate with constipation. By then, however, it was grown commercially in England. *See* Wood, *The Silk Road*, p. 14.
† Indeed, Tibet founded its empire precisely for access to the Silk Road trade: it was a vital source of revenue.

tradition, the anticipated world savior, the Saoshyant, will be welcomed by a disciple named Karashapa.[2] It is also clear that, for many Central Asians of the early Middle Ages, Amitabha, the Buddha of Boundless Light, was hardly to be distinguished from the Persian god of light. And Tibet's other religion, Bon, seems to have been influenced by Zoroastrianism. Both traditions speak of a Bridge of Judgment, over which the soul must pass, or from which it will fall to perdition.

Christianity was also an important force throughout central and eastern Inner Asia at this time. There was a Christian community in Bactria by 196. In the first quarter of the seventh century, there were missionaries preaching in China. By the middle of that century, there were bishoprics both in Samarkand, the Sogdian capital, and at Kashgar, two of more than two hundred such bishoprics east of the Oxus River. And we know from a letter of Patriarch Timothy I, head of the Chaldean Christian Church (whose spiritual home was and remains Baghdad), that a century and a half later, there were considerable numbers of Tibetan Christians. Writing to his friend Severus, sometime between 795 and 798, Timothy mentions that he is preparing to anoint a metropolitan for the "land of the Tibetans." Given that a metropolitan is a bishop who exercises not merely diocesan but provincial powers, it is clear that this community must have been a reasonably important one.[3]

No major power in the region actually adopted Christianity, but again its influence was keenly felt. There are those who wonder whether the universalisation of the Buddha in the Mahayana tradition was not to some extent in response to the similarly universal claims made for the Semitic God.

Another important, and in some ways more successful, movement of the time was Manichaeism. Here, too, it was the Sogdians who played a major role in its dissemination in the East. Founded by a third-century Persian named Mani (who met his end flayed alive on the orders of the king), Manichaeism was a highly syncretic collection of beliefs. Mani's followers believed him to incarnate the Christian Holy Spirit, yet they also drew inspiration from Buddhism and from the Jewish prophetic tradition. (Significantly, there were pockets of Jews living all the way along the Silk Road and there was an important Jewish community in China itself.) The Manichaeans held that the world is radically polarized between light and darkness, between good and evil. The purpose of religion was to release the particles of light stolen by Satan and imprisoned in the human brain. In practice, its adherents were vegetarian—the elect did not even prepare their own food for fear of damaging these light particles—and highly ascetic. So successful was Manichaeism that, for a time, Buddhists, Christians and Muslims alike regarded it as their principal rival. Its most famous exponent, after Mani himself, was the North African saint Augustine of Hippo, one of the world's most influential philosophers and, of course, a famous convert to Christianity. Describing his years as a Manichaean, Augustine spoke of its "absurd trivialities" and of how its doctrines concerning the souls of plants had led him to believe "that a fig weeps when it is plucked, and that the fig tree, its mother, sheds milky tears."[4]

But for all the efforts of Zoroastrian, Christian and Manichaean missionaries, Buddhism's hold over the popular imagination remained secure until the triumph of Islam during the second half of the first millennium. This may seem ironic—that the area most closely associated with the crudely fundamentalist Taliban movement should once have been at the epicenter of Mahayana Buddhist culture; but rather than conclude that the people of this vast region have exchanged a gentle faith for a militant one, it is safer to note that it is ideologies (not religions per se) that all too easily become militant. After all, Buddhism itself has at different times been allied to nefarious political movements. During the first half of the twentieth century, institutional Buddhism developed ever-closer links to the imperial fascist cult

in Japan. A well-known photograph of a squad of monks carrying rifles and drilling under the approving gaze of a military
supervisor permits no doubt as to the depths of the association.
In Tibet, too, there is, as we shall see, a long-established tradition of monastic involvement in martial enterprise.

4

A Lion Among Men

According to the fourteenth-century scholar-monks[*] who composed the first "modern" histories of Tibet, Songtsen Gampo, Chenrezig's first Tibetan incarnation, was thirty-second in the royal line since the first king of Tibet.[†] The first was Nyatri Tsenpo, who is said variously to have come down from the sky, to have been the exiled king of another Tibetan province or to have been the deformed son of an Indian king. All agree that he had eyes that closed upward like a bird, and hands and feet webbed like a goose. Some authorities also cite turquoise eyebrows, whiskers like a tiger and a full set of conch-white teeth at birth. It was these marks that are said to have caused his father to order him placed in a casket and pitched into the Ganges. Fortunately, the baby was discovered by a peasant who rescued him and brought him up. But when the boy found out about his ancestry, it is said he fled, full of grief, to the Himalayas. There he encountered

---

[*] The most exalted of whom is Bu'ton Rinpoché, who memorably concludes one of his works with a description of himself as "Bu'ton with the large mouth and resembling a parrot."
[†] Actually, not all agree precisely: according to some, he was thirty-first, and to others thirtieth.

some priests who asked him where he had come from. Not understanding them, Nyatri pointed to the sky. This was enough to
convince the priests that he was a god. They proclaimed him
king at once and bore him away, carried aloft on a throne—hence
his name. Nyatri means, literally, "the Neck-enthroned One."

Nyatri Tsenpo is said to have reigned until his son was old
enough to ride a horse (the time when boys came of age among
most nomad peoples, it seems). Nyatri then ascended a magical
rope and disappeared back into the heavens whence he came,
"like a rainbow." The first seven kings of Tibet all possessed
such a rope. This explains why none of them was buried. The
first to be interred was Drigum Tsenpo, who accidentally severed
his during a fight. Thereafter the royal house was earthbound.

Drigum died without issue, but his queen dreamed that she
had intercourse with an emanation of Yarlha Shampo, the royal
mountain, in the form of a man whose body was entirely white.
When she awoke next morning, she saw a white yak rise from
her pillow and gallop off. Obscenely, the offspring of this union
began life as nothing more than a clot of blood the size of a fist.
At first, the queen was inclined to throw her issue away but,
seized with compassion, she decided to keep it even though it
had neither eyes nor a mouth she could feed. Placing the object
inside a yak horn, she rolled it into the hem of her trousers,
where she left it for several days. When she looked again, she
saw, to her joy, that the yak horn contained a baby boy. It was
this child who became the next king of Tibet.

According to the monastic historians, the twenty generations
that passed between this reign and that of the first king to come
into contact with the *buddhadharma*, Lha ThoThori Nyentsen,
saw the rise and development of Tibet's pre-Buddhist Bon religion. Actually pronounced "Pön," the Bon religion survives to
this day and even has quite a following among modern-day
consumers of religion in the West. But scholars are divided over
what form Bon took during the pre-Buddhist era. Many Tibetans

still consider Bon as, if not an evil tradition, at least a benighted one. In contrast to the lofty, universal concerns of Buddhism, Bon is often portrayed as being preoccupied with narrow, this-worldly matters. Initially, Western scholars considered it a shamanistic religion, with an emphasis on direct communication between its priests and the spirits of the natural world. But this is no longer accepted. While some propose that Bon was originally a royal cult, focused on the divine person of the king, others maintain that it was never anything more than a heterodox form of Buddhism and that the royal cult was something else again. Today, the casual observer is hard put to distinguish even Bon monastics from their Buddhist counterparts. Both wear the same maroon robes; both meditate and chant their prayers in similar fashion. The only immediately recognisable difference is the direction in which Bonpos (Bon practitioners) circumambulate their shrines and temples. They go widdershins, to use the Celtic term: the "wrong" way. Both Buddhists and Celtic Christians leave holy places on the right. Bonpos go anticlockwise. Similarly, the Bon swastika, a symbol so closely identified with it that the tradition is often referred to by Buddhists as "Swastika Bon," turns left. For Buddhists and Hindus alike, it turns right.

Bonpos themselves refer to their tradition as Yungdrung Bon, the "eternal Bon." According to their own historians, its founder, Tonpa Shenrab, came to Tibet a credulity-stretching forty thousand years ago, from a western land they call Tazig.* This, most assume to have been located in modern-day Iran. But while Buddhists have, at best, tended to be disdainful of Bon, actually it has a formidable literature. Its earliest scriptures are said to have been written in the language of Zhang Zhung, the ancient name for what is now western Tibet. But while these scriptures

---

* Shameful as it is to relate, I was once condescending enough to ask the young and very gifted abbot of a Bon monastery, who was at the time pursuing studies at Oxford University, whether he believed this. "Of course," he replied, a little coolly.

are said by Bonpos to antedate Tibetan translations of the Buddhist scriptures, on the assumption that the Zhang Zhung script was developed before the Tibetan, this has not been established beyond doubt. What is beyond doubt is that, though Buddhist scholars have long accused Bonpos of plagiarizing Buddhist scripture and adapting it for their own purposes, while this certainly did happen, Buddhists have themselves plagiarized Bon texts.

From a modern perspective, the traditional history of Tibet's first encounter with the *buddhadharma*—though charming—is clearly mythical. Once, when the sixteen-year-old* Lha ThoThori Nyentsen was sitting on the roof of his palace, a casket fell from the sky—or was borne there on a sunbeam, depending on the authority.† This was found to contain two books of scripture and a small golden stupa.‡ Unfortunately, these scriptures were written in Sanskrit and, Tibet being at that time completely unlettered, nobody could read them. They thus became known as the Secret, and the king had to be content with a prophetic dream, the meaning of which would be revealed five generations hence. In due time, according to legend, seeing that the moment was auspicious, Chenrezig, the Compassionate One, manifested a ray of light from his head, illuminating the Land of Snows. The focus of his beam was the Jampa Mingyur Ling, the Palace of Immutable Loving Kindness, where now King Namri Songtsen resided with his consort, Driz Tokarma, princess of Dri. That night, she conceived a child.

When nine months had passed, and the tenth had begun, she gave birth to a son. At the sight of him, the Buddhas gave their

---

* As, by tradition, Tibetans believe a person to be fully human from the moment of conception, a baby is reckoned to be a year old at birth. Here, then, the king would have been fifteen according to Western reckoning.
† Modern Tibetan scholars generally construe "fell from the sky" in terms of "sudden appearance." According to another tradition, the texts were brought to Tibet by two—presumably Indian—monks.
‡ Full-size stupas generally contain the earthly remains of high lamas.

blessing, the Bodhisattvas made auspicious pronouncements, the deities caused flowers to fall like rain and the earth shook in six different ways.[1]

The boy, named Songtsen Gampo, succeeded his father as king at the age of twelve. One of his first enlightened acts was to send a minister, together with sixteen companions, to India, with a view to finding a script suitable for the Tibetan language. The minister, Thonmi Sambhota, remained abroad some years. There he studied Sanskrit and other languages, together with their grammar, spelling and scripts. When he returned, he brought with him several Mahayana Buddhist texts as well as an alphabet he had devised for the Tibetan language. This was comprised of thirty consonants, to each of which could be added four vowel sounds. It remains in use unmodified to this day.

The king was delighted and immediately announced his withdrawal from public life in order to study with Master Thonmi. During this time of seclusion, having mastered the new alphabet and grammar, and learned Sanskrit, he began to translate into Tibetan Lha ThoThori Nyentsen's Secret, as well as the other Buddhist works Thonmi had brought with him. Not that he entirely forswore his kingly duties. Desiring to reform the morals of the people, Songtsen Gampo drew up the Great Code of Supreme Law, comprising ten divine precepts and sixteen articles of earthly conduct.*

Now sixteen, and in want of a wife, Songtsen Gampo sent the

---

* The ten divine precepts began by stating that the good should be rewarded, the evil punished, and contained the following strictures:

> *Those who quarrel shall be punished.*
> *Murderers shall pay blood-monies, great and small.*
> *Thieves shall repay the price of goods stolen,*
> *Plus eight times the value; nine times the value in all.*
> *Adulterers shall have their limbs severed and shall be banished to another land.*
> *The tongues of those who lie shall be cut out.*

See Gyaltsen, *The Clear Mirror*, p. 107.

Great Minister mGar (the "m" is silent) to the kingdom of Nepal to ask for the hand of the sovereign's daughter. The minister took with him a great caravan of pack animals and provisions, together with five gold coins and a wonder-working helmet of lapis lazuli as the bride price. At first, King Amshuvarnam of Nepal was reluctant to accede to mGar's entreaties on behalf of his master; but he was persuaded when he became convinced of the Tibetan king's supernatural powers. The princess, whose name was Tritsun, was both a great beauty and a devout Buddhist who brought with her what was to become one of Tibet's most precious possessions: a statue of the Buddha as a child—Buddha Akshobya—that had been blessed by Buddha Shakyamuni himself.

Songtsen Gampo's next initiative was to engage the faithful mGar in a more difficult enterprise: to obtain for him the hand in marriage of the daughter of Taizong, T'ang emperor of China. Undaunted, mGar took with him as bride-price seven gold coins and a wonder-working suit of armor made of lapis lazuli, together with a still larger caravan of pack animals and provisions. On his arrival in China, mGar discovered, to his dismay, that he was not the only suitor for the princess's hand. There were delegations from India, from the Uighur people and from the Persian king of wealth,* all intent on the same prize for their rulers. How could he, a poor man from the wild, distant Land of Snows, compete with these four giants? Nevertheless, with his gifts and his clever answers to the emperor—and especially with his assurance that Songtsen Gampo would support the princess's Buddhist faith—mGar won the right to contest for her hand. He now had to fulfill four tasks.

The first he found easy enough. A hundred mares in a pen had to be reunited with their foals, which stood in an adjacent pen—no mistakes allowed. mGar simply made a hole in the wall separating the two groups and mares and foals infallibly reunited themselves with one another.

---

* To eastern Asians, Persia was the Eldorado of its day.

The second task mGar found just as easy. He had to find his way back to a room, after spending only one night there, in a building with dozens of identical rooms. He was taken to it after dark, and led away before daybreak. Prior to leaving, however, the wily Tibetan lit a stick of incense, the smell of which led him unerringly back when he returned later in the day.

mGar's third task gave him equally little trouble. The emperor possessed a large piece of coral through which a tiny hole twisted and turned. This mGar must thread. Taking a length of silk, he tied it to the leg of an ant and let the insect do the work for him.

The final task was more of a challenge. He had to identify the princess from among a hundred maidens—some sources say three hundred—identically attired. Fortunately, mGar was able to discover from one of the princess's handmaids that her mistress would be the only one wearing real flowers in her hair. So he waited to see which one of them the bees were attracted to. There was nothing the emperor could do now but let his daughter go.

Like her Nepalese counterpart, Princess Wengchen—for that was her name—was a great beauty and a fervent Buddhist. Tradition identifies her as an emanation of Tara, Chenrezig's female aspect, while Tritsun is identified as an emanation of Bhrikuti, Tara's wrathful aspect. Wengchen brought with her to Tibet many fine belongings, including, most importantly, the self-originated Jowo statue, which, like that of the Buddha Akshobya, had been blessed by the Buddha himself. This was to become—as it remains today—Tibet's single most precious material possession.

Together with his new brides, Songtsen Gampo now set about building temples to house the two precious Buddha images. Wengchen, who was skilled in the art, performed a divination to determine where these should be constructed. No doubt some-what to Songtsen Gampo's surprise, she announced that the kingdom of Tibet itself took the form of an ogress lying on her back, her legs and arms wantonly splayed. The lake at Otang, just outside Lhasa, Wengchen perceived to be the ogress's heart: precisely the spot at which the first temple, the Ramoché, should be built. The lake was duly drained and construction begun. This temple was to house the statue brought by Princess Tritsun.

The other temple, the Jokhang—literally, the Jo[wo] building—built to house the Jowo statue, proved immensely difficult to build, falling down frequently during the construction process. It finally transpired that the plot on which the temple was to stand lay directly above an immense underground lake connected to an area in the far northeast of Tibet. The curious thing about this was that, so long as nobody in central Tibet knew about the link, the water would remain where it was. But as soon as knowledge of it was obtained, it would flow from west to east. Fortunately for the king, one of his agents came upon the information by chance—and the water duly gushed from Lhasa to what is now the lake at Kokonor. Spanning sixty-five miles across and forty miles from top to bottom, it is no small body of water—and all of it from beneath the Jokhang in Lhasa, the building of which continued without further hindrance.

Songtsen Gampo went on to build many other shrines in order to completely subdue the ogress. There were shrines for the Subjugation of the Borderlands, shrines for Further Subjugation and shrines for the Subjugation of the Regions, 108 in all. That done, he ruled wisely and mercifully for many years before merging, at the age of eighty-nine, with the Jowo statue itself, in open confirmation of his status as an emanation of the mighty Chenrezig.

Give or take a later embellishment or two, the foregoing summarizes the traditional history of Songtsen Gampo, the first and greatest of the dharmarajahs* or religious kings, and of the

---

* The Tibetan for "dharmarajah" is *choegyal*.

introduction of Buddhism to Tibet. The narrative is a striking example of the way in which fact, fable and religious piety mingle in the Tibetan imagination. Yet we cannot afford to dismiss it as mere folk tale, for it is this very story—this interpretation of events—which inaugurates the institution of the Dalai Lamas.

The great Buddhist historians of the fourteenth century depicted the reign of Songtsen Gampo as a golden era during which the king introduced the twin blessings of wise government and the teachings of the Buddha. At the same time, they linked him and two of his royal successors personally with Chenrezig, the father of the Tibetan race. This had the effect of establishing that Chenrezig did not merely operate outside Tibet, but rather that the relationship between Chenrezig and Tibet is actually grounded in the very nature of the world itself.[2]

Here, though, we need to say something about traditional Tibetan historiography as it comprises a genre unknown in the West, although it resembles Christian hagiography. Known as *chos'byung*—meaning, literally, "religious history"—this is the story of the spread of the doctrine in Tibet as construed by some of its most eminent practitioners. At first glance, it looks less like history than a literature of wishful thinking. But saying this, we need to recognize that the saintly writers of these accounts were motivated not by any desire to falsify the past; instead, they were driven by the need to provide a picture of the past despite having access to almost no contemporary records. As for their numerous attempts to forge documents in order to legitimize past glories (whether real or fictitious), these can be attributed to a desire to explain events in the context of what they knew about Buddhism.[3] Hence, given that Songtsen Gampo introduced the doctrine to Tibet, it follows that he must have been an incarnation of Chenrezig; given that Wengchen brought the Jowo statue to Tibet, it follows that she must have been an incarnation of the goddess Tara. If this logic does not satisfy the modern mind, it is important to recognize that, in arguing for a more objective account of events, history as we moderns write it is also geared toward a predefined goal—what we call objective truth, the truth that allegedly tells us what actually happened.

Yet though we may approach such objectivity, it can only tell us certain things. It may suggest that, in reality, Songtsen Gampo was a ruthless leader and a warmonger, but it tells us nothing of the nature of the world, still less of how we should live our lives. Conversely, what we might call the mythic component of Tibetan history is very much concerned with how we should conduct our lives.

We could do little more than acknowledge these different approaches to the past were it not for the work of Sir Aurel Stein. Born in Budapest in 1862, Stein was educated first at Oxford, then with the British Museum, before he sailed to India to take up a post as principal of the Oriental College at Lahore in 1888. In the early 1890s, he began a second career as an explorer and archeological surveyor of central and eastern Inner Asia. Stein made a total of four expeditions into the region and it was on the second of them, to Dunhuang, formerly an important Silk Road entrepôt, in western Turkestan (now in China's Gansu province) that, during 1906, he made his greatest discovery— or had his greatest stroke of luck, depending on one's point of view.

Dunhuang was home to a Buddhist community from 366 until its conquest by Genghis Khan in 1227. During this time, a huge complex of caves lying adjacent to the oasis town was colonized by successive generations of Buddhist faithful who transformed them into temples and shrines. These they adorned with thousands of thrilling frescoes executed in the Greco-Buddhist style of the Gandhara school, many of them preserved to this day by the desiccating winds of the Gansu–Sinkiang Desert, at the threshold of which Dunhuang stands. In fact, it was not Stein who actually discovered these. They were already known to Western archaeologists thanks to the work of a Hungarian geological survey which had come upon them back in 1879. It was Stein's destiny to arrive at Dunhuang shortly after the site's self-appointed caretaker, Wang Tao-Shih, a former soldier turned Taoist priest, had unearthed a walled-up antechamber to one of the cave shrines. Inside, he found a library containing thousands of document scrolls. When Wang revealed the existence of this magnificent repository—which turned out to have been sealed during the early years of the eleventh century and left undisturbed since—Stein realized its significance immediately. He spent the next several weeks desperately trying to persuade the timid but—so he said—cunning Wang to permit him to take the library away with him. In what has been described as the greatest archeological heist of all time, he eventually managed to obtain several hundred of the total of well in excess of ten thousand scrolls. He did so by convincing Wang—many would say cynically—of his devotion to the Chinese pilgrim Xuanzang, who had passed this way praying to Chenrezig during the early part of the seventh century. It was surely this great Buddhist, argued Stein, who had arranged that he and Wang should meet. It was also Xuanzang who, through Stein, would rescue the precious documents for translation and publication by modern-day scholars for the benefit of the Buddha's twentieth-century devotees. Put like this, it became easier for Wang to accept the explorer's offer of a donation of five thousand rupees for the shrine which, using funds raised entirely at his own initiative, he was restoring, as Stein relates, garishly and in the meanest of taste.*

---

* What Stein did not at first appreciate was the sheer variety of this extraordinary find. A majority of the scrolls were written in Chinese (which he did not read), among them the earliest known example of woodblock print, datable to 868 CE. But there was vastly more treasure besides. Among his haul were documents written in Uighur, Sogdian, Runic Turkic, Brahmic, Sanskrit, and Tibetan. Moreover, the content of the texts, together with another batch carefully selected a year later by the polyglot French philologist and Sinologist Paul Pelliot (who had mastered not only classical Chinese but also Arabic, Persian, Turkic, Japanese, Mongolian, Manchu, and Tibetan), was extremely varied. Alongside a great deal of Buddhist literature, there were important collections

Most important from the point of view of modern Tibetan scholarship was the discovery of documents among this collection that provide a more or less complete history of ancient Tibet. Now known as the *Old Tibetan Chronicle*, these cover the period of Tibetan history from the time of Songtsen Gampo until the collapse of his Yarlung* Dynasty, two centuries after he died. In scholarly terms, this was a sensation. A whole epoch of history was now open to cross-checking against a contemporary account. Moreover, in enabling a comparison with accounts of the later religious historians, the discovery of the *Old Tibetan Chronicle* allows us to see clearly the way in which Buddhism came to shape Tibetans' view of themselves. It also helps us understand the origins of Tibet's troubled relationship with China. And, by enabling us to trace Chenrezig's lineage through the dispassionate eyes of pre-Buddhist writers, it permits us to see the history that lies behind the creation of the Dalai Lama institution.

In the first place, the *Old Tibetan Chronicle* presents a far less flattering portrait of Songtsen Gampo and his world than that claimed in the great Buddhist histories of Tibet. The period of Tibetan history from the beginning of the reign of King Songtsen Gampo until the death of Rapalchen in 838 is known as that of the dharmarajahs, the religious kings. There were eight in all,

---

of Manichaean writings as well as of Syriac (or Nestorian) Christian scripture and liturgies. There was also much secular literature, including, for example, Confucian manuals of etiquette more exacting by far even than anything dreamed up in high Victorian England. *The Family Instructions of the Grandfather* set down rules of conduct for young men:

> *When his father goes out to walk*
> *The son must follow behind.*
> *If on the road he meets a senior*
> *He puts his feet together and joins his hands.*
> *In front of a senior*
> *He does not spit on the ground.*

* Some scholars prefer the term Pugyal.

and two besides Songtsen Gampo are acclaimed as incarnations of Chenrezig. Of them all, certainly three and probably four of the eight were assassinated, including two of the Bodhisattva kings. Indeed, its picture of ancient Tibet fits Hobbes's ghastly maxim perfectly. For many Tibetans, life was indeed nasty, brutish, and short.

To give just one eye-watering example of how nasty, the chronicle records that a certain Spug Gyuntang, fearful of disclosing to his wife a plot he is engaged in, roams the mountains at night rather than sleep with her. When eventually he returns they quarrel, so he bites her tongue out and she bleeds to death.[4]

From the chronicle, we also learn that Songtsen Gampo's father, Namri Songtsen, who had begun the work of unifying Tibet under his crown, was murdered in 620 when Songtsen was still a minor. A general insurrection ensued, culminating in more than one execution of convenience at court. These disturbances were largely quelled by a faithful minister, Myang. But then Myang himself was cleverly implicated in a plot by a ruthlessly ambitious courtier named Zutse. Myang was killed in the battle that followed the storming of his castle. The plotter now seized this moment to make an attempt on Songtsen Gampo's life. When it failed, Zutse committed suicide. Thereupon Zutse's son took his father's severed head to Songtsen Gampo, for which demonstration of loyalty he was permitted to retain the family fief. Later, Songtsen Gampo's own younger brother began to cause trouble for the king. The pretender duly died in his bed by fire, so the chronicle tells us, because of the treachery of a servant.[5] The atmosphere in the court of the Divine Mighty One Magically Manifest (to give Songtsen Gampo his full title) must have been bracing in the extreme.

As to the reality of such events as the promulgation of Songt-sen Gampo's Great Code of Supreme Law, this, if it existed, does not survive. The excerpt quoted earlier is from a mid-four-teenth-century source based on popular tradition. But from the legal documents that have come down to us from the Dunhuang library, we gather that Tibet's was explicitly a warrior culture, more akin to Homer's than that of either Buddhism or our own. The T'ang annals themselves speak of Tibetans as a people whose "military discipline is strict," noting that "they prize death in battle." Cases of cowardice were turned over to the will of the people. A fox's tail was attached to the head of the fainthearted one at which, we are told, a great crowd would assemble and the victim would be put to death. Similarly, the penalties for misdemeanor in the hunting field demonstrate very clearly "the stern demands of honor and discipline of a rugged, even militaristic society."[6] In the case of injury to persons of high rank, the penalty was death. Where there was little or no disparity in status between the two parties, this was commuted to payment of blood money (though the death penalty was exacted if this went unpaid).

There were also severe penalties for those who failed to go to the assistance of others injured in accidents on the hunting field, with forfeiture of property (including womenfolk) in prospect for those found guilty. Similarly, if your dog caused a third party to be thrown from his horse, the penalty was up to a maximum of "banishment to a desert place" and a quarter of all treasure and cattle forfeited by your family. There was, however, a system of rewards for rescue: a daughter or a sister or, if there was neither, or if an objection were made, then two hundred *sang* to be paid in recognition of valor.[7]

More striking still, as an example of life in ancient Tibet, was the custom, noted by Chinese and Tibetan records alike, of five or six select individuals dedicating themselves to the monarch as "common fated ones." Originally, it seems, this meant that they literally shared his fate: alive they enjoyed the same privileges. When he died, they were ritually slain:

The day when the sovereign dies, all the Men of the Same Fate during the day and the night indulge in wine. The [next day], when they are to be buried, they are stabbed in the [legs], so that they bleed to death. When they are then about to bury the living with the dead, there is, moreover, a trusted man among the relatives who, using his sword, cleaves their brain and cuts them out. He also takes four small pieces of wood, as great as a finger, and pierces their [chest] on both sides. When the four or five men are completely dead, they are buried with the dead [king].[8]

As late as 790, there is mention of a group of sworn companions whose duty it was to accompany the sovereign in death, though there are grounds for believing that by then this shared death was symbolic.

Continuing the work begun by his father, of unifying Tibet's disparate tribes and clans, Songtsen Gampo succeeded brilliantly—in fact to such a degree that he was able to extend his influence into neighboring territories. This he did with a mixture of guile and main force. Songtsen Gampo's ploy to obtain control over Zhang Zhung well illustrates his methods. First, he married his sister to the king. Then, when his brother-in-law began to cause trouble, Songtsen arranged for her to lead him into an ambush, on the pretext of joining Songtsen's hunting party. Thereafter, Zhang Zhung was easily co-opted into Songtsen's growing polity.

Not that Songtsen Gampo was shy of more conventional methods of domination. He personally led his troops into battle with the A-zha people, who lay between Tibetan-controlled territory and China, forcing them to pay tribute.* Nor was he afraid of taking on much more powerful enemies. In addition to subjugating Nepal and parts of upper Burma, on September 12,

* The Chinese for "A-zha" is *Tu yu hun*.

638, Songtsen Gampo had the audacity to launch a raid on Sung Chou, a garrison town within the border region of China herself.* The intention of this raid was not, of course, to subjugate on a permanent basis even a small part of China; but it was not merely an exercise in booty-gathering either. The king wanted to be noticed.

Following the idiom of the day, it is clear that Songtsen Gampo desired to augment his power at home by forging marriage alliances with those territories over which he could not hope to exercise direct control for any length of time. He thus took wives not only from the Tibetan feudal aristocracy, but also from the Mi-nyan people of upper Burma and, as we have seen, from Nepal.† A Chinese wife would have been the most desirable prize of all. It would signify that Tibet had obtained most-favored status with the emperor. And Songtsen Gampo felt that such status was his due.

For their part, the Chinese emperors were in the habit of granting brides to those barbarian (and anyone who was not Chinese was a barbarian) chieftains with whom it seemed politic to develop alliances. It was one way of beginning the process of civilizing them. Letting them have silk was another. Such grants did not come without a great deal of cultural baggage, however. They were closely bound up with the tribute system that governed China's foreign relations. From the Chinese perspective, the emperor was Son of Heaven and therefore preeminent among all who lived under heaven. It followed that all men should honor and pay tribute to him. But while this principle was generally enforceable within China herself, the attitudes of other peoples were much less readily conformable to this principle. They too should, by rights, honor the one who held heaven's

---

* According to Schafer, *chou* means, literally, "land bound by water," or "island," but came to be used to denote an administrative district, generally with a town or city as its capital.
† Though legend is adamant about this, some scholars, notably Tucci, have doubted whether Songtsen ever did receive a Nepalese princess.

mandate; but because they were uncivilized, and ignorant with it, generally they did not. Nonetheless, the emperor, as befitted his office, was generosity, not to say munificence, itself. He was always ready to bestow his favor on any who would come before him and submit. In deserving cases, he might even grant a member of the imperial household—though certainly not a daughter—as a bride in recognition of the fidelity and good standing of a foreign ruler. This was particularly likely when the barbarians in question were so troublesome that a way must be found of bringing them into line.

In 635, a request by Songtsen Gampo for a matrimonial alliance was turned down by the imperial court. The Tibetan king was duly affronted. It was in response to this rebuff that he launched his infamous raid on Sung Chou. The Tibetan monarch was, in effect, alerting the Chinese that he represented a force to be reckoned with. The fact that, ten days after occupying the town, his army was seen off by a superior Chinese force can have done nothing to detract from the impression his daring made. So when subsequently Songtsen Gampo sent Great Minister mGar, popularly known as mGar the Conqueror, with five thousand ounces of gold and several hundred "precious baubles" at the head of an embassy to the Chinese court, "to beg," in the words of the Chinese records, "forgiveness for his [Songtsen Gampo's] crimes," we need not suppose that this was his motive at all. He wanted a bride, just as legend tells us. And this time he was given one. Indeed, though of course there is no mention of mGar's four tasks, the T'ang annals further state that the Tibetan envoy gave such a good account of himself, and so impressed the emperor with his clever replies, that he himself was also offered a princess. mGar declined, however, on the grounds that he was already married (and, we may suppose, knew what was good for him). But humorous legend adds that following his success, mGar took such a long time to return home that in the meantime he fathered a child on Songtsen Gampo's princess.

According to the *Old Tibetan Chronicle*, Wengchen, the princess, was not actually intended as a bride for Songtsen Gampo himself but for his son and heir, GungTsan, who, when he came of age, would assume power in the place of his father. It seems, however, that GungTsan never took full control of Tibet's affairs, ruling only as viceroy from 641 to his death at the age of eighteen in 646. Songtsen Gampo then reassumed power, taking as his own his son's wives. Songtsen Gampo himself died, and was buried with a squadron of ritually slaughtered horses, in 649 or 650. Wengchen died in 680. These dates are reasonably certain, though that of Songtsen Gampo's birth is not. But we can be reasonably sure that he did not live to be eighty-nine, as the religious historians assert. He was likely nearer to forty.[9]

These dates make Songtsen Gampo a near contemporary of Taizong, T'ang emperor of China, who reigned from 626 until his death, also in 649. Regarded as one of the greatest of all the Chinese emperors, Taizong was not only an accomplished military leader but also a capable scholar and calligrapher—the very model of a Confucian monarch—who "attracted able ministers, established close relations with his advisers, accepted criticism, and lived frugally."[10] Under his direction, imperial troops gained control of Inner Mongolia and swept deep into Central Asia to establish garrisons at the great Silk Road trading centers of Kucha, Khotan, Yarkand, Kashgar, and elsewhere. He also saw to improvements in the examination system governing public appointments and established scholarships for poorer students. Not that he was incapable of ruthlessness. At the time of his accession, he ordered his two brothers and all their ten sons executed. And, in the end, he did become somewhat corrupted by his immense personal power and prestige. He began to overlook affairs of state in favor of long and costly hunting expeditions. And on one occasion he had a palace that had taken about two million days to construct destroyed on the grounds that its site was too hot and the building's style too elaborate.

But well might Songtsen Gampo have congratulated himself on obtaining a princess from so great a monarch. It seems, indeed, that he took the alliance very seriously. In 646, Songtsen sent another embassy led by the faithful mGar, bearing a letter written in flowery language to congratulate the Son of Heaven on his victory (short-lived, as it turned out) over Korea. This was accompanied by a ewer in the shape of a swan, seven feet tall and made of solid gold.[11] Then, in 648, Songtsen Gampo sent troops to the assistance of the emperor's mission to India.[12] And while there has been scholarly debate over whether Thonmi Sambhota really did invent the written language, there is no doubt that one of the first uses to which Tibetans put their new-found literacy was in setting up a Chinese-style chancery.[13]

This early contact with China inaugurated something of an enthusiasm on the part of Tibetans for all things Chinese, an enthusiasm which continued beyond the reign of Songtsen Gampo. Throughout the T'ang era, the sons of Tibet's aristocratic families were sent to China to be educated. On one occasion, a Tibetan royal embassy formally requested ten copies of the Chinese classics—which included the works of Confucius, Mencius and Sun Tzu. Unfortunately, this only elicited a frosty internal response, saying that to meet it would be like "giving weapons to brigands or one's possessions to thieves."

From the Tibetan perspective, the most important aspect of the contact between China and Tibet was the royal family's exposure to Buddhism. It seems likely that the *buddhadharma* was already known in parts of Tibet, having entered from Central Asia; but it was from China that the Tibetan kings took their religion, even if it is unclear to what extent Songtsen Gampo himself can properly be described as a Buddhist. There is no evidence from the Dunhuang library that he ever formally became one. It is also not true that he founded 108 Buddhist temples, though we can date the founding of the Ramoché and Jokhang temples approximately to his time, along with perhaps ten more.[14]

Yet there seems no reason to doubt that he at least took an interest in his wives' religion. And it is surely significant that, in 649, the new emperor of China, Emperor Gaozong—physically weak (he had frequent attacks of incapacitating dizziness), indecisive, mother-dominated and not actually a believer himself—conferred on the Tibetan monarch the Buddhist title of Pao-Wang: Precious King, or King of Jewels.[15] This is of particular interest from the point of view of the cult of the Dalai Lamas because the term Pao-Wang was an epithet of Amitabha, Buddha of the Western Heavens, whose activity Avalokitesvara-Chenrezig manifests. It is possible that this event marks the origin of the tradition that Songtsen Gampo was himself an incarnation of Chenrezig.

5

The Later Dharmarajahs

The incomparable Songtsen Gampo was succeeded, in orderly fashion, by his grandson, Mangson, in 650, or thereabouts, but as he was still a minor, Great Minister mGar assumed the role of regent. While making no attempt to usurp the throne—presumably because the sacral character of the dynasty could not be transferred—not only did mGar retain this position until his own death, he even succeeded in passing it to his son. Like the Shogun families of Japan, and the Ranas of Nepal, for a time that of mGar rose to be more powerful than the monarchy itself. There was some justice in this. T'ang historians record a cutting, if diplomatic, reply to an inquiry after the Tibetan king's health at the reception of an embassy to Chang'an. The Tibetan envoy stated that Mangson was a diligent ruler, but could not be compared with his grandfather.[1]

Before mGar Senior died, in 667, he had done much to consolidate the conquests of Songtsen Gampo. Toward the end of his life, Tibetan troops had begun to raid the Chinese-controlled Silk Road settlements of Khotan and Kashgar, generally in alliance with local Turgis tribesmen. This set the pattern for what was to follow for the best part of the next two centuries. Interrupted only by brief interludes of peace following treaties proposed by one side or the other, a period of almost constant conflict with China ensued. And if at first sight the story of the Tibetan Empire seems remote from that of the Dalai Lamas, in reality it is not. It is precisely the glory of this era to which Chenrezig's later incarnations lay claim. The period is also vitally important from the perspective of Sino-Tibetan relations. Not that, to start with at least, there was an open breach between the two thrones. There are records of at least two important embassies during Mangson's reign—although it is difficult to know quite what to make of the Chinese historians' assertion that the first took a gift of a hundred wild tarpans and an ass fifty feet tall.[*]

The second embassy, which arrived during 658, took with it, more plausibly but hardly less marvelous, the gift of "a golden city, populated by golden horsemen, and the figures of horses, lions, elephants, and other animals," testifying to Tibetans' facility as goldsmiths, even at this early phase in their culture.[2] Indeed, to "judge by records of tribute and gifts from Tibet to T'ang, which over and over again list large objects of gold, remarkable for their beauty and rarity and excellent workmanship, the Tibetan goldsmiths were the wonder of the medieval world."[3]

The first clash with T'ang came in 670 when Tibetan forces, in an enterprising and daring campaign, moved north and seized control of the Tarim Basin by sacking the city states of Khotan and Kashgar. The Tarim, comprising the great depression separating the Kunlun and Tien Shan mountain ranges, and including the fearsome Taklamakan Desert, is home today to China's nuclear-testing stations. Then, it was skirted to north and south

---

[*] Tarpans were a breed of small, dun-colored horse, originally from the Russian steppes but recently extinct.

by the great Silk Road. Control of these two of China's so-called Four Garrisons put the southern route into Tibetan hands.

King Mangson died in 676, having personally made almost no impression on Tibetan history. He was succeeded by Du'song, a man of very different mettle, though he never succeeded in establishing himself as absolute ruler of Tibet. At that time, Tibetan fortunes were considerably bolstered by their defeat of the Chinese army, which tried to dislodge the upstarts from the Tarim garrisons. This put Tibetan troops in control of the whole of China's frontier south of Qocho and with it the northern trade routes as well. For a generation, the Silk Road trade with Central Asia was held in Tibetan hands, prompting a student of the Chinese Imperial Academy to remark that the emergence of Tibetan power was more than merely a temporary phenomenon. "I am afraid," he wrote prophetically, "that the pacification of Tibet is not something you can expect to accomplish between dawn and dusk."[4]

It was only in 689 that the T'ang armies began a concerted effort to take back control of the Tarim. At the first attempt they were again repulsed. Three years later, however, they succeeded and a leading member of the mGar clan was himself put to the sword. When another Tibetan army suffered heavy losses at the hands of the Chinese in 693–4, King Du'song took the opportunity to move against the house of mGar. The monarch invited a large number of the clan—about two thousand of them—to a royal hunting party where he ambushed and routed them completely.

At the same time as annihilating his mGar rivals, King Du'song sued for peace with China and renewed a now long-standing request for a second marriage alliance with T'ang. Given the circumstances, this appears at first sight almost as brazen as Songtsen Gampo's proposal more than half a century earlier. The Tibetans were demanding a concession even in defeat. Yet from the Chinese perspective, it cannot have been entirely without appeal. If granted, it might win them another period of peace and cooperation with these increasingly troublesome barbarians. Accordingly, although the proposal was not accepted at once, it was not turned down either.

When, in 699, T'ang secured a further victory over the Tibetans in their quest to regain control of eastern Central Asia, the last of the mGar chieftains committed suicide and it looked as though Du'song would finally be able to assume full control of Tibet. At that moment, however, his mother, the formidable Tri (Queen) Ma'lod, seized power and took the position of regent while her son had to remain content with command of the military. Following his death in action in 704, Tri Ma'lod became undisputed ruler of Tibet. Her first action was to depose Du'song's son, the rightful heir to the throne, and install another royal child known as Mé Ag'tsom who was then just a year old.

It is striking to note that in her chicanery, the queen was to some extent mirroring the coup undertaken in China by her contemporary and diplomatic friend, the Empress Wu. (The two women were in direct contact until Wu's death in 705.)[5] A concubine of Emperor Gaozong, Wu Zeitan manipulated the succession first by causing various crown princes to be poisoned and installing her third son, Zhongzong. But, after just six weeks, she repented of her decision and replaced him with another son whom she subsequently kept a virtual prisoner at the Inner Palace. During the six years of her son's nominal reign, Wu Zeitan began to promote herself as empress in waiting, an immensely ambitious undertaking given that Confucian ideology had no place for a female on the throne. Turning to Buddhism for legitimization, she seized on a Mahayana text which prophesies that a future *cakravartin*, or "universal monarch," will be a woman. Her supporters, among them a prominent monk of doubtful piety, went a stage further and proclaimed her an incarnation of Maitreya, the future Buddha. Such was popular enthusiasm for Buddhism in China at the time that this enabled her to usurp her son. She thus became the first—and last—woman to ascend, after the customary three refusals, the Dragon Throne. Her reign, remarkable for its brutality even by the standards of the day, lasted fifteen years from her accession in 690. In an act of the cruelest revenge, one of her first deeds as empress was to cause Gaozong's widow, together with a now aging concubine, to have their limbs amputated and what remained of them tossed in a vat of wine to drown.

It was at least partially due to the good relations between Empress Wu and the Tibetan queen that, in 707, the T'ang court now provisionally acceded to Tibet's long-standing petition for a new marriage alliance. The original request was for one of Wu Zeitan's own daughters. Instead, she had "earmarked eventually to receive that dubious honor one of her nieces, the princess Ching Ch'en . . . on whom she conferred imperial privileges."⁶ With the empress by this time dead and her son, the weak and ineffectual Emperor Zhongzong, recently re-enthroned, Ching Ch'en finally departed for Tibet in 710.⁷ She arrived to find herself betrothed not to a graybeard, as perhaps she feared, but, hardly more enticingly, to a boy of eight—the future king, Mé Ag'tsom.

At this time, Tri Ma'lod was still very much alive and we have no reason to suppose that Ching Ch'en and her retinue were not well-received. But two years later, in 712, the old lady died and the rapprochement with T'ang she had so assiduously promoted ended soon after. Although a Chinese embassy was received at the Tibetan court in 713, the following year saw Tibetan troops sweep across the Yellow River and raid deep into Chinese territory precisely at harvest-time, carrying the year's labor back to Tibet. This agricultural banditry developed into an annual event, causing the region to be nicknamed the "Tibetan grain estates" by bitter Chinese locals.

This cannot have made life easy for Ching Ch'en, whom we know to have kept up a correspondence with her relatives at home all her life: she would no doubt have come under intense pressure to use her influence to bring the Tibetans back into line. But the pressure was not from one side only. In 721, she wrote to Chang'an, then capital of China, urging the emperor to accept Tibetan terms for a new peace treaty. By pushing west into Central Asia and forming an alliance with the Arab armies that had begun to penetrate the region, Tibetan troops were once again threatening the Chinese hold over the Silk Road trade. When Mé Ag'tsom's terms for peace were refused, Ching Ch'en made plans to escape to Kashmir, though in the end she did not go. Perhaps she felt that a series of defeats subsequently inflicted on the Tibetan army by her countrymen would redress the situation in China's favor. But then her husband, now a vigorous twenty-five-year-old, traveled east to lead a new campaign against the Chinese, attacking and capturing the important border garrison at Kua Chou in a thrilling victory of Tibetan arms. As it was recorded in the *Old Tibetan Chronicle*, "the many riches of the Chinese being taken out to the Western Regions . . . having been amassed in Kua Chou were all confiscated by the Tibetans who thereby once again found great wealth. Even the ordinary people joined in covering themselves with good Chinese silks."[8]

Two years later, in 732, the two powers came to new terms in a treaty recorded in bilingual inscriptions on stone pillars erected in their respective territories. Significantly, the Tibetans now refused to accept the traditional Chinese token of vassaldom when they went to Chang'an to sign it. This was comprised of one half of a bronze (some authorities say golden) fish, the other half of which was kept at the Chinese court. Effectively a *laissez-passer* for the barbarian envoys that carried them, these fish halves were emblematic of the bearer's subservient status. In declining to accept one, the Tibetan envoy adroitly signified Tibet's claim to equality with T'ang—an equality the Chinese were forced to concede again and again.

The first time was in 736, when Tibetan troops marched into Turkestan, causing T'ang to revoke the treaty just four years after it was signed. The Chinese responded with an invasion of the Tibetans' northeastern territory, hoping thereby to forestall the possibility of Tibetan troops forming up with the Turgis tribes in the west. King Mé Ag'tsom had recently entered into a formal alliance with their king, the *qaghan*, by granting him a Tibetan princess. That the Chinese were not entirely successful is, however, suggested by the defeat inflicted by the Tibeto-Turgis axis on some twenty petty fiefdoms in the Pamirs to the far west. Following this, once again, as the Chinese historians put it, "tribute ceased to arrive."[9]

T'ang now replied with further attacks in the east, this time on three fronts simultaneously. They were successful on two of them, prompting Mé Ag'tsom himself to lead the counterattack. This "unusually brutal" action of 741 saw the destruction of an important Chinese town, the slaughter of its inhabitants and the subsequent occupation of a strategic Chinese fortress.[10]

Despite this setback, T'ang continued to pour troops into the region. By the end of the decade, the Chinese had retaken almost all of their former territories in central and eastern Inner Asia from the Tibetans, who had, in the meantime, become embroiled in domestic turmoil. So severe was this that it led, in 754, to the assassination of the king.

The source of trouble at the Tibetan court is far from clear, but it seems likely that it represents the culmination of long-standing resentment toward Princess Ching Ch'en and the growing influence of her Buddhist faith. It also marks the first of a series of reversals for the supporters of the new religion, testifying to the bitter ideological contest it precipitated among the Tibetan leadership. Although there were at this time neither any monasteries nor any ordained Tibetans, and though the religion cannot have spread far beyond the palace, it seems to have been identified politically with the progressive, pro-Chinese faction at court. As for the princess herself, she seems to have been very pious. We know, for example, that she gave personal protection to a community of monastic refugees from Khotan. But following her death in 739, in an outbreak of smallpox, there was a general reaction against Buddhism, which was blamed for having angered the national gods. This in turn suggests a reassertion of the values of the old religion by conservative chieftains, and a purging of the pro-Buddhist, pro-Chinese element at court.

On to this scene of internal disintegration and external reversal came the new king, the second royal incarnation of Chenrezig, Trisong Detsen, "manifesting himself as the best of men."[11] Born in 742, the offspring of Mé Ag'tsom and his Chinese bride, Trisong Detsen was old enough, at fourteen, to ascend the throne immediately. But no sooner had he done so than, according to the later historians, the anti-Buddhist faction at court intensified its attacks on the new religion and, in acts of sacrilege unsurpassed until the Cultural Revolution twelve hundred years later, unleashed an iconoclasm that virtually obliterated it. Temples were either destroyed or, as in the case of the Jokhang, turned into slaughterhouses. Sheep carcasses were hung from the hands of the holy statues and, the Buddhist historians tell us, their necks garlanded with entrails.[12]

Though the young incarnation was privately sympathetic to Buddhism, it was not until later in his long reign that Trisong Detsen came out firmly in favor of the new faith. Nor was his conversion entirely uncontested. It seems that eighth-century Tibet was something of a spiritual battleground with Christian, Islamic and Manichaean missionaries all targeting the country. In the meantime, under Trisong Detsen's leadership, the Tibetans began once again to throw themselves back into central and eastern Inner Asia. In China, a rebellion against the elderly (and lately infatuated) Emperor Xuanzong during 756 gave them an opportunity to reassert themselves, which they were quick to seize. Within a few years, Tibetan forces were encroaching on the eastern part of what is now Gansu province. Then, in 763, they mounted an audacious raid on Chang'an, the Chinese capital.

Astonishingly, the world's largest city fell to the Tibetans. And not only that, they were even able briefly to set up their own puppet emperor.*[13] Though he lasted no more than three weeks before being overthrown, this was still a breathtaking feat of arms, and utterly humiliating of T'ang.† And though again this Tibetan operation was a raid and not an invasion as such, the storming of Chang'an, which had more than a million inhabitants, was a remarkable episode and one which left the important grazing lands to the west of the Chinese capital in Tibetan hands for many decades.

To understand how the highlanders were able to exploit T'ang weakness to such a degree, we need to know something about Tibet's war machine at this time. In the first place, the country was kept on a permanent war footing. Administratively, Tibet was divided into first three, then as their territory grew, four "horns," or regions, under the command of a *ru-pön* responsible for both military and civil governance: there seems to have been little distinction between the two. Each of these four horns was further subdivided into smaller units under the authority of military commanders responsible for raising troops and supplying them with the necessities of war: troops, horses, rations for both man and beast, armor and weaponry.

On active service, wherever the Tibetan armies were victorious, they immediately pressed into service those who fell into their clutches. Prisoners were kept at first in large pits (certainly dug by themselves). The most important were then questioned and, if necessary, tortured, before being tattooed and assigned

* This was Guang-bu Huanti-ti.
† It is worth noting that the *chos'byung* historians hardly deigned to mention this feat, their concerns being primarily religious.

duties. Literate prisoners were appointed to administrative tasks and tattooed on the arm. Ordinary prisoners were pressed into service as soldiers and tattooed on the face.[14] From documents found by Sir Aurel Stein on another of his expeditions to the region, we learn that Tibetans were stern masters. "At the beginning of the first spring month of the Horse year, on examining the soldiers . . . one of the Khotanese serving as cooks . . . having many times caused annoyances, it was decided that he should be put to death."[15] But so remote were some of the outposts that they were forced to occupy, it is evident that keeping them adequately supplied was not always an easy task. "To the tiger soldiers as far on as Ho-to Gyumo, letter petition of the Glin-rins soldiers. We, a sergeant and a corporal, both having mountain sickness . . . having run short of food and provisions, have the kindness to send them soon." For similar reasons of remoteness, there was also the familiar problem of providing for the soldiers' other basic requirements: "There being for the males not a single female companion, the ruler-in-chief is begged to send at once many serving women."[16] Nor was it always possible to find suitable men for the task of administering these far-flung acquisitions: "The Home Minister Tshan-to-re is an insane mother-ravisher, sister-ravisher, an insatiate wine-bibber, a death-child, who deserves to die nine times—in fornication and wine a gourd and a sieve. Having ravished all the matrons who came in his way, great and small, he should be expelled to Sin-San."[17]

Other documentary survivals from the period tell us something of how Tibetan troops operated in the field. A marching column would typically be comprised of horsemen leading, followed by archers and "dagger-armed soothsayers"—perhaps the equivalent of a detachment of modern-day intelligence and signals operators?—followed by spearmen, bringing up the rear. A Chinese account notes:

Men and horses all wear [link] mail* and armor. Its workmanship is extremely fine. It envelops them completely, leaving
an opening only for the two eyes. Thus, strong bows and sharp
swords cannot injure them . . . When they do battle, they must
dismount and array themselves in ranks. When one dies, another
takes his place. To the end, they are not willing to retreat.[18]

In 783, the monarchs of Tibet and China concluded a new
treaty, again on the initiative of the Chinese, who desired to relieve
pressure on the frontier.[19] This treaty defined the border between
their respective territories and confirmed Tibetan dominion over
east Turkestan, Gansu and a large part of modern-day Szechuan
province. It did not satisfy the Tibetans for long. In 787, their
troops captured first Dunhuang and then, in 792, Khotan. For
the second time, the whole of the Silk Road trade (now greatly
expanded) lay in Tibetan hands. Given that just a century and
a half before, Tibet was comprised of little more than an array
of more or less mutually hostile tribes of so little consequence
it had barely come to the notice of the Chinese, this expansion
of Tibetan power was an extraordinary achievement.

If the second half of the eighth century saw the high-water
mark of Tibetan military expansion abroad, domestically the
same period was of even greater consequence to the future history
of Tibet. It was at this time that Trisong Detsen began to take
a serious interest in Buddhism. He invited to Tibet a famous
Indian Buddhist monk, Shantarakshita. Not yet entirely
convinced that its advocates did not practice black magic, the
king also sent two ministers to India to inquire into the validity
of the Buddhist teachings. These ministers reported back their
findings after two months, as a result of which the king acquired
"firm faith that the doctrine was good" and formally adopted it.

---

* This was made of intricately woven leather.

This inaugurated a power struggle between those sympathetic to Buddhism and advocates of the old religion which was to last until the dynasty fell two centuries later. Almost at once, the king's conversion precipitated a violent reaction among the still-powerful supporters of the old religion. Buddhism was no longer associated with China, but it was so strongly disliked by many that, following an outbreak of natural disasters, which were again blamed on Buddhism for having angered the national gods, the king had no option but to compel Shantarakshita to leave and await a more propitious time. A year or so later, however, the Indian sage was back and, at his instigation, another Buddhist master was invited to Tibet. This was Padmasambhava.*[20]

As we shall see, subsequent accounts elevate Padmasambhava to the dignity of a second Buddha. So far as the historical record is concerned, it seems that he was a wonder-worker who specialized not just in subjugating demons hostile to Buddhism, but also in the entirely practical science of water miracles. Some modern scholars speculate that, for all his spiritual credentials, Padmasambhava was, preeminently, an irrigation expert. This is made the more likely given that we know the Swat Valley, whence he came, had complex irrigation systems in place at this time. Apparently using gabions, he "trained rivers and lakes," caused water to "spurt forth in arid lands," and transformed sandy plains into meadows, creating many lush and fertile fields.[21] These scholars further argue that it was the power that Padmasambhava's "water miracles" placed in the hands of ordinary people that caused the landowning classes to take against him. Whatever the correct interpretation, there followed a new court revolt against Buddhism such that before he was able to complete his work, Padmasambhava was ejected from Tibet on the orders of the king himself. It would even appear that Trisong Detsen was party to a plot to

* Literally, "the Lotus Born."

assassinate him as he made his way home. Fortunately, Padmasambhava, being clairvoyant, knew of the plan and caused his would-be assailants to be "frozen like a painting, unable to speak" and passed through them.[22] Leaving Tibetan territory, he uttered a famous and telling prophecy—that in future, the divisions in Tibet would not be between Buddhists and non-Buddhists, but among the followers of the doctrine themselves.

Despite the evident controversy surrounding Padmasambhava's mission, the king did not renounce his faith. In 775, or just after, Tibet's first monastery was consecrated by Shantarakshita, who must have survived the purge of his co-religionist. This was Samye, a building quite as ambitious and impressive as any building in Inner Asia at this time. Although first damaged (during the eleventh century), then burned down (during the seventeenth), then again ruined in an earthquake (during the early nineteenth), Samye was rebuilt each time according to the original plan. What we see today is thought not to be greatly different from the eighth-century original, and an extraordinary achievement it remains. Said to have been modeled on the great Indian center of monastic learning at Odantapuri—which not only does not survive but its actual location has been forgotten—Samye is constructed on the plan of a mandala, taking the form of a three-dimensional rendering of the Buddhist *abhidharma* universe.

Around the same time as founding Samye, Shantarakshita also ordained the first Tibetan monastics: fifty sons and daughters of "noble and genteel" families. Then, in 779, Trisong Detsen published an edict declaring Buddhism to be the state religion of Tibet. No longer were men to have their eyes put out, nor women their noses cut off for apostasy as the old religion demanded. Instead, all of the court ministers were on oath to protect the holy doctrine. For now, the king had won his battle with the reactionaries.[23]

This must truly have seemed the inauguration of a new and

glorious era. T'ang was at bay, the Silk Road trade lay entirely in Tibetan hands, and, as if to lay claim to heavenly glory as well, the king had officially embraced the new religion. Small wonder that later tradition proclaimed him a manifestation not only of Chenrezig but of Vajrapani too—the embodiment of the Buddha's power.

Yet no sooner had the Tibetan court officially embraced the new religion than Padmasambhava's awful prophecy began to be fulfilled. Within the matter of a few years, a doctrinal dispute erupted, splitting the nascent Buddhist community in two. In essence, the dispute was between a faction that accepted the possibility of achieving enlightenment in a sudden flash of inspiration (the subitists) and another which claimed that this— essentially Chinese—development in Buddhist thought was heretical and that enlightenment could only be achieved after persistent effort (the gradualists).

Given the strength of feeling that the controversy aroused, it is not surprising to read in the victors' histories that the doctrine of instant enlightenment drove its adherents mad. One leading proponent is said to have gashed himself, two others to have crushed their own testicles, and yet another to have set fire to his head.[24] Trisong Detsen resolved the crisis by holding a great debate at Samye. Himself presiding, the king quickly found in favor of the gradualists and expelled the leader of the subitists, a Chinese monk named Hashang Mohoyen. Nothing more was heard of him, though it is said that four of his accomplices subsequently took revenge and murdered the leader of the gradualist faction—by squeezing his kidneys.[25]

The last years of Dharma King Trisong Detsen's reign are obscure. It seems that the sudden-enlightenment dispute must in some way have played into the hands of the old religionists, who succeeded in engineering his abdication in 797. He died three years later, possibly assassinated by or at the behest of his first wife, who was one of their number. But if there is doubt over the cause of Trisong Detsen's death, there is none that the dowager poisoned his son Muni Tsanpo. A supporter of the Buddhists himself, the young king had attempted to move against the supporters of the old religion. The dowager now tried to set up another son, Mu'rug, but he had drawn the hatred of the Na'nam clan during his brief reign and they opposed his candidacy. It seems that on one occasion, the late king had been holding private discussions with his great minister when Mu'rug attempted to gain entry. The Na'nam guard at the door moved to prevent him, whereupon Mu'rug drew his sword and killed the man. As a result of this opposition, the old queen was forced to enthrone still another son, Senalek, though Mu'rug effectively held power until he was himself assassinated by his Na'nam enemies in an act of revenge.

Senalek's reign proved to be a worthy one. With both his mother, who died soon afterward, and Mu'rug out of the way, he too actively supported Buddhism, taking the unprecedented step of appointing a monk as his great minister. Abroad, the Tibetan armies continued to hold the Chinese at bay in the east, while far to the west (more than fifteen hundred miles away!) Tibetan troops participated in a siege of Samarkand. And to the north, they threw a bridge over the Yellow River at Wul-lan in order to raid into Uighur territory.

When Senalek died—of natural causes—in 815, he was succeeded by his youngest son, the third and last of the kingly incarnations of Chenrezig. King Rapalchen was, according to the religious historians, so devout that he had extensions woven into his hair in order that when conversing with members of the *sangha*, the monastic community, they could sit on his locks. Rather more plausibly, a Chinese account from this time describes the king occupying a sumptuous golden domed tent, decorated with tigers, leopards and fierce reptiles executed in gold.[26] But Rapalchen was a weak ruler who suffered poor health and paid little attention to affairs of state. His primary interest lay in the propagation of Buddhism. During his reign, the number of translations of Buddhist texts multiplied, monasteries were endowed with royal patronage and many new temples and shrines were built. He also granted further privileges to the *sangha*, while making it a crime, punishable by amputation of the fingers, to point at and mock the clergy. Nonetheless, the empire remained sufficiently strong and T'ang sufficiently weak for the two dynasties to have signed, in 821, the last of their peace treaties.

In 838, no doubt in reaction to Rapalchen's excess of piety, there was a new revolt against the crown. Once again, the old religionists asserted themselves. The accounts differ as to what happened to Rapalchen—some say he was inside his palace, others that he was drinking *chang*, or barley beer, in his garden— but all agree that the king was murdered by two ministers who twisted Rapalchen's head around until his neck broke.

6

Like a Beggar Saying He Is King, Like a Donkey Dressed in Lion's Skin

Rapalchen was succeeded by Lang Darma, his elder brother. Seniority did not guarantee succession—more or less any male member of the ruling family was eligible—but precisely why Lang Darma was not crowned in the first place is unclear. Most likely the younger son had better suited a largely pro-Buddhist court. What is clear, however, is that Rapalchen's murder was the culmination of a carefully orchestrated series of events.[1] In addition to his trichological eccentricities and his legal protection of the clergy, Rapalchen also decreed that every monk should be maintained by no less than seven households apiece. This was tantamount to a new tax and was bound to be unpopular given that the majority of families were not Buddhist themselves. As the present Dalai Lama's brother has written, with cool understatement, Rapalchen "let his fervor carry him too far."[2]

The first sign of trouble was the forced exile of the king's own son.* The royal soothsayers, the priests of the old religion,

* Some authorities say brother.

predicted that if he did not go, Rapalchen's life would be in danger and the country itself liable to harm. Next, the king's monk chief minister was successfully, though wrongly, convicted of conducting an illicit affair with the queen. He was duly executed, most likely by being sewn in animal skins and thrown into a river.* The queen then committed suicide.[3]

The saintly Rapalchen's subsequent assassination gave the Buddhist historians the opportunity to vent their spleen against the old religionists. Following his death, "the power of the sovereigns diminished like winter rain. The Laws of the Ten Virtues disintegrated like a rope of rotten reeds . . . Evil actions raged like swirling tempests, while kindly thoughts were forgotten like last night's dreams."[4] They are especially bilious toward Gyal-To're, one of the assassins, whom they portray as evil personified. And while it is tempting to assume that they are exaggerating, the T'ang historians concur. He was, they report, cruel, perverse and over-fond of women and hunting. It was inevitable, say the worthy Confucians, that with ministers like this the Tibetan state should fall.[5]

And fall it did, if not immediately. Lang Darma's reign lasted four, perhaps six years (the dates in the various accounts do not agree exactly), but at any rate long enough for him virtually to expunge Buddhism from the land, according to the traditional histories. Monks and nuns were forcibly laicized. Some were compelled to become butchers, others to become hunters, still others to marry. The doors of the temples and monasteries were bricked up and daubed with caricatures of beer-swilling monastics, their contents destroyed. The story is told of a learned cleric encountering a monk hunting wild animals with his robes hitched up, a bow and arrow in his hands and feathers on his head. Unable to believe what he was seeing, the master besought his companions: "Am I an old man who has lost his mind?"

---

* This being the usual method of execution right up until the twentieth century.

'It is not you who is mad," they replied sadly.

The climax came when news of the harm being done to the holy doctrine finally reached the ears of Lhalung Palgyi Dorje, a hermit meditating in a cave some miles to the east of Lhasa. Feeling great compassion for Lang Darma, he knew there was only one thing to be done.

Taking some soot and some oil, Lhalung blackened his face and hands. He then blackened a white horse. Next he dressed in a long black cloak with a white lining and put a black hat on his head. (This story is beloved of every Tibetan schoolchild to this day.) Armed with an iron bow and a quiver of iron arrows, he mounted up and rode to Lhasa. Leaving his horse tied up close to the river and, keeping his weapons hidden, he made his way on foot to the center of the town. There he found the king reading the inscription on the stone pillar erected in front of the Jokhang. Going up to Lang Darma, the hermit made as if to prostrate before him. In Buddhist countries, this is performed by sinking to the knees, then throwing the body flat on the ground, arms outstretched, before standing and repeating the action twice more. On his first prostration, Lhalung, concealing his movements within the voluminous sleeves of his cloak, took an arrow from its quiver. On the second, he bent his bow. On the third, standing up, he fired directly at Lang Darma's heart. As the king fell dying, a great cry went up from the crowd and, in the confusion that followed, Lhalung ran back to where his horse was tethered. Vaulting on to its back, he threw off his hat, reversed his cloak so that it was white side out, and urged his steed into the river. On reaching the opposite bank, it emerged with the soot washed away. Both horse and rider were now all white where before they were all black. In this guise, as the "white demon of the skies," Lhalung escaped east, arriving eventually in the province of Kham, where he spent the rest of his days.

Another, slightly different tradition, recounted by the present Dalai Lama's elder brother, tells how Lhalung, riding to Lhasa, took part in a ritual Dance of the Black Hats in order to get close to the king. According to this version of events, it took three arrows to kill Lang Darma, though how his assassin could have made good his escape after this is difficult to imagine. In either case, we are faced with the same conundrum: one of the great heroes of Tibetan Buddhism is not a martyr for the faith but a regicide.

For this phase of Tibetan history, we are almost entirely reliant on the religious historians. It is difficult to discern how much of it "actually happened"; but this is largely irrelevant. The more important question is, rather, how Lhalung Palgyi Dorje can be said, as all the authorities assure us he did, to have had compassion for the king.

The answer is that, according to a certain—puzzling—strand within Buddhist thought, there may be certain instances when individuals, through their sinful actions, put themselves in danger of falling into the lowest hells (and thus beyond the reach of help). In such instances, it may be an act of compassion, provided that the motive is entirely pure and selfless, to kill them in order to prevent that person from harming themselves and others still further. In other words, in certain circumstances, murder is not murder at all, but an act of kindness.

The assassination of Lang Darma, for which we can only hope he was properly grateful, precipitated the final collapse of the empire. By the middle of the ninth century, the majority of Tibetan-controlled Silk Road towns and fortresses had fallen to the Chinese. In 851, Khotan, arguably the most important of them, regained its independence, and in the same year, the governor of Dunhuang submitted to T'ang.

Although a son of dubious paternity born to one of Lang Darma's queens was set up as king by the anti-Buddhist nobles, another, Örung, was held by the Buddhist party to be the true heir. Neither succeeded in gaining universal recognition. Örung was murdered while his nephew fled to the far west of Tibet. There he founded a new Buddhist kingdom comprising present-day Ladakh and Gu'ge.* In the meantime, two rival warlords emerged in central Tibet. Again, neither was able to gain complete mastery. One simply disappears from the chronicles; the other's head ended up (say T'ang sources) being sent in offering to the imperial court at Chang'an.[6] Finally, early in the tenth century, there was a rebellion among the chieftains of central Tibet that obliterated the last vestiges of centralized power.[7] The simultaneous desecration and looting of the royal tombs symbolized the final destruction of the old religion. With this, the sacral character of the dynasty was lost without hope of retrieval.

So far as Lang Darma's persecution of Buddhism is concerned, not much is known beyond what the religious historians tell us. There are, however, increasing numbers of scholars who dispute the traditional view of his role in it. The earliest Tibetan account, from the Dunhuang library, makes no mention of Lang Darma's violent death, an omission that accords with the two Chinese sources available to us.[8] More remarkable still is the suggestion that there was, in fact, no persecution of Buddhism. On the contrary, it suggests that the king actually supported the new religion. But this is greatly controversial among Tibetans. When the document was first brought to public attention by a Tibetan academic during the 1980s, his account, issued by the Tibetan government in exile's own publishing arm, caused such a furor that the book was withdrawn from sale. To deny Lang Darma's culpability is, among traditionalists, to deny one of the founding myths of the Tibetan nation. But the implication is that, in place of a violent persecution, there was simply a diminution in royal patronage of the monastic community.

* Pronounced "Goo-gay."

It is instructive to note that, also at this time, Lang Darma's contemporary, Emperor Wuzong, had initiated one of China's periodic persecutions of Buddhism.[9] One wonders, therefore, whether the two events might not have been in some way conflated by the later historians as they looked back on the turmoil that followed the fall of the Tibetan royal dynasty. They bear significant resemblances. In China, thousands of monasteries were destroyed and literally hundreds of thousands of monks and nuns were forced to disrobe and return to lay life— along with many thousands of Christian and Zoroastrian clergy for good measure. And although Wuzong's suppression of Buddhism neither lasted long nor accomplished his ambition of the wholesale destruction of the religion (he died in 846, sent mad and finally poisoned by the immortality potions to which he was addicted, just a year after giving his orders), Buddhism in China never recovered its former prestige.*

The outcome of the two persecutions, however, was quite different. Whereas in Tibet the collapse of Buddhism was coterminous with the collapse of the old religion as well, in China, the persecution saw a restoration of the traditional Confucian order and a reassertion of the emperor's authority over all his subjects. In Tibet, the opposite happened, and within half a century of Lang Darma's death, the country had fallen into a state of anarchy both temporal and spiritual.

The form this temporal anarchy took was Tibet's reversion to the disparate array of mutually hostile tribes and clans that obtained before the rise of the royal dynasty. Only with the founding of the great monasteries from the twelfth century onward, in devotion to which these groups began to set aside their antipathies, did some sort of concrete political authority reappear. And even then, marked regional rivalries remained.

---

* Let it be said, however, that the present Dalai Lama is optimistic of a great revival of the religion in China. "After all," he says, perhaps stretching a point, "the Chinese are a Buddhist people."

The result was that Tibet remained largely disunited for a full four hundred years from the death of Lang Darma in 842 until the Mongol conquest of Tibet during the middle of the thirteenth century. And it was not until the seventeenth that, under the Great Fifth Dalai Lama, the whole country united, more or less, under a single indigenous ruler.

As for the outbreak of spiritual anarchy that occurred following the fall of the dynasty, the source of this was Tibetan enthusiasm for tantra, a late development within Indian Buddhism. To those who accept them as authentic, the final and highest teachings of Buddhism are contained within the liturgical, ritual and scriptural tradition of the tantric "cycles." These cycles, elements of which are revealed only to initiates, consist in practices held to be so powerful they are capable of enabling individuals to attain enlightenment during the course of a single lifetime. As such, they expound their own philosophy, are situated within their own cosmology, and have their own standard of morality.* Further, not only do they hold out the promise of fast-track liberation, they also promise access to visions, ecstasies, and the command of supernatural powers. It is of the tantricists especially that are told tales of magic-working mystics, of solitary meditators who after years of training are able to levitate, and of thaumaturges able to bring down rain or even hail at will. Most controversial of all, it is also of tantric practitioners that are told tales of sexual mastery so complete they are able to transmute the moment of orgasm into the direct apprehension of the bliss of emptiness.†

In the turmoil of post-dynastic Tibet, it was doubtless inevitable that the magical and sexual components of tantric practice came to be emphasized at the expense of the philosophical and the scriptural. Some scholars believe that this corruption was

---

* Though Tsongkhapa for one denies that the tantras depart from Mahayana orthodoxy.
† The sexual yogas are not unique to tantra, however.

precipitated by contact with Shivaite—that is, non-Buddhist—
tantricists, such as the Goraknaths, then active in Bengal.* Yet,
given the centrality of tantra to the Tibetan tradition, we cannot
afford, as some of the earliest writers on the subject did, to dismiss
tantra's sexual and magical rites as mere degeneracy.† Though
they constitute only a part of the tantric inventory, it is entirely
orthodox for Tibetans to believe that every candidate for enlightenment must, at some point during the endless cycle of birth,
death and rebirth, master the sexual practices.‡

To situate the sexual rites of tantra within their proper
context, it is necessary to know something of the rationale
behind tantra as a whole. In common with orthodox Mahayana
teaching, the tantras take as their starting point the notion that
all sentient beings contain within them the "seed of enlightenment." In a sense, we are enlightened already. Tantric practice aims therefore to break down the barriers that separate us
from our innately enlightened condition. To do this, a variety
of techniques are employed, the sexual rites comprising just
one. Also used are magical practices centerd on the repetition

---

* The Goraknaths are notable for having developed techniques to free the
mind and cleanse the soul which make yoga as it is generally practiced in the
West look anaemic in comparison:

> Squatting in water reaching to the navel, with a tube inserted in the anus,
> one should contract the *adhara* [sphincter]. [This] washing is the *basti karma*
> . . . The *basti karma*, performed with water makes calm the humors, the
> sensory and motor faculties, and the seat of thought and feeling; gives glow
> and luster [to the body] and good digestion . . .

Adapted from Briggs, *Gorakhnath and the Kanphata Yogis*, p. 328.

† L. A. Waddell wrote of how "this yoga parasite, containing within itself the germs
of Tantricism . . . soon developed monster outgrowths which crushed and cankered
most of the little life of purely Buddhist stock yet left in the Mahayana" with the
result that "even the purest of all the Lamaist sects . . . are thorough-paced devil-
worshippers." *See* Waddell, *The Buddhism of Tibet or Lamaism*, pp. 14 and 152.
‡ On the one occasion I heard the present Dalai Lama discuss the sexual rites
in detail, he made clear his allegiance to the principle. But whereas he found
the subject hugely amusing, a considerable proportion in the audience seemed
tensely serious.

of certain secret verbal formulae, or mantras. Then there is a type of meditation known as "deity yoga" wherein practitioners visualize themselves as a particular deity. And finally, there are transgressive acts in which the tantric yogin offers to the gods substances that are conventionally considered impure: blood, semen, feces, urine and human flesh. Historically, the traditional site for these practices was the *ghat*, or cremation ground—hence Chenrezig's incarnation as the "Yogi of the Burning Ground."* And while to the outsider, revulsion seems the appropriate response to these particular rites, to many Tibetans, the exploits of the tantricists lend them a certain pious glamour.

The most highly realized, and thus the most admired, tantric yogin is the one who can engage in such activities without suffering any adverse mental or emotional response. Of such people, it is often claimed that they could drink a cup of water or a cup of urine with equal detachment. The aim here is not indifference, but equanimity: the ability to treat adversity with complete dispassion. Nonetheless, there are important reasons why tantric practice remains controversial even among those who accept its validity. For while in most cases, it would seem that if there is any harm in them, it would rebound only to the detriment of the yogins themselves, certain tantric rites seem so extreme as to call into question the whole enterprise. Among the documents recovered from Dunhuang is one that describes a practice referred to euphemistically as "deliverance" but which clearly entails the killing of living creatures.[10] It seems that sacrifice, even of human beings, has at times been part of the tantric repertoire.

Given that abstention from killing is a defining precept of the religion, it seems extraordinary that such rituals could ever have

---

* It will be remembered that, not content with simply meditating there, he did so lying on top of the corpses.

found a home within Buddhism, and, indeed, perhaps they never did. Pressed on the point, most will argue that the more extreme rites were never meant to be taken literally. But while today the impure offerings called for in the rituals are represented symbolically with colored water and barley dough, there seems little reason to doubt that, in the troubled atmosphere that followed the collapse of the Yarlung Dynasty and in the absence of the discipline imposed by the monasteries, such outrages did occasionally occur in tenth-century Tibet. Because the tantric yogin is held to be beyond dualism, beyond mundane conceptions of right and wrong, and thus beyond conventional morality, the notion that for the holy all they do is holy can never be far away.

The dangers of tantric antinomianism were recognized early on. An eleventh-century priest chieftain, Yeshe Ö, castigated the renegade tantricists in a famous ordinance which could stand for any over-liberal interpretation of religious tradition:

> *You tantricists, living in villages,*
> *Have no connection with the Three Ways,*
> *And yet you claim to follow the Mahayana.*
> *Without observing the rules of the Mahayana,*
> *You say, "We are Mahayanist."*
> *This is like a beggar saying he is king.*
> *To claim to be Mahayanist though one is not*
> *Is like a donkey dressed in lion's skin.*

The trouble was that, for many Tibetans, tantra was the very thing which made Buddhism attractive. According to the testimony of a Nepalese missionary active in Tibet during the twelfth century, the people were generally inattentive when he preached the classical Perfection of Wisdom teachings, but when he expounded the tantras, "their astonishment knew no bounds."[11]

7

Lama Drom and the Followers of the Doctrine

Chenrezig's fourth earthly manifestation in Tibet was the eleventh-century missionary and monastic Lama Drom Tönpa. His birth in 1004 means that there was a hiatus of some 166 years between the death of King Rapalchen and the appearance of his successor incarnation. According to tradition, this delay is to be accounted for simply by saying that until then, the circumstances were not ripe for Chenrezig's next appearance. Even so, it is necessary to know something of developments in the intervening period in order to understand fully the significance of Drom Tönpa's contribution to the history of the Dalai Lamas. The three key figures of this time are Yeshe Ö, scourge of the tantricists, Rinchen Zangpo, the great translator, and Dipamkara Atisha, Drom Tönpa's spiritual mentor and teacher.

A remote descendant of the Yarlung Dynasty, Yeshe Ö was hereditary chieftain of the tribes occupying the southwestern province of Gu'ge. An ardent Buddhist, Yeshe Ö took holy orders at an early age. Soon after, he handed over secular power of

Gu'ge to a regent, while retaining ultimate control by virtue of his personal prestige. By this means, Yeshe Ö established a form of rulership that was to be repeated many times over the next five hundred years, culminating in the institution of the Dalai Lamas themselves.

In spiritual terms, Yeshe Ö regarded himself as an upholder of orthodoxy. Another edict he issued against the freelance yogins accused them of being "less clean than pigs and dogs." But Yeshe Ö may also be said to be the inaugurator of what has come to be known as the second diffusion of Buddhism in Tibet. Tibetans have traditionally regarded Lang Darma's reign as marking the end of Buddhism's first brief but glorious dawn in Tibet. This was followed, according to the tradition, by several decades of utter darkness during which only a few scattered remnants of the faith kept the tradition from being extinguished entirely. But this is very much a central Tibetan perspective. It is clear that, in Gu'ge at least, the faith flourished. Yeshe Ö founded a major monastery at Tholing at the end of the tenth century, and it was at his urging that direct links were established with Buddhism in India, its native land. Dubious of the provenance and authenticity of many of the teachings then in circulation, he sent a party of twenty men to India in a bid to locate texts and teachings that were truly authoritative. Of these men, only two returned, one of them being Rinchen Zangpo, the rest having succumbed to the languorous heat and insidious diseases of the subcontinent.

It is said that during a life spanning a full ninety-seven years, Rinchen Zangpo mounted a total of three such missions to India, albeit by the time of the third he had mastered the art of *gang dyok*, or swift-footedness, enabling him to cover in six days distances that would ordinarily have taken six months of travel.*

---

* The most striking anecdotal evidence for this practice is to be found, somewhat unexpectedly, in *Conundrum*, an account of the author's gender reassignment by Jan Morris, the great Welsh travel writer (pp. 75–6). Speaking on the subject of such apparently paranormal phenomena, the present Dalai Lama

These missions added scores of the basic texts and commentaries subsequently translated and collected in the Kangyur and Tengyur, a body of scripture often (but always erroneously) referred to as the Tibetan Bible.*

For this, Rinchen Zangpo is regarded as among the first rank of Lotsawa, the great translators, whose wholesale rendering into Tibetan of Indian Buddhist literature, over a period amounting to little more than a couple of centuries, must rank as one of the greatest literary enterprises in human history. It is as if the entire literary output of the ancient Greco-Roman world were to have been snatched from the dying embers of the republic, transported to some unknown province beyond its farthest boundary (say the Highlands of Scotland), and translated into a literary language created expressly to convey the most profound wisdom of one culture to another that hitherto was virtually unlettered. Well might Rinchen Zangpo have been accounted a saint when he died in 1055.

Meanwhile, following Rinchen Zangpo's first visit to India and toward the end of his life, Yeshe Ö was—to use the terminology of the sources—"inspired" to invite to Gu'ge the man who was, by reputation, the most learned and accomplished Buddhist teacher then living: the great scholar-saint Dipamkara Atisha. At that time, Atisha was teaching at Vikramasila, the monastic university and stronghold of the faith in Magadha, part of present-day Bengal in northeastern India. According to

---

once pointed out to me that, from a traditional Tibetan perspective, the idea of one man levitating was just about conceivable, but the idea of four hundred people flying through the air in an iron bird would have been dismissed as completely unimaginable.

* Comprised of more than a hundred volumes each, the Kangyur and Tengyur are, respectively, the collected scriptures and commentaries translated from Sanskrit. Both are considered authoritative, yet they do not have the same status as the Bible in the Christian tradition. While for Christians the Bible is the definitive revelation of God, in the Tibetan tradition the Buddha's word is continuously revealed. Although the Kangyur and Tengyur are closed, the Buddhist canon thus remains open to further revelation.

tradition, Yeshe Ö's first attempt to persuade Atisha to come to Tibet was unsuccessful, even though he sent a bar of gold in offering to the great man. Undaunted at this rebuff, Yeshe Ö immediately set about collecting treasure in order to make a much larger offering, which would, he hoped, persuade Atisha of the deep faith and desire for teaching of the Tibetan people.* To this end, he led revenue-gathering missions into neighboring lands—some have suggested they were actually raiding parties—in order to raise the necessary funds.[1] And it was on one of these missions that he fell into the hands of a Qorluk chieftain. The Qorluk were a nomad people of Turkic origin, converts to Islam, whom we know to have invaded Gu'ge briefly around 1035. It is said that Yeshe Ö's captor offered him his freedom back at the cost either of accepting Allah or of his own weight in gold. The former course being unthinkable, it fell to his great-nephew, Changchub Ö, also a monk, to try to raise the necessary funds. When, finally, Changchub and his compatriots had collected what they hoped was a sufficient quantity of gold, they returned to the warlord. Unfortunately it turned out to be an amount short of the required weight, equivalent to that of the old man's head. At this point, however, the saintly captive intervened. Physically broken by his captivity, he argued with his would-be savior that, since he must now be near the end of his life anyway, there was little point in paying the ransom. Better that it should be put toward the cost of bringing Atisha to preach among the Tibetans. Besides, in none of his previous lives had he sacrificed himself for the sake of the *buddhadharma*. His present situation gave him the precious opportunity to be of some use to the holy faith by means of his suffering and death. In sorrow and tears, therefore,

---

* Monetary offering of this kind is a feature of Buddhist culture that sets it apart from the Western religious tradition. The Christian mission is generally construed in terms of self-sacrifice for the love of God and His Son, its reward the number of souls saved.

Changchub Ö took leave of his old great-uncle and, returning home, sent the gold to Atisha.

This time, the Tibetan's entreaties to the master were successful. In recognition of Yeshe Ö's sacrifice, Atisha finally accepted their invitation. The priest chieftain of blessed memory was meanwhile put to death.

If there were other reasons for Atisha's change of heart, the first was probably the fact that in India, Buddhism was now at a low ebb. Resurgent Hindu sects that practiced tantra* and borrowed freely from Buddhism—recasting Buddha Shakyamuni as an *avatar*, or incarnation of Vishnu the Preserver—had begun to blur the distinctions between the two religions, and, because Buddhism was, as it remains, so heavily dependent on monasticism,† it was always at the mercy of royal caprice. In the first place, though the merchant classes were their principal benefactors, the monasteries required royal patronage in order to function; then, when they became wealthy in their own right, they were dependent on royal sufferance. The Indian kings had the unwelcome habit of withdrawing their support when it suited them to do so. And, on occasion, short of money, or simply greedy, they were not above plundering the monasteries of their riches. At the turn of the first millennium, Buddhism was in just such a precarious position. Not only did the Pala Dynasty no longer support Nalanda, the most important of the monastic universities, but, more dangerous still, northern India had recently come under attack from the idol-destroying Ghaznavids. These Muslim converts of Central Asian origin were "ferocious in war and plunder."[2] Looting and defiling temples and treasuries, they carried off slaves of both sexes by the hundred thousand in a series of raids spanning several

---

* In fact, tantra was almost certainly an ancient Indian tribal practice before ever it found its way into either Buddhism or Hinduism.
† In Buddhist estimation, the doctrine is only established where the *sangha*, the monastic community, is established.

years. In such circumstances, Tibet may have looked to Atisha as a safe haven for the faith—as indeed it proved.

Born in 982,[3] Dipamkara Atisha* was the scion of a noble Bengali family.[4] He is particularly revered on account of his association, whether real or fondly imagined (there is much debate on the point), with the eighty-four *mahasiddhas*, or "great adepts," who appeared in India between the ninth and twelfth centuries. These were tantric yogins, all of whom, it is believed, attained enlightenment during their earthly lives as wandering miracle-workers. Few of the eighty-four are actually identifiable as historical figures, but the *mahasiddha* tradition has nonetheless had immense impact on the evolution of Buddhism in Tibet, given Tibetans' great appetite for tantra. A typical example of the great adepts is Savaripa the Hunter. It is said that he was brought to recognize the danger his profession was putting him in by Chenrezig himself. The Bodhisattva manifested as a fellow hunter able to shoot a hundred deer with a single arrow and promised to teach Savaripa his secret if he would forsake eating meat for a month. At the end of this time, Chenrezig revealed, in a vision of hell, the appalling fate that lay in store for Savaripa if he did not cease killing. The hunter repented of his evil ways and ended his days a great teacher of the faith.

Judging by the names of many of the eighty-four, it is clear that redemption is one of the principal concerns of the *mahasiddha* tradition.[5] Other examples are Kankaripa the Lovelorn Widower; Lalipa the Royal Hedonist; Tantipa the Senile Weaver; Aryadeva the One-eyed; Duryipa the Courtesan's Brahmin Slave; Babaha the Free Lover; Kucipa the Goiter-necked Yogin. Arguably the best-loved in Tibet is Naropa. According to one tradition, Naropa was a wood-gatherer, the offspring of a mixed-

* "Atisha" translates as "Great Lord."

caste (and therefore forbidden) union. According to another, he was the Brahmin son of an altogether respectable aristocratic family. He earned his own soubriquet of Naropa the Dauntless through the faithful service he rendered to Tilopa, yet another of the *mahasiddhas*. It is said that Naropa had to endure countless beatings, insults and other signs of displeasure over the course of twelve long years before Tilopa so much as spoke to him. Yet this example of unswerving devotion is held up as the very model of the guru–disciple relationship.* And though it may appear to be still another exaggeration on the part of the hagiographers, very likely there is a strong element of truth here. Even today, prospective disciples are urged not to take anyone as a teacher before they have scrutinized them assiduously over a period of at least twelve years.†

When Atisha finally arrived in (western) Tibet—he was granted three years' leave by his university—he was met by an escort of some three hundred horsemen commanded by four generals who greeted him with song.[6] He was then taken to Tholing, where he set about teaching, helping to translate the scriptures and, most importantly, writing his classic exposition of the faith *The Lamp to the Path of Enlightenment*.

When his three-year leave of absence from Vikramasila expired, Atisha left Gu'ge for India via Purang. This was an important

---

* "Guru" is the Sanskrit word for "teacher."
† As is to be expected, the vast majority of the literature concerning the eighty-four *mahasiddhas* is of a legendary character. We do, however, have one eyewitness account of Naropa from the hand of one of those sent to invite Atisha to Tibet:

> I went to the spot, and a great throne had been erected. I sat right in front of it. The whole crowd started buzzing, "The Lord is coming!" I looked and the Lord was physically quite corpulent, with his white hair bright red [stained with henna], and a vermilion turban bound on. He was being carried [on a palanquin] by four men and chewing betel-leaf. I grabbed his feet and thought, I should listen to his pronouncements! Stronger and stronger people, though, pushed me further and further from his seat and finally I was tossed out of the crowd. So, there I saw the Lord's face, but did not actually hear his voice.

trading post at the junction of the Indo–Nepali border, said to have been home to Sudhana, a previous incarnation of the Buddha Shakyamuni. It was here, in an event that was to change the lives not only of the two men themselves, but also the course of Tibetan history, that Atisha first made the acquaintance of the one who was to become his chief disciple and spiritual successor, Drom Tönpa. As one might expect of so auspicious a meeting, it was foretold to Atisha in a dream by the goddess Tara herself. The two men duly met in the road, just as Atisha was preparing to leave, Drom Tönpa saying not a word but "following the Master as if he had associated with him before."[7]

Though arguably the least colorful of Chenrezig's Tibetan incarnations, Drom Tönpa is also one of the most important. Born into an ancient family living in a district to the northwest of Lhasa, Drom's mother died early. His father remarried, but it seems that the boy quarreled with his stepmother. One day, he upset the cow that she was milking, whereupon she beat him. He left home soon after to live with a (Buddhist) teacher whose attendant he became. His duties included grinding the barley for the household's *tsampa* supplies and, outside, looking after the cattle which he defended with "arrow, lance and sword."*[8] Despite the fact that these responsibilities must have occupied much of his time, the young man became in due course very learned and an accomplished translator of Sanskrit. Several of his renderings—said to be remarkable for their purity and accuracy—are to be found among the collections of the Kangyur and the Tengyur.

Besides his qualities as a translator, Drom was also gifted with great powers of persuasion. His first act on making the master's acquaintance was to induce him to change his plans to return to India. He did this by presenting Atisha with a

---

* *Tsampa*, the staple diet of Tibetans, is most frequently mixed with tea, but beer, water, milk and yogurt are also used. It is kneaded into small balls and eaten by hand. I can think of no analogy for its taste.

petition signed by the recusant faithful of central Tibet. Follow-ing the disintegration of the royal house, political power in the two provinces of U (corresponding roughly to western Tibet) and Tsang (corresponding roughly to central Tibet) now lay in the hands of rival chieftains. Many of these derived their authority either from being or from having associations with quasi-Buddhist holy men. We have almost no reliable records for the period, but it would appear that the collapse of the ruling house and, with it, the authority of the Old Religion, saw the gradual emergence of a nominally Buddhist priestly ruling caste. According to the religious historians, Atisha, when he went to meet an assembly of these aristocrats and priest chieftains, thought at first that he had made an error in submit-ting to Drom's entreaties: "If you have so many priests in central Tibet, you have no need of me here." But on drawing closer and seeing that they were dressed in elaborate clothes, mounted on magnificent horses and that they displayed the luxurious trappings of wealth, he realized that his presence was indeed required. Properly educated in the faith, they would under-stand that the *buddhadharma* has no place for such extravagant displays of affluence.[9]

Thereafter, the two men, Drom Tönpa and Atisha, embarked as master and disciple on an extended tour of the region. On the whole, they were warmly received, although on one occasion the trumpeters heralding the master's arrival caused the inhabitants of a village to flee under the impression that war had broken out. On another, a young bride who, as a mark of her respect for Atisha, made him an offering of her wedding ornaments was rebuked furiously by her parents. "You have given away all the valuables to [this] greedy Indian who always runs after rich presents." At this, she threw herself into the river and drowned.[10] On a third occasion, Atisha uncovered a plot to murder him.[11] It is clear, however, that in the great majority of places, Atisha was well-received by the local populace, who embraced his teachings eagerly. When he reached Lhasa, it is recorded that a series of three rainbows rose above one of the mountains overlooking the valley in which it stands.

Part of the reason for the success of Atisha's mission is that, for the first time in Tibet, Buddhism was being propagated as a mass movement. While previously it had come down to the common people from their rulers and ministers, now, thanks to Lama Drom, as he is popularly known, it was being preached to them in the villages and farmsteads where they lived and worked. This was something entirely new, and was enthusiastically received by a people whose traditional faith was in disarray.

Yet what is also remarkable about Atisha's mission is that it was successful despite the fact that, although he was a renowned tantric master, he rarely expounded the secret doctrines of the tantras, and then only to a select few. It was later said that this neglect was actually the result of a "demon having penetrated the heart of Tibet." A less colorful tradition makes a puritan Lama Drom responsible for Atisha's neglect of tantra, suggesting that the zealous layman was always on the lookout for "persons of immoral conduct" whom he would expel from the master's classes.[12] This strand of thought holds that Lama Drom, in his desire to see strict moral conduct established in Tibet, actually prevented Atisha from promulgating the tantric or *vajrayana* teachings. Further, it holds that although Lama Drom himself received many secret teachings and initiations from Atisha, he deliberately, and wrongly, failed to pass them on. This is almost certainly unfair.[13] There is no suggestion that during their time together, Lama Drom was anything less than an exemplary disciple, still less that he ever tried to usurp Atisha's authority. It is more likely, therefore, that Lama Drom's conservative outlook reflected the master's own. Atisha clearly felt that Tibetans should be firmly established in the straight way before further exposure to the Diamond Path of tantra.

Instead of teaching the tantras widely, Atisha promoted devotional and meditative practices centered on Chenrezig. This was a strategy that is of crucial significance to the history of the Dalai Lamas, for it is in connection with these practices that the association of Drom Tönpa and, later, of the Dalai Lamas with Chenrezig originates. In his teachings, Atisha would frequently illustrate points of doctrine by referring to the previous lives of Lama Drom. And the previous life stories* that he used as examples were none other than those contained in the traditional *Thirty-six Lives of Avalokitesvara* [Chenrezig] *in India.* Atisha clearly identified Lama Drom as a manifestation of Chenrezig. He did not—at least as far as we know—propose the three religious kings as links between Lama Drom and the thirty-six. That part of the tradition comes from elsewhere. It is even possible to imagine that Atisha did not mean this association to be taken literally, that this was merely a teaching device. But it was this linkage that effectively inaugurated the spiritual lineage that saw Lama Drom's successors claim absolute power over Tibet in the person of the Dalai Lama.[14]

In 1054, Atisha took ill and, after a rapid decline in strength, died at the age of seventy-two, some twelve years or so after arriving in Tibet. Lama Drom was stunned with grief. It seems that he withdrew from public life for a full two years before gathering around him a select group of disciples and, in 1056, founding Reting Monastery. Located two days' journey to the northeast of Lhasa, Reting became one of the most important— and one of the richest—monasteries in all of Tibet. It came also to be one of the most influential both in political and spiritual terms. Today, though badly damaged several times during its history—most recently, and most severely, during the ravages of China's early occupation of Tibet during the 1960s—it still stands surrounded, unusually for this part of Tibet, by the forest of

---

* Or "Jakata Tales," as they are commonly known.

juniper trees that is said to have sprung from the hairs on Drom Tönpa's head.[15]

The first monastery to be founded in Tibet during this second diffusion of Buddhism, Reting was also the first to be associated with a distinctive Tibetan Buddhist school or sect. As the mother monastery of several subsequent foundations, it became the center of the Kadam tradition.* The stated aim of the Kadampas, who looked to Atisha and Drom Tönpa as joint founders of the order, was to teach the full range of Buddhist teachings. In practice, however, and in keeping with their founders' example, the Kadampas emphasized decisively the classical Mahayana teachings. They also laid particular stress on academic study and on monastic discipline—this in conformity with Atisha's dying words to Lama Drom that the *sangha*, the monastic community, on which the dharma, or the Buddhist path, depends is in turn dependent on the *vinaya*, the canon of monastic discipline. The Kadampa teachings were thus resolutely orthodox in outlook, in sharp contrast to the spiritual free-for-all that had characterized the preceding centuries.

When he founded Reting,† Lama Drom announced that he was giving up worldly life for ever,‡ a vow to which he remained faithful until his death in 1064—apparently of leprosy—and in keeping with which he "taught his disciples disgust toward the world."[16] And, although it seems he did pass on Atisha's tantric teachings to a carefully chosen few—he even translated some tantric literature—he remained extremely reticent with regard to its practice.[17] This caused Milarepa, the great twelfth-century mystic, *tantrika*, and poet to exclaim (according to one, arguably

---

* On one view, "kadam" means, literally, "the followers of the doctrine."
† Intriguingly, the present Dalai Lama has stated that he feels a particular spiritual connection with the place, and adds that it is his fondest hope one day to retire there.
‡ Though he remained a layman all his life, never seeking ordination. It is a remarkable coincidence that St. Benedict (480–550), the father of Christian monasticism, was likewise a layman all his life.

biased, source) that had Lama Drom done as he should and taught them freely, "by now Tibet would have been filled with saints!"[18]

During Drom Tönpa's lifetime there were not more than sixty "ascetics" (to use the language of the sources) resident at Reting, but after his death the monastery expanded rapidly. By the fifteenth century it had become one of the most important institutions of the later Gelug tradition, itself known as the New Kadampa school. Hugh Richardson, the British (subsequently Indian) political officer resident at Lhasa, describing a visit in 1950, reported a still-flourishing community, which treasured images of both Lama Drom and Atisha. He even saw some books that had belonged to the latter carefully preserved there. But if Reting was of immense significance to the development of Buddhism in Tibet, there were, as we shall see, two occasions when its political role was to play an important part in the destruction of Tibet during the twentieth century.

As to Drom Tönpa himself, he can fairly be regarded as the father of Tibetan monasticism. Although lifelong commitment to poverty, obedience and chastity seems impossibly—and unnecessarily—arduous to us moderns, it proved hugely attractive to Tibetans (as indeed it did to medieval Europeans). At its height, perhaps as many as 2 percent of the entire male population lived as monks.

8

Ozer and the Treasure-Revealers

Between the death of Drom Tönpa in 1064 and the birth of
Gendun Drub, the First Dalai Lama, in 1391, Chenrezig's lineage does not manifest straightforwardly as successive incarnations. Instead, two distinct series of incarnations appeared. The
members of the first, a series of five, are considered to be joint
reincarnations of King Trisong Detsen and of Padmasambhava,
the great miracle-worker and mystic whom the monarch invited
to Tibet during the eighth century. The second series comprises
a further eight incarnations, several of whom were in fact contemporaries of the Dalai Lamas themselves and the last of whom
lived during the fifteenth century. But while from the outsider's
perspective, the logic behind this seeming jumble of lives is hard
to follow, from a Buddhist point of view, the lack of a clear succession presents no particular difficulty. Nor does the idea that a
given individual could be said to be the reincarnation of not one
but two contemporaneous historical figures. For a start, the reincarnation lineage* itself is not necessarily to be taken as a strictly

---

* In Tibetan, this is *tung-rab*.

consecutive line. In the second place, the seeming confusion may be said simply to be a reflection of the way the universe exists: as a dynamic, ever-changing, ever-fluid process in which things and events arise and disappear not in conformity to some grand design, but only as a result of the collective karma of countless sentient beings.

Of the thirteen incarnations that separate, more or less, Drom Tönpa and the First Dalai Lama, two may be said to have had a profound impact on Tibetan history: Nyangré Nyima Ozer (1136–1207) and the man known to history as Phagpa (1235–80), friend and teacher of the Mongol emperor of China, Kubilai Khan.

If, as we shall see, Phagpa's legacy on Tibetan history is overwhelmingly political, then Ozer's was chiefly spiritual. As a key figure in the renaissance of the Nyingma, or Old School, tradition,* Ozer certainly had a major, and direct, impact on the evolution of Buddhism in Tibet. But in saying that his significance is mainly spiritual we must not overlook the fact that, in the Tibetan context, there is no very clear distinction to be made between the two spheres—the spiritual and the political—any more than there is a distinction to be made between the natural and the supernatural.[†] Within the traditional Tibetan worldview, politics is more to be understood as something that follows on from the spiritual.

Despite his importance, of all the historical figures within the Dalai Lamas' lineage, Ozer is the one we know the least about. He was born in Lhodrak, south of Lhasa, the son of an accomplished

---

* This is the first of Tibet's four principal sects or traditions. The others are the Kagyu, the Sakya and the Gelug.
† This may seem somewhat surprising, yet even in the West no clear demarcation emerged until the modern era: "There have always been distinctions between, for instance, the sacred and the profane, higher beings and worldly beings and so forth, but in the 'enchanted' worlds that humans inhabited in earlier times, these two kinds of reality were inextricably interwoven." Taylor in Wrathall (ed.), *Religion after Metaphysics*, p. 48.

lay *tantrika* who was himself the scion of an old aristocratic family. He thus combined, as one modern commentator puts it, "the privilege and authority of aristocracy with the unfettered unorthodoxy of the lay tantric practitioner."[2] At just seven years old, Ozer began to have visions which "exhilarated him for a whole month" at a time.[3] As a teenager, he seems also to have undergone something akin to the "dark night of the soul" described by John of the Cross, the sixteenth-century Spanish mystic, when he experienced three successive "disasters": the rending of the sky, the quaking of the earth and the shaking of a mountain. Subsequently, his behavior caused many people to suspect he had gone mad. But when he left impressions of his hands and feet in rock, it became clear that there was something special about the boy. Such obvious signs of spiritual accomplishment authenticated the visions he began to have of Padmasambhava. And when the master directed him to places where he had concealed "treasure" during his sojourn in Tibet during the eighth century, Ozer was hailed as a great seer.

Today Ozer is acknowledged as one of the inaugurators of what has come to be known as the treasure, or *terma*, tradition. The *terma* tradition is one of the most remarkable and distinctive features of Tibetan Buddhism. Derived from the insight that Padmasambhava, the Lotus Born,* was not merely a great *tantrika* but actually a second Buddha, it holds that during his time in Tibet he concealed numerous "treasures"—mainly scriptures, but also statues and other devotional artifacts—predestined to be revealed in later times by highly realized practitioners with a special karmic link to him. Ozer was one of the first, and greatest, of these revealers, though discoveries have continued to be made down the centuries. There are

---

* Padmasambhava is the Sanskrit form of his name. In Tibetan it is rendered, somewhat less euphoniously to Western ears, as Urgyen.

still, at the time of writing, a number of acclaimed treasure-revealers, or *tertön*, at work.*

From an orthodox Nyingma perspective, the *terma* tradition can be taken entirely at face value. Yet it would be wrong to suppose that this is because Tibetans are any more credulous than supposedly sophisticated moderns. From the beginning, they have been alive to the possibility of forgery and deception, and much effort is expended in distinguishing genuine from false treasure. But while modern sensibilities would require any items supposed to have been buried during the eighth century to be tested and analyzed for authenticity before they could be accepted as genuine, Tibetans have tended to be much more interested in the qualities of the individual claiming to have discovered them. The criteria are different, but in general terms, the approach is just as skeptical.

Besides his acclamation as a *tertön*, Ozer is especially significant to our story for another reason, however. In several of his visions, he met with the *dakini*, or goddess, Yeshe Tsogyal, who is said not only to have been one of King Trisong Detsen's wives (though her name is unknown among contemporary records), but also to have been Padmasambhava's tantric (sexual) consort while he was in Tibet. During one of these visions, Yeshe Tsogyal directed Ozer to a building known as the Copper Temple, where she revealed a book, written by her, containing the life story of Padmasambhava. It recounts the master's doings in Tibet and purports† to show that, far from being turned out of Tibet after just a few months, as dynastic records show, in reality he worked his miracles there for fifty-six years before returning home.

---

* In fact, not all treasures are physical objects. Sometimes Padmasambhava (currently residing in *takching kandoling*, the land of the *dakinis*, or goddesses) imparts teachings and scriptures to the seer in visions and apparitions that arise during states of advanced meditation.
† This is not a word a believer would use.

The biography of Padmasambhava, revealed by Ozer during the latter half of the twelfth century, represents a vital moment in the history of the Nyingma sect and in the formation of the "modern" Tibetan national consciousness. On the one hand, it crystallizes the efforts of those faithful to the earlier tradition of Buddhism in Tibet who, no doubt stung by the success of Drom Tönpa's Kadampas, sought to validate their own practices rather than accept the new orthodoxy. Not all were renegade *tantrikas* of the sort that Drom Tönpa was so determined to thwart. On the other hand, Ozer's *The Immaculate Life Story* shows that Padmasambhava's mission to Tibet was in fact of far greater significance than even his most ardent supporters had grasped. He was, in fact, a fully enlightened being—the Guru Rinpoché[†]—a second Buddha. Not only did he instruct the sovereign and his ministers in the holy faith, but he also confronted the local gods and demons who, up until then, had dominated Tibet's supernatural landscape. The biography recounts how Padmasambhava was on his way through Tibet when

> three male and female *yakshas* . . . gathered all the icy winds of the three northern plains into one and blew them on to Master Padma and his retinue. The retinue was almost paralyzed, and even the Master felt a slight chill. But then Master Padma span a wheel of fire . . . and the snow mountains where the *yakshas* lived melted like butter touched with a red-hot iron.[4]

Only he did not destroy the gods. Instead he converted them and bound them over as protectors of the new faith.

Ozer's biography also reveals that Padmasambhava played a vital role in the construction of the Samye Monastery. Remain-

---

[*] Literally, "precious teacher."

ing in meditation, he commanded the "eight classes of gods and demons" to assist in the building work. By rolling building materials down the mountainside into the valley, "what the gods and demons built by night exceeded what the humans built by day."[5] Finally, the biography reveals that Padmasambhava was the one who "invited" the god Pehar to Samye to act as its resident protector deity, an event which, as we shall see, comes to have enormous significance in the development of the Dalai Lama institution, and indeed in relation to the Shugden controversy.

The Lotus Born did not, however, have any delusions about the innate sanctity of the people he was dealing with. In his *General Testament to the Tibetan People of Future Generations*, he admonishes them without compunction:

> *Kings, ministers, and people of Tibet, the primitive borderland,*
> *You are a race of red-faced demons lacking compassion and*
>   *goodwill.*
> *Your father's race is a monkey with little modesty or shame*
> *And your mother's race is a rock demoness, quarrelsome and*
> *hostile to the Dharma.*
> *You are a race of beastly people, full of craving toward wealth.*[6]

But perhaps most significantly of all, Ozer's Padmasambhava particularly commends Chenrezig to the Tibetan people, emphasizing the extraordinary benefits arising from the recitation of Chenrezig's sacred mantra *Om mani padme hum*: "all needs and wishes are granted when you supplicate the precious wish-fulfilling jewel [i.e. Chenrezig himself], but the merit of uttering the six syllables just once is even greater."[7]

Thus from the perspective of the Dalai Lama institution, Ozer and his treasures provide the link between the modern (that is, Buddhist) era and the earlier period when the Tibetan Empire ruled much of Inner Asia. They also provide the means by which the Dalai Lamas are connected with the whole Nyingma tradition and thereby to the large percentage of the population that even today follows the Old School. Before the supremacy achieved by the Gelug from the time of the Fifth Dalai Lama onward, the followers of the Nyingma tradition can be assumed to have comprised somewhere between a tenth and a quarter of all Tibetans, including much of the aristocracy, and the majority of those who lived beyond the reach of the various centers of political power, such as the nomadic element of the population.

Whether or not the treasure discovered by Ozer is genuine in terms that could be accepted today, its effect continues to have an impact on people's lives well into our own times. It articulates an understanding of history that is precisely in keeping with Tibetans' traditional outlook on the world and, in so doing, actually legitimizes and strengthens it, while re-situating it within a Buddhist framework.

This traditional or folk outlook, similar as it is to the folk worldview of all pre-modern cultures, is of such importance to the Tibetan understanding of the world that it is essential we have some insight of it. Any history of Tibet that does not give some account of what the great French Tibetologist R. A. Stein (not to be confused with Sir Aurel Stein) called Tibet's "nameless religion" is likely to leave the reader guessing as to the real motives behind many of the most important events in Tibetan history. For while the Tibetan folk universe may seem quaint, exotic, even charming, from a modern perspective, this is to romanticize it. And romanticism points invariably to patronization. There is nothing quaint, exotic or charming about the world that, traditionally, Tibetans have lived in.

9

The Nameless Religion: Tibet's Folk Tradition

As anyone who has been there will testify, much of Tibet's land-scape is so barren and desolate as to bludgeon the beholder. Ippolito Desideri, the seventeenth-century Italian Jesuit mission-ary to Tibet, wrote of its "dreadful and tedious solitude" and of its "frightful caverns on inaccessible mountains." Yet, from the perspective of the folk tradition, it brims with life: there are gods of one sort or another—sometimes whole hosts of them—on every plain, in every tree and shrub, in every river, lake and waterfall. There is no mountain, no valley, no field, nor any village with-out its presiding deity. All unusual rock formations, all precipices, all mountain crevasses are likewise the abode of some unseen spirit. And not only these: the birds of the air, the fish of river, lake and stream—each have their protective numena. Look up into the heavens (and you have never known them until you have looked up to the night sky through the brisk, evaporating air of the Tibetan uplands): each planet, each star, the sun, and the moon—all have their attendant divinities. As do the Ten Directions themselves: from west (which always takes prece-dence in Tibet), through northwest, north and all the way around the compass (making eight), above and below (making ten). And everything besides: every tool, every table, every house, every hoe; this bed, that book, my hat, your cooking pot; the doorway, the window, the hearth. In short, there is nothing, animate or inanimate, that is not conceived of as falling under the aegis of some supernatural being.

Nor is it possible ever to escape the attention of these gods. Every individual is born with a complement of *lha*, or *dii minores*.* There are regional variations as to their number, but it is generally assumed there are five: the life god, situated at the heart; a male god at the right armpit; a female at the left; an adversary god (who deals with our enemies) at the right shoulder; and a local god at the crown of the head. In connection with these, it remains customary in parts of Tibet to plant a *bla'shing*, or "soul tree," at the birth of every child.[1]

All this might indeed seem very quaint if it were not for the nature of the gods: the enchanters of the Tibetan universe should not be confused with the lame spirits of modern children's fairy tales. They are conceived of not as vanishing wraiths, but as mounted warriors, armored, and wearing copper helmets adorned with feathers. They carry weapons and ride on antelopes, yaks, wild asses, wild dogs. Their habitation is a lake of blood or a castle of copper. To look at, they are hideous: this type has one eye, that type has one leg, another has no skin. Many have diabolical consorts, and the more powerful among them have large retinues of godlings too.

Worse still is their nature. They are haughty, touchy, prone to anger, and slow to forgive. Once their bile is aroused, they often persecute their victims out of all proportion to the supposed offense. And their doings are seen in every event outside human control. They may not be directly responsible—there is also karma to consider—but it is certain these

---

* "Minor deities" in Tibetan and Latin respectively.

supernatural beings are caught up in them somehow. One of the most common ways in which their activities are felt is when illness strikes. The gods are also invariably implicated in all such mishaps as crop failure, storm damage, rockfall, fire, and flooding. Your watch stops for no apparent reason? Some spirit is angry with you. Your car won't start? You have failed to propitiate a local deity. Thunderstorms are their work, too: the thunder itself is the roaring of celestial dragons; lightning occurs as they spit fireballs.* And what is an eclipse if it is not some heavenly being attacking and seizing the sun or moon and attempting to swallow it whole? Small wonder that, in olden times, everyone left their tents or took to the streets as the sky darkened, with a fearful yelling and screaming and banging of their pots and pans.

As one might expect, there is a hierarchy among this hidden host. Mountain gods are vastly more powerful than the spring-dwelling *lu*. And certain of them are more important to one class of people than to others. For the nomadic population, the tent gods are of supreme importance. Associated principally with the hearth, these are:

> strange jealous creatures [that] swarm at the rising of the smoke in a new tent, and take proprietary though at times perverse interest in the new hearth. Because of their displeasure, children die or are born dead. Their spiteful blows bring blindness, strange swellings, and the swift rotting of anthrax . . . What tent can hope for peace if the hearthstone spirits are angry?[2]

To say that the gods of folk tradition are involved in every calamity, and to say that they are haughty, touchy, and vindictive,

---

* You would have in your possession a wish-fulfilling jewel if ever one of these strikes a tree and you are able to find it among the blackened branches.

is not to say that they are all intrinsically evil. Most are considered to be of a neutral disposition. There are, however, certain supernatural phenomena that are invariably dangerous to humanity. One example is the *gson'dé*, a kind of spirit that takes over women, especially at night. Their hapless victims become the demon's playthings, bringing misfortune and lingering illness—venereal disease no doubt being one of them—to everyone she has dealings with when possessed. Then there are the *shi'dre*, a form of malevolent ghost. These are brought into being most often in cases of murder. The victim is transformed at the point of death, and thereafter pursues remorselessly the perpetrator of the crime. Then there are the *rollang*. These take over the body itself on the point of death. Transformed into zombies, they kill anyone who crosses their path.

So varied, and so comprehensive, is this supernatural order that, in the words, arguably somewhat exaggerated, of another great Italian student of Tibetan culture, Giuseppe Tucci, "the Tibetan lives in a permanent state of anxious uneasiness; every physical or spiritual disturbance, each illness, every uncertain and threatening situation, leads him to embark upon a feverish search for the cause of the event and the appropriate means to ward it off."[3]

As we have seen, in Ozer's treasure text, *The Immaculate Life Story*, the conversion of Tibet's indigenous gods was undertaken by Padmasambhava. Unfortunately, it turns out that the Lotus Born was unable to complete this task, owing to the dissent of powerful sections of the population who remained loyal to the old gods. Consequently, not all were converted. Some were—and a few continue to be—hostile to the new faith. Fortunately, for all their malice, even the most powerful of gods are biddable. Dealt with appropriately, they may even take your side. If not, at least it is often possible to appease them and prevent them from taking against you. Many different types of apotropaic magic are used to achieve this. In the first instance, there is the mental and verbal propitiation of prayer. The advantage of prayer is, of course, that it can be offered up at any time and in more or less any circumstances. To increase its efficacy, it is usual to combine prayer with other offerings, most often of food and of woodsmoke—preferably juniper, or certain aromatic types of rhododendron. Incense is also used. On those occasions when the gods show signs of intractability, or when they have actually been offended, it is usual to perform deeds especially pleasing to them. Such meritorious activities include, for example, redeeming animals destined for slaughter, carving prayers on rocks, and commissioning monks to chant prayers on one's behalf.

The gods also require to be propitiated before any particular activity. When traveling, offerings are made at the home of any deity encountered en route: at the base of a tree, at the top of a rise, at the edge of a lake. Usually all that is offered is a prayer and a stone added to an existing cairn. But on special occasions, weapons are taken to the abode of the mountain gods, and prayer flags too, inscribed with Buddhist imprecations—for to layman and deity alike, the *buddhadharma* is the most powerful magic of all.

In ancient times, before the advent of Buddhism, the more powerful gods were able to demand even human sacrifice, not to mention hecatombs of yaks and horses. The arrival of the *buddhadharma* brought new technology. It became possible to use methods still pleasing to the gods but not actually requiring blood sacrifice. In place of the *shen* priests of yore, Buddhist holy men became available to perform rituals to protect the individual from the depredations of hostile forces, or exorcisms when malignant powers had visited individuals or settled at some place nearby. Such rituals could either be performed by peripatetic yogins, or by orthodox Buddhist monks who specialized in the practices of tantra. If it were a matter of choice, then reputation would be the deciding factor. A freelance yogin with a good track record would always be preferred over monastic officialdom. A high lama famed for his spiritual attainments would be better still.

Where protection is sought—perhaps before the outset of a hazardous journey (and all journeys of any length in Tibet were hazardous before the advent of modern communications)—it is also customary to perform a *do*. This ritual is essentially concerned with the concept of ransom. An image, usually in the form of a small sculpture made from butter or dough, is offered up in the expectation that, satiated with this, the gods will forbear from harming the individual on behalf of whom the ritual is performed. They accept these images not because they are now prepared to accept inferior offerings. The power of the *buddhadharma* is such as to render them actually more desirable than the god's original choice of victim.

In desperate circumstances, it nonetheless remains customary to use a live scapegoat in place of an image, though again no blood is spilt. Tibet's first Western-trained doctor describes in his autobiography how, when he fell sick with a mysterious illness at the age of about thirteen, his family called on the services of monks from their local monastery. For several days, they recited prayers and chanted, but when the boy's condition continued to deteriorate, his parents resorted to more drastic measures in addition. They bought a sheep that was destined for slaughter—the choice of animal being determined by the fact that he had been born in a Sheep year, reckoning according to the Tibetan lunar calendar. It was then painted and kept "almost as a pet." When this, too, failed to bring about any improvement, a ritual using a human scapegoat was performed. This entailed finding another youth to participate, since "it was believed that, in this ritual, my disease would be transferred to the other boy." For this reason, "only a very poor family was likely to allow one of its children to take part." Accordingly, Dr. Pemba's parents found an indigent who would participate in exchange for some payment to his family.

Unfortunately, the ritual did not work. At first, everyone was perplexed. But when Dr. Pemba's family "found out that, the day before my illness, I had been awful enough to urinate in the stream where a fierce deity was believed to live, they were sure this had brought on my illness." They began to leave offerings of food at the water's edge, and begged the deity to relent. "I suppose he forgave me, because in a few days, I became much better." Even so, the thoroughly modernized Dr. Pemba doubted there really had been malevolent forces at work. "I think now that it was meningitis." This characteristically modern viewpoint does not, however, consider the question of why he should have been struck with the disease in the first place.

Another vital aspect of the traditional relationship with the supernatural is the ceaseless effort to discover what the future holds. Many and varied are the ways in which this is attempted. Astrology—adapted in large part from the Chinese system, though Indian methods are also used—has always held an important place in the Tibetan seer's repertoire. But divination by means of scapulimancy (using the shoulder blades of sheep) is practiced too, as is interpreting the "language of ravens." Here it is said, for example, that if a raven caws in the northeast between first light and midmorning, a female guest is soon to arrive. If a raven caws from a tree while one is traveling, there will be neither food nor water. And if it catches at your hair with its beak when you are traveling, this is a sign of impending death. There are also elaborate compendiums of "dos and don'ts" for particular days. One of the most famous is *The Mirror of Omens*, compiled by the seventeenth-century monk Karma Chakme. (He wrote it not as a guide, though it is used as such, but as a record of superstitious customs.) This suggests that cutting your hair on the first day of the month "will affect your lifespan and health." If you buy a dog on the twelfth day, "it will be a manifestation of evil."*

Among many other forms of divination practiced by Tibetans, that of *'mo* is still popular and widely used. This is performed by placing in a vessel two or more balls, traditionally of barley dough, distinguished from one another with dye or by pieces of paper with possible answers written on them and concealed inside. The balls are then rotated more and more swiftly—accompanied by appropriate prayers and invocations—until one flies out, propelled by centrifugal force. Though simple enough in operation, conducting a *'mo* is a grave and serious business. The correct spiritual outlook and motivation are essential if it is to be accurate.†

These practices may seem to place the Tibetan folk tradition far from the more lofty concerns of Buddhism, with its emphasis on compassion and on the stilling of the mind; but it is important to realize that, in Tibetan religious culture, there is no clear distinction between the two. While it would be out of the question for a Christian to pray to any such deities, even though in pre-Christian times they were no less important than in the Tibetan folk tradition, the Tibetan herdsman who prays to his local mountain god considers himself an orthodox Buddhist nonetheless.

It is difficult to tease out precisely which beliefs and practices in Tibet pre-date Buddhism, but it is clear that the folk tradition sustains an understanding of the world that is quite different from that elaborated in Buddhist thought. While, for

---

* Another popular belief holds that if a baby looks backward through its legs it will soon be joined by a brother or sister. I have found this to be entirely accurate, even in cases where the impending arrival of that sibling is unexpected.
† The present Dalai Lama himself is known to be well-practiced at this form of divination. He is said sometimes to perform them for friends.

example, Buddhism proposes a universe that has existed *ab aeterno*, Tibetan folk mythology speaks of *creatio ex nihilo*:

> *First there was nothing. All was emptiness.*
> *Within this emptiness, life gradually began to form.*
> *Within this life, light and a ray appeared.*
> *Light is the father and the ray is the mother.*
> *Within the light and the ray, darkness and obscurity became manifest*
> *Within them, a soft breeze like breath appeared*
> *Then within this breeze, a whitish frost,*
> *And within this frost a whitish dew.*
> *From the union of the frost and the dew,*
> *A lake, like a mirror emerged.*
> *A layer formed on the lake and rolled itself into an egg.*
> *Out of this egg, two eagles emerged . . .*

The first gods were the offspring of these two great birds.

Much of this mythology is bound up with genealogies and the tales of god-men and heroes who were the progenitors of this or that tribe. Like the Olympians, the ancestral gods are conceived of as being members of large and quarrelsome families. Sons and fathers argue and challenge one another to fight. Brothers compete with one another for land and possessions. One god, knowing he will be the cause of strife if he favors one or other of his sons, strangles himself with his bootlace when they both ask him to dine at their separate dwellings. But then they fight over his corpse. Similarly bathetic is the story of the wife who, in order to protect her husband, changes herself into a frog; but her strategy fails and he is murdered by his rivals just the same.

Preserved mainly by wandering bards, the epic deeds of the ancestors are still recounted in rhyme and in song, most often at events such as the harvest festival, or at regional games and horse races. Elements of this earlier dispensation are also preserved in the wedding songs it remains customary in parts of Tibet to sing when the bridegroom's family comes to fetch the bride. Taking the form of riddles, these tell of the old gods and of the natural world of the pastoralist:

> *Who catches the wild yak by the horns?*
> *Who seizes the tiger with his hand?*
> *Who picks up water with his lasso?*
> *Who builds a castle out of sand?*
> *Who strikes water with a sword and wounds it?*
> *Which bird can give birth?*
> *Which beast of prey lays eggs?*
> *Who follows the footprint of the pheasant running over rock?*
> *Who sews a cloak for the slatey ground?*

Each question has its prescribed answer. The bird that can give birth is a bat. He "who catches the wild yak by the horns" is Makchen Rampa; he "who seizes the tiger with his hand" is Saya Pecho, these being two powerful ancestral deities.

Certain popular prayers invoking good fortune likewise testify to an earlier outlook:

> *May the eagle, king of birds . . . protect my life from the Lord of Death.*
> *May the red tiger with black stripes whom no one would dare defy, protect my body from illness . . .*
> *May the turquoise dragon, lord of sound who produces lightning, protect my wealth from all forms of pernicious opposition by expanding it like a lake in Summer . . .*
> *May the white lion with turquoise mane, without rival, remove the obstacles from my path . . .*
> *May the horse galloping with the magical speed of the clouds prevent the glory of my soul from being scattered by the hindering wind.*[4]

So while the aboriginal gods are now, for the most part, re-imagined as Buddhist deities, it is the ancestral gods to whom Tibetans, even today, cry out as they reach the saddle of a mountain pass, adding a stone to the cairn, *"Lha'gyal'lo!"*— "May the gods be victorious!" And it is the memory of these gods, and of the pre-Buddhist tradition, that informs Tibet's two most singular institutions: the wrathful deities (*tro'wo*), of which Dorje Shugden—the deity implicated in the murder of Lobsang Gyatso—is an important example, and the Dalai Lamas themselves. Both occupy a position precisely at the intersection of the Buddhist and folk traditions.

From a folk perspective, the wrathful deities are understood principally as protectors. They are held to protect both individuals and groups—such as a tribe, a family or the members of a particular monastery—from harm. Because of their wrathful nature, it is also believed they can be persuaded to visit harm on the enemies of those whom they protect. When, for example, China launched its invasion of Tibet in 1950, the country's protector deities were invoked to bring calamity on the People's Liberation Army. Monasteries made mystical bombs, in the form of dough pellets charged with spells and incantations, and tossed them in the direction of the advancing troops.

From a strictly Buddhist perspective, the wrathful deities comprise two different kinds of spirit: the *yi'dam* and the *cho'kyong*. The *yi'dam* are deities invoked in meditation and ritual to assist the practitioner in overcoming what the present Dalai Lama has defined as "all those negative emotions which undermine our inner peace: hatred, anger, pride, lust, greed, envy and so on." The *cho'kyong** are wrathful deities whose primary concern is defense of the faith. They can in turn be divided into a further two categories: those whose concerns are mundane and those whose concerns are supra-

* Or *S(r)ung'ma*, as they are also known.

mundane. The supra-mundane *cho'kyong* are considered to be the wrathful manifestations of fully enlightened beings—of Buddhas and Bodhisattvas, in other words. The mundane *cho'kyong* are worldly spirits—such as mountain gods or, as in the case of Dorje Shugden, malicious spirits—that have been converted and bound over as protectors of the *buddhadharma*. As an entailment of this brief, they are also believed to be concerned with the earthly well-being of individual practitioners of the faith, though ultimately it is actually that person's faith and practice they are concerned to protect.

Of course, the mundane protectors are much more numerous than the supra-mundane. But just to complicate matters, a mundane deity may be a manifestation of a supra-mundane deity. An example of this type is Dorje Drakden, the protector deity of the Dalai Lamas and the god who serves as one of the three state oracles of Tibet. Although apparently only a lowly *yaksha*, he is in fact the wrathful manifestation of Pehar, the protector invited to Samye by Padmasambhava.

We are not to suppose that, because these deities are wrathful, they are, as it were, permanently angry. According to the present Dalai Lama, Dorje Drakden can be very gentle. Referring to the deity's possession of its medium, he recounts how "when I was small, it was very touching . . . [He] always took great care of me. For example, if he noticed that I was dressed carelessly or improperly, he would come over and rearrange my shirt, adjust my robe and so on." At the same time he is "very reserved and austere, just as you would imagine a grand old man of ancient times to be." But this is not the attitude of most Tibetans. For most layfolk fear mixed with a profound respect would be the more characteristic emotion. Given their representation in Tibetan iconography, this is not entirely surprising. With their leering mouths and popping eyes, necklaces of freshly severed human heads, and belts of writhing snakes or garlands of human entrails, they stand with their feet submerged in pools of blood, or with one foot resting on a corpse. Multi-limbed, not to say many-headed, they are often shown holding aloft the flayed skin of a sinner and, clutched to their breast in obscene and explicit sexual union, a consort, her eyes burning with lust. Admittedly, to Western sensibilities, there is something slightly comical about them. Their bodies are rather squat and they have a vacant, sometimes almost apologetic expression. But few Tibetans could look at them dispassionately. Most would prefer to hurry past: lingering might be the cause of unwelcome attention.

Of course, to an educated Buddhist—and, traditionally, these would be a small minority, even within the monasteries—this iconography is quite differently understood. Every characteristic has a meaning, precisely defined: the number of eyes, of heads, of limbs, the raiment, are all symbolically related to the higher practices of yoga tantra. But while the whole concept of protector deities is highly refined within the Tibetan scholastic tradition, the relationship between protectors and laity tends to be shamelessly mundane. For example, Dorje Shugden is popularly invoked not only as a defender of the faith, but as a god of material wealth. Certain others are called upon when people desire to attack their enemies. (The Thirteenth Dalai Lama was himself the victim of at least one such attack.)* Nonetheless, the wrathful deities have always had an important role in Tibetan political life. And nowhere is the political dimension of the cult more apparent than in the institution of the Dalai Lamas themselves.

---

* The present Dalai Lama often warns against the dangers of having a partial understanding of the wrathful and protector deities, likening their propitiation for favors to "mere spirit worship." But this is orthodoxy speaking. From a folk perspective, spirit worship is precisely what religion is all about. The *buddhadharma* is, in this sense, just superior magic.

10

Priests and Patrons, Phagpa, and the Sakya Ascendancy

The next important incarnation of Chenrezig was Lodro Gyaltsen, otherwise known simply as Phagpa,* meaning, literally, Noble One. A direct descendant of the founder of the Sakya sect, his father—fifty-two at the time of his birth—was the younger brother of Kunga Gyaltsen, then the abbot of Sakya Monastery and thus head of the order. Regarded to this day as one of the greatest figures in the second diffusion of Buddhism in Tibet, Kunga Gyaltsen, generally known as Sakya Pandita, or Sa-Pen for short, was famous throughout Tibet for his wisdom and learning. Sakya Monastery was likewise known for the scholarship of its monks, for its many contributions to literature, and for the excellence of its artists. Its main source of inspiration was the Hevajra tantra, a body of teachings and liturgical rites brought to southern central Tibet from India during the very period when Atisha and Drom Tönpa were evangelizing further north. By now, however, the popularity of Drom Tönpa's Kadampas was beginning to wane

* The "h" is aspirated, hence the "p" remains hard, so *not* "Fagpa."

somewhat. The Kadam teachings eschewing tantra in favor of learning were just too austere and too focused on discipline for most Tibetans.[*1] The Sakya teachings, by contrast, offered all the color, passion and promise of the hidden mysteries of the Diamond Path.[†]

As a result of this success, Phagpa was heir to a very considerable benefice comprised of lands and estates that spread deep into central Tibet. And from the very first, it is said, he showed unmistakable signs that, like his uncle, he was destined for greatness. It is said that, as a child, he could sleep with his eyes open,[2] that at two years old he was reciting lengthy tracts of scripture, that by the age of seven he was declaiming to crowds "gathered together in full thousands."[3]

Phagpa's childhood cannot have been entirely serene, however. The great Mongol warlord Genghis Khan had died in 1227, but the Mongols themselves, whose homeland lay adjacent to Tibet's northern frontier, were as strong as ever. And if their reputation hammered terror into the psyche of the peoples of western Europe—by 1241, the barbarians were within striking distance of the gates of Vienna, having trashed and torched their way through the Russian principalities—how much more conscious of the Mongols must their near neighbors have been. Matthew Paris, the great medieval chronicler of the West, wrote that the

---

[*] A famous Kadam text warns that:

> As *alcoholic drinks are the root of moral infections, drink them not;*
> As *woman is the root of moral infections, look not on her;*
> As *covetousness is the root of moral infections, hoard not money;*
> As *to move about is the root of evil, go not roaming.*

[†] This should not, however, be taken to mean that the Sakya teachings are somehow less authentic than those of the Kadam. What we are really talking about here—as in any comparison of the sects—is more a question of emphasis than of fundamental doctrinal difference. By way of analogy, one might think of the contrast between "smells and bells" Anglo-Catholicism and the more austere "chapel" Christianity, both variants of Protestantism, both of which accept Jesus as savior, and both of which accept the Trinitarian nature of God.

Mongol cavalry rode horses so tall they needed ladders to be mounted and so voracious they fed off branches "and even whole trees." The Tibetans no doubt knew better—that not only was the Mongol cavalry unrivaled, but the bows they carried were accurate up to more than six hundred yards; that they were experts in siege warfare, in bridge-building, and in the black arts of disguise, deception, espionage, and psychological warfare; that their communications using smoke, colored flags, and, at night, lanterns, was unrivaled; and that in terms of both ferocity and discipline they left all other warriors far behind.

No doubt, too, the Tibetans were acutely aware of the Mongols' ruthlessness:[*] how when prosecuting a siege they would "take the fat of the people they kill and, melting it, throw it on to the houses [with the result that] wherever the fire falls on this fat, it is almost inextinguishable."[4] And doubtless they knew of Mongol dauntlessness: how they would eat whatever they found, including, *in extremis*, mice, leeches and even human flesh. More than likely, the Tibetans would also have heard about the Mongols' drunkenness. The Franciscan missionary John Plano of Carpini, sent by the Pope to remonstrate with them for their unwarranted invasion of Europe, was aghast to find that "drunkenness is considered an honorable thing by them."[5] When they reached capacity they would vomit before continuing.[†6]

The young Phagpa, then, was born into a world overshadowed by the threat of disaster at the hands of the Mongols. He was not five years old when it struck. In 1240, troops under Prince Godan, a grandson of Genghis, stormed south as far as Reting

[*] For example, after a savage battle at Liegnitz in Poland, they sliced off an ear from each of their victims, collecting nine full bags of them.
[†] John Plano was equally astounded to find a chapel in a tent close to that of the Great Khan's, where Nestorian Christians rang the Hours and chanted the Divine Office. In fact, Genghis's favorite wife was a devout Christian, and he himself made regular gifts to the priests—though they too were given to drink. William of Rubruck, another Franciscan missionary, spoke of the Nestorian priests he encountered "howling as they chanted in their drunkenness."

Monastery, which they sacked, and Gyal Lhakhang, a more recent monastic foundation, which, having laid it waste and butchered five hundred of its inhabitants, they then set ablaze. This assault was not an invasion as such, however. Its purpose seems to have been threefold. First, it is clear that the Mongols wanted to discover what riches Tibet held, and what obstacles there might be to acquiring them. Second, it is likely they meant to make it clear to the Tibetans that any demands they might make of them—whether of tribute or for troops to assist them in their campaigns—required instant obedience. But it seems they also had a third purpose in mind. As both Marco Polo and the Franciscan missionaries relate, Tibet's holy men had a reputation throughout the East for their prowess as magicians.* For this reason, their religion was highly regarded by the Mongols, whose own spiritual tradition was centered on the relative crudities of shamanism. It seems that part of Godan's intention was to explore the possibility of appropriating Tibet's Buddhism for use by the Mongols, and the reason for this was that the Mongols, like previous barbarian empire-builders, needed a universal religion, of which they could be the earthly leaders, as a means of unifying the peoples under their rule.

Various different stories are told about how Godan chose Sakya Pandita as the man to instruct him in the faith. The Sakya's own historians relate that the general who led the raid reported back to the prince that the chief lama of Drigung Monastery was the wealthiest man in Tibet, that the chief lama of Taklung was the most sociable, but that the lama of Sakya—Sakya Pandita—was the most spiritual. As a result, it was Sa-Pen who, some time later, received a letter from Godan instructing him to proceed to the Mongol's court at Liangzhou (situated in present-day Gansu province in China). "I, the most powerful and prosperous Prince

---

* Marco Polo was a Venetian merchant who met Kubilai Khan and traveled extensively throughout the Mongol Empire during the late thirteenth century.

Godan, wish to inform Sakya Pandita, Kunga Gyaltsen, that we need a lama to advise my ignorant people on how to conduct themselves morally and spiritually . . ." So far, so cordial, but the letter ended more ominously: "I will not accept any excuse on account of your age or the rigors of the journey . . ." Sa-Pen was already sixty-two at the time, but he duly set out—perhaps fortified by the knowledge that although according to the Mongols' code of honor they would not spill the blood of an enemy leader, they habitually circumvented their own prohibition by tying them into sacks and trampling them under their horses' hooves.

There must, however, have been more to Godan's summons than is preserved in the Tibetan records since, when he left Sakya in 1244, Sakya Pandita took with him the nine-year-old Phagpa—his heir—and the boy's six-year-old younger brother, Dorje. The reason for this was a cruel but simple one. Following the idiom of contemporary Central Asian politics, the two young aristocrats were to be left with the Mongols, brought up by them and then used as agents of the Mongol court. In effect, they were held as hostages.

On arrival at Godan's court, Sa-Pen found that the prince himself was absent, attending the *quriltai*, which would elect the new Great Khan following the death of Genghis's son Ogodei. When the two men finally met, in 1247, the Sakya historians tell us that the saintly Sakya hierarch gave Godan religious instruction and won, his trust to the extent that Godan appointed him as his regent in Tibet. Following this success, Sa-Pen, seeing a way to augment the prestige of Sakya Monastery, wrote a letter to all those holding positions of authority in his homeland. In this, he describes Godan—somewhat audaciously—as a Bodhisattva, warning his countrymen that if they do not submit to the Mongols, they can certainly expect to be forced to pay tribute. He warns that, among other items, gold, silver, ivory, large pearls, tiger-, leopard-, wild cat-, and otter skins would be demanded of them—before reminding his countrymen that Godan's "various vassals are many," including the Chinese people themselves. Actually, this last was somewhat of an exaggeration. At that stage, the Mongols held only northern China. But it was a telling point. Resistance was useless. They should accept as their inevitable fate either Sakya rule or ruin itself.

Unsurprisingly, central Tibet's disparate factions chose the former option, though not without misgivings and not for long. Indeed, it appears that the Tibetan passion for quarreling soon overcame their fear of the Mongols, with the result that, in 1252, they were duly visited by something like a full-scale invasion. The new Great Khan was Mongke, another grandson of Genghis, who took a personal interest in Tibet. Brushing aside Godan's alliance with Sa-Pen, Mongke inaugurated a two-year campaign, that was undertaken with the ferocity and ruthless vigor for which the Mongols were rightly feared, "killing, looting, burning houses, destroying temples, and injuring monks."[7] Thereafter, Tibet was divided into thirteen myriarchies, or administrative districts, whose representatives reported directly to Mongke's court. As a result, the Mongols remained substantially in control of Tibet for the greater part of the next century.

There is, however, another side to the story of the Mongols' subjugation of Tibet. As Sakya Pandita had recognized from the beginning, the Mongols' interest in Buddhism gave him, on behalf of Sakya, a precious opportunity for evangelism. So while he was clearly alive to the political capital to be made from the alliance with Godan, actually his greater purpose was the religious conversion of the Mongols. And it was this sacred mission that, on his deathbed, he entrusted to Phagpa, as he presented him with his prayer wheel and his begging bowl.

Sa-Pen died in 1251, just before Mongke's invasion.* Thus

---

* Godan died soon after—from sorrow at the loss of his beloved teacher, according to the more pious sources, though drink is the more likely direct cause.

Phagpa found himself, at the age of sixteen, abbot in exile of the Sakya Monastery and head of its sect, but in a most uncertain position with respect to the Mongol leadership. No doubt he longed to return home. Instead he found himself summoned to the court of Kubilai Khan, yet another of the Mongol chieftains, who was at that moment preparing, with fastidious attention to detail, to wage war on the kingdom of Ta-li (modern-day Yunnan province). This was preparatory to a final thrust against the Song Dynasty in southern China.

As with Godan and Sakya Pandita, Kubilai's interest in Phagpa was primarily a religious one. It is clear that, at this time, Kubilai already harbored ambitions to seize the khanate (the overall leadership of the Mongols) from Mongke, if ever the opportunity arose. In the meantime, he sought to make a name for himself as a conqueror and ruler. Very likely he saw Phagpa as someone who could help him in both these endeavors. On the one hand, there was the promise of the superior spiritual firepower offered by the tantras. An important aspect of the Hevajra tantric cycle propagated by the Sakyapas is devotion to Mahakala, a wrathful form of Chenrezig and one of the great protector deities of the Tibetan Buddhist pantheon. With him on Kubilai's side, the campaign against Ta-li was bound to be successful. On the other hand, Kubilai, in common with the rest of the Mongol leadership, was conscious of the need for a universal creed as a means to sustain his rule over the conquered territories.

This was a perennial problem for barbarian usurpers. The Toba Wei, a nomadic people of Turkic extraction originating in Manchuria, who had come down from the steppes and conquered northern China during the fifth century, faced exactly the same difficulty. Needing an ideology to counter the highly developed Confucian culture of their Chinese subjects, Buddhism looked the logical answer. As one tribal leader put the matter, "Buddha, being a barbarian god, is the very one we should worship."[8] Thus although no doubt the conversion of many barbarians to

Buddhism was entirely sincere, in the case of the Toba Wei leadership, the motives were starkly political. A remarkable feature of Toba Wei rule was the close relationship between the clergy and the structures and institutions of power. In a move that prefigures the identification of Songtsen Gampo and, much later, the Dalai Lamas with Chenrezig, the first Toba Wei emperor was proclaimed Tathagata—a synonym for the Buddha himself.

It is quite likely that Kubilai was aware of this tradition whereby the steppe rulers turned to Buddhism. It is also more than possible that he knew of the tradition whereby Buddhist rulers could be identified as earthly forms of a divine being. If he could obtain such recognition for himself, it would bolster his chances of winning the khanate. But he could not just proclaim himself a god: he needed someone to do so for him.

When the two men finally met after Kubilai had successfully overcome Ta-li, Phagpa gave Kubilai instruction in the basic tenets of the Buddhist faith and initiated the Mongol prince into the preliminary mysteries of the Hevajra tantra. As a result, Phagpa, for his part, gained a new and powerful patron for Sakya, to say nothing of the bounteous gifts Kubilai bestowed on the still teenaged Tibetan—a record of which is carefully preserved by the Great Fifth in his history of Tibet. They included a jade seal, a cloak ornamented with gold and pearls, a cloak ornamented with precious stones, an official headdress ornamented with precious stones, a golden parasol, and a golden throne, together with other items including an ingot of gold, an ingot of silver, horses, camels, tea, cloth, and silk.[9] It is also reported that Phagpa created such a favorable impression on Kubilai's senior wife, Chabi, that she presented him with a magnificent pair of earrings that he was able subsequently to sell for an ingot of gold and five thousand ingots of silver. This he used to endow the assembly hall at Sakya with a golden roof.[10] But most importantly, or so the Great Fifth says, following their meeting, Kubilai made a gift to Phagpa of the thirteen myriarchies, or administrative districts, of Tibet.

The Great Fifth Dalai Lama was, however, mistaken. It was not within Kubilai's power as a mere prince to grant Phagpa rule over the thirteen administrative districts. All that he actually granted Phagpa on this occasion was an edict exempting members of the *sangha* from taxes, and from military service, and religious freedom for all.*[11] Nor was there anything either new or remarkable in this: it had been general Mongol policy since the time of Genghis himself.† On the other hand, there is no doubt that Kubilai was sufficiently impressed with the Tibetan to have summoned him again the following year in order to consecrate the stupa, or burial monument, of his uncle, Sakya Pandita.

In the meantime, however, Kubilai became interested in another Tibetan lama. This was Karma Pakshi, head of the Karma-Kagyu sect and a man reputed to possess extraordinary magical powers. The various branches of the Kagyu sect were Sakya's greatest rivals and it seems they hoped that Karma Pakshi might be able to lure Kubilai away from his patronage of the Sakyapas. To this end, the great Kagyu master visited the prince at court where, according to the tradition's own historians, he succeeded in mesmerizing Kubilai with his ability to glide on water, soar in the air and reduce stones to dust.‡[12] It is unlikely that Phagpa was actually present on the occasion of Karma Pakshi's meeting with Kubilai, though some accounts suggest he was. According to these, it was only at the insistence of Chabi, Kubilai's senior wife, that he deigned to show

* By contrast, all Mongol males were liable from the moment they could manage a horse up until the age of sixty.
† Edward Gibbon, the great Enlightenment historian, notes sarcastically in his *Decline and Fall of the Roman Empire* that there was a "singular conformity to be found between the religious laws of Zinghis Khan and of Mr. Locke" (the philosopher) and contrasts favorably the Mongol attitude to religious freedom at the time with the Roman Church's preoccupation with the Crusades.
‡ According to another version of events, he conjured up a pair of elephants before levitating in front of the assembled company.

himself the Karmpa's superior. Requesting her to fetch a sword, Phagpa, in an anatomically challenging maneuver, deftly beheaded himself and severed each of his limbs in turn. To the astonishment of his audience, he then miraculously transformed these five body parts into Buddhas, which rose slowly and serenely into the sky.

The next event in Phagpa's life for which we have corroborating evidence is another contest, albeit one of a nature more political than spiritual. This took the form of a public hearing, arranged by Kubilai himself, to settle a row between China's Taoist and Buddhist communities. At issue were a number of Taoist scriptures that purported to show that the Buddha Shakyamuni was merely one of eighty-one incarnations of their founder, Lao Tzu. On this supposed fact, the Taoists based their claim that the Buddhist religion was in fact Lao Tzu's instrument to convert the barbarians. Also infuriating were the Taoist scriptures themselves, which flagrantly plagiarized the Buddhist sutras. But most vexing of all, in more recent times, the Taoists had succeeded in appropriating no fewer than 237 Buddhist temples in China and reconfiguring them as their own. The controversy had been simmering for decades, if not centuries, and Kubilai sought to settle it once and for all.

The debate began with the Buddhists questioning the Taoists about their claim that Buddhism had originated with Lao Tzu. If that were the case, the Taoists could surely explain some of the rules concerning Buddhist ordination. Their leader countered that he was not interested in such minor matters. His Buddhist opponent then asked what was meant by the Taoist claim that Lao Tzu himself became a Buddha. To this the Taoist replied that a Buddha was a person good in the highest degree. The Buddhist replied that there had been numerous such good people in the history of the world. Why were they not all called Buddhas? Clearly the Taoists did not know the meaning of the term. Yes,

the Taoist leader replied, of course they did. It meant "to realize heaven, earth, yin, yang, human-heartedness, righteousness,
and knowledge." The Buddhist countered that this was precisely
what Confucius had taught. Why, then, was Confucius not called
a Buddha? To this question, the Taoist could find no reply.

At this point, Phagpa himself stepped in, cleverly extracting
from the Taoists the admission that since the *Tao-te-ching* was the
only work left behind by Lao Tzu himself, these other scriptures of theirs must be forgeries. Kubilai himself now broke in
to remark (stretching a point) that while Lao Tzu was known
only in China, the Buddha was known the world over, so how
could the two be compared?

The debate was a complete triumph for the Buddhist party,
and a personal triumph for Phagpa, who, let us remember, was
still only twenty-three years old. Not only had he shone, but he
had done so in public and in the sight of Kubilai.

Seventeen Taoist clergy were duly forced to convert, the 237
expropriated temples were returned to the Buddhists, and the
offending scriptures banned. It was a supremely lenient settlement in the context of the times. But Kubilai, as ruler of half
China already, could not afford to completely alienate the substantial proportion of his subjects who followed Taoism. This was
true even if these did tend to be the uneducated peasantry,
attracted to its practices for their supposed ability to confer
immortality by means of alchemically generated elixirs (of jade,
gold, mercury and other substances).*

Either just before or just after the Buddhist–Taoist contest,
Kubilai declared himself personally for the holy faith taught by
Phagpa by requesting the lama to bestow on him the *abhisheka*

---

* Kubilai was less clement when, in 1271, he discovered that some Taoist
clergymen, still seething at their humiliation, had deliberately set fire to one
of their own temples in the capital and accused the Buddhists of arson. He
had two of the ringleaders executed; one more had his nose and ears cut off;
and six others were cast into exile.

ceremony that would initiate him into the higher mysteries of the Hevajra tantra. Naturally the Tibetan sources construe this as a genuine conversion on the part of the prince, but while it is certainly true that Kubilai became an ardent supporter of Buddhism, it is by no means certain that he became a Buddhist in any profound sense of the word. His devotion to drink and to the chase suggest otherwise. In later middle age, Kubilai was so gout-ridden after a lifetime of overindulgence that the only shoes he could tolerate were sewn from fish skins especially imported from Korea. And, according to Marco Polo, his fascination with hunting was so extreme that whenever he took to the field, he was accompanied by lions, leopards, and lynxes "trained to hunt wild boars and bulls, bears, wild asses, stags, roebuck, and other game." Hunting is, of course, forbidden to followers of the *buddhadharma*.

Part of the problem in deciding the question of Kubilai's personal faith comes from his habitual presentation of himself as all things to all men. To the Chinese Mandarins whom he employed, Kubilai assumed the pose of an upholder of the Confucian system, regularly sacrificing to the ancestors and promoting such practices among the people. To the Tibetan and Chinese *sangha*, he portrayed himself as a devout Buddhist. To the Muslim community, he acted as a protector. To his European visitors, such as Marco Polo, he predicted mass conversions among his people to Christianity, even going to the extent of requesting the Pope to send him a hundred missionaries.* And toward the Taoists he was generally lenient, as we have seen.[13] Yet, it is doubtful whether he ever really ceased to be

---

* Tsepon Shakabpa notes in his political history of Tibet that Phagpa, in his autobiography, mentions that Kubilai was at this time friendly with a Westerner. I have been unable to verify this, but if true it might go a long way to settling the great scholarly debate over whether Marco really did ever visit China, since this is surely the man he is referring to. Doubts arise on account of a number of striking omissions in Marco's great travel book. He does not mention foot-binding, for example.

a barbarian at heart. He continued always to take part in the Mongols' traditional rituals as well.

Nonetheless Kubilai did take a personal interest in Buddhism, and for a very particular reason—a clue to which can be found within the Hevajra tantra cycle itself. In common with the other tantras, the defining metaphor of its ritual system is the transformation of the initiate into a *cakravartin*, or universal monarch.[14]

According to religious historians, this, together with its avowedly military symbolism, derives from the fact that the tantric cycles had come to maturity at a time when Buddhism in India was under intense pressure. On the one hand, the monasteries had the loss of royal patronage to contend with. On the other, they were under more or less constant threat from India's Muslim invaders.* In one way, tantra can be seen as a sort of psychological defense mechanism. For Kubilai, the world ruler in waiting, the symbolism was clear. The prince would also have been aware of the Buddhist concept of the *cakravartin*, whose archetype was, as we have seen, Ashoka. Ashoka's territories had covered all India, as far south as Bangalore as well as much of Central Asia, including Bactria (part of present-day Afghanistan), and his name was a byword for political power in Buddhist culture.

According to our Tibetan sources, before agreeing to bestow the *abhisheka* ceremony on Kubilai, Phagpa, in a gesture of determined orthodoxy or of stunning diplomatic finesse, according to taste, suggested to Kubilai that it might be better to wait for the time being. In the present circumstances, Kubilai would not, unfortunately, be able to fulfill the conditions laid down for the initiation. These stated that, once granted, the lama must at all times take precedence over the one whom he has anointed. This would obviously create problems for Kubilai, who deferred to no man. At this point, we are told,

---

* Indeed, the Kalachakra tantric teachings are replete with references to a coming conflagration in which the followers of Buddha will emerge victorious in a final battle with the followers of the Prophet.

Kubilai's wife came to the rescue, suggesting that Kubilai might yield precedence to Phagpa during private religious ceremonies and teachings, while, at public gatherings, Kubilai could retain his authority. It was a brilliant solution. The arrangement suited both parties, and Phagpa was able to proceed with the first of the three initiations that he would, at intervals, bestow on Kubilai over the course of the next sixteen years.

From now on the relationship between the two men was configured in an entirely new way. Phagpa was no longer merely Kubilai's chaplain but, in religious terms, his co-equal. Similarly, Kubilai was no longer merely Phagpa's patron, but also a supplicant. For according to the Buddhist understanding of the priest–patron relationship, the patron is one who must be deemed worthy of the priest's ministrations; he must also be worthy of bestowing gifts on the priest (and this quality of worthiness is of course to be determined by the priest himself).*[15]

In earthly terms, Phagpa's consecration of Kubilai reconfigured their relationship in like fashion. If Kubilai was henceforth acknowledged as a *cakravartin*, Phagpa's earthly status was similarly raised to that of religious king. And it was to this status that the Great Fifth Dalai Lama was alluding when, in his autobiography, he made the startling claim, "I am Phagpa."

Kubilai's conception of himself as a world leader came a step closer to reality when, during the following year, 1259, Mongke died. More or less immediately, Kubilai declared himself Great Khan—but then so did his brother, Arigh Borke. One remarkable feature of the Mongol Empire was that its leadership was an entirely family affair. Having no abstract concept of political authority, rule of conquered lands was divided up between brothers and cousins according to their standing within the family. Nor was succession to the khanate by primogeniture. Instead, it was open to any member of the family to claim if he could

---

* In Tibetan, this is *mchod yon*, pronounced "chö yon."

generate enough support from the remainder. In cases, such as
now, when the leadership was disputed, settlement was reached
by force of arms. Four years of intermittent fighting were to pass
before Kubilai finally emerged victor. But even then he struggled
to defend himself against claims that his assumption of the khanate
was invalid. Conservative Mongols felt that he was too closely
associated with sedentary China to be a fitting leader, a charge
that was to grow in force the more firmly in control of China that
he became. Kubilai's attempts to project himself as a *cakravartin*
can thus be seen in terms of his effort to counter this accusation.

After declaring himself Great Khan, Kubilai moved to establish his personal authority over Tibet by recalling the representatives Mongke had sent there following the 1252 invasion. In
January 1261, Kubilai appointed Phagpa to the dignity of national
preceptor, giving him at least notional responsibility for Tibetan
affairs.* The Tibetan sources also allege that Kubilai decreed
from now on that all other sects were to be proscribed. However,
Phagpa magnanimously insisted they be allowed their freedom.
But this is unlikely: such a decree would have been almost impossible to enforce, and anyway complete religious tolerance was a
feature of Mongol rule. On the other hand, it is certain that Kubilai did move against the Kagyu sect. He caused Karma Pakshi
to be arrested and banished to southern China for eight years,
for having had the temerity to support Arigh Borke in the brothers' struggle for paramountcy.†

As national preceptor, Phagpa was now not only a member
of Kubilai's inner circle but an official of high standing within
the Mongol government. This meant that he kept company
with a group of advisers and officials drawn from a wide variety of ethnic and religious groups. Kubilai made it a point to

---

* This is clearly the event to which the Great Fifth was referring.
† Kagyu historians relate how Karma Pakshi was set on top of a burning pyre
for three days. He was sent south only when it became apparent to his captors
that no flame could harm him nor chains could hold him.

govern with personally selected representatives from every major community within his empire. And not only did he employ these men as his representatives in their own countries, it was a particular feature of Kubilai's rule in China that he staffed many departments with non-Chinese, as a means to weaken the grip of the Mandarin class which traditionally ruled the country. He had, for example, Uighur military advisers, a Nestorian Christian as one of his senior secretaries, and Central Asian Muslims acting in different capacities.

Though he must have longed to return home, for the time being Phagpa was thus forced to remain in exile—for the most part in Kubilai's camp in Kambaluk, the Mongol capital. But he was by no means idle. Not only did he continue, even at this distance, as abbot of Sakya Monastery—sending a major subvention of funds in 1262—he also threw himself into his personal mission to evangelize the Mongols. To this end, in addition to public teachings, he kept up a steady flow of catechetical letters and exhortations to various members of the princely families. Unlike his uncle—whose exposition of Indian logic written in mnemonic verse, accompanied by a lengthy commentary, remains a standard text on the subject—much of Phagpa's literary output was devoted to the tantras, though he did compose an important rhyming treatise on karma. Phagpa also made a significant contribution to Tibetan literature by commissioning the translation from Sanskrit of a series of handbooks concerned with poetics. These had an immediate impact on Tibetan literary style, which, as a result, became markedly more elaborate, more subtle, and more intricate in its use of rhetorical devices. But arguably the greatest of Phagpa's collected works is the book he wrote for one of Kubilai's sons, outlining the principles of the faith. This is the *shes bya rab gsal*, known in English as *Prince Jingim's Textbook of Tibetan Buddhism*. It remains one of the great classics of Tibetan literature.[16]

Phagpa was still at court when, in 1264, Kubilai finally

succeeded in forcing his brother's surrender. At this point, Kubilai moved swiftly to consolidate his hold over northern China. In an important symbolic gesture, he shifted his headquarters to the site of the old Chin capital in the northeast, where he founded the entirely new city of Ta-tu—modern-day Beijing. Simultaneously, he inaugurated a number of new administrative offices, including the Tsung-chih Yuan, the Office for Buddhist Affairs, which, from now on, would be responsible for steering developments in Tibet.

As part of Kubilai's latest thinking on Tibet, Phagpa was to return to Sakya, accompanied by his younger brother Dorje. Having been just six years old on arrival at court, Dorje had in the meantime been thoroughly Mongolized, even to the extent of marrying one of Godan's daughters. A detail in an important *thangka*, or painting on silk, still kept at Sakya, depicts him showing off his skills by skewering two geese with a single arrow while an approving Kubilai looks on. Continuing the archery theme, it is said that on his arrival back at Sakya, Dorje ran up on to the roof of the main building and fired an arrow into the mountainside behind. From the spot where it landed emerged a spring with curative powers.

The brothers reached Sakya during the early part of 1265, Phagpa himself having traveled via Lhasa. It is not hard to imagine the rejoicing there must have been. The lama occupies a place in Tibetan society that combines all the modern elements of celebrity and prestige granted to entertainment-industry stars with all the old-world values attached to kingship and clerical authority. And like a modern-day sporting hero, the lama is very much the possession of a given community. We may be sure that in Phagpa's case, the people of Sakya took enormous pride in his triumphant return. He had been tutored by the great Sa-Pen, whose reputation even today transcends sectarian rivalry; he had won the confidence of the most powerful man in the world; he had gained for himself a reputation as a scholar and a teacher of genius. And now here he was, back among his own people, to rule, so it seemed to them, in the manner of one of the religious kings of old.

Today, the most significant legacy of Phagpa's homecoming is the magnificent, if austere, Lhakhang Chenmo, or Great Temple, that he caused to be built on the southern side of the Trum-chu River, opposite the community's original monastery. Looking more like a fortress than an ecclesiastical building, it is built with walls ten feet thick and fifty feet high, a fact which partly accounts for its excellent state of preservation.* The other reason for its survival, and for the survival of its magnificent contents too, is that, for modern China, the building symbolizes the subjugation of Tibet from now on. According to them, Mongol rule over Tibet via Kubilai's Office for Buddhist Affairs marks the incorporation of Tibet into the Chinese state. Of course, this ignores the fact that the then emperor was not Chinese but a Mongol, that Mongol intervention in Tibet pre-dated the establishment of the office, and that Kubilai did not in fact become emperor of all China until 1279. Nor indeed does it acknowledge the fact that Kubilai clearly saw Tibet as a territory distinct from China (otherwise he might have been expected to have ruled it as a Chinese province). Yet it is on this basis that the Chinese communists claim that Tibet is, and indeed always has been, an inalienable part of China.

Phagpa's rule in Tibet lasted just three years. In 1267, he was summoned back to Kubilai's court. The reason for this is unclear, but there can be no doubt that Phagpa faced serious opposition to his rule from the other sects. A famous Kadam scholar circulated verses satirizing the Sakya hierarch that ended by asking, "How could holy men / Become officials like dogs?" And either

---

* It contains a copy of the *Prajnaparamitra* sutra in a hundred thousand verses, written in gold lettering on pages that measure 6' by 2'6" as well as a conch shell held to be the remains of the Buddha in a previous existence in which he was born as a shellfish. This was given to Phagpa by Kubilai on the occasion of the Mongol's second *abhisheka* initiation.

just before or just after the summons to return, Dorje died in circumstances which gave rise to widespread suspicions of foul play.[17] This was followed shortly afterward by a raid on Sakya territory by troops loyal to the Kagyu monastery of Drigung.

At first sight, this attack looks foolhardy; but it seems the Drigung leaders were putting their trust in their relationship with Hülegü, Kubilai's other brother, and hoping that this might save them from retribution. It did not. Kubilai immediately dispatched a punitive expedition to crush the rebels. This he followed up with Tibet's first census,* which, together with the institution of the fabled Mongol postal system[†] and the subsequent codification of the law, marked Kubilai's assumption of direct rule over Tibet. Yet the Drigung raid shows that Phagpa's rule was by no means welcomed by all Tibetans. Indeed, there is evidence that throughout this period there was continued resistance, outside Sakya, to Mongol rule.

Back in China, Phagpa retained both his title and his office. Indeed, Phagpa's civil career was to scale new heights, suggesting that his time in Tibet was not seen as any sort of personal failure. As a mark of Kubilai's continuing esteem, the emperor commissioned him to devise a new alphabet as a means to the unification of his realm. Because so many languages were spoken by imperial officials, necessarily there were as many different written languages. Life would be made much simpler if these could at least share the same script. The Tibetan's solution, known as the Phagpa square script, and presented to Kubilai two years after his return to court, was a triumph. It was capable of rendering phonetically the three principal court languages, Mandarin, Mongol, and Tibetan, as well as Sanskrit, employing

---

* It came up with a figure for central Tibet of some 223,000 households, suggesting a total population of perhaps a million or so. This figure does not, however, include the nomadic population, nor the itinerant tradesmen and cultivators who made up a substantial proportion of the whole.
† Astonishingly, this was capable of delivering mail over distances of up to 250 miles a day.

a distinctive alphabet that had the further merit of lending itself to printing. Kubilai immediately ordered it to be used for all official documents, and set up a number of academies to teach and disseminate it throughout the empire. But, though technically a brilliant contribution to a noble ideal, ultimately the Phagpa script failed. This was due not to any fault either of Phagpa or his alphabet, but simply because, in the end, Kubilai found himself unable to persuade enough of his officials—the majority of them deeply conservative Confucians—actually to use it.

Nonetheless, in recognition of this service to the empire, Kubilai promoted Phagpa to the dignity of *tisri* (in Chinese, *ti shih*) or imperial preceptor. This was a standing office of the imperial government, which meant that, from now on, Phagpa "enjoyed extraordinary honors, disposed of large means, and exerted a paramount influence"[18] in relation to the Office of Buddhist Affairs, and hence over the government of Tibet itself. This did not mean that Phagpa could do anything significant without first gaining Kubilai's approval, but it did mean that, within Tibet, his decrees had the same validity as Kubilai's.

Phagpa's promotion coincided with a shift in his living quarters from within the capital to Lin-t'ao, some distance outside it, where he resided from 1271 to 1274, pursuing his monastic vocation, teaching, and adding to his already substantial literary output. He did return to the capital at the end of this period, but not for long.

Having conferred the *abhisheka* initiation on Kubilai for the third time, Phagpa resigned his office as imperial preceptor preparatory to returning to Tibet for good.* Quite what arrangement he came to with Kubilai at this point is uncertain, but there

---

* Inevitably, the Sakya historians make extravagant claims for the munificence of Kubilai's thanks offerings to Phagpa on the occasion of this final ceremony; but one in particular is questionable. It is suggested that it was Mongol practice to drown annually, for the purposes of population control, some hundreds of thousands of Chinese and that, on this occasion, Phagpa requested that from then on Kubilai desist. Whereas one would certainly expect this to be celebrated in the Chinese chronicles, the story appears nowhere but in the Tibetan sources.

is no reason to suppose that their relationship was anything less than entirely cordial. On the contrary, it is clear that Kubilai was conscious of being to a considerable degree dependent on Phagpa for his legitimation as emperor. Since their first meeting some two decades earlier, Kubilai had steadily increased the number of lama officials within his administration, despite the antipathy of the Mandarins toward them. It is as if Kubilai desired to give his regime a distinctly religious character, rather in the manner of the Holy Roman emperors in the West, in the knowledge that the more people that came to accept Buddhism (which he promoted assiduously as the state religion) and the more convincingly he could project himself as a *cakravartin*, the more secure became his claim to sovereignty over all the territories he had conquered.*

On the occasion of Phagpa's final homecoming, Tibet was enduring one of its frequent bouts of instability. Despite Kubilai's determination to see the place brought to heel, neither he nor his successors ever succeeded in doing so for more than short periods at a time. "From the early reign of Kubilai on, we read over and over again in the Basic Annals . . . of rebellions of Tibetan tribes, of invasions against Mongol-held garrisons and of punitive campaigns against them."[19] The subjugation of the "greatest thieves and criminals on earth," as Marco Polo unflatteringly described the Tibetans, proved beyond the capabilities even of the Mongols. On this particular occasion, it took the troops of three Mongol princes more than six months to dislodge the rebels blocking Phagpa's route back to Sakya.

The rejoicing at Phagpa's homecoming was, we may be sure, again prolonged and intense. It is not difficult to imagine him presiding over a whole series of religious ceremonies, each of them

* These now included Burma, Korea, and Vietnam as well as China, Tibet, and the lands that lay in between them. Only Japan evaded his grasp. Perplexingly, modern-day China does not lay claim to these other territories, though it would seem to have no less grounds for doing so than it has in respect of its claim to Tibet.

employing the whole panoply of Tibetan monastic ritual: the senior monks and lamas richly brocaded, the altars and statues freshly clothed in silk, every one of hundreds of butter lamps brightly burning, as the *dung-chen*, or great horns, announce the Noble One's arrival in short blasts of booming bass. Then, as the crowd settles, the low insistent chant of the choir led by the depth-trawling *profundo* of the *umze*, or chant master—intermittently offset by the shrill note of human thigh-bone trumpets and a dissonant clash of cymbals—begins to mount the eerie threnody peculiar to Tibetan liturgical form. There would have been tantric dances too, the performers clad in vivid costumes, their heads adorned with the curious tasseled crown of the *tantrika*, or their faces masked with the likeness of a grinning skull, eyeballs intact but staring madly, in urgent reminder of the transience of mortal existence. We know that for several days Phagpa gave religious teachings, while as many members of the Sakya community (which included all those affiliated to it by reason of birth, property, or employment and therefore certainly numbered tens of thousands) attended as possible. And he would have received countless petitioners, the most important first, to be sure, but eventually the most humble, the awestruck peasantry with their pleas for succor, for guidance or for intervention.*

Meanwhile, Kubilai's troops continued their operations in Tibet. It was thus against a background of continuing resistance to Mongol-backed Sakya rule that, in the following year, Phagpa invoked a general synod. The members of every monastery and religious community—and there were by now several thousand such foundations of one denomination or another—were invited to attend. It is said that some seventy thousand clerics made the journey, in return for which they were each given a tenth of an

---

* Very little in the relationship between the people and the *sangha* has changed over the centuries, and modern visitors can see for themselves the trembling devotion many Tibetans continue to have for the hierarchs and teachers of their faith.

ounce of gold, while, in addition, every third monk present was given a new set of robes[20]—both grants being made by Prince Jingim, Kubilai's son and heir apparent.[21] Ostensibly, the synod was an entirely spiritual affair—and an ecumenical one at that: it was presided over not by Phagpa but by a leading Kadam scholar. But there is no doubt that there was a political angle too. This was an attempt at "pacification" by other than military means.

Such was his authority, such was the esteem in which he was held, and such were the memories of what had happened when Drigung attacked Sakya a decade earlier, that for the time being Phagpa succeeded in restoring peace to Tibet. There are no further reports of disturbances in the central Tibetan region until after his death in 1280. Yet it is likely that he was murdered.

It seems that, some years previously, Phagpa had been involved in the dismissal of Sakya's chief administrator. Now the same man had secretly written to Kubilai in Phagpa's name calling for military intervention in the hope of obtaining reinstatement. Hearing that troops were on their way and aware that Phagpa would be bound to find out that they had been fraudulently summoned, the deposed administrator arranged for poison to be administered to the saintly hierarch. It is related that Phagpa taught on the eighteenth day of the eleventh month of the Iron Dragon year. He was then ill for three days. On the fourth, Phagpa departed this life with his prayer wheel and tantric thunderbolt clasped in his hands.

At his cremation, it is reported that the smoke of the funeral pyre formed a white lotus on which Phagpa himself sat serenely as it rose slowly heavenwards. Suddenly a thumb bone spat from the flames. This proved to have five tiny Buddha images engraved upon it.* Yet, to the consternation of those present, not all his

---

* Tibetans believe that such relics are often found where the individual concerned has attained significant spiritual realization. The present Dalai Lama once showed me some in his possession: minute Buddha figures carved—but not, as he explained, by human hand—into fragments of bone.

ashes were white as is generally to be expected where a high degree of sanctity has been achieved; some were black.* Different explanations are offered to account for this. Some say the black content was a symbolic reference to the fact that, at Phagpa's death, there still remained some Tibetan, Mongolian and Chinese officials who had not embraced the *buddhadharma*. Others suggest a material explanation—that the black remains indicate that Phagpa really was poisoned. Whatever the truth of the allegation, Kubilai was swift and ruthless in his response.

An army of seven thousand battle-hardened soldiers, backed by a large body of militia and commanded by General Sangko, marched directly into central Tibet, storming the deposed official's headquarters and putting him to death. It then proceeded to Sakya where Sangko sent out detachments of troops to strengthen the Mongols' military positions throughout Tibet. In addition to these, when eventually he returned to China, Sangko left behind a force of nearly 160 men at Sakya itself. These deployments constituted the first permanent occupation of Tibet by imperial troops.†22

Phagpa's life thus ended as it had begun, in the shadow of Mongol violence. Indeed, his whole existence was caught up with the Mongols' avowed desire to subjugate all the peoples of the earth. But while the Chinese claim that it was he who delivered Tibet into their hands is clearly unsustainable, so is the Tibetan claim that Phagpa ruled Tibet in the dignity of one of the religious kings of old. On the other hand, it is evident that, in preaching the *buddhadharma* to Kubilai and his court, and in

* For a moving impression of what this would have meant to Phagpa's followers, see the passage describing the corruption of Father Zossima's flesh in Dostoyevsky's *Brothers Karamazov*.
† Sangko was apparently of Tibetan extraction though brought up as a Uighur (pronounced *Weega*). He later rose first to be Kubilai's finance minister, then his prime minister. But absolute power corrupted him absolutely. He was executed in 1291 and is today one of the bogeymen of Chinese history, being especially reviled for having sanctioned the desecration of the Song Dynasty tombs.

his work as a government official, Phagpa did succeed in keeping the Mongols at arm's length. There may have been numerous troop incursions into Tibetan territory, but while Phagpa was alive, there was no wholesale ransacking of the country. At the same time, it is evident that, despite the enormous difficulties he lived under—an exile for most of his adult years—Phagpa was an exemplary monk, faithful both to his people and to their traditions. It is no surprise to hear that the present Dalai Lama draws great inspiration from his example.

11

The Lineage of the Sacred Words: An Alternative Tradition

As we have seen, following the fall of the royal dynasty, and with it the Tibetan Empire in Central Asia, the first religious group to come to the fore in Tibet was the Kadam sect, founded by Drom Tönpa, the fourth of Chenrezig's earthly manifestations in Tibet. Chenrezig (and hence the Dalai Lama, too) is also associated with both the Nyingma sect, via Ozer the Treasure-revealer, and with the Sakya sect, via Phagpa. But Chenrezig is further associated with the Kagyu tradition, that of Phagpa's rival Karma Pakshi—which has generally opposed the Dalai Lamas.

The place to begin any survey of the Kagyu tradition is with Jetsun Milarepa (1052–1135), one of Tibet's most popular saints. Born into a wealthy family tracing its descent from a famous Nyingma lama, Mila's father died when he was just seven years old. Unfortunately, as happens even in the best families, the deceased patriarch's intentions were ignored and his property was appropriated by his brother. Worse still, though they remained on it, Mila and his mother and sister were now compelled to do the "work of donkeys" and provided with food "fit only for dogs."[1] Humiliated, the boy's mother conceived a plan to send Mila in search of a yogin who would teach him black magic in order that they might avenge themselves of this injustice.

As soon as the boy came of age, she sent him off with all the money she had managed to save. After several false starts, he finally found a teacher who, moved at his story, agreed to teach him the black arts. Mila proved quick to learn and it was not long before the two of them, master and pupil, withdrew for fourteen days of continuous spell-chanting. At the end of this time, the deities he had been invoking came to Mila bearing the severed heads and bleeding hearts of thirty-five of his relatives gathered that day for a family wedding. The lives of two of these would be spared, the deities explained, if he so desired. Delighted, Mila begged that this would happen in order that they might know "my vengeance and my justice." Thus it was that Mila's hated uncle and aunt survived when the building in which the others were rejoicing came crashing down on their heads.

Not content with this, Mila then conjured a hailstorm that entirely obliterated the best harvest his uncle's village had seen in years.* But almost no sooner than he had done so, Mila was overcome with remorse for the evil he had committed. Experiencing a sudden and miraculous change of heart, the youngster became filled with a desire to practice religion. "My longing for the teachings so obsessed me that I forgot to eat. If I went out, I wanted to stay in. If I stayed in, I wanted to go out. At night sleep escaped me . . ." Half-crazed with sorrow,

---

* Hailstorms were, as they remain, the scourge of Tibetan farmers. Frequently producing hailstones as large as golf balls, and often materializing out of serenely blue skies, they are easily capable of flattening a field of standing corn. As remains current practice in some parts of Tibet even to this day, it was customary to pay a tithe either to a local monastery or to a holy man for prayers and rituals to subdue the evil spirits whom, it was universally believed, were responsible for bad weather.

he began to search for a lama who could help him atone for his sins and set him on the path to enlightenment.

Many trials later, Mila eventually managed to attach himself to Marpa, a great tantric yogin who had traveled widely in India and studied (like Atisha) under Naropa the Dauntless—one of the eighty-four *mahasiddhas*. Thereupon, he entered an arduous apprenticeship, lasting many years. Marpa, recognizing a future saint, but mindful of the young man's sin, was almost impossibly demanding of his new pupil. He hardly deigned to speak to the young man, and then only to chastise him. Rather than teach him, the great guru set Mila the task of building, successively, three towers, several stories high. On completion of each one, Marpa ordered Mila to destroy it, saying that he had been mistaken, or drunk, or momentarily insane when he had given the original order. Again, a fourth time, he told Mila he must build a tower. When it was half complete, Marpa ordered Mila to take it down and remove a stone that some of his other disciples had placed in its foundations, on the grounds that Mila had not put it there himself. Bursting with frustration, Mila did as he was told. Marpa then instructed him to put it back and to rebuild what he had just destroyed.* By now, Mila was close to despair. His back ran with blood and pus from the sores that had opened up on it. When he complained, Marpa replied with kicks and blows and curses. In desperation, Mila ran away to another teacher, only to be sent back when it became clear that Marpa had not released Mila from his vow of obedience. Finally, when Mila was on the verge of suicide, Marpa gave him the first of a series of initiations that were to enable him to achieve enlightenment in a single lifetime.

Following several more years spent with Marpa, now studying the *buddhadharma*, Mila returned to his village where, after visiting his now derelict home, he retreated to meditate in a cave

---

* This one survives: it stands nine stories high and was later roofed with gold.

among the mountains that rose above it. There, having exhausted his food supplies, Mila subsisted for the remainder of his years largely on nettles boiled in water. He is depicted in Tibetan iconography as emaciated, with straggling hair, Struwwelpeter fingernails and green all over (from eating nettles), with his hand cupped to one ear, symbolizing the harmonious melody of the songs by means of which he imparted his wisdom.

Word of Mila's spiritual accomplishments began to spread. In due course he began to attract disciples to whom he taught the various meditative techniques he had now mastered. Among them was a great proficiency in *tum'mo** yoga. This constitutes one of the more remarkable practices within the Tibetan tradition. First reported by Alexandra David-Neel, the doughty French theosophist, in her 1932 travelogue *Magic and Mystery in Tibet*, *tum'mo* enables practitioners to raise their body temperature at will. To the astonishment of a team of observers sent to India from Harvard Medical School half a century later, it turned out that not only is the practice capable of producing this effect, but it enables meditators to raise their body temperature by up to 15°F (8.5°C).[2] On a night when the outside temperature fell to -4°F (-20°C), observers witnessed monks meditating—to all intents and purposes naked—for a full eight hours without so much as a shiver.

By the end of his life, Milarepa (the suffix *-repa*, meaning "cotton-clad," was added in recognition of his unworldliness) was universally attested a saint. Tragically, though, his death was brought about by poison administered at the hand of a jealous monk. Desiring to prove that the wisdom acquired from book learning within the monasteries was superior to that of Milarepa's solitary and unstructured meditation, the monk reasoned that if Milarepa really were a saint, he would know by clairvoyance that what he was about to consume would kill him. Milarepa did

---

* Literally, "fierce woman."

indeed know, but he took the poison anyway. He was old now so there was no point in refusing the tainted food if, by means of example, he could save his murderer. Recognizing at last Milarepa's selflessness and virtue, the monk assassin became a devotee, while the master, lingering a short while, cautioned his pupils against following the letter but not the spirit of the holy law:

> *What good is meditating on patience*
> *If you will not tolerate an insult?*
> *What use are sacrifices*
> *If you do not overcome attachment and revulsion?*
> *What good is giving alms*
> *If you do not root out selfishness?*[3]

The life of Jetsun Milarepa is significant to our story not because he features in the spiritual lineage of the Dalai Lamas, but because he is considered a founding father of the Kagyu (literally "Lineage of the Sacred Words")* sect. Alongside Drom Tönpa's Kadampas and Phagpa's Sakyapas, the Kagyupas are the third major school deriving from the second diffusion of Buddhism in Tibet. From its inception during the early twelfth century, the sect divided into several distinct branches, of which the Drigung, the Pakdru† and the Karma were the most important. Placing greater emphasis on yoga than the Sakyapas, greater emphasis on tantra than the Kadampas, and greater emphasis on monasticism than the Nyingmapas, Kagyu spirituality exhibits a marked bias toward the ecstasy of yogins like Milarepa, a tendency which reached its full flowering in the tradition of *nyön'pa*, or holy madmen, whose principal exemplars lived toward the end of the fifteenth century.

---

* This is Dr. Thupten Jinpa Langri's translation.
† Correctly, *phag mo grub pa*.

The most famous of the *nyön'pa*, who needless to say were not mad at all, was Drukpa Kunley (1455–1529). Besides having, like Milarepa, a genius for the spontaneous composition of spiritual songs, Drukpa Kunley was an enthusiastic *chang* (barley beer) drinker, flute player and fornicator. He fathered children on many different women, one of them a fifteen-year-old nun. He was also a fierce critic of the monasteries, once remarking that he had tried to visit hell, but had found the way barred by a band of monks.* According to his advocates—and, like Milarepa, Drukpa Kunley is a hugely popular figure throughout Tibet—all this seemingly outrageous behavior was, in reality, nothing of the sort. The young nun was, for example, a goddess; his other lovers were likewise tantric consorts far advanced on the path to liberation. As for his propensity to inebriation, this too was in appearance only.

If this interpretation seems in danger of dressing up profanity as saintliness, it would be quite wrong to suppose that the tradition of the holy madmen rests solely on the credulity of the ignorant. As with the treasure-revealers, the *nyön'pa* first had to overcome a skepticism that is not merely the preserve of the supposedly rational modern world.†4 Tibetans have been only

* In this, and in certain other respects, Drukpa Kunley resembles Piers Plowman, the creation of William Langland (c. 1330–80), the great English critic of degenerate monasticism. Hugh Richardson once remarked that Tibet has no tradition akin to that of Piers, but he was surely mistaken.

† Further evidence of Tibetans' natural skepticism is implicit in the tales of Agu (the name is derived from *akhu*, meaning "uncle") Tönpa, a seminal figure in Tibetan folklore. Behaving in many ways like a *nyön'pa*, Agu Tönpa is, as everybody knows, nothing but a rascal. An inveterate seducer of nuns, he is a trickster whose exploits are recounted as bawdy entertainments. In one story, for example, he manages to become the bride of a rich man—and thereby to make off with a complete suite of wedding jewelry. In another, he succeeds in "taking the veil" and entering a nunnery, where he sleeps with all the prettiest nuns before being found out. On still another occasion, he takes his revenge on his employer by convincing the man to eat his, Agu Tönpa's, excrement. Then there is the one about how he buys a crop of magic penises from a farmer whose field has been cursed, and sets up his stall outside a nunnery. Inevitably, the abbess buys the largest one of all, but she is confounded when, on one fateful occasion, she forgets it when called away from her community and sends her host's servant to collect the reliquary in which she keeps it . . . Everyone has a favorite Agu Tönpa story.

too keenly aware of the possibility that ill-intentioned individuals might try to pass themselves off as holy madmen. There have also been plenty who have claimed to be *nyön'pa* who were genuinely unhinged. Trimon Shapé, a member of the Thirteenth Dalai Lama's cabinet, seems to have been one such. When he lost his position, he was seen, bizarrely dressed, singing, and dancing in the Lhasa marketplace. On the other hand, there is also little doubt that there have been individuals who have succeeded in passing themselves off as *nyön'pa* and enjoyed themselves at others' expense. A recent example of an exponent of the *nyön'pa*'s so-called "crazy wisdom" is Chögyam Trungpa Rinpoché (1939–87), a hugely influential figure in American Beat culture—the poet Allen Ginsberg was an early disciple. Like Drukpa Kunley, Trungpa was an enthusiastic drinker and philanderer who, by the end of his short life, was often barely coherent when teaching. Yet to his followers, this too was all in appearance only, the illusory pranks, designed to instruct, of a fully enlightened being.

The tradition of holy madmen, which may be said to have been inspired by Milarepa (and which is not without its parallels in the Western religious tradition) is one of the special contributions of Kagyu spirituality to Tibetan Buddhism.[*] It has, however, a much wider significance—and relevance to our story—in that it crystallizes a particular strand in Buddhist thought that is resorted to time and again (if often in good faith) when appearances seem to suggest dubious motives. The most obvious case in point is the example of the Sixth Dalai Lama, who was, as we shall see, a dedicated wine-drinker and seducer of women.

---

[*] St. Francis of Assisi described himself and his followers as *jongleurs*, or jesters, for God. To the consternation of his audience, he once preached a sermon naked. St. Simeon (390–459) and his fellow Stylites lived on top of pillars—in the case of Simeon, the last of the series on which he resided was sixty feet high and just six feet wide—from which they preached against the licentiousness of the age. In Russian Orthodoxy, too, there is a tradition of holy fools.

The influence of the Kagyu sect on Tibetan history derives not just from its spirituality, however. Politically, the school drew much of its support from the eastern province of Kham, as a result of which many of its monasteries lay outside Sakya jurisdiction. Free from outside interference, the Kagyu sect—and, specifically, the Karma-Kagyu sub-sect—developed in a way which was to be of immense significance for the future history of Tibet in general, and for the Dalai Lamas in particular. For it was the Karma-Kagyupas that instituted the practice of succession by reincarnation.

Today, the Karmapa—as the head of the Karma-Kagyu sect is known—is incarnated in a youth of Hollywood good looks, born to nomadic parents in 1985. Like the Dalai Lama himself, he is believed to be a reincarnation of Chenrezig, though according to one way of reckoning, the Karmapa institution pre-dates that of the Dalai Lama by a full three centuries. Karma Pakshi, the miracle-worker worsted at the court of Kubilai Khan by Phagpa and the second in the Karma-Kagyu lineage, recognized himself as a *tulku*,* the earthly manifestation of a fully enlightened being. Thereafter, the sect appointed as leader the one (invariably a child) deemed to reincarnate his predecessor.

To begin with, the practice of recognizing successive incarnations was confined to the most important figures within the Kagyu tradition, but it proved so successful as a means of succession that in due course it became the way in which the majority of influential lineages were sustained.[5] Only the Sakya kept to the old hereditary principle. In 1959, it is estimated that some two thousand *tulkus* were identified in this way.[†]

Following Phagpa's death, the eclipse of the Sakya sect by

---

* More correctly, *sprul sku*, meaning, literally, "emanation body."
† As to the question of whether it is really possible by this means genuinely to ascertain the rebirths of successive individuals, much depends on what one means by the term "reincarnation." As we have seen, Buddhism does not accept the existence of soul. Instead, Tibetan philosophers talk in terms of "streams of consciousness" that carry within them "karmic imprints." There is no idea

the Kagyu was not far off. This came about mainly due to developments in China where the Mongols' Yuan* Dynasty went into progressively steeper decline when Kubilai Khan himself died in 1294. Spiritual degeneracy was also a factor. Considerable numbers of Sakya monastics had taken up office within the government and, as might be expected, some had grown more fond of the comforts attendant on political power than on the austerities of the cloister. These became detested by the Chinese for their high-handedness, as well as for the impunity their position gave them. In 1308, for example, a band of Tibetan monks stole fuel from a civilian, but instead of the clerics being punished, the plaintiff himself narrowly escaped a lynching. During the following year, some monks assaulted a princess, but again they escaped punishment. And the last imperial preceptor (still a Sakya lama) is credibly reported to have supplied the emperor with aphrodisiacs and to have encouraged him in vice as a means of obtaining favor.[6]

So far as the Mongols' continuing—though by now largely nominal—rule of Tibet was concerned, they remained heavily reliant on the relationship with Sakya. Sakya relied in turn on the reputation of the Mongol army. As Mongol power declined, so this reputation began to seem less threatening, and, by that time, Sakya itself was anyway losing ground within Tibet to the various Kagyu sects. The reason for this was twofold. On the one hand, as we have seen, there was a certain cooling of the great monastery's spiritual ardor. On the other was the rise of a new secular power in central Tibet, the Pakdru Dynasty.

---

that individual "A" is crudely incarnated in individual "B," though this is certainly how most uneducated people understand the principle. It is also worth noting that there have been many cases when incarnations have been disputed. The present Dalai Lama's younger brother is convinced that his identification as a high incarnation was a mistake and has long lived as a layman, and the present Karmapa's identity is contested by some. There is a pretender whose followers maintain that he is the "real" Karmapa.
* Pronounced "Wan."

During 1322, the Sakya lama appointed a young man, Chang'chub Gyaltsen, as governor of the Pakdru myriarchy. In so doing, he signed the Sakya government's death warrant. Again, although not a member of their spiritual lineage, Chang'chub Gyaltsen is closely bound up with the story of the Dalai Lama. In particular, his nationalism greatly inspired the Fifth Dalai Lama. One of Chang'chub's first acts on taking up his governorship was to attack the neighboring province of Yazang, in a bid to restore territory lost during the period of office of his predecessor, a weak and feckless relation. Although Chang'chub's campaign was a success, it immediately brought him into conflict with Sakya. A court hearing convened in 1325, during which a high official was suitably bribed, led to a judgment in favor of Yazang, to whom Chang'chub was ordered to return the land. So began a long and protracted feud, which saw, in the first instance, Chang'chub Gyaltsen refusing to hand back his hard-won territory and then disobeying an order to relinquish his post as governor.[7]

A decade later, in a bid to recapture their land, Yazang troops launched a major attack on Chang'chub Gyaltsen, whom they captured. He immediately instructed his subordinates not to surrender, whatever might become of him. To preclude the possibility of being forced to sign anything, Chang'chub destroyed his seal of state—actually in the presence of his Yazang captors. Complaining of a cold, Chang'chub requested some herbs to inhale. A brazier was brought in and the infusion set to boil. As the vapor began to rise, Chang'chub pulled his cloak over his head and drew out the sandalwood seal, dropping it into the flames. Unsurprisingly, his captors took exception to this, and Chang'chub was stretched on the rack, then bound and flogged. He received further beatings over the next few days: 135 lashes in all. It was only when it became apparent that Chang'chub had the overwhelming support of the people that he was given a conditional release. But his troubles were far from over. Now Sakya itself, recognizing Chang'chub Gyaltsen as a threat to its authority, struck with an assault on his headquarters during the summer of 1348. Chang'chub retaliated by marching on an important Sakya outpost, looting its estate and cutting down its trees—a "savage and devastating act of war" which seems nonetheless to have been routine in those days.[8] Sakya counter-attacked, in turn cutting down all the trees in the vicinity of Chang'chub's fortress and torching both houses and temples, forcing him on the defensive. But when the Sakya forces themselves faltered, Chang'chub went on the attack once more. The eventual result was a total victory for Pakdru. In the words of the Great Fifth, "the heads of the enemy and their banners were handed over like symbols of victory."[9]

Several challenges to Chang'chub's authority were launched over the next few years, but none was successful. Instead, Chang'chub further strengthened his position, while that of Sakya continued to decline. By now, Sakya's claim to administer the whole of central Tibet on behalf of the Yuan Dynasty was no more than a polite fiction. The emperor (by this time Toghon, who is said to have spent much of his time closeted with young Korean girls, emerging only to take part in elaborate tantric orgies conducted in the palace grounds) continued, for his part, to hand out gorgeous titles. But with Toghon not having the resources to deploy troops to enforce his will, relations between the two courts were reduced to little more than empty symbolism. In 1357, the emperor, forced to recognize the new power in Tibet, conferred on Chang'chub Gyaltsen the title of T'ai Situ.

A year later, the Sakya lama was murdered. The circumstances are obscure, though Chang'chub Gyaltsen himself is in no way implicated. There seems instead to have been an internal struggle which culminated in an attack on the monastery itself by one of its former ministers. The happy result for

Chang'chub was that he was now cast in the role of savior of Sakya. Personally leading the Pakdru troops, he took the besiegers in the back and, according to the Great Fifth, "after many killings, arrests and suicides by drowning" completely destroyed them. A total of 464 prisoners were taken, and all had their eyes put out. Chang'chub Gyaltsen himself now emerged as master of the whole of central Tibet, a position he maintained until his own death in 1364.

According to contemporary histories, Chang'chub Gyaltsen, having entered the novitiate as a boy, remained a monk throughout his life. This seems implausible given his martial exploits.[*] But we have no reason to disbelieve the claim that he spent the remaining years of his life reorganizing the government of central Tibet while personally living an exemplary life and observing all the precepts of a monastic vocation. Neither alcohol nor women were allowed within the precincts of government and, in accordance with the *vinaya*, the canon of monastic rules, Chang'chub Gyaltsen took no food after midday.[†] As part of his repatriation of government, Chang'chub Gyaltsen abolished the Mongol system of myriarchies and replaced it with a network of *dzongs*, or fortresses, each governed by a local *dzongpön*, or magistrate. He also replaced Mongol law with legislation modeled on what he took to be the code drawn up by Songtsen Gampo. As a means to improving agriculture, he inaugurated the practice of holding annual farming competitions throughout central Tibet. And, in a move designed to reassert Tibetan national identity after a century of Mongol influence, Chang'chub Gyaltsen banned the wearing of foreign dress, expelled all who had adopted Mongol customs and instituted

---

[*] It is not, however, unheard of for a person to take vows, repudiate them and then, later on, profess them once again.
[†] The present Dalai Lama follows this particular rule as closely as he is reasonably able. He may occasionally take a cookie or two to sustain himself while traveling and in other special circumstances.

the practice whereby government officials would wear the imperial regalia of the earlier dynastic period during the traditional
New Year celebrations. In all this, of course, his aim was to
foster Tibetans' natural pride in their country and in themselves as a people.

Behind all these developments, and influencing them
profoundly, lay the recent discovery and popularity of one of
the most important of all *terma* texts, the *Pema thang yig.**
Revealed by the renowned *tertön*, or treasure-revealer, Orgyen
Lingpa, this continued the tradition of Ozer's *The Immaculate
Life Story of Padmasambhava*, glorifying Tibet's imperial past
and purporting to prophesy the Mongol menace—the havoc it
would bring, and the humiliation of the people forced to observe
foreign customs.[10] But whereas the effect of Ozer's treasures
was to give new life to the Nyingma tradition, that of the *Pema
thang yig* was to revivify Tibetan national consciousness itself.
And it was this resurgence that Chang'chub capitalized on. The
time of Pakdru's supremacy under Chang'chub is regarded as
another brief golden age in the history of Tibet, a time of peace
and stability when, it is said, even an old woman carrying a
sack of gold on her back could travel unmolested. Chang'chub
differed from other important figures in Tibetan history in one
important respect, however. He never sought to win political
power for his own Kagyu sect. Instead, he was content to allow
Sakya to maintain its now symbolic relationship with the
imperial court in China. It was a policy error which has cost
Tibetans dearly. Chang'chub's failure to sever entirely Sakya's
relationship with the Yuan Dynasty has allowed the Chinese
to maintain that they have had an unbroken relationship with
Tibet since Kubilai's time.

Before he died in 1364, Chang'chub wrote a lengthy
autobiography, at the end of which he admonished his succes-

---

* Literally, *The Treasure Text of Guru Padmasambhava.*

sor to observe that the decline of Sakya could be attributed to the fact that "the disciples [became] more important than the lamas, the state servants [became] more important than the state officials, and the women became the most powerful of all." As it turned out, the power of Pakdru hardly outlived Chang'chub Gyaltsen himself. Yet his brief reign as paramount leader of central Tibet provided the inspiration for a very different type of rule that was to emerge from the political and spiritual turmoil of the next two and a half centuries: that of the Dalai Lamas themselves.

12

Tsongkhapa and the Dance of the Yellow Robe

Between the death of Phagpa, in 1280, and the birth of Gendun Drub, the First Dalai Lama, in 1391, only one other member of Chenrezig's spiritual lineage is an historically attested figure (though there are several that are not). This is Lodro Gyaltsen Zangpo, another Sakya lama, who was an almost exact contemporary of the First Dalai Lama. The brief hagiography given in the biography of the Great Fifth states that he was "the best of lamas" who had visions of several important deities. There is mention that when he visited the eastern province of Kham, the Karmapa "showed many signs of envy."[1] Historically speaking, however, his life and work had no great impact. And despite his contribution, there was a hiatus of over a century during which no incarnation manifested. In the interim, Chang'chub Gyaltsen restored Tibet's political autonomy, while in the religious field the most important figure is the man known as Tsongkhapa* or, to his followers, Je Rinpoché.†

---

* Literally, the "Man from the Valley of Onions."
† Literally, and more exaltedly, "Precious Lord."

Although arguably Tsongkhapa (1357–1419) is, in both religious and political terms, the single most important figure in
Tibetan history after Padmasambhava himself, and although the
institution of the Dalai Lama could not have occurred without
him, Tsongkhapa does not belong to Chenrezig's lineage. Instead,
he is considered to have been an emanation of Manjushri,
Bodhisattva of Wisdom. But since the history of the Dalai Lamas
makes no sense without some understanding of Tsongkhapa and
the spiritual revolution he inaugurated, it is to him that we now
turn.

Born in eastern Tibet* of humble parentage, throughout his
life Tsongkhapa eschewed the miraculous in favor of scholarship
and personal virtue. It is said nonetheless that a tree planted on
the spot where he came into the world was itself possessed of
magical properties. On every leaf, it bore that character of the
Tibetan alphabet with which his name began—a property attested
to by two French Lazarist priests who saw it on the way to Lhasa
from China in 1845. "We . . . looked at the leaves with burning
curiosity and were dumbfounded to see that, sure enough, on
each leaf were well-formed Tibetan characters."[†2]

At a young age, Tsongkhapa was presented to Rolpai Dorje,
the Fourth Karmapa, for consecration as a novice monk. The
great hierarch, sensing immediately the boy's potential, did
not perform the usual initiation ceremony. Instead, he conferred
a more extensive one, prophesying that the boy would grow
up to be a great spiritual leader.[3] Thereafter, Tsongkhapa began
his education at Drigung Monastery, where he studied medicine. He went on to be tutored by some of the greatest

* The present Dalai Lama hails from the same province of Amdo, which, for
some Tibetans, has much the same reputation as Nazareth had in biblical times:
"Can anything good come out of Nazareth?"
† Less than a hundred years later it had apparently died and been replaced by
a sapling. But while Thupten Jigme Norbu, the present Dalai Lama's eldest
brother, asserts in his autobiography that this replacement tree perpetuated
the miracle, today the legend seems to have died out.

teachers of the time. The young Tsongkhapa proved a brilliant student and is said to have been able to memorize two whole pages of text—equivalent to perhaps a hundred lines of verse—a day. His particular bent was toward logic, Madhyamaka philosophy, and rhetoric, although he also displayed a particular enthusiasm for the *vinaya*, the ancient code of monastic discipline.*

Having completed his formal education, Tsongkhapa sought out and took teachings from some of the greatest teachers of each sect. He finally settled, at the unusually advanced age of forty, at Drom Tönpa's old monastery of Reting, having been ordained a monk in the Kadam tradition.† The Kadam school was the one he felt closest to—despite the fact that he was originally inducted as a Kagyu novice and despite the fact that his single most important teacher had been a great Sakya scholar. A vision of Atisha he experienced soon after confirmed in him the conviction that it was his destiny to revive the now declining Kadam school.

Tsongkhapa's most significant legacy was thus the New Kadampa, or as it came to be known, the Gelug school, which came into being in the early part of the fifteenth century. Yet although he is properly regarded as its founding father, it was his disciples—among them Gendun Drub, the First Dalai Lama—who actually created the Gelug institution. During Tsongkhapa's lifetime, his followers were either known as the Gandenpas (after the monastery he founded) or as the New Kadampas. So far as he himself was concerned, his aim was not to found a new sect, but rather to breathe new life into Drom Tönpa's school by returning it to its roots as a bastion of doctrinal orthodoxy and moral rectitude.

---

* Considered a distinct branch of learning, the *vinaya* is summarized in 253 rules for monks—263 for nuns.
† It was at Reting that Tsongkhapa composed his great treatise, *Stages of the Path to Enlightenment*, one of the most important works of Tibetan literature.

Tsongkhapa is often described as the Luther of Tibetan Buddhism; but this is somewhat misleading. He neither over-turned any practices then current nor—at least from his own point of view—introduced any innovations in doctrine or ritual. As he saw it, those changes he did make reflected more appro-priate emphases. Certainly he did not see himself as a revolu-tionary, stressing instead decorum, the primacy of doctrine over subjective experience, and the adequacy of reason as a spring-board to enlightenment. This program, coupled with his own brilliance and great personal integrity, won him a following that was to explode into a mass movement.

Tsongkhapa's growing fame soon reached the ears of Emperor Chengzu of China, who invited him to preach at court. But Tsongkhapa refused, sending a disciple in his place.* Tsongkhapa was himself too preoccupied, not only with teaching and with the administration of the monastery he had founded at Ganden, just outside Lhasa, but also with the Monlam Chenmo, or Great Prayer Festival, he had recently inaugurated.

The Great Prayer Festival was another important legacy of Tsongkhapa to his people. Co-opting the already well-established New Year Festival, it grew quickly to become the most impor-tant event in the religious and cultural life of all Tibet. It also served to establish Lhasa as the center of the Gelug's religious and, later, political power. Combining theatrical, sporting, and other traditional folk events with the full pageant and prestige of the religious community, it attracted pilgrims from every part of the country, and became a sort of Buddhist Haj that every Tibetan would try to attend at least once.

During Tsongkhapa's lifetime, Monlam was a more modest affair than eventually it became, but it followed the same basic

* This is a good example of China's standing in relation to Tibet during the Ming Dynasty. When the Mongol warlord Godan Khan summoned Sakya Pandita, Sakya Pandita had gone at once, knowing what the consequences would be if he did not. Tsongkhapa felt no such compulsion.

pattern from its inception. On the penultimate day of the twelfth month (bearing in mind that, until recently, Tibet followed a lunar calendar), a votive offering, accompanied by a solemn performance of *cham*, or tantric dancing, was made to purge the old year of its accumulated negativity (sin) and misfortune. Then on the last day of the year, there were prayers at Ramoché, the temple built by Songtsen Gampo's Chinese bride. The New Year festivities began, on the first day, with the Priest's New Year, followed on the second by the King's New Year. On the third, the preparations for the Great Prayer itself began, followed by the initial ceremonies on the fourth. The Monlam Chenmo took place on the sixth day. But the festival did not end there. On the tenth was the Gathering of the Skygoers, at which the government consulted the oracle concerning prospects for the year ahead. Then, on the fifteenth day, came the feast of the Great Miracle, commemorating the Buddha's defeat of the heretics and the first preaching of the dharma. On the nineteenth, there was the Brilliant Evocation of the Glorious Goddess, followed, on the twenty-fourth—after almost a month of public events—by the casting out of the votive offering of the Great Prayer. Interspersed with all these were military parades in ancient armor, horse races, archery contests, running races, trials of strength, and a terrifying event (with frequent injury to participants) which, by way of a sort of hereditary punishment, involved members of a particular clan climbing up a pole at least forty feet tall and performing a jig on the tiny platform at its summit. There were also endless dances, both formal and informal, and, on the part of the laity, continuous feasting, drinking, and carousing. Some remarkable film, shot in color by a British delegation to Tibet in 1937, captures something of the atmosphere of the traditional Monlam Chenmo. Before the backdrop of the mighty Himalayas, and testifying to the loss of a remarkable culture following China's occupation of Tibet in 1949–50, there are flickering vignettes of slow, solemn pageant, of extravagant fire-offerings made to the gods, of tantric dance and ritual—the performers clad in costumes of sumptuous brocade—all enacted among great crowds of eagerly staring lay-folk.

It is recorded in Tsongkhapa's biography that, on the occasion of the first Monlam Chenmo, in 1409, ten thousand monks took part. The donations made to the clergy included over 100 pounds of gold, 40,000 pounds of butter, more than a quarter of a million sacks of *tsampa*, 416 bricks of green tea, 163 bricks of black tea, the cured meat of 2,172 yaks and sheep, and live cattle to the value of a further 225 pounds of gold.[4]

As to the nature of Tsongkhapa's religious reforms, he, like Drom Tönpa, insisted on the importance of monasticism to Buddhist practice and the central place of learning in a disciplined environment. This was in contrast to what he saw as the laxity, both academic and moral, prevalent at the time. By now both the Sakyapas and the Kagyupas had been somewhat corrupted by political power, by wealth, and by their contacts with the Chinese court.[*] Like the generally non-monastic Nyingmapas, followers of both traditions accepted marriage among members of their religious communities, and neither was strict in their attitudes toward the consumption of meat and alcohol. Tsongkhapa insisted that his followers be celibate, teetotal and—where possible—vegetarian.

As might be expected, he also took a stern view of tantra. This is not to say that he denied its validity: on the contrary, he was an advocate. But the sexual practices were, he insisted, only for those far along the path to enlightenment. For the vast majority, and certainly for all monks, they were to be reserved to the imagination in complex meditational exercises, and then only at the end of arduous and lengthy preparation. Still, it is widely held that he was undertaking just such meditative practices at

---

[*] The Kagyu had established independent relations with the (Chinese) Ming Dynasty, which succeeded the Yuan in 1368.

the point of his death, with the result that he attained enlightenment soon after expiring physically.

Arguably Tsongkhapa's greatest achievement—and the glory
of the Gelug tradition—was his elaboration of the classical
Madhyamaka understanding of reality.* This states that all
phenomena are empty of intrinsic existence. An object, such
as a table, cannot be said to exist except in dependence on its
causes and conditions: the molecules and atoms that comprise
its matter on the one hand, and the actions of the carpenter
who fashioned the wood into a piece of furniture on the other.
This is not to say that the table does not actually exist, but
rather that its existence is not separable from the complex nexus
of causes and conditions from which, as it were, the table
emerges. We cannot finally isolate the property that constitutes
"tableness."

At first sight, there is nothing particularly controversial in
this; but then consider the idea of self. Tsongkhapa maintains
that the notion of person likewise arises out of a complex web
of causes and conditions. Beyond that, the self does not exist.
The self that is falsely imagined to exist seems not to be
identical with the body, since if we hurt our foot, although we
say, "I am injured," clearly, it is the body that is injured and
not the "I." Yet, Tsongkhapa, following the Indian Madhyamaka masters, argues that this does not mean the self is identical with the mind. We can imagine that, given the chance to
exchange our unenlightened mind for one that has attained the
transcendence of true insight, we are likely to take the
opportunity to do so. For Tsongkhapa, this suggests that there
is a sort of core belief in the existence of self that is not what
we refer to when we speak of the mind, but still it is false. He

* For this, he drew on the greatest philosophers of the Indian tradition, Nagar-
juna, Vasubhandu, Dharmakirti, and Candrakirti. These, in turn, took inspiration from Avalokitesvara's famous discourse delivered from the Vulture's Peak:
form is emptiness, emptiness is not other than form.

further argues that the self is not identical with emotion. When something upsets us seriously, we may say, "I am angry." Yet here again, the "I" of this sentence is not identical with the feelings that are being experienced. Thus, according to Tsongkhapa, the self is not the emotions it experiences, nor is it identical either with perception or with consciousness itself, nor is it the aggregate of them, nor can it be found separate from them. In fact, the self does not exist. It is a mere projection, arising out of ignorance of the true nature of reality. Conventionally, the person exists and the table exists. But Tsongkhapa wants to show that, finally, all phenomena are empty of intrinsic existence. The ultimate nature of reality is in fact emptiness itself.*

This startling conclusion looks, at first sight, entirely nihilistic, and yet, paradoxically, Tsongkhapa's whole aim in philosophy was to argue against nihilism. For him, there was an inescapable link between epistemological skepticism, philosophical nihilism, and moral relativism, and it was precisely these that he sought to repudiate. He did this by arguing for the ultimate equation of the doctrines of dependent origination and emptiness, and by proposing a way to reconcile this with the doctrine of cause and effect, or karma. Recognizing, however, the ease with which his teaching on emptiness could be misconstrued, he emphasized the importance of students having a robust appreciation of the phenomenal world. For Tsongkhapa, philosophy was not merely an exercise in abstruse argumentation. For him, it was the very fact that we cling so tenaciously to our habitual notion of self that is the cause of our suffering, and thus the very thing that prevents us from attaining liberation. If the individual practitioner is to make any genuine spiritual progress, he must first possess this key insight. He must then meditate on it continuously until not only does he assent to its truth intellec-

* The Sanskrit word for emptiness is *sunya*.

tually, but eventually he comes to have direct experience of the emptiness of intrinsic existence of all phenomena.

It is clear that Tsongkhapa's emphasis on the intellectual framework for spiritual practice was at least in part motivated by a desire to overcome what he took to be the general lack of philosophical and analytical rigor then prevailing in the monasteries. In his teaching and his writings, Tsongkhapa continually emphasized the indispensability of reason—of ratiocination—and the importance of the discursive analysis of philosophical problems. His work was bountifully rewarded. Though it seems hardly plausible today, Tsongkhapa's call for academic excellence, coupled with doctrinal purity and personal probity, proved hugely attractive. Within his own lifetime, thousands heeded it and flocked to join the great monastic universities of Ganden (founded by himself), of Drepung and of Sera (founded by disciples of his). Within two hundred years of his death, the Gelugpas (the word means, literally, and self-consciously, the Virtuous Ones) had spread throughout Tibet and into China, Mongolia, and India. By then the Three Seats (as these, the main Gelug monasteries, had come to be known) had a population of something like twenty-five thousand monks. The world had seen nothing like this since the great Benedictine expansion in Europe of the early Middle Ages.* And, as in that case, the Gelug ascendancy inaugurated a spiritual revolution that was to have profound political consequences.

One of the reasons for the success of the Gelug revolution was that, from the beginning, it attracted some of the most able men of the day.† Several of Tsongkhapa's closest disciples became important figures in their own right, and, among these, few did more to propagate the cause of the Gelug tradition than

---

* Even the largest Benedictine foundations were home to no more than a few hundred monks, however. The only Christian communities of comparable size are to be found in Ethiopia.
† There were relatively few Gelug nunneries. Today, however, it is among women that Tsongkhapa's call to the monastic life is having the most spectacular success.

Tsongkhapa's disciple Gendun Drub, the man who came post-humously to be recognized as the First Dalai Lama.

Another important factor was the tradition's meritocratic nature. Success in Gelug terms was largely to be measured in terms of academic achievement. This is not to say that the Gelug monasteries were open only to scholars. On the contrary, only a relative few would ever be destined for academic honors. The remainder, once they had reached a certain stage, joined the group that was chiefly responsible for the liturgical work of the monastery—its daily propitiation of the protector deities, its observances of the great Buddhist festivals, and so on. Furthermore, although there was a good deal of crossover, there existed another large portion whose principal function was to look after the practical side of running the monastery: cooking, collecting fuel and provisions, or collecting taxes from families living on the monastery's estates. The great majority of monasteries also engaged in business of one form or another, and monks were required for these too. One of the most profitable activities was the provision of loans (at an interest rate typically of 25 percent per annum) which, because debt could be inherited, also had the benefit of tying families into dependence on the monasteries.

Nevertheless, it was the scholars, and, among these, the tiny minority who went on also to become spiritual adepts—masters of meditation, like Tsongkhapa himself—for whom the Gelug monasteries, and indeed those of the other sects, existed. Each one was a center of spiritual as well as academic excellence. There was thus keen competition between them, sharing as they did the same academic curriculum and texts. This competitiveness in turn helped ensure that standards were maintained. Yet while the Gelug movement was successful to the point where the earlier traditions—Nyingma, Sakya and Kagyu—all declined in the face of the Gelug's superior ability to attract members[*] (at least until the nineteenth

[*] Many Gelug monasteries began life belonging to one of the other schools that had either been abandoned entirely or had declined to the point where they could offer no resistance, spiritual or moral, to the Gelugpas.

century, when a non-sectarian coalition of these three sprang up), this success did not come without its own problems. Because orthodoxy was so highly prized by them, and because dissent from the doctrines taught by Tsongkhapa was seen, at best, as ingratitude toward the Master, the tradition was inherently conservative.* As time passed, the Gelug curriculum became increasingly rigid, while innovation of any sort was regarded with the deepest suspicion. It is thus not surprising that in due course there began to emerge a fundamentalist element that remains powerful to this day. Typified by dedication to Dorje Shugden, the protector deity linked to the murder of Lobsang Gyatso with which this book begins, Gelug fundamentalism nonetheless constitutes something of a paradox, given the fresh look Tsongkhapa had taken of all that had gone before him. Yet it does seem that there is something in Tsongkhapa's thought that lends itself to political application. When he died, in 1419, Tsongkhapa had given Tibet not only a revitalized monastic movement but also, in the three great monasteries of Ganden, Drepung, and Sera, a nucleus of power that would see the Gelug sect raised to political preeminence under the Dalai Lamas.

* When Gendun Choephel, the brilliant twentieth-century Gelug scholar and polemicist, began to speak out against some of Tsongkhapa's theses, he was, on one famous occasion, physically beaten up for his trouble.[5]

13

Gendun Drub, the "First" Dalai Lama

Gendun Drub[*] (1391–1475), the man posthumously raised to the dignity of First Dalai Lama, was born of humble parentage in the year of the Iron Sheep of the seventh calendrical cycle at Gurma, not far from Sakya. Compared with some of his near contemporaries, it could be argued that his spiritual attainments, like his ancestry, were not of the very first rank.

According to the present Dalai Lama's brother, Gendun Drub's family were originally nomads hailing, like Tsongkhapa, from the eastern province of Amdo. By the time of Gendun Drub's birth, however, they had been assimilated to the Sakya clan and were now living in central southern Tibet. It is said that on the night he was born, a gang of bandits raided the tented camp in which, as pastoralists, the family was living. Fearing for the baby's life, as well as for her own, Gendun Drub's mother hid her newborn in a cleft in some nearby rocks. When she returned the next day—trembling with anxiety at what might have befallen him—

[*] In "Drub" the "r" is almost silent, the "b" is pronounced more like a "p" and the "u" is short, as in "put."

she found the baby not only unharmed, but being guarded by a large raven. All agreed that this could only be an emanation of Mahakala, a wrathful form of Chenrezig himself.

The young Gendun Drub was tall and fleet of foot, attributes which earned him the nickname Sha'ring, or the Tall Deer. From an early age, he showed leanings toward the spiritual life, being an avid carver of *mani* (prayer) stones.[*] When, in his seventh year, his father died, Gendun Drub was presented to the Narthang Monastery, a local Kadampa foundation, where his uncle was already a monk. Gendun Drub may not have been the greatest scholar of his generation, but he was still an exceptional student, advancing twelve grades in twelve years. On receiving full ordination, the future Dalai Lama left Narthang and traveled widely throughout central Tibet. During the course of the next twenty years, he took teachings and initiations from many of the leading masters of the day. He also made lengthy stays at two important Nyingma monasteries, where he deepened his knowledge of tantra. Among his many teachers was the famous Bodong Choklay Namgyal, a man revered, among other things, for being Tibet's most prolific writer. Indeed, given that his collected works are reputed to run to some two thousand volumes, he must surely be among the most prolific writers ever. It is said that he would dictate up to four different works simultaneously[†] as he circumambulated a stupa, with a scribe placed at each corner. Bodong nevertheless recognized in Gendun Drub an equal—in intellect if not prolificacy—honoring him with the title Tam'che Kyen'pa, "All-Knowing One," a soubriquet conferred subsequently on each of the Dalai Lamas.[‡]

---

[*] This remains a popular pastime among pious Tibetans, who carve or paint prayers or invocations on to pebbles, rocks, and stones.

[†] Saint Thomas Aquinas is also reputed to have been able to do this.

[‡] The present Dalai Lama has frequently insisted that this is not to be taken literally, claiming, with disarming candor, that far from being omniscient and therefore able to recall past lives, he often finds it difficult to remember what he did the day before, let alone anything he might have done in a previous incarnation.

But the event which was to have the greatest impact on Gendun Drub's life came when, at the age of twenty-four, he was presented to Tsongkhapa, the master being then in his fifty-eighth year. According to Gendun Drub's biographer, Tsongkhapa immediately recognized the younger man's potential and, in a highly symbolic gesture, tore a piece from his own robe. This he presented to Gendun Drub, prophesying that this new pupil would be the savior of the *vinaya*, the canon of monastic law. As it turned out, Gendun Drub's jauntily named treatise, *A Hundred Thousand Sayings on the Vinaya*, would indeed become, as it remains, a standard work on the subject.

Besides his enthusiasm for the *vinaya*, it is clear from Gendun Drub's collected works that his other main preoccupations were logic, Madhyamaka philosophy, liturgy, and hymnology. An important aspect of his spiritual practice was Gendun Drub's reverence for Palden Lhamo, another of the great protector deities, whose cause as chief guardian of the Gelug sect he did much to advance. Palden Lhamo's characteristics are somewhat alarming to those unfamiliar with the Tibetan universe:

The body is of a dark blue color . . . in her right hand she brandishes a club over the brains of those who have broken their promises to her; in her left hand, on a level with her heart, she holds a skull-cup filled with blood and other substances used in exorcism. Her mouth is open and between her sharp teeth she gnaws on a human corpse. As she does so, her joyous yelps resemble roaring thunder. She has three red, round eyes, which gleam like lightning. Her yellowing hair stands on end and her eyelashes and beard blaze like the fire which flames up at the end of cosmic eons. In her right ear she wears a lion, in her left, a snake. On her head she wears a diadem of five skulls, while around her neck is draped a garland of fifteen freshly severed heads, dripping blood . . ."[1]

Small wonder that the Victorian missionaries who first encountered these deities thought the Tibetans worshipped devils. But if it is natural to be taken aback at this apparent obsession with the macabre, it is worth remembering that their function is to aid sentient beings in their quest for enlightenment. Gendun Drub makes this plain in a hymn to Mahakala:

> *Homage to Mahakala, the Great Black One,*
> *Wrathful emanation of the Bodhisattva of Compassion.*
>
> *Homage to Mahakala, whose implements are*
> *The skull-cup of blissful wisdom and the knife*
> *of penetrating methods, severing negativity—*
> *The Black Lord of ferocious appearance*
> *Whose voice causes all on earth to tremble.*[2]

Gendun Drub's meeting with Tsongkhapa secured the young monk a place as the last and youngest of the great man's "heart sons"—the inner circle of disciples he named as his spiritual heirs. Gendun Drub is not, however, regarded as the foremost of them. That distinction belongs jointly to Gyaltsab-Jé (1364–1432) and Khedrup-Jé (1385–1438), who are recognized as the greatest men of their time after the master himself.

Gendun Drub's crowning achievement was the foundation, in 1447, of the Gelug's fourth great monastery, Tashilhunpo. Dedicated to the memory of Tsongkhapa, Tashilhunpo is not, as might be expected, the one most closely associated with the Dalai Lamas. Instead it became, by a curious twist of karma, the seat of the Panchen Lamas, the spiritual heirs of Khedrup-Jé, who, thanks to their own relationship with China, came for a time to be plausible rivals to the Dalai Lamas. Today, the Panchen Lamas are famous for having two claimants to the see of Tashilhunpo: one recognized by the present Dalai Lama and taken into house arrest by the Chinese, the other recognized by China but by almost no one else.

The site chosen by Gendun Drub for this, the Gelug's first major community outside the Lhasa area, was one where, traditionally, the dead of the locality were brought for sky burial. The remains of the highest lamas were either embalmed or cremated, the poorest were simply tossed into a river, but the remains of people of middling rank would be taken to such sites, cut into small pieces, their bones then pulverized and mixed up with *tsampa*, and offered to the local vulture population. The stone slab on which this grisly performance (even now a common method of disposal in Tibet) took place is still to be seen.

A fine craftsman, Gendun Drub supervised the building of Tashilhunpo himself, calling in artisans from among the Newar community of Nepal and fashioning at least two important images—those of Tara and Mahakala in the abbot's private chapel—with his own hands. Indeed, so closely involved with the monastery was he that when, some three years after construction began, Gendun Drub was offered Tsongkhapa's throne at Ganden, symbolizing overall leadership of the Gelug sect, he refused, saying that he was still needed at Tashilhunpo. After a further three years, however, it was functioning sufficiently well to be able to house upward of three thousand monks.

Although early on the Gelug remained largely aloof from politics, Gendun Drub's success in establishing Tashilhunpo gave them a position of major strategic importance in southern Tibet. This came to be of increasing significance as the power of the Pakdru Dynasty (founded, it will be remembered, by Chang'chub Gyaltsen) began to wane. Elsewhere in Tibet, the Gelug made slower progress. Although they succeeded in founding a major monastery at Chamdo, several weeks' trek to the east of Lhasa, the Karma-Kagyu sect remained dominant throughout the eastern province of Kham. At the same time, much of the eastern and border regions were governed, as central Tibet had been following the fall of the empire, by petty princelings and tribal chiefs whose loyalty lay either with the Nyingma sect or with

Bon, the religion of the royal period and earlier, albeit that Bon had in the meantime come to look more and more like a form of heterodox Buddhism. On the southern and southeastern borders, there remained several tribes, such as the Mishmis and Lohpas (or Abors), who, ethnically unrelated to the Tibetans, maintained their own customs (which were reliably reputed to include eating their enemies) and had little to do with the majority.

As to the situation abroad, there was less danger during Gendun Drub's lifetime than there had been for many generations. To the west, in what is today the Baltistan region of Pakistan, there remained a community of Tibetan tribes, settled since the empire period. Although converted to Islam early on, this remnant of Tibet's imperial greatness acted as a buffer between the Tibetan heartland and the more militant followers of the Prophet further west. From the Muslim point of view, Tibetans are polytheists and thus legitimate targets of forced conversion. There is no record of any attempt to mount such a campaign from that direction, however. The threat came instead from the south. By the beginning of the thirteenth century, the (Muslim) Mughal invaders of India had laid waste to the whole of the north of the subcontinent. From the monasteries of Kashmir in the west, via Nalanda—the greatest of all the monastic universities—in the center, to Vikramasila in the east (whence Atisha had come), Buddhism lay in ruins. A pitiful story, dating from the end of the thirteenth century, tells of a Tibetan pilgrim who, searching for scriptures among the ruins of the university of Nalanda, came across one lonely monk teaching Sanskrit to a handful of students among the piles of rubble. But there is only one account of a Muslim attack on central Tibet, and that occurred back in 1205, when the hitherto successful warrior-missionary Ikhtiyar-ud-din mounted an invasion. Taking an army equipped with ten thousand horses, he marched toward the Himalayas, but the resistance he met with was such that he was repulsed at the first stronghold he came up against. Not only that, when he turned for home, he found his exit route obstructed, all the vegetation burned, and neither food nor fodder for his now much-depleted war machine. When he finally made it back, it was without a single horse: it had been necessary to eat them all. Following this debacle, and apart from a small amount of trade, until the time of British India, there seems to have been little contact between Tibet and India.

To the east, the Mongols' Yuan Dynasty had been replaced, in 1368, by the self-consciously ethnocentric Ming Dynasty. Taking a keen interest in the history of the glorious T'ang Dynasty, the Ming began to revive China's ancient customs and traditions. This led to a revival in Confucian culture, although during the dynasty's early years, the court continued to favor Buddhism—this despite lingering resentment toward the Yuan's many Tibetan monk officials. The first Ming emperor, Taizu (r. 1368–98), had himself spent a number of years in a Buddhist monastery during his youth, and even gave Buddhist teachings from time to time. The third Ming emperor, Chengzu (r. 1403–24), was heavily influenced, especially—if paradoxically—in military matters, by a Buddhist monk official who "prepared soldiers and armaments for the rebellion [against the second emperor, whom Chengzu overthrew] and constantly made strategic decisions as it unfolded."[3] Having heard of the fame of the Fifth Karmapa as a miracle-worker, Chengzu went to considerable trouble to persuade the young hierarch to visit him at Nanjing. The Karmapa eventually acquiesced, arriving at court in 1407. There he produced a stunning series of twenty-two miracles, one for each day of his visit.[4] Among them were a pulsating cloud, a rain of flowers—some fully open and some in bud, "their stems and upper parts like crystal"—and numerous apparitions, including, on one day, the appearance of the gods in the distance "adorned with precious jewels and riding on blue lions and white elephants."[5] The emperor was so impressed that he had a list of these miracles recorded on a scroll six feet tall and thirty feet wide, and written in five different languages—Chinese, Tibetan, Arabic, Mongol, and Uighur—which was then delivered to the Karmapa's headquarters at Tsurphu.

Despite such cordial relations between the emperor and Karmapa, Tibetan relations with China were not universally friendly. Ming attempts to secure a monopoly of the trade in Chinese tea in exchange for Tibetan horses did nothing but provoke large-scale smuggling.[6] And there were periodic military clashes—in the borderlands between the two countries—just as there had always been. The principal cause of these was Ming's desire to secure China's borders against further Mongol incursions from the north. Ming interest in T'ang history reminded them that the Tibetans had long been a source of trouble. There was thus a keen desire to "pacify" them, to use the traditional term. Yet the important point to note, against modern Chinese claims, is that following the collapse of the Yuan Dynasty, Tibet ceased to have an administrative relationship with China. The Ming emperors, even those who were not particularly sympathetic toward Buddhism, continued to hand down gorgeous titles—"Propagation Prince of the Doctrine" was a favorite—to leading members of the Tibetan *sangha* who traveled to Nanjing on tribute (in other words, trading) missions, as of old. But this they did without favoring one sect over any other. Still less was there any attempt to use one of the sects as an instrument of government, as in the case of Sakya rule on behalf of the Mongols. Reflecting its position during T'ang times, Tibet was seen as a tributary state, along with most of the rest of South-East Asia; but it was not one of Ming's fifteen administrative provinces. Tellingly, when, in 1654, a government official drew a map of the Ming Empire, Tibet was not included among the dynasty's dependencies.[7]

Finally, to the north, the Mongols, following their loss of China, were engaged in a period of infighting that would keep them occupied for the best part of two hundred years. It was thus, against this relatively benign background, that Gendun Drub spent the last two decades of his long life at Tashilhunpo, accepted as the Gelug's principal spokesman and leading scholar. There he wrote, taught, and meditated in a career that was blessed with many visions, including notable encounters with Tara (Chenrezig's female aspect) and with Mahakala. When he died, aged eighty-four, in 1475, it is said that his body transformed into that of a youth, and began to shine brilliantly, until it reached such a pitch of radiance that few could bear to look on it.

14

A Mad Beggar Monk

Gendun Gyatso, the Second Dalai Lama, was born in 1475, a Wood Sheep year. Because it was not until the time of his successor that the institution actually came into being, he was not, of course, recognized as Dalai Lama during his lifetime. It is not even clear that he was ever formally recognized as Gendun Drub's reincarnation. Instead, and most unusually, he simply came forward and announced himself as the saintly hierarch's authentic successor. And if at first he met with—understandable—skepticism, by the end of his life, few doubted his claim. Indeed, had the Dalai Lama institution not come into being, it is certain that Gendun Gyatso would nonetheless occupy a stellar position within Tibetan Buddhist history. Regarded by the present Dalai Lama as the greatest of the early Dalai Lamas, he is considered by the Gelug sect as one of the most accomplished of all its scholars. He is also highly regarded by the Nyingma sect for his attainments within many of their spiritual practices. And by Tibetans in general he is held in the highest regard for having bequeathed to them access to the mysteries of Lhamo Lhatso, a body of water in southern Tibet renowned for its ability to induce visions in those with appropriate credentials.

Born into a family with a long history of involvement in the religious life, Gendun Gyatso's ancestry was impeccable. Although they had originally been Khampas—that is, natives of the eastern province of Kham, famous for its fierce and determinedly independent warrior tribes and clans—it is recorded that during the ninth century, Gendun Gyatso's forebears had been summoned to assist in the building of Samye Monastery by King Trisong Detsen himself. As a result, they had come into contact with Padmasambhava, the Lotus Born, and were present at the tantric ceremonies during which he invoked and bound over Tibet's guardian deities as protectors of the *buddhadharma*.

Following Samye Monastery's completion, the family settled in Tsang province, where they evolved a spiritual lineage that was handed down from father to son, such informal, non-institutional arrangements being a common feature of the Nyingma tradition. Gendun Gyatso's great-grandfather and grandfather were both highly regarded spiritual masters, and in addition to his Nyingma practice, Gendun Gyatso's own father, Kunga Gyaltsen, was a disciple of Gendun Drub. On the female side, Gendun Gyatso's ancestry was equally illustrious. His paternal grandmother became a hermit at the age of thirty-five. Not only did she shut herself away, she actually had herself bricked up into her cell. This custom, maintained among Tibetan spiritual virtuosi to this day, entails the meditator being immured in a cell with only a small, curtained aperture through which food is passed. This aperture is in turn sealed with a (removable) brick so that light is allowed in to the least extent possible.* After forty-four years of solitary confinement, the old lady fell ill and

---

* Lieutenant Archie Jack, a British army officer who visited Lhasa privately during 1938, was shown one of these cells on a visit to a monastery. It was explained to him that the crashing and bumping noises he could hear coming from inside were due to the hermit having mastered the art of levitation.

was finally released from her cell shortly before she died. This enabled her to meet her young grandson, for whom she prophesied a great future and who, in return, composed a hymn in her honor.

Gendun Gyatso's mother, Ma Cig Kunga, was likewise a highly accomplished spiritual practitioner and had been recognized as the incarnation of an important thirteenth-century yogini.* Given that she was an initiate of several important tantric cycles, it is probably safe to assume that she was also her husband's tantric sexual consort, even if this risks raising an unwarrantedly lurid image in the mind of the modern reader. When she died, her son kept the top of her skull for use as a ritual chalice.

As was only to be expected in the circumstances, Gendun Gyatso's birth was attended by numerous signs and wonders, including a rainbow that appeared in the cloudless sky above, and his childhood was distinguished by an unusual piety. His biography relates that Gendun Gyatso "never cried or misbehaved, and his body only gave off the sweetest fragrances, even when he messed himself."[1] But the boy's most exceptional characteristic was his claim—made at a very early age and then with increasing frequency—to be the reincarnation not only of Gendun Drub but of Lama Drom, the great evangelist himself.

This was highly significant for two reasons. Firstly, it seemed to bear out a prophecy made by Gendun Drub that he would reincarnate, even though at the time the system of reincarnating *tulkus* was not recognized within the Gelug tradition. Secondly, because Atisha had spoken of Lama Drom as an incarnation of Chenrezig, and as a successor to the thirty-six famous Indian incarnations of Chenrezig, this self-proclamation placed him squarely in line with some of the most exalted beings within the Buddhist tradition. It is hardly surprising, therefore, that it took many years before his claims were generally accepted.

---

* A female yogin. "Cig" is pronounced as if there was an "h."

While still a boy, Gendun Gyatso was initiated into the lineages held by his father. At twelve, he was accepted as a novice at Tashilhunpo, the monastery founded by Gendun Drub. This first sojourn at Tashilhunpo was not a happy experience. Although he clearly saw himself as having a special destiny, it is evident that not everyone shared his certainty. On one occasion when he was seated on Gendun Drub's teaching throne, he behaved in such a way as to cause a former, now elderly, disciple of the First Dalai Lama to doubt that he was the authentic incarnation. Whereas the First had been quiet and somewhat introverted by nature, Gendun Gyatso was outgoing and somewhat haughty in his demeanor.

Remarkably, the question of Gendun Gyatso's authenticity as Gendun Drub's reincarnation is not given as the reason for the calamity that befell him in 1492, when he was forced by the then abbot to leave Tashilhunpo. According to his official biography, there were actually three reasons for this. The first, "outer," reason was that the monastery's administrators were worried that the prestige attaching to the boy threatened their own positions. If, as no doubt seemed likely, the abbot was to step aside in Gendun Gyatso's favor, the power and privileges they enjoyed would be taken from them. They therefore engineered his expulsion. The second, or "inner," reason put forward was that, by some unspecified misdeed, Gendun Gyatso had incurred the enmity of a powerful local deity. The third, or "secret," reason given is that the whole episode was a mystical drama, deliberately enacted by the abbot himself, as a means of enabling Gendun Gyatso to reach his full potential—something that would not have been possible otherwise.

To the modern mind, only the first of these explanations seems plausible. This is especially so when it is remembered that the whole question of reincarnating holy men and women was controversial among the Gelugpas of the time. Tsongkhapa seems to have felt that it was not entirely in keeping with the *vinaya* injunction that monks were not to own property, given that high lamas would automatically inherit from their predecessors. It is also notable that Tsongkhapa himself did not take rebirth.

Despite the personal calamity of expulsion, it seems that no particular ignominy attached to Gendun Gyatso's move from Tashilhunpo. He joined Drepung Monastery the following year, where he became pupil to one of its leading teachers. And so brilliant a student did he prove that Gendun Gyatso is reported to have accomplished in three years what would require of the average student twenty. It is said that the relationship he developed with his guru could be compared with the pouring of nectar from one vessel into another. It is just as well that Gendun Gyatso was a fast learner. In 1498, serious unrest broke out in nearby Lhasa, with the result that the two principal Kagyu subsects, the Karma and the Sharmapa, long jealous of the Gelug's prestige, gained control of the city.* They succeeded in this thanks to the assistance of their patrons, the princes of Tsang, who now wielded the dominant secular power in central Tibet. The loss of Lhasa was a major blow to the Gelug. It meant that they also lost control of the New Year Festival, and with it the Monlam Chenmo (together with the enormous gift-revenues it produced), which was handed over to their rivals. For the next twenty years it was not safe for Gelug monks even to be seen in Lhasa. And, to add further insult to the Gelug's injured feelings, both the Karma and the Sharmapa built monasteries opposite, and in direct competition with, Ganden and Sera. According to Gendun Gyatso's biography, the reason that in all the next twenty years he only ever spent a few months at Drepung, of which he was appointed the abbot in 1517, was the huge demand for his presence at different monasteries and holy places throughout the land. But this looks like an overly cheer-

---

* Bear in mind, however, that this was no city in the modern, Western, sense of the word.

ful interpretation. There can be no doubt he was a great teacher. Nor is there any doubt that he had a large and eager following. But the real reason for these two decades of wandering was surely the desire (whether on his part or of those closest to him) to keep away from danger.

That said, Gendun Gyatso's enthusiasm for taking teachings and initiations from as many of the important lineage-holders then living would have kept him away from home a great deal anyway. Besides also seeking out the riches of the Kadam tradition, he showed a keen interest in the spiritual wealth of the Nyingma tradition. This eclecticism earned him a reputation for such openness that he was popularly known as the "Yellow Hat Master Without Sectarian Bias"—though to be sure his ecumenism did not extend to the Kagyu tradition.

For a full decade from 1498, Gendun Gyatso did not, probably because he could not, settle in one place for more than a few months at a stretch. He spent much of his time in missionary work, notably in western Tibet. Then, in 1509, he founded a monastery of his own, Chokhor Gyal, in southern Tibet. He had recently met his most important guru, Norsang Gyatso, at a nearby hermitage, and it was in this place that he established his credentials as a highly accomplished spiritual master in his own right. Under Norsang's guidance, Gendun Gyatso achieved direct insight of *sunya*, the ultimate—empty—nature of reality, a sure sign that he was far advanced along the path to enlightenment.*
Precisely what such direct apprehension of emptiness entails is, of course, impossible to guess. Even those who do know have been unable to say much about it. Mere words are too clumsy. But we do know that, for Gendun Gyatso, the event was of such importance that he desired to build a permanent memorial of it.

* Though, of course, as emanations of Chenrezig, Gendun Gyatso and the other members of the Dalai Lamas' spiritual lineage are all considered to be enlightened already. From this perspective, their earthly guise is merely a form of role-play.

Situated at a remarkable fifteen thousand feet and over-looked by three important mountains, each considered the abode of a powerful protector deity, Chokhor Gyal's buildings seemed, according to Gendun Gyatso's autobiography, "to rise up by themselves . . . It was as though we humans would build during the day, then after dark, the spirits of goodness would work all night."[2] As a result, he gradually came to understand that the site was of even greater significance than he had thought. A series of dreams and visions convinced Gendun Gyatso that the body of water known as Lhamo Lhatso, which lay four hours distant, was one of the principal residences of Palden Lhamo, the great protector goddess whose cause his predecessor had done so much to further. What was more, he realized that it lay within his grasp to unlock the spiritual power of the lake itself. In a further series of visionary encounters, the location of the key—a ritual dagger—that would enable him to do so was revealed. Following initial propitiations, Gendun Gyatso took this dagger, accompanied by ten ritual masters, to the shore of the lake, where he invoked the goddess. It is said that almost immediately the color of the water began to change, passing successively through each color of the rainbow. Then, just as suddenly, it cleared to reveal countless images of the gods and goddesses of the Tibetan pantheon. Finally, and still in the sight of all present, the lake began to bubble, as if it were boiling, before turning the color of milk. It was a true miracle. Thanks to his own power, Gendun Gyatso had made the power of Lhamo Lhatso available to all those "of pure mind and conviction." Not surprisingly, the lake became an important pilgrimage destination of the faithful, and especially for those searching for the incarnations of high lamas. Famously, it was here that Reting Rinpoché, the regent appointed following the death of the Thirteenth Dalai Lama, received a vision of the whereabouts of the present Dalai Lama when he visited during the summer of 1935.

Gendun Gyatso's unlocking of the power of Lhamo Lhatso is considered by Tibetans to be his most important legacy, an incomparable gift to his people. It coincided with an unexpected development in his own life. Several times during the years following his forced departure from Tashilhunpo, he had written requesting an audience of the abbot. In each case, there had been no reply. Then suddenly, in 1511, there came a message from the man himself. "It seems as though my guru, the omniscient Gendun Drub, has indeed taken rebirth," it began. Begging Gendun Gyatso to return to Tashilhunpo, the abbot signed himself humbly "your little disciple." Welcome though this *volte-face* must have been, it put Gendun Gyatso in a quandary. Despite the assistance of the gods, the building work at Chokhor Gyal was not yet complete, and Gendun Gyatso feared that if he were to be away for any length of time, momentum would be lost. On the other hand, he could hardly refuse Tashilhunpo's concession. He resolved, therefore, to divide his time between the two communities, spending roughly five months of the year at each. This he did until a revival of Gelug fortunes enabled him to return to Drepung in 1517. A year later, he was able to preside over the first Great Prayer Festival to have been conducted by the Yellow Hats, as the Gelug were popularly known, for twenty years.

The sources are coy about how, precisely, the Kagyu sect lost to the Gelugpa their position of preeminence in Lhasa, noting only that the relationship between the sects at this time could be compared with that "between a bat and the sunlight."[3] There is no reason to doubt the claim that throughout the intervening period, for fear of attack, Gelug monks would routinely forsake their headgear in favor of the anonymous red worn by the other sects. We can assume, therefore, that the Kagyupas did not relinquish their hold over Lhasa without a struggle, even if it is difficult to know to what extent the monks themselves were involved in any fighting. As to any possible involvement in the crisis on the part of Gendun Gyatso himself, it is clear that—as we would expect of so highly realized a spiritual master—he kept himself entirely aloof from the turmoil in which his contemporaries were involved. In his writings, he often referred to himself ruefully as "the wandering monk Gendun Gyatso."

Returned to Drepung, Gendun Gyatso continued to oversee both Tashilhunpo and Chokhor Gyal. This meant that, although based at Drepung—where he built a permanent residence for his lineage, the Ganden Phodrang*—he continued to spend much of his time traveling.

Again as we might expect of so accomplished a spiritual practitioner, the tribulations of this peripatetic lifestyle seem not to have affected Gendun Gyatso unduly. It certainly did not prevent him from being a prolific writer, especially of *nyam'gyur*, the spontaneous spiritual songs of the *mahasiddhas*, for which Milarepa and others had become famous. Nor, apparently, did these wanderings do anything to undermine Gendun Gyatso's sense of his own destiny, even if some of the other sobriquets he gave himself might seem to suggest otherwise. Besides also calling himself the "Melodious Laughing Thunderbolt," he sometimes referred to himself as the "Yogi of Space." On occasion, he even spoke of himself as an "irreligious hermit from Tsang, the mad beggar monk Gendun Gyatso." Actually, these apparently self-deprecating terms all refer to his spiritual attainments. The word "beggar" refers not to a mendicant in rags but to one who has succeeded in overcoming all forms of attachment. And "mad" denotes the fact that the perceptions of the one who has apprehended emptiness directly (a "yogi of space") are as different from the perceptions of ordinary mortals as those of a madman are.

Gendun Gyatso kept traveling right up to the last year of his

---

* This became the residence of the Dalai Lamas for the next hundred years, and is also the name by which the Dalai Lama's government is known.

life when, at the age of sixty-seven, and defying his closest advisers, who were concerned for his health, he undertook an arduous journey ostensibly in order to visit one of his most important patrons, the sick wife of the Pakdru leader. According to his official biography, however, Gendun Gyatso had another motive for making the trip. By means of the necessary rituals and propitiations, he wanted to prepare for his rebirth in that area, knowing that he was shortly to relinquish this life. Returned to Drepung that winter, he duly began to weaken, though he continued to receive students and visitors in his room to the very end. This came during the third month of the following year, in 1542. For four days, it is reported, Gendun Gyatso sat with his chief disciples in continuous meditation. On the evening of the fourth day, the sky "filled with rainbows and a rainfall of flowers fell from the heavens." He then spoke his last words, before returning to his meditation, withdrawing into the clear light of *dharmadatu*—or emptiness—and finally expiring three days later. In confirmation of Gendun Gyatso's sanctity, a great many relics were found among the ashes following his cremation. Nobody could now possibly doubt that he had indeed been the authentic reincarnation of Gendun Drub, just as he had said. Nor could there be any doubt that he himself would soon be reborn in order to carry on the work of the great Tsongkhapa. Thus it was that, with renewed—and still more violent—unrest shortly to break out between the Gelugpas and the Kagyupas, the search for Gendun Gyatso's reincarnation began almost immediately.

15

Sonam Gyatso, the Ocean Lama

Sonam Gyatso, both Third and First Dalai Lama, was born at Tölung on February 28, 1543, a Water Hare year. He is said to have emerged from the womb untarnished, clear as crystal, and adorned with countless marks of perfection. As with his predecessor, Sonam Gyatso's breeding was impeccable. His father's family traced their descent from Ma Rinchen mChog, a saint revered for his translations of the scriptures during the first diffusion of Buddhism in Tibet. More recently, the family had been high dignitaries during the time of Sakya rule. At the time of Sonam Gyatso's birth, they governed one of the central districts. His mother, for her part, was the daughter of a famous exorcist.

The boy's discovery and subsequent acclamation as the true reincarnation of Gendun Gyatso came about over a period of just under three years and in the face of mounting evidence. A medium channeling Mahakala, who in his raven-headed form had protected the First Dalai Lama as a baby, handed down a prophecy declaring that Gendun Gyatso's rebirth was imminent. Not long afterward a lama, granted a vision of Tara, Chenrezig's female form, announced that Gendun Gyatso had now taken rebirth. Meanwhile, the boy himself began to show signs of being particularly gifted. He appeared, even though still only an infant, to have access to the heavenly realms through dreams and visions. And when he was just two years old, an important ecclesiastic saw him and became convinced he was the reincarnation of a great master, though of which he did not know. Inevitably, rumors about the boy began to spread. Eventually, these reached the ears of Sungrab Gyatso, the Second Dalai Lama's close confidant, chief personal attendant, and the man in charge of identifying and confirming his late master's successor.

Hearing about the young prodigy, Sungrab remembered that at Tölung, on his visit to the wife of the Pakdru chieftain during the last year of his life, Gendun Gyatso's horse had stumbled, necessitating a change of mount. Could this have been an indication that it was here that his own change of body was to be found? A third prophecy, this one handed down by the Nechung oracle, confirmed that the boy in question was indeed the hoped-for reincarnation. Subsequently, Sungrab took a small party of monks to the boy's household where— to general astonishment and delight—he called each by name, even though he had never met them before. An auspicious rainbow then formed in the sky directly above, and there was a rainfall of flowers. On this occasion, the child prodigy was left with his parents, but a year later Sungrab returned as head of an official delegation from Drepung Monastery in order to take the boy home to the Ganden Phodrang, the palace built by his predecessor. Of course, even at this stage, the Dalai Lama institution had not been created. The young *tulku* was recognized simply as the *chöje*—literally, religious lord—of Drepung. On coming of age, he would be enthroned as abbot. In the meantime, amidst great rejoicing, he was initiated as a novice monk by the then abbot, who conferred upon him his full religious name: Sonam Gyatso Tenpai Nyima Chokley Namgyal.* His induction as a novice over, the precious child left Drepung with Sungrab almost immediately, traveling directly to Chokhor Gyal in order to be (re)introduced to the Second Dalai Lama's chief disciples. It is said that he remembered the names of many.

At the end of 1546, Sonam Gyatso returned to Drepung, where he began his monastic education. According to the present Dalai Lama's elder brother, he quickly excelled his teachers in both knowledge and wisdom. In recognition of this, he ascended the Ganden Throne at a mere nine years of age. At ten, he presided over Monlam Chenmo, the Great Prayer Festival, for the first time. Then, having completed his basic training and received initiation into the main tantric cycles, he began to divide his time between Drepung and Chokhor Gyal, just as "he" had done during his previous incarnation.

There may, however, have been other factors at work in Sonam Gyatso's speedy ascent of the monastic ladder. No doubt he was a brilliant student. And no doubt, too, there were compelling spiritual reasons for this continued shuttling between Drepung and Chokhor Gyal. But the unrest, and the threat of unrest, that overshadowed central Tibet throughout the fifteenth, sixteenth, and seventeenth centuries must have had a part in it. During Sonam Gyatso's minority, the Pakdru Dynasty established two centuries earlier by Chang'chub Gyaltsen was still—nominally— the leading power in central Tibet. Its system of district fortresses, or *dzong*, headed by a *dzongpön* empowered to raise taxes locally, was still in place, but Pakdru's authority over these districts was limited. During the previous century, the lords of Rinpung had come close to usurping Pakdru altogether. Now they too were in retreat before the rising power of the militantly Kagyu-support- ing chiefs of Tsang.

* Literally, "Glorious Meritorious Ocean, Sun of the Doctrine, Victorious in All Directions."

As it turned out, however, the threat to the Gelugpas from the chiefs of Tsang was as nothing to the reemergence, the following year, of the Mongol threat. In 1566, a relative of Altan Khan, the new strongman of the East, invited the Tibetans of the Three Rivers region of the northeast to submit to him. They were quick to do so.

Following the collapse of their Yuan Dynasty back in 1368, the Mongols had split into three distinct groups: those of the west, the center and the east. Their disunity was greatly exacerbated by the revenge exacted on them by Ming forces during the first half of the fifteenth century. The Chinese army penetrated as far as the Mongols' ancestral capital of Karakorum and burned it to the ground. But now, a century later, it was clear that the barbarians of the north were on the verge of unity once again, while Ming power was waning. In 1542, Altan Khan's troops massacred or captured some two hundred thousand Chinese, rustled a million cattle and horses, and torched thousands of dwellings in western China.[1] Seven years later, Altan actually succeeded in capturing the then emperor when the "Son of Heaven" was foolish enough to allow himself to be persuaded to launch a campaign against the Mongols.* A year later, the barbarians laid siege to the Chinese capital for three days. Although they failed to take it, they subsequently established themselves in a threatening position to the west of the city from where they were able to control the horse trade.

At the same time, there was a power struggle within the Mongol leadership itself. In 1559, Altan (a Tümat, or eastern Mongolian) succeeded in capturing Karakorum from the western, Oirat, Mongols. By the end of the following decade, he had established control over the majority of Mongolia's disparate tribes and welded eastern, central and western regions into a

---

* He was well treated and eventually allowed home, where he resumed his reign until his death in 1567.

single unit. By 1560, Altan had invaded and taken control of China's Qinghai province. In 1566, he took up a position in northeastern Tibet. The Ming responded to these unwelcome developments on their doorstep by refusing to recognize Altan and denying him all trade. By the early 1570s, however, Altan's position was so strong there was nothing they could do but acquiesce in his demands and grant him the easiest terms.

It is clear that Altan Khan was intent on recapturing China for the Mongols. For the time being, however, he was content to consolidate his position and muster his forces. By now, Altan's dominion was no less extensive than that of Genghis during his heyday. He lacked only one thing—the very thing that would give him the security to launch his bid for China's Dragon Throne: legitimacy. In spite of Altan's preeminence as a military leader, he lacked authority in the eyes of his own people. By tradition, no one who was not directly descended from Genghis could claim authority to lead the Mongolians as a whole, and Altan was from a different tribe. He therefore needed some other quality to justify his position. It is said that, following the invasion of the Three Rivers region of Tibet (presumably undertaken to put further pressure on the Ming), Altan was "awakened a little" to the *buddhadharma* by a lama whom his forces captured and brought to court. More than two hundred years had passed since the collapse of the Yuan Dynasty. In that time, Buddhism had more or less died out among the Mongols. In its place, the vast majority had returned to the shamanism of old. But from then on, we are told, Altan began to "pray in the six syllables," using the sacred mantra of Chenrezig: *om mani padme hum*. It seems highly likely that doing so also awakened in him the idea that he could use the Buddhism of Tibet to advance his cause. Evidently, he was aware that Kubilai had used his relationship with Tibet's leading holy man to present himself as a *cakravartin*, a universal monarch, in his effort to establish legitimacy in the eyes of the Chinese. Perhaps he, Altan, could establish a similar relationship, and use it as a means to justify himself to his own people. This, then, was almost certainly the motive behind Altan Khan's subsequent move into Tibet during 1573: not so much the desire for conquest, but the desire to re-establish Mongol links with Tibet's religious hierarchy.

Shortly after this incursion into Tibet, one of Altan's lieutenants, who had himself converted to the faith, is reported to have told Altan that Chenrezig himself had appeared in bodily form and was then living in central Tibet. At once, Altan dispatched an embassy to Sonam Gyatso beseeching him to visit the Mongol court. Understandably, on arrival at Drepung, the khan's embassy occasioned great consternation. But remarkably, the Tibetan scholar-saint declined to accept the invitation, sending a subordinate instead. How did Sonam Gyatso dare to do so? What made him think he could get away with refusing Altan is a mystery. No doubt he was aware that Tsongkhapa had turned down the Ming emperor's invitation. No doubt, too, he consulted with the protectors; he was a particular devotee of Dorje Drakden and of Palden Lhamo. But we are entitled to wonder whether the gods themselves were acting on information unavailable to us? Perhaps the situation in central Tibet was such that Sonam Gyatso dared not absent himself. We know for certain that there was another outbreak of unrest during 1575, when Tsang forces attacked several Gelug strongholds to the south of Lhasa.[2] We also know that sometime during the same year, Sonam Gyatso was called to mediate between his own people and forces loyal to the Sharmapa. It may be that refusing Altan's request seemed the lesser of two evils.

Altan, of course, was unwilling to take no for an answer. In 1577, a second embassy arrived, this time bringing with it camels, horses, and provisions for Sonam Gyatso and his entourage. This time, the Tibetan did not refuse. What made him change his mind—what made the gods change their minds—we do not know, but it is entirely possible that Sonam Gyatso, for his part, now recognized an opportunity to win for the Gelug a powerful new patron.

Departing Drepung during the depths of winter, Sonam Gyatso was seen off by a gathering of thousands of emotional well-wishers.* Many, fearing that they would not see him again, begged him to stay. Their misgivings were entirely justified. He never returned.

Sonam Gyatso was escorted by a large number of monks from the Three Seats (the great monasteries of Ganden, Drepung, and Sera) as far as Dam, ninety miles or so to the north of Lhasa. This was the last human habitation before the mighty Chang'tang, the mountainous desert stretching some eight hundred miles east to west and three hundred north to south, through the eastern quarter of which Sonam Gyatso's route lay. It is one of the most inhospitable areas of the globe. Hardly had the saintly hierarch and his party said their last farewells than they were swallowed up in a blizzard. With visibility reduced to a few feet, they were soon lost. An incredible 170 days passed before they finally saw another settlement.

It is said that during the journey, the still young (he was not yet thirty-five) Sonam Gyatso had to contend with numerous demons. The fact that many of the Mongolians' pre-Buddhist deities appeared subsequently in the Tibetan pantheon testifies to his success in subduing them. For Sonam Gyatso, it seems, the boundary between mundane reality and the supramundane was never fixed. He reports in a piece of autobiographical writing that, on one earlier journey within Tibet, he encountered first a single-headed Srin'mo, or ogress, then a two-headed one, then a monster Srin'mo with eleven heads, the uppermost one of which was that of a horse. Each of these deities was entirely friendly, however. But then a four-header

* Almost four hundred years later, a similarly emotional crowd gathered there to bid farewell to the present Dalai Lama as he left for a state visit to China in 1954.

tried to pull Sonam Gyatso from his mount. Fortunately, this miscreant was chased off by two further apparitions, enabling him to continue his journey: "Thus I arrived happily." Sonam Gyatso also reports that, on reaching the banks of the Yangtze River, he found it so swollen as to be impassable. Undaunted, he sat down in meditation, making the hand gestures of a wrathful deity. Immediately, the waters began to subside and he and his party crossed it no less easily than Moses and the Israelites had crossed the Red Sea.[3]

It was summer 1578 when the Tibetans arrived at the Mongolian outpost of Chahar. There they found a meat-eating and kumiss-drinking* nomadic people living in felt tents, raising goats, sheep, and horses, and devoted to the terrifying and bloodthirsty gods of their ancestors. Sonam Gyatso was particularly horrified to learn that the khan himself would daily assuage his gout by having the belly of a mare sliced open and plunging his foot into its entrails.[†] Welcoming the Tibetans with a guard of a thousand cavalrymen, Altan then proceeded side by side with Sonam Gyatso to his headquarters, where he showered gifts on his guest: a mandala constructed from five hundred ounces of silver; a golden bowl brimming with jewels; twenty bolts each of white, yellow, green, and blue silk; a hundred horses, ten of which were white, their saddles ornamented with precious stones.

It was a lavish occasion. And it was at this moment that the institution of the Dalai Lamas was born: at the ceremony that followed, and the two men granted each other new titles. Sonam Gyatso proclaimed Altan Khan the reincarnation of Kubilai and, identifying himself as Phagpa, pronounced Altan "Religious King, Brahma of the Gods." The khan responded by referring to the Tibetan hierarch as the "Taleh [literally, ocean] Lama," the word being rendered in Tibetan as "Dalai."

---

* Fermented mare's milk.
† I am grateful to Professor Don Lopez for bringing this choice insight of Mongolian history to my attention.

Some scholars doubt whether too much should be read into the meeting, and question whether Altan Khan intended anything more than mere courtesy at this stage, given that the word *taleh* is simply a translation of "Gyatso"—which itself means ocean, one of the Dalai Lama's names. Nonetheless, as the great French Sinologist Paul Pelliot pointed out, the word Genghis is a palatized form of the Turkic *tengiz*, which again means ocean.[4] Genghis Khan was thus Ocean Khan, the khan whose power and prestige were as limitless as the great ocean surrounding the world. A curious circularity emerges, though how far either side was aware of this we can only guess. To begin with, at any rate, it is unlikely that Sonam Gyatso and his fellow monastics attached much importance to the title. It is not at all certain that, during his lifetime, Sonam Gyatso was thought of as the Third Dalai Lama. Nor indeed can we be sure there was any assumption that his successor would bear the title. What we do know is that there was no thought of the title denoting an institution, still less that the term Dalai Lama denoted the supreme spiritual and temporal ruler of Tibet. Sonam Gyatso himself was just one high lama among many. From his successful mediation in sectarian disputes, it is evident that his prestige in some degree transcended his identity as a Gelug lama. But in no sense did this give him political power over his countrymen. All this still lay far in the future. Much more significant at the time was the proclamation issued by the Mongol leader, following this exchange of titles, setting out a new Buddhist law for his people. From now on, blood sacrifice and blood restitution were outlawed.[*] When a man died, no longer were his wives and horses to be slain and buried with him, and in place of the tent god idols to which the Mongols habitually offered specially slaughtered animals, they were permitted only to keep an image of Mahakala, the Gelug protector. To him, they might offer milk and butter.

[*] On pain of death, somewhat ironically.

Toward the end of that year, 1578, letters arrived from Tibet urging Sonam Gyatso to return home. He declined to do so on the grounds that Mongolia was proving to be a fertile mission field: he was received with great honor and enthusiasm wherever he went. Sonam Gyatso finally departed Altan Khan's territory, having consecrated several new monasteries and won countless converts to the faith, almost two years after his first meeting with the Mongol leader. His intention now was to travel down to Kham, Tibet's largely lawless southeastern province.

In 1580, at Lithang, an important settlement situated some twelve hundred miles east of Lhasa, the newly styled Dalai Lama founded what was to become the Gelug's largest monastery in the region. Hitherto, most people living in and around Lithang had been devotees either of the Nyingma or of the Karma-kagyu schools. There were even some adherents of the old Bon religion, who, when they became aware of Sonam Gyatso's presence, are said to have brought down hailstones and lightning on his camp. To this he responded by drawing his ritual dagger and "dancing in the attitude of a wrathful deity."[5] This turned the weather back on them, at which display of superior magic the Bonpos, duly chastened, came and offered their repentance and were converted to the true faith. From Lithang, where he seems to have been based for a full four years, Sonam Gyatso journeyed northwest to Chamdo—again stopping to preach and teach everywhere that pilgrims gathered. It is reported that, much like the present Dalai Lama, Sonam Gyatso evolved a daily routine whereby it made little difference whether he traveled or stayed in one place. Rising early in the morning, he would undertake several hours of prayer before conducting the business of the day. Some said he never slept.*

---

* If true, this much is in marked contrast to the present Dalai Lama, who makes no secret of the fact that he makes sleep a priority. He further claims always to sleep soundly and well.

It was at Chamdo that, in 1583, Sonam Gyatso learned of Altan Khan's death, an event which brought to an end the dream of re-establishing the Mongol Empire. The Mongols remained powerful for another century and more, but no leader ever again succeeded in uniting what was becoming an increasingly divided people. On hearing the news, Sonam Gyatso set out to return to Mongolia. Proceeding to the court of Durung Khan, Altan's son and successor, Sonam Gyatso spent the last two years of his own life ceaselessly preaching, teaching, and conferring initiations in what was to prove an enduring conversion of Mongolia's tribesmen to the Buddhism of Tibet.* Just before Sonam Gyatso died, in 1588, an envoy arrived from the Ming emperor inviting him to pay a visit to Beijing. Although the Tibetan hierarch is known to have accepted the invitation, his meeting with the emperor did not take place. Some historians say that Sonam Gyatso was actually on his deathbed when the envoy arrived, but all are agreed that it was in Mongol territory that the First and Third Dalai Lama was lost to the world. And it was there, among strangers, that he was found again.

---

* One of the joys of the present Dalai Lama's life has been to welcome back into the fold members of the Mongolian *sangha* following the fall of the Soviet Union. A Buddhist renaissance continues there apace.

16

Yonten Gyatso, Son of the Eastern Hor

Sonam Gyatso died in Mongolia on April 21, 1588. He was cremated there and his ashes were sent back to Drepung. It was an inauspicious time. The Mongols, themselves without strong leadership, had resumed their habit of internecine strife. This made life more than usually perilous for those Tibetans living in the far northeast. Two years later, no less than 165 tribes—74,710 Tibetan persons in all[*]—submitted to the Ming. This they deemed preferable to continual harassment by the Kokonor Mongols.[†] Nonetheless, and much to the surprise of the Gelug community remaining in those parts, rumors about a possible rebirth in the area began to circulate. These were investigated by Tibetan monks living locally and an enthusiastic report was sent back to Drepung. At first, the possibility that Chenrezig might have chosen to be reborn a son of the Hor (as Mongolians

[*] Whether or not "persons" extends to include women and children is unclear. *See* Schram, quoted in Smith, *Tibetan Nation*, p. 107.
[†] This event surely undermines the Chinese claim that Tibet was a dependency of the Ming. If it was, how could the Ming have been said to have accepted the submission of the people who were already under the emperor's sway?

are known to Tibetans) must have seemed remote; but following two authoritative prophecies and the rejection of a rival candidate from the Lhasa area, a delegation from Drepung was duly assembled and dispatched to the Kokonor region. Presently situated in China's Qinghai province, the Kokonor* itself is Tibet's largest inland body of water. Measuring approximately sixty miles east to west and fifty miles north to south, the surrounding lands were in former times so fertile that, according to the French priest Abbé Huc, who passed that way during the 1840s, the grass grew to the height of his camels' bellies. Today, woefully overgrazed, the Kokonor region is more famous for being home to the Chinese government's nuclear-testing facilities. Then, however, it was home to a boy born into the family of Prince Sechen, a grandson of Altan Khan, on February 15, 1589, barely forty-eight weeks after the demise of Sonam Gyatso.[1]

Helpfully enough, a number of signs manifested during his mother's pregnancy: a rainbow clothed the tent in which she conceived him; the day after his conception, she had numerous auspicious dreams; others clearly heard the six-syllable mantra of Chenrezig emanating from her womb. But if all these were promising indications, the boy's family was less conventional from a Tibetan perspective. The Mongols being but recent converts to the way of the Buddha, the family had no history of spiritual attainment, and no links to the saints of olden times. On the other hand, the boy—who was unusually large—was encouragingly precocious. At seven months, he had slept for a full three days before waking and explaining that during this time he had visited Tibet, and when the delegation from Drepung finally arrived, he quickly proved to their collective satisfaction that he was indeed the rebirth of the Dalai Lama. The late Sonam Gyatso's personal treasurer was among their number. With him he brought his former master's

---

* Literally, the Blue Lake.

rosary and ritual instruments: his hand bell, drum and *dorje*, or thunderbolt. These the boy correctly identified as his own from among a selection of similar objects. And most importantly, he convinced the treasurer, who had known Sonam Gyatso intimately over many years, of his authenticity. Great, then, was the rejoicing among the delegates.

But brief was its duration. To the Tibetans' dismay, the boy's father refused to let them take him away from home. Ordinarily, *tulkus* are sent to a local monastery just as soon as they are identified. When the necessary preparations have been made, the child is then sent to the monastery with which his lineage is associated. But Prince Sechen demanded that he remain at home. Not until he was thirteen years old was the longed-for incarnation permitted to leave for his spiritual homeland—and it seems that this was the last of a whole series of dates proposed by the authorities at Drepung. Perhaps this reluctance on the part of the family—who were after all highborn Mongolians— explains why the party eventually sent from Drepung to escort him to Tibet included not only senior members of the monastic establishment, but also several high-ranking members of the Tibetan nobility.

Traveling at first along the perimeter of the Great Wall of China (recently rebuilt), the new Dalai Lama's party made slow and suitably stately progress back to central Tibet. At every halt, pilgrims and well-wishers, many of whom had been blessed by the previous incarnation, turned out to see him. It is also recorded that the new Dalai Lama spent a lengthy period at Tongkor, where his predecessor had established a diplomatic office staffed with both Tibetan and Mongolian officials. As a result, his journey home took almost three years to complete. On arrival in central Tibet, the new incarnation's first important engagement was at Reting, the monastery established by Drom Tönpa, where, following a tradition established by Gendun Gyatso, the Second Dalai Lama, he preached a sermon from the lama's throne. At the conclusion of the sermon, a light rain fell and rainbows spread in all directions, an auspicious sign that recalled those that had accompanied his two predecessors' homilies. The Dalai Lama's second major engagement was at the Jokhang, then, as now, Tibet's holiest shrine. There, at the unusually late age of fifteen, he was finally initiated as a novice monk by the first Panchen Lama.* It was then, too, that he gave up the long hair which until now he had worn after the fashion of a young Mongolian aristocrat. Following the *tra'phü*†—correctly, *skra phud*—ceremony, Yonten Gyatso, as he would be called henceforth, embarked on the last leg of his journey to Drepung. The monastery, which largely survived the depredations of the Cultural Revolution intact, stands just five miles northwest of Lhasa. By the turn of the seventeenth century it was home to nearly ten thousand monks, all of whom turned out to greet the new Dalai Lama. Now, at last, he was able to begin his monastic education.

In 1604, the young Dalai Lama presided over his first Monlam Chenmo. To the delight and amazement of the crowd, he is said to have spoken without a trace of Mongolian accent. People remarked that he could have been a native of Tölung, where his predecessor had been born, or was this wishful thinking? The Gelugpa's traditional enemies were anxious at the sight of the squadrons of Mongolian cavalry that had accompanied Yonten Gyatso from his homeland. Indeed, given that these troops showed no sign of leaving, many of the Gelug's supporters were equally apprehensive. It seems, too, that the Dalai Lama's own court was acutely sensitive about the foreign origins of the new incarnation.

These mixed emotions found their expression in an incident that occurred some time later that year. A letter addressed to Yonten Gyatso from an unnamed Kagyu lama, written in verse

---

* Strictly, the Panchen Lama institution had not yet been recognized.
† That is, hair cutting or tonsuring.

form and using language that was archaic and obscure even by the standards of the day, was received by his attendants. Nobody could quite understand its meaning, but it seemed to urge that the Dalai Lama study carefully the words of the Buddha. This could either be taken at face value or to suggest that, if he did not, he would be misled by his teachers. The boy's staff were duly outraged. In what came to be regarded, even within Gelug circles, as a major error, instead of simply replying in an equally obscure manner, they sent a strongly worded protest directly to the Karma hierarchy, arousing much ill-feeling. As a result, a rumor began to spread that those closest to the Dalai Lama were unable to understand poetry. This in itself was a considerable insult. Such ignorance was taken as a sign of a poor education. Less than a year later, another literary insult surfaced. This one took the form of a prayer inscribed on a *khatag** presented to the famous self-originated statue of the Buddha brought to Tibet by Songtsen Gampo's Chinese wife, and housed in the Jokhang temple. Apparently written by the Sixth Sharmapa, it too was seen as a veiled insult. Yonten Gyatso's Mongolian cavalry escort immediately set out for the Sharmapa headquarters and raided its stables. This led to a counterattack by the king of Tsang, who was the Sharmapa's chief patron. Following what must have been a bloody encounter, the Mongolians were forced to retreat from Lhasa. This left the Gelug temporarily without protection and the Dalai Lama himself in a dangerous position.

Yonten Gyatso's extended pilgrimage throughout central and southern Tibet, begun in 1606, should thus be seen in the light of the Gelug's need to secure approval for the new incarnation. By taking him to places associated with his illustrious predecessor, and with the spiritual heroes of Tibetan history—Songtsen Gampo, Padmasambhava, Atisha, Tsongkhapa and others—the

---

* A silk scarf, given in offering to both individuals and deities. They often have prayers inscribed on them.

Gelug hierarchy clearly intended to impress on the disparate clans and tribes of Tibet that here was the legitimate heir to this legacy. It produced mixed results. At Chokhor Gyal, the monastery founded by the Second Dalai Lama, close to the miraculous lake Lhamo Lhatso, he was suitably well-received. And when he reached the Yarlung Valley, home of the religious kings and, latterly, the Pakdru Dynasty, he was given a great welcome. However, it was at the Pakdru headquarters at Neudong that Yonten Gyatso was the butt of yet another double entendre. It is customary for Buddhist prelates in positions of authority always to take precedence over their secular counterparts. Accordingly, the cushions on Yonten Gyatso's throne were arranged in such a way that they were higher than those of the chieftain, but when he sat down on them he sank into them to such a degree that he ended up sitting lower down. There is no suggestion that the chieftain was himself responsible for this humiliation. It appears rather to have reflected the feelings of his court—and indeed of many others.

At Tashilhunpo in 1607, Yonten Gyatso fared somewhat better. One of the men appointed to tutor him on his arrival in Tibet was a lama almost unknown at the time other than for his exceptional modesty. This was Lobsang Chokyi Gyaltsen, a scholar-saint later to become the Great Fifth Dalai Lama's principal tutor and recognized as the First Panchen Lama. Then serving as abbot of Tashilhunpo, Chokyi Gyaltsen showed his pupil particular courtesy by traveling a considerable distance out from the monastery in order to welcome him. On the other hand, the king of Tsang, whose forces had routed Yonten Gyatso's Mongolian escort and whose headquarters at Samdruptse virtually overlooked Tashilhunpo, refused to offer any assistance whatsoever. This was an unambiguous insult. Unexpectedly, however, when the Dalai Lama's party reached Gongkar on its way back to Lhasa, he received a letter from the Sixth Sharmapa himself. On offer was the possibility of a meeting that might lead to reconciliation between the two sects. Unfortunately, although the Dalai Lama was in favor of dialogue, his court opposed the suggestion. In particular Yonten Gyatso's senior attendant was emphatically against the idea and the Dalai Lama gave way to him. As a result, nothing came of the Sharmapa's gesture and Yonten Gyatso was instead hurried back to Drepung. There he remained for much of the next five years, pursuing his religious studies. In the meantime, the Pakdru made one last attempt to take back to itself some of the prestige it had lost, annexing several properties in the vicinity of their Neudong headquarters, properties they had lost some years earlier. As the Tsang were now the leading power in central, southern, western, and even parts of northern Tibet, this move amounted to open insurrection.

Realizing that serious trouble was in the offing, Lobsang Chokyi Gyaltsen contacted the Dalai Lama, urging him to do all he could to forestall unrest. In the idiom of the day, this meant not diplomacy but the relentless propitiation of the wrathful deities. To the extent that Lhasa did not become embroiled in the fighting that duly broke out, Yonten Gyatso's efforts can be regarded as successful, and the appearance of the Mongol cavalry at precisely this juncture can be perhaps attributed to the gods.[2] But that the Tsang chieftan now gained control of Neudong itself suggests that his success in persuading the wrathful deities to take the Gelug side was only partial.

Two years later, a delegation from the Ming court is reported to have arrived at Drepung with an invitation from the emperor. The Dalai Lama's presence was requested at the forthcoming inauguration of a new temple at Nanking.* This presented Yonten Gyatso with an opportunity to make his mark on the political events of the day. But once again he was unable to overcome the suspicions of his court and of his chamberlain in particular. Instead it was agreed only that he would bless the temple in a

---

* The Ming records make no mention of this, however.

ceremony to be conducted on the roof of the Ganden Phodrang, scattering barley to the wind. In his history of Tibet, the Great Fifth Dalai Lama notes that this resulted in the temple keepers having to sweep up barley by the bushel load some two thousand miles away. But given his other, less than entirely complimentary comments about Yonten Gyatso, there is also room to wonder whether the Fifth really believed what he was saying.

Later on, in 1616, Yonten Gyatso is credited with another miracle. Following an attack of rheumatic fever, he traveled in search of a cure to a hot spring made famous by Padmasambhava, whose footprints were imprinted on a boulder nearby. While there, he is said to have been taunted by a local Nyingma yogin on account of his Mongolian origins. Yonten Gyatso responded by asking whether his abuser would believe him if he said that he himself was an emanation of Padmasambhava. Thereupon, uttering wrathful mantras, he impressed his own footprints on a boulder. But the spring itself seems to have had no such miraculous properties. The Dalai Lama died of a further attack of rheumatic fever a few months later, shortly before his twenty-ninth birthday.

17

Lobsang Gyatso and the Unification of Tibet

According to Tsybikov, a Russo-Buryat explorer, Yonten Gyatso was poisoned. Whether this story—heard by him at the beginning of the nineteenth century—is true, we can only guess. What is certain is that the Fourth Dalai Lama was not only ineffective in providing the Gelug with reliable lay patronage, but also something of an embarrassment. Following Altan Khan's death, the Mongol tribes had once again divided into mutually hostile factions. The eastern tribes had begun to assert themselves at the expense of the western. And it was the western, Oirat, Mongols with whom Yonten Gyatso was connected. Crudely put, the Gelug had backed the wrong horse. To make matters worse, the king of Tsang, their sworn enemy, was busy seeking alliances of his own among the Mongols, via intermediaries in the form of Kagyu missionaries. For while the king had been willing initially to acknowledge the spiritual claims of the Dalai Lama, the refusal by Yonten Gyatso's court to grant him an audience had turned him against the Gelug. And when it became clear that an illness from which he was suffering was caused by the late Dalai Lama's sorcery, he became bent on revenge. The king banned the search for the new incarnation throughout the territory he controlled. By now this included much of central Tibet, along with the whole of the south and west. It was thus into a world fraught with danger that the future Great Fifth Dalai Lama was born.

According to his biographer, the child came into the world on the same day of the week and in the same lunar month as Buddha Shakyamuni himself—that is, Saturday, October 21—in the year of the Fire Snake (1617) at the castle of Chongye, not far from the old royal burial grounds.[1] It is further recorded that his birth was accompanied by a rain of flowers.

This time, the Dalai Lama's father was a minor aristocrat, from a family that had supplied *dzongpön*, or district governors, to the Pakdru regime for several generations. The father's religious affiliations were both Gelug, through an ancestor who had been a disciple of Gendun Drub, the First Dalai Lama, and Nyingma, through a much earlier familial connection with Samye. The baby's mother, herself prophesied in scripture—"the woman whose womb is like a *lon-then* flower"—was of aristocratic descent.[2] She also had important connections with the Jonang sect (which her son would later outlaw), while a cousin was a senior lineage holder within the Drukpa-Kagyupas.

Such a variety of associations within Lobsang Gyatso's family undoubtedly contributed to the catholic approach he took in his spiritual practice. This was in marked contrast to a number of important Gelug hierarchs both of his time and later as the traditions became increasingly narrowly focused and exclusive. Yet it is important to realize that, for the average layman, the distinction between the various schools has always been somewhat blurred. If, for example, a family's local monastery was a Sakya foundation, one could expect it to be loyal to the Sakya tradition; but if one of its children came to be recognized, as quite often happened, as an incarnation of a lineage belonging to a different sect, this would cause no undue difficulty. The ties to Sakya would remain, but new ones would open up.

The year following Lobsang Gyatso's birth was particularly inauspicious for the Gelug. The king of Tsang now attacked and finally overthrew the last vestiges of Pakdru power before marching on Lhasa. Taking control of the town, his troops proceeded to Drepung and Sera and sacked them both. Assisted by their lay supporters, the two monasteries put up a vigorous fight, but they were no match for the Tsang militia. It is said that they left the "rice heap" (the literal translation of Drepung) littered with the bodies of slaughtered monks. Meanwhile, the surviving brethren fled to Taklung Monastery, several days' journey to the north. Originally a Kagyu foundation, Taklung had increasingly come under Gelug influence (underlining a degree of fluidity even within the sects themselves).

Following this attack, a number of smaller monasteries were forcibly converted to the Kagyu tradition. At the same time, the king ordered that two military camps be built, one cutting Drepung off, the other blocking the main route to Lhasa. Back at his headquarters, he sponsored the construction of a new monastery, Tashi Zilnon—"Subjugator [or, more politely, Out-shiner] of Tashi." The name referred directly to Tashilhunpo, the First Dalai Lama's monastery at the edge of Shigatse, above which this new Kagyu foundation was built. Making best use of the height advantage, its builders lost no opportunity to harass their rivals by rolling boulders down on them from above.

In the meantime, the beleaguered Gelug waited in hope for news of Yonten Gyatso's reincarnation. Though officially there could be no search, Sonam Rabten, the Fourth's *chamzö*, or chamberlain—evidently an ambitious man given that he was only twenty-two at the time of his late master's death—was already making his own inquiries. Reports had begun to circulate concerning not one but three infants, all of whom showed exceptional promise. One was of course Lobsang Gyatso, who came from Chongye. Another was Drakpa Gyaltsen, later to be identified with Dorje Shugden, the wrathful protector deity and chief suspect in the murder of the Fifth Dalai Lama's namesake almost four centuries later. Nor was it just the Gelugpas who became interested in the little boy from Chongye. He also attracted the attention of both the Drukpa and the Karma sects of the Kagyu tradition, and possibly that of the Jonang too.* Fortunately for the Gelug, Sonam Rabten was ahead of their rivals. Having alerted the Fourth Dalai Lama's tutor (the future Panchen Lama), he organized a rendezvous at Reting Monastery. There, before its sacred Buddha image, the two men performed a divination, in response to which the gods revealed that Lobsang Gyatso was indeed the reincarnation of the Precious Protector. Accordingly Sonam Rabten set out for Chongye with a view to confirming the auguries and removing the child to safety.

Meanwhile, the king of Tsang's administration of central Tibet had quickly run into difficulty. In 1619, a group of Mongolians appeared in the vicinity of Lhasa, where they set up camp, causing intense speculation as to what their intentions might be. It was generally agreed that their numbers were "too small for an army, too large for a gang of bandits." Ostensibly pilgrims, they remained a year doing nothing before suddenly—having secretly been in contact with Drepung all along—attacking the two Tsang camps. Lulled into a false sense of security, the Tsang militia was caught completely unprepared. Immediately, the king of Tsang dispatched reinforcements from Shigatse.†

A major bloodletting seemed certain. But at this point, the Gelug hierarchy called on the Panchen Lama to negotiate a truce. It seems they calculated that Tsang's army might be needed one day to see off the notoriously fickle Mongolians, should they

---

* It was his mother's kinsman, Taranatha, the great Jonang master, who gave him his birth name.
† At the time, Shigatse was in fact known as Samdruptse.

turn on the Gelugpas themselves. The "Peace of Chakpori" negotiated by the Panchen Lama thus has the flavor of a delaying
tactic rather than an outright victory for the Gelugpa. In return
for a significant bribe, paid by the Gelugpa themselves, the
Mongols agreed to stay their hand. Tsang would meanwhile
dismantle their military camps outside Lhasa and return the
monasteries they had taken two years earlier. The king of Tsang
still did not agree to permit the search for the new Dalai Lama,
however.

It was thus in great secrecy that Sonam Rabten conducted the
confirmatory interview with the boy from Chongye. That he was
certain of the boy's potential is made clear by the Great Fifth's
later admission, in his autobiography, that he failed completely
to identify correctly the items belonging to his predecessor. An
official "showed me some statues and rosaries,* but I was unable
to distinguish between them. When he left the room, I heard
him tell the people outside that I had successfully passed the
tests. Later, when he became my tutor, he would often admon-
ish me and say, 'You must work hard since you were unable to
recognize the objects.'"[3]

But there could be no general rejoicing, nor could the boy be
taken to Drepung for initiation. Instead, he was taken to
Nankartse, several days' journey to the south of Lhasa. Had his
identity become widely known, it is certain that the king of
Tsang would have sent for him to be arrested, if not killed. So
when the king died suddenly during 1622, it is easy to imagine
the relief felt in Gelug circles. Seizing the opportunity offered
by this welcome turn of events, the Gelug hierarchy was quick
to announce the coming again of the Precious Protector.

Despite even Tsang's acceptance of his candidate (the new
king being still a minor, the Tsang court was not in a position
to withhold recognition), Sonam Rabten's problems were not

---

* Among them were some that had belonged to the Fourth.

yet over. The excitement among the Mongols was immense: he must go at once to their homeland. Had not the *chamzö* spirited the boy from Drepung down to a fortress in southern Tibet, the clamor might have been irresistible. As it was, Lobsang Gyatso spent the next two lonely years as virtually a prisoner. The experience was not wholly negative, however, for it was during this time that Lobsang Gyatso, still only six years old, gave the clearest indication yet of the qualities that were to mark him out as truly exceptional. Whether during a ritual or a period of quiet meditation is uncertain—he himself did not have a clear memory of the event, taking on trust the testimony of the monk in whom he had confided at the time—he experienced the first of many visions he was to receive during his life. That first, hazy memory was of Tsongkhapa appearing on the altar at the foot of which the young novice sat. Later visions were to be far more dramatic. Some were to contain long prophetic discourses handed down by different saints, gods, and goddesses. Others took the form of celestial journeys through time and space to the heavenly realms. Still others took the form of mystical initiations performed by fully enlightened beings. And there were to be encounters with wrathful deities, their consorts and emissaries, not to mention miraculous healings, bodily transformations, and sensory experiences both terrifying and ecstatic. Most remarkable of all is that these extraordinary spiritual irruptions should have been preserved in the Great Fifth's *Sealed and Secret Biography*. This extraordinary document provides a precise and detailed account of Lobsang Gyatso's experiences, worked up from notes written, in most cases, immediately afterward. To begin with, the young Dalai Lama's visionary experiences were infrequent. He had another aged ten and another at seventeen. They did not begin in earnest until 1641, just when the political situation in Tibet was at its most dangerous. But thereafter they occurred most often in conjunction with, or just prior to, significant earthly events. They seem also to reflect the Dalai Lama's growing, if controversial, virtuosity as a Nyingma practitioner.

The dreams and visions of the Fifth Dalai Lama present an unusual problem for a modern historian. It is quite clear that Lobsang Gyatso, as head of state, based many of his most important decisions on them. In this, he was by no means unusual. Each of the other Dalai Lamas did the same. The Fifth is unusual only in having left a more or less complete record of his prophetic spiritual experiences. But in fact it is not just the Dalai Lamas—including, it must be emphasized, the present one—who made decisions according to the interpretation of what we would call supernatural counsel: traditionally, any Tibetan would do the same. Just as today we moderns might check the weather forecast before embarking on a journey, or consult a stockbroker before making an investment, so for Tibetans it was, and to a considerable extent still is, natural to take account of dreams and intuitions and to consult holy men where the interpretation was doubtful. Yet it would be wrong to conclude from this that the supernatural is somehow more real for Tibetans than it is for us moderns. On the contrary, from the Tibetan perspective, not merely is it incorrect to talk of a distinction to be made between the "natural" and the "supernatural" realms, but in fact it is incorrect to speak of a "supernatural realm" at all. The gods and deities of the Tibetan worldview are in a sense continuous with, and in fact, part of, the natural world.

For now, Lobsang Gyatso's initiation into the ancient Nyingma tradition lay safely in the future. In the meantime, his life was dominated by the Gelug curriculum for student monks. Heavily biased toward philosophy, this followed broadly the same pattern then as it does today, albeit whereas most novices are expected to take around sixteen years, the Dalai Lamas, enjoying the individual attention of the best teachers, have generally completed their formal studies in considerably less time. From about the age of eight, and under the tutoring of the great Chokyi

Gyaltsen, the first Panchen Lama, Lobsang Gyatso spent a year or so learning the basics of philosophical logic together with the rudiments of philosophical analysis: what makes an argument and so forth. As part of this introduction, he was instructed in the principal tenets of the different philosophical schools within the Indo-Tibetan tradition. After this introduction came a year of *tsema*, the study of epistemology (or theory of knowledge) according to Buddhist principles. From this followed the most important part of a novice's studies: the five years or so devoted to *pharchin*, the Perfection of Wisdom literature. This covers meditation theory and practice, the generation of *bodhichitta* (the desire to attain enlightenment for the benefit of all sentient beings), and, most importantly, of *nyingje*, or compassion. These three disciplines may be said to comprise the nuts and bolts of the Buddhist path. Lobsang Gyatso spent the next two or three years studying Madhyamaka (middle way) philosophy, with particular attention to its exposition by Tsongkhapa. Finally, he undertook a period devoted to the study of *vinaya*, the code of monastic discipline of which the First Dalai Lama was a specialist, and *abhidharma*—that is to say psychology and cosmology. Today, the Gelug academic curriculum culminates in a series of public debates which, at the highest grade, confer the title *lharam geshe* or, loosely, "learned doctor." In Lobsang Gyatso's time, there was no such universally recognized system of examinations: it was indeed he himself who instituted them.*[5]

In due course, the Fifth Dalai Lama was to become a highly proficient scholar. Meanwhile, at around the age of sixteen, he received the first of many initiations into the teaching and practice of the Nyingma tradition. This marked a turning point in

---

* There are no written exams at all. Writing within Gelug circles was taught only to a minority of pupils. A certain degree of suspicion attached to the practice: many considered it the high road to heresy. As as result, according to the present Dalai Lama, even brilliant scholars might barely be able to write their own names.

his life and he now began to incorporate Nyingma rituals into his own daily practice. At the same time, he embarked on a life-long involvement with *dzog'chen*. This distinctively Nyingma body of tradition seems to many conservative Gelugpas to smack of the old Chinese heresy outlawed by King Trisong Detsen at the great debate held at Samye during the ninth century. Concerned at what they saw as a dangerous straying on the part of the young Dalai Lama, a number of influential members of the hierarchy now began to wonder whether the Dalai Lama was a true Gelugpa at all. Indeed, it was this turn toward the ancient tradition that lies at the heart of the Shugden controversy. During the time of the Fifth, it seems as though the champion of the Gelug purists was none other than Drakpa Gyaltsen, the candidate passed over in favor of Lobsang Gyatso. Installed in what was known as the Upper Chamber at Drepung, Drakpa Gyaltsen, himself a high incarnation, grew up to be a fine scholar and an inspirational figure in his own right, with a significant following among sections of the Mongol nobility.

At around the same time as the young Dalai Lama's conversion (or subversion, as some would have it) to Nyingma practice, the situation in central Tibet began to deteriorate, following a period of relative calm. From 1634, or thereabouts, the new king of Tsang—now grown to adulthood—forged an alliance with the king of Beri (one of Tibet's easternmost districts). An adherent of the old Bon religion, the king of Beri declared himself the enemy of the *buddhadharma* and set about persecuting the clergy throughout his territory, paying particular attention to the Gelug community in Lithang. Worse still, a new Mongolian strongman, Legden Khan, who seems to have been in touch with Tsang, had emerged in the Kokonor region. When he set out with an army with the declared intention of attacking central Tibet, the hierarchy called a hasty conference. Likening their sect to a "butter lamp flickering in a raging storm," they concluded that their only hope lay in forging a new alliance among the Mongols.

To this end, Sonam Rabten himself, representing the Dalai Lama, was dispatched to trawl the Hor tribes for a new patron-protector of the Gelugpas.

Fortunately for the Gelug, Legden's army was struck down by smallpox and scattered before it could inflict any damage. Even more happily came news that Sonam Rabten had succeeded in securing an alliance with Gushri Khan, leader of the Qoshot Mongols. Won over to the faith, Gushri agreed to support the Gelug. Their troubles were not yet over, however. Almost immediately a new threat emerged. Arsalang, another Mongol chieftain, began to lead his troops toward central Tibet. Unlike Legden, who was intent on conquest, Arsalang's concern was merely plunder. Fortunately, Gushri managed to intercept him and persuaded Arsalang at least to spare Gelug interests. When Arsalang reached Lhasa, he greatly surprised the terrified populace by throwing himself down at the feet of the Dalai Lama.

The Dalai Lama himself wrote that Arsalang's conversion was the result of his successful propitiation of the protector deities. The teachings he bestowed on the chieftain were not so effective, however. Not to be deprived of his spoil, Arsalang turned his attention to the Kagyupas instead, fighting an engagement which almost certainly caused the death of the Shamar Lama, a saintly man reputed to have memorized no less than thirty-two volumes of scripture.[6] Fortunately, the Kagyu magicians were no less adept at the black arts than Lobsang Gyatso. They duly cursed the Mongolian and sent him mad. He is reported to have run amok and killed several of his own people before being assassinated, apparently on the orders of his own father.

Having survived the threats posed successively by Legden Khan and Arsalang, the Gelugpas could rejoice in having won for themselves, in Gushri Khan, a powerful patron. Accordingly, they gave him a rapturous welcome when he arrived in Lhasa during the latter part of 1637. It is unclear precisely how long he stayed, but we do know that the Dalai Lama, now twenty years of age, not only initiated him into the Gelugpa tradition, but also, following the example of the Third Dalai Lama, conferred on the Mongol chieftain the title of religious king— *choegyal* in Tibetan—and defender of the faith.

The following year, Gushri Khan toured much of central Tibet. That this was less a triumphal excursion than a show of strength is suggested by the interception of a letter from the king of Beri, who was still active in the east. Evidently alarmed by developments in Lhasa, the king had written to his ally, the king of Tsang, calling for a fresh attack on the Gelug, to include destruction of the Three Seats. Observing that there had been ceaseless wars and sectarian conflict since the arrival of the Jowo statue (brought to Tibet by Songtsen Gampo's Chinese wife), he stated his intention of seeing it thrown in the river.* Aghast, the *chamzö* urged the Dalai Lama to call Gushri Khan to arms. Not only must the king of Beri be destroyed, but it was time also to declare war on Tsang. Lobsang Gyatso accepted that for his persecution of the faith, the king of Beri must be done away with. But toward the king of Tsang, he took a milder approach, saying:

I am supposed to be a lama. My duty is to study religion, to go into meditation and to teach others . . . It seems to me unnecessary to cause any more disturbance in the country . . . Our relations with the Tsang faction are not as bad as they were last year. They are not persecuting the Gelugpa now, and the harm caused to Drepung and Sera monasteries back in 1619 was, in fact, the fault of the Gelugpa for refusing to give the Tsang ruler an audience with the Fourth Dalai Lama.[7]

---

* A hideous sacrilege, since this was how the corpses of the poor were traditionally disposed of.

Accordingly, Lobsang Gyatso instructed Sonam Rabten to compose a letter to Gushri Khan authorizing an attack on the king of Beri, but requesting that his troops return to Mongolia directly thereafter.

Sonam Rabten, for his part, took a very different view of the matter. Clearly a political, if not a spiritual, visionary, he recognized in the king of Beri's letter a *casus belli* that could propel the Gelug to preeminence throughout the whole of Tibet. He therefore disobeyed the Dalai Lama.

It was the custom of the day to accompany written communications with supplementary oral instructions. Where secrecy was paramount, these might entirely contradict the contents of the letter. Writing many years later, the Dalai Lama noted that, in this case, "the tune of the flute" seemed to have been transformed into "the song of the arrow." Gushri Khan duly fell on Beri "like a red and black whirlwind" and the king was captured and executed during the closing weeks of 1640.[8] The joyful news of his destruction reached Lhasa during the following Monlam Chenmo. It was especially well-received when it was further reported that the many monks imprisoned by the dharma-destroyer had also been freed. All Kham, as far east as Lijiang in modern-day Yunnan province (where hitherto the Kagyu had been the dominant sect), was now delivered to the followers of Tsongkhapa. But delight turned to consternation when rumors began to circulate that, following this success, Gushri Khan had not returned home as requested. Instead he was on the march to central Tibet. Telling Sonam Rabten that this time he had gone too far in his schemes, Lobsang Gyatso announced that he was determined to intervene. But it was too late. Even as they were discussing the matter, an urgent message arrived from Gushri. The Panchen Lama must immediately be summoned to safety as an attack on Tsang was imminent. Accordingly, Sonam Rabten drew up a letter containing the fiction that two of Gushri Khan's wives had embarked on a pilgrimage to central Tibet.

The senior queen, having fallen ill, was unable to travel beyond Lhasa. The Panchen Lama should therefore come without delay. The elderly prelate duly set out, only to be turned back on the orders of the king of Tsang, who had in the meantime received word that the Mongol army was on its way. Mindful of the "Peace of Chakpori" negotiated by the Panchen Lama in 1621, the king urged him to intervene once more. But Sonam Rabten had already met with Gushri and led his army into Tsang. The Mongols were beyond recall.

Gushri Khan made directly for Shigatse, the capital of Tsang, meeting with little resistance en route. Sonam Rabten for his part—throwing off all pretense of neutrality—followed, taking over the administration of former Tsang strongholds as they fell. When they reached Shigatse itself, however, the Mongols found that the king had erected an impregnable stockade around the perimeter of his fortress, itself situated on a hill. Moreover, the accuracy of the Tsang archers prevented the Mongols from closing with the enemy. Days turned to weeks and still Gushri Khan's troops were kept at bay. Toward the end of 1641, Sonam Rabten's nerve began to fail. It was his turn now to suggest mediation. At this, Lobsang Gyatso lost patience with him:

I have never spoken a harsh word to you, but today I am so disturbed that I have no alternative but to reproach you. Did I not tell you a number of times that it would be unwise to engage in a war with the Tsang ruler? He is not as insignificant as you think. How can I possibly attempt to mediate when it is already widely known that we sent an official to guide Gushri Khan to Tsang? Even if I did bring about an end to the fighting, the Tsangpa forces would take their revenge as soon as Gushri Khan departs for his own country. I made up my mind we would have to fight the Tsangpa ruler on the very day Gushri Khan's messengers arrived telling us to bring the Panchen Lama to safety. We must now go through with this war, which you have so carelessly begun. If Gushri Khan wins, well and good. If he loses we shall have to leave Lhasa and find some other country to live in.[9]

Chastened, Sonam Rabten responded by taking a detachment of monks from Drepung and Sera, and marching them to the assistance of the beleaguered Mongols. On the way, they attacked and took an important fortress at Dongkar, before proceeding to Shigatse itself. There they replenished Gushri's stocks of food, fodder, and munitions, and assisted in the construction of new catapults.

At precisely this moment of crisis, the Dalai Lama, presiding over an assembly of monks, experienced a startling vision. In front of the altar at which he sat, a large human head with macabre face rose up, its mouth opened wide, and into which a cascade of smaller heads fell "like grain poured into a sack."[10] This the Dalai Lama took as a sign of the success of the rite he was conducting to implore the deities to grant a favorable outcome to the war on Tsang. Shortly afterward, on the first day of the Water Horse year (1642), several of the Dalai Lama's attendants at the Ganden Phodrang were alarmed to hear a sound like a woman's piercing scream somewhere in the distance. And on the second day, during the rite of atonement, Lobsang Gyatso experienced a vision of Palden Lhamo, his personal protector deity, dancing in the sky. To begin with, he was skeptical of what he had seen, and doubtful of its significance. But then came the first reports of the fall, on the eighth, of Shigatse *dzong*.

In Lhasa, there was great rejoicing. Prayer flags were hoisted and incense was burned in celebration. For his part, Gushri Khan immediately invited the Dalai Lama to Shigatse, where a great ceremony would be held.

Arriving at the beginning of the fourth month, Lobsang Gyatso was received by the Mongol chieftain, accompanied by the whole of the Mongol army, and with Sonam Rabten at his side. In the ceremony that followed, Gushri was formally installed as the patron, protector, and king of all Tibet, while Sonam Rabten, still officially the Dalai Lama's chamberlain, or *chamzö*, was made Gushri's regent. The khan then made an offering of the *mendel tensum* to the Dalai Lama—a mandala symbolizing the body, speech, and mind of a fully enlightened being—in recognition of his position as supreme spiritual head of state.[*]

[*] Some scholars argue, persuasively in my view, that this arrangement superseded the established principles of *mchod yon* relations. Gushri Khan remained patron-protector, but it was Sonam Rabten, not the Dalai Lama, who took on the role of priest-protector. The Dalai Lama himself was now elevated to a still higher plane in his role as an object of worship and means by which merit was obtained. *See* Seyfort-Ruegg, "The Preceptor-Donor Relation in Thirteenth Century Tibetan Society and Polity, its Inner Asian Precursors and Indian models."

18

The Great Fifth

The tumultuous events of 1642 marked the climax and fulfill-
ment of a long leaning toward unification in Tibet, begun by the
Sakya hierarchs under the Yuan Dynasty and furthered by the
nationalism of Chang'chub Gyaltsen and his heirs. So it was that,
for the first time in eight hundred years, Tibet was once again
under the rule of one man. For now, that man was Gushri Khan.
But it was this arrangement that paved the way for the emergence of the Dalai Lama himself as supreme head of state, both
spiritual and secular.

Before returning to Drepung, Lobsang Gyatso took the
opportunity to obtain preliminary ordination from the Panchen
Lama at nearby Tashilhunpo Monastery. Having recently
embarked on a lifelong study of the subject, he also founded
a small school of medicine within the precincts of the fortress
so recently vacated by the king. The Gelug hierarchy meanwhile began immediately to assert its ascendancy. Tashi Zilnon,
the Kagyu monastery founded by the king of Tsang, was demol-
ished at once. Today, save for its wooden planking, which was
carried off to Lhasa to replace the flooring of the Jokhang, not

a trace of it survives. Simultaneously, all the Gelug monasteries that had been forcibly converted were taken back, while several smaller monasteries were themselves requisitioned to the Gelug sect (though these were returned as relations between the two schools improved). The larger Kagyu foundations were permitted to remain functioning, albeit with restrictions on the number of monks they could house.

No sooner had he returned to the Ganden Phodrang than the Dalai Lama succumbed to an illness so severe some believed him to have been poisoned. Whatever the cause, Lobsang Gyatso lost the power of speech. He himself was convinced that the cause of his illness was spiritual impurity contracted during the violent rite he had performed against the king of Tsang. Two months later, however, Lobsang Gyatso experienced a vision during his conduct of a ceremony in the chapel dedicated to the protector deity Mahakala. Several individuals appeared and conferred an initiation on him. At the same time, he felt that Sonam Rabten and others were looking on disapprovingly at his participation in a Nyingma ritual. When he came back to mundane reality, he found that he had totally recovered from his illness.

One of the first executive decisions the Dalai Lama took on returning to Lhasa was to name it—as opposed to Drepung— the headquarters of the new government of which he was now nominally leader. The government of central Tibet itself would henceforth be conducted according to the principle of *chö'si sung'drel**—literally, the union of the secular and the spiritual— whereby ecclesiastical and lay affairs both came under the jurisdiction of the one authority.

Considering the centuries that had elapsed since Tibetans last enjoyed stable government under a single leader, it is not surprising to learn that genuine unity was not achieved quickly. It could

---

* Or *chos srid zung 'brel.*

be argued that it was never achieved at all. Because the government was, in effect, the agency of the Gelug sect, all those who remained loyal to the others were, in some degree, disenfranchised. While at the lay level, the high degree of respect accorded the *sangha* meant that this was generally no more of a problem than it is in a modern democracy when the individual's preferred party is not elected, it did mean that there was a certain tension built into the system. Areas such as Sakya, whose monastery had long governed local affairs, were, to begin with, largely exempt from what amounted to a general program of centralisation under the Gelug. But problems arose whenever the Gelug pressed their claims too strongly.

The first major test of the Gelug sect's new authority came within just a few months of the fall of Tsang. Insurrection broke out in Gyantse, Tibet's third largest urban center. Another rebellion followed in the Kongpo region, on the eastern edge of central Tibet, where several Gelug monasteries were burned to the ground. At one of these, more than five hundred monks were reported killed. Gushri Khan reacted mercilessly. It is said that in the campaign to crush the rebels, some seven thousand were killed and many more captured. Recognizing that while the deposed king of Tsang still lived, he was likely to remain a figurehead for opponents of the new regime, the decision was taken to put him to death. This was duly accomplished in standard fashion by sewing him into a leather bag and throwing it into Lhasa's Tsangpo River. It seems that, while inclined to clemency, Lobsang Gyatso's interpretation of what it meant to be the earthly manifestation of Chenrezig, the Bodhisattva of Compassion, meant that he could still be brisk when it came to matters of justice, saying that "no pity should be wasted on those who had to be executed for their crimes."[1] The execution of the king of Tsang must at least have had the Dalai Lama's tacit approval. But the Dalai Lama did intervene on behalf of the rebel leaders themselves, successfully pleading for their death sentences to be commuted to life imprisonment.

Although Lobsang Gyatso's contribution to the governance of Tibet was at first limited, certain of his innovations were to prove immensely significant. One such innovation was the institution of Pehar as the wrathful protector of the Ganden Phodrang, as the Gelug government was—and remains—known.* The story of how this happened tells us much about the way Tibetans have understood the contiguity between natural and supernatural.

Originally said to have been brought to Samye by Padmasambhava, it seems that Pehar moved of his own accord to a small Nyingma foundation lying half a stage to the east of Lhasa on the banks of the Kyichu River. Sometime around the period we have been discussing, he had a quarrel with its senior lama. This resulted in the lama's order that there should be no depiction of Pehar in the sanctuary of a new chapel that was then under construction. To this the deity retaliated by manifesting as a boy who came to offer help to the monks working on the new building. In return for his many services, the boy's only request was that, somewhere on the wall, the monks should paint a small picture of a monkey with a stick of burning incense in its hand. To this, the monks readily assented. The following night, Pehar slipped into the image of the monkey and, using the stick of burning incense, set the building ablaze. Realizing what had happened, the lama responded by setting a cross-thread demon trap by which means he was able to capture the deity. Placing Pehar in a box, the lama cast his prisoner into the river. Some days later, this box was seen, presumably in a vision, by Lobsang Gyatso, who ordered that it be brought to him, cautioning that on no account should the box be opened. Perplexingly, the closer the monk who brought it ashore came to Drepung, the heavier the box became. At last, unable to restrain his curiosity any longer,

---

* It will be remembered that the Gelug government is named after the Dalai Lama's residence at Ganden.

he lifted its lid. Somewhat anticlimactically, the box proved to contain nothing more than a pigeon which flew immediately into a nearby tree. When he heard what had happened, the Dalai Lama admonished the monk and ordered that a shrine be built around the tree. In due course, this shrine was incorporated into the adjacent monastery of Nechung.² When subsequently the deity* possessed one of the Nechung monks and his identity became clear, he began to be consulted both by the Dalai Lama and by the Ganden Phodrang for advice on political matters as well as for insight of the future.

Besides maintaining close relations with Pehar, Lobsang Gyatso was also particularly close to three other wrathful protectors. These were Palden Lhamo (whom we met at the miraculous lake close by Chokhor Gyal Monastery), Begtse, and Gonpo Dramzey (the raven-headed emanation of Mahakala who protected the First Dalai Lama as a baby). Begtse seems originally to have been a Mongolian war god who became attached to the Dalai Lama lineage during the time of the Third's visit to Altan Khan in 1575. Some texts suggest that he lives in a cemetery. Others state that he resides in a castle that rises from the center of a lake of boiling blood. Begtse himself, his body bright red in color, his limbs thick and short, his mouth open with warm blood bubbling at the corners, emerges from a sun lotus standing with one leg on the corpse of a man, the other on the carcass of a horse. In his retinue are numerous minor deities, including a group of twenty-one butchers, similarly red in color, and clad in the flayed flesh of humans.† Some nibble at a heart, others at a lung or liver, while still others sip blood or brains from skull-cups.

* To be precise, Dorje Drakden, one of Pehar's lieutenants.
† In Tibet, butchery has traditionally been regarded as the lowest occupation of all. From the time of the Fifth, it has been the preserve of the Kashmiri Muslim community that settled just outside Lhasa during the mid-seventeenth century.

Not only were these wrathful deities central to Lobsang Gyatso's worldview—as they remain for many Tibetans, including the present Dalai Lama—but they were also central both to his spiritual practice and to his academic interests. He invariably performed Begtse rituals on the last day of every month, while Palden Lhamo was the focus of his New Year rituals. Later in life, the Fifth would compile a vast compendium, containing many rituals, prayers, and hymns of his own composition, devoted to these *dharmapalas*.

This monumental book was only one among many, however. Lobsang Gyatso's collected works exceed in number those of all the other Dalai Lamas combined. Relatively few are read today. But of those that are, his history of Tibet, completed on November 14, 1643, is one of the most important. Poetically entitled *The Melody of the Queen of Spring*, not much of what it contains would pass for history in a modern academy. Yet in the context of the scholastic culture in which he worked, the Fifth's historical method is decidedly radical. Not only did he go to great lengths, by comparing different sources, to verify dates, but he also contrasted and criticized the opinions of previous chroniclers. He created thereby one of the most valuable historical documents of his time.

One of the most important passages in Lobsang Gyatso's history of Tibet is concerned with his relationship with Gushri Khan. For the Fifth, the Mongolian's motives in coming to Tibet were purely religious. Indeed, he tells us that so great was the devotion born in Gushri when the khan first became acquainted with the *buddhadharma* that the chieftain bruised his forehead making protestations in the direction of Lhasa. It is clear that from the Dalai Lama's perspective, in political terms, Gushri was no more than the guarantor of the Ganden Phodrang government. This seems a fair assessment, given that, following Tsang's final defeat, Gushri left all decision-making to Sonam Rabten, and himself lived a retired life, spending the summers among the pasturelands of Dam and wintering at

Lhasa. But as might be expected, the Chinese court took a different view of the matter. China itself had recently been conquered by the Manchus, northern barbarians who had overthrown the Ming Dynasty in 1636. And for the Manchus, the relationship between Lobsang Gyatso and Gushri Khan presented a possible means to an end. Because between them the Dalai Lama and the Panchen Lama had "the absolute allegiance of all the Mongol tribes," it appeared that, by himself patronizing the Gelugpas, the Manchu emperor could hope to obtain the Dalai Lama's assistance in keeping the Mongols at bay. Of course, it was an exaggeration to suppose that the Gelugpas had the allegiance of all the Mongols. On the other hand, it is highly significant that the Manchus did not see the relationship as in any sense usurping a pre-existing relationship with Beijing. Had Tibet been an "inalienable part of China" (to use the stock phrase of the Chinese Communist Party), we could have expected the court to have been hostile toward Gushri for having encroached on Chinese territory. Instead, they saw an opportunity to use the Mongols' newfound piety as a weapon against them. Accordingly, though the new emperor, Shunzi, was just six years old at the time, the Manchus issued a formal request to the Dalai Lama to visit at the Tibetan hierarch's earliest convenience.

This, Lobsang Gyatso was at first minded to refuse altogether. But a year later, Zurchen,* his Nyingma teacher, wrote telling him of a dream in which Lobsang Gyatso had announced that he was going to China and that he, Zurchen, must accompany him. Though another six years were to elapse before he actually set out for China, Lobsang Gyatso came in due course to realize that the dream had been prophetic.

In the meantime, the Dalai Lama, again at Zurchen's instigation, began work on a project that was to play a pivotal role in the acquisition of absolute power by the Dalai Lama

* Otherwise known as Chöyong Rangrol.

institution, namely the construction of the Potala Palace. Unquestionably one of the architectural wonders of the world, the
Potala is, after Everest, Tibet's most famous landmark.* Despite
the Chinese Communist Party's heedless transformation of Lhasa
into an almost characterless modern city, the thousand-chambered
Potala still dominates the sprawl. Inaugurated in 1645 with a
mandala drawn on the site by Zurchen, the original plan called
for a single structure, the White Palace, to be built around a small
temple erected by Songtsen Gampo for his Nepalese wife. It was
later added to with the construction of the Red Palace, the whole
providing accommodation not only for the Dalai Lama himself,
but also for government officials and the monks of Namgyal, the
"monastery within a monastery" that had hitherto served the Dalai
Lamas from within the precincts of Drepung. The Potala's importance to Tibet lay less in the fact that it became the seat of political power, however. More important was its symbolic power. First,
through its association with Songtsen Gampo, it provided an immediately recognisable link with the old empire. Secondly, the very
name given to the new building recalled the four Potalaka, the
celestial residences of Chenrezig. It thus proclaimed itself his residence, here on earth, in Lhasa, Tibet.

Just four years after work began, Lobsang Gyatso moved into
the White Palace, and with him came the administrative officers
of the Ganden Phodrang government. Paintings of the building
as it then was show it to have been considerably smaller than it
became by the end of the century, but even so, its speed of
construction suggests enormous effort. To mark the opening of
the new building, there were public processions, dances, and
competitions, including equestrian sports, archery, wrestling,
weight-lifting, and board games.† These proclaimed not only its

---

* To Tibetans, Everest is known as Chomolongma, which may be translated as
the "nun riding on an ox's back."
† The festivities are depicted in an impressive series of frescoes, still extant,
on the walls of the palace.

physical opening but also denoted the Potala's status as a public space, a place of pilgrimage to which all Tibetans would aspire to journey at least once in their lifetime.

In the intervening period, Lobsang Gyatso continued his religious studies, both with the Gelug tradition under the supervision of the Panchen Lama, his senior tutor, and as a Nyingma master, in which capacity he went under the secret name of Dorje Thokmetsel. He also continued his literary activities, completing his biography of the Third Dalai Lama in 1646. So far as the Gelug administration was concerned, at this time its chief difficulty, following Gushri Khan's crushing of Tsang, Gyantse, and Kongpo, lay in the far south in what is today Bhutan. There, a rebellion against Gelug rule resulted in troops being sent to intervene, but they were dealt a humiliating defeat. Government troops were again dispatched in 1647 and again defeated, their arms subsequently put on display at the nearby fort of Paro, where they remained, to the shame of all patriotic Tibetans, until the beginning of the twentieth century when the fort burned down.

The situation throughout the rest of Tibet was generally stable, mainly due to the continued presence of Gushri Khan and his army. But it can also be attributed in part to the growing success of the Ganden Phodrang. The government had begun to extend its authority throughout all Tibet, a fact borne out by the observation that it seems to have had little difficulty in suppressing, throughout all but the very far east of the country, the Jonang sect. Ostensibly, this was on the grounds of heresy. Exponents of the Jonang teachings were deemed to hold views on the nature of emptiness that not only contradicted Tsongkhapa's but, according to their Gelug critics, took them dangerously close to theism. But perhaps more at issue was the fact that its leader, Taranatha, who, as we saw earlier, was a kinsman of the Dalai Lama's mother and the bestower of his birth name, in the period immediately prior to his death in 1635, had disgraced himself in Lobsang

Gyatso's eyes. It is not precisely clear what Taranatha's crimes were. Suffice to say that, for Lobsang Gyatso, he was a "lecherous villain without equal."[3] Nor is it clear why the whole tradition should have to be suppressed, its chief monastery re-consecrated as a Gelug institution, and its precious library of printing blocks put under lock and key.* But whatever the proximate reasons for the suppression, its thoroughness remains something of a blot on the Fifth Dalai Lama's reputation for generosity toward non-Gelugpas.

A better reflection of the Dalai Lama's reputation is the number of foreign dignitaries who came to Lhasa to pay their respects and offer gifts. These included an emissary of the king of the Kathmandu Valley (Nepal did not yet exist as a nation state) and, it seems, from Shah Jahan, the great Mughal conqueror of India. And, between 1649 and 1651, at least another two embassies arrived from the court of the Qing (pronounced "Ching") emperor, repeating his earlier request that the Dalai Lama visit Beijing.

Despite Zurchen's earlier dream and despite knowing there existed a prophecy that one of the Dalai Lamas would convert all Tibet, China, and Mongolia to the way of the Buddha, Lobsang Gyatso remained undecided as to whether he should accede to this request. Toward the end of 1651, however, he experienced the first of many visions that would eventually persuade him that now was the acceptable time for such a visit. The first of these occurred while the Dalai Lama was staying at Chokhor Gyal Monastery. The next occurred during the eleventh month (reckoning by the Tibetan calendar) while burning juniper leaves on the tomb of Songtsen Gampo, when Padmasambhava appeared to him surrounded by a vast retinue of attendants. And on the first day of the following year—that of the Water Dragon—he

---

* It is also somewhat puzzling that these were not destroyed. They finally became available once more during the early part of the twentieth century when they came into the possession of the Ri med (pronounced Ree-mé), or Non-sectarian, movement.

saw Palden Lhamo dancing in the sky and announcing that this year was the year for "propagating religion."

Halfway through the Great Prayer Festival of 1652, the Dalai Lama abruptly and unexpectedly handed over responsibility for its conduct to another senior lama and returned to Drepung. There he performed a number of private rituals. Having carefully reflected on his visions and undertaken further investigations, including precise scrutiny of certain prophetic scriptures, the Dalai Lama made up his mind to leave for China during the third month. That this was the correct decision was confirmed to him when he had another vision in which Padmasambhava announced that it was he, the Fifth Dalai Lama, who was "destined to subdue the barbarians." The Lotus Born then imparted instructions concerning the way in which the Dalai Lama should protect himself during the journey. Two days later, Lobsang Gyatso experienced yet another vision. In this, he saw scenes of India, Nepal, China, Kashmir, and Shambala (the hidden kingdom of the north), before meeting with Yeshe Tsogyal, wife of King Trisong Detsen, consort of Padmasambhava and author of the *Pema thang yig*, the treasure revealed by the Dalai Lama's spiritual forebear, Nyangré Nyima Ozer. Then, in sexual union with the queen, Lobsang Gyatso experienced the non-duality of bliss and emptiness. Subsequently, while performing the atonement rite of Palden Lhamo, he saw the goddess gallop across the sky riding her mule. As she did so, the earth shook. Finally, another goddess appeared to him and led him through the sky to a rocky mountain, the summit of which reached to the heavens. There, in a cave, he saw an ordinary-looking yogin, whom he supposed to be another manifestation of Padmasambhava. Touching the Dalai Lama's head with a vase, in a gesture of initiation, this final apparition of the master dissolved into light and disappeared into Lobsang Gyatso's heart. This was his last vision before departing for China. Whatever else it and those preceding it reveal, they leave us in no doubt that, for the Dalai Lama, his visit to China was principally a spiritual enterprise.

One of the most important ways in which the Dalai Lama conducted his mission was by means of elaborate public ceremonies dedicated to Chenrezig, whose incarnation he now openly professed himself to be. During the course of the next eighteen months, he was to conduct a total of sixty-seven such ceremonies before the large crowds that turned out to pay him respect. In so doing, he did much to spread the cult of himself as the Bodhisattva's earthly manifestation, and thereby to increase the power of the Dalai Lama institution itself. Although it might seem that his promotion of Chenrezig's cult was little more than an exercise in self-aggrandizement, the visions suggest that, even if this is to some extent true, Lobsang Gyatso was principally motivated by a desire to propagate what he thought was the correct interpretation of the *buddhadharma* itself.

The Dalai Lama traveled slowly, taking almost twice as long to complete his journey to the borderlands as an ordinary trading caravan. Partly this was due to his religious duties, which included not only the public ceremonies but also meetings with local lamas, chieftains, and monastic officials. But the size of his entourage was also a factor. Although many would have been porters, among the three thousand personnel accompanying the Dalai Lama were his Mongol escort, a dance troupe, thirteen government officials representing each of its different departments, and numerous other monks and members of the Gelug establishment, along with their attendants. The leisurely pace this enforced suited the Dalai Lama well, however. No matter what else occupied him, Lobsang Gyatso never allowed his official duties to stand in the way of his literary work. During the course of the journey, he was able to complete his biography of Yonten Gyatso, the Fourth Dalai Lama.

Five months after setting out, but little more than halfway

to Beijing, the Dalai Lama sent a letter on ahead to the emperor. In this, he proposed that they should meet outside the Great Wall, at Keritaka. It was an extraordinarily bold suggestion, but one that makes clear the Dalai Lama's conception of himself as paramount leader of the Tibetan people. That the Manchu court even considered the proposal testifies to the respect in which they held him (not to mention his Mongol divisions). In the end, however, although the emperor himself was minded to acquiesce, an agreement was reached whereby he would "run into" the Dalai Lama while on a hunting expedition in Beijing's southern district.* Even this was a major break with protocol. Ordinarily, the emperor would meet foreign dignitaries only within the precincts of the Forbidden City.

While waiting for a reply, the Dalai Lama and his party progressed to Keritaka, which lay on China's northwestern boundary. One practical reason for suggesting this as a meeting place was the Tibetans' fear of contracting smallpox or some other epidemic disease that flourished in China's unfamiliar climate. As it happened, the Emperor's court was for its part nervous of the large size of the Dalai Lama's party, particularly since there had been such a poor harvest that autumn.† A great number of meetings took place between Tibetan and Chinese officials before a compromise could be reached. In the meantime, the emperor sent one of his uncles as an emissary bearing a letter of welcome together with sumptuous gifts for the Dalai Lama. It was finally agreed that from Keritaka, the Dalai Lama would proceed with an entourage of just three hundred. But as a sign

* This arrangement is recalled by the diplomacy developed by the U.S. Department of State whereby on visits to Washington the Dalai Lama has on occasion been officially received by the Vice President while the President has, fortuitously, been in the same building. This has allowed the two leaders to "run into" one another without invoking the full symbolism of an official meeting.
† Or perhaps this was just an excuse.

of the esteem in which the emperor held him, the Tibetan leader would be accommodated in the Yellow Palace, which was even now in the process of being especially constructed for him. To judge by the account of these negotiations in his autobiography, the Dalai Lama was entirely happy with the arrangements, as he was with the emperor's honors and gifts. Most importantly, he was satisfied that the emperor recognized him as the "legal king, of whom there was not the like in Tibet"—in other words, that it was he, Lobsang Gyatso, who was ultimately paramount leader of Tibet, over and above Sonam Rabten or Gushri Khan (neither of whom accompanied him).[4]

Commenting later on the tenor of the negotiations themselves, the Dalai Lama recorded how "for two or three days numberless people kept arriving on horses, camels, or oxen. The ceaseless sound of salutations . . . oppressed my ears. For days together, I gave blessings and flowers to every one of three thousand persons. The silk presentation scarves fell like snow and piled up [as high] as haystacks." Then, on December 22, 1652, "holding in his hand the sword of office and [other] symbols and preceded by men and music, the emperor's personal envoy arrived, surrounded by two thousand riders, with umbrella, banner, and fans raised on both right and left, all in proper order, as if in the assembly-ground of the Lord of the Immortals himself . . ."[5]

Of his first meeting with the emperor himself,* the Dalai Lama wrote how he "entered the outer wall which was raised in front of the emperor, and progressed gradually† . . . From this spot, when I had covered the distance of four arrow shots I dismounted from my horse. The emperor descended from his Throne and advanced a distance of ten fathoms. He seized my hand with his hand . . ." The two men then drank tea together and exchanged pleasantries.

---

* Most likely this took place on January 14, 1653.
† It was not, of course, the case that the two men should meet literally during the course of a hunt.

Subsequently, the Dalai Lama remained two months in Beijing, during which he celebrated the Tibetan New Year, received the emperor at a great banquet to mark the occasion, was himself granted a grand reception over which the emperor presided and during the course of which were exchanged the customarily long-winded titles appropriate to the occasion, gave numerous teachings and initiations, received representatives of the local monastic community, handed down instructions concerning the proper organization of monasteries, and experienced a vision of his personal goddess of wealth—no doubt in anticipation of the bounty he would take back to Tibet with him. For though from the Dalai Lama's perspective the missionary aspect of his visit was the most important, from the Tibetan perspective generally, the economic benefits were no less significant.

While there can be no doubt that the Tibetans' hopes of economic gain from Lobsang Gyatso's visit to China were amply fulfilled, it is not clear that the visit was entirely successful in other respects. During early February, the Dalai Lama memorialized the emperor, explaining that the "climate of this country does not suit me and I have been ill. My companions, too, have been ill. I pray that the emperor allow me to return." Whether illness really was the reason for wanting to go back to Tibet is uncertain. We only know that the Tibetans remained acutely fearful of the danger of contracting unfamiliar diseases from China's vast population. But it is reasonably clear that the Dalai Lama left Beijing sooner than originally intended. It seems possible he had concluded that the deities had exaggerated somewhat the spiritual riches to be gleaned from the Chinese mission field.*

Part of the reason for the relative failure of the visit can no doubt be attributed to the character of the emperor himself.

---

* Or maybe it was sufficient that he had planted the seed of the *buddhadharma*. Perhaps it will fall to a later incarnation to reap the full reward of the Fifth's mission.

Although in his autobiography the Dalai Lama is full of praise for the young Shunzi (he was just fifteen years old at the time), describing him as "the very pattern of a fearless lion" and "very hospitable," the truth is that he was hotheaded to the point of instability. When his favorite concubine died a few years later, the emperor first contrived to follow suit. When he failed at this, he determined to renounce the world and become a monk. He was prevented from doing this as well and died a broken man in 1661. There was also the age-old problem of the relationship between the emperor of China and the *buddhadharma*. Shunzi, encouraged by his (Mongolian) mistress, was certainly sympathetic toward Buddhism (as, under the influence of Jesuit missionaries, he had earlier been to Christianity). But, as Son of Heaven and leader of all China, his officials dared not permit him to risk alienating the hundreds of millions of his subjects who followed Taoism, nor the literati who generally followed Confucius, by identifying himself too closely with the Dalai Lama.

On the eighteenth day of the second month, therefore, Lobsang Gyatso attended a great farewell banquet at which he was given gifts "as generous as before" and, on the twentieth, departed Beijing once again in the company of more than three thousand officials and associates of the emperor's court. His first prolonged halt was at Keritaka, where he remained two months preaching and teaching, conferring initiations, giving audiences, and conducting rituals both publicly and privately. During one of these, he experienced a vision of Songtsen Gampo and both his Chinese and his Nepalese consort. This, he felt sure, was a sign of his capacity to bring happiness to the Tibetan people—if not, he might have added, to the Chinese.

From Keritaka, the Dalai Lama eventually set out for the Kokonor region during May 1653. Just before doing so, he received a final letter from the emperor, accompanied by still more gifts, and with these a gold seal, all of which were handed over with great rejoicing. However, though the Chinese Communist Party today makes much of this seal, saying that it somehow "proves" that the Dalai Lama accepted the emperor's authority over Tibet, Lobsang Gyatso himself clearly thought little of it, noting that its translation into Tibetan (it was inscribed in Tibetan, Chinese, and Mongolian) was very poor.

Staying first at Kumbum, the monastery erected to mark Tsongkhapa's birthplace, the Dalai Lama progressed via several Gelug foundations in Amdo until he reached the Mongol heartland after a further three months. As he went, Lobsang Gyatso redistributed the wealth received from the emperor. Much of it was used to restore those monasteries which had been damaged during the great suppression of the Gelug conducted by the king of Beri, but Lobsang Gyatso also spent some of it on private acts of charity. At Sining, for example, near where the present Dalai Lama was born, he ransomed the life of a criminal fettered and thrown in prison for theft. This cost him three hundred measures of silver and shows that, even as Dalai Lama, he could not usurp the local legislature.

Finally, during the tenth month, the Dalai Lama began the homeward journey to Lhasa, arriving at Reting Monastery toward the end of 1653. Six days out from the capital, Gushri Khan and Sonam Rabten came to welcome him home. The Panchen Lama would have come too, but at eighty-two his age told against him and he sent a representative in his stead. With these dignitaries came most of the population of Lhasa and the outlying area, all of them to express their relief at having the Precious Protector safely back. Yet, evidently a man of great physical stamina, Lobsang Gyatso hardly rested at all. Within a few weeks, he set out once more, this time for a tour of Tsang. Accompanied by Gushri Khan and several other Mongol chieftains, he traveled via Chokhorling as far as

Tashilhunpo. There, at the comparatively late age of thirty-seven, he presented himself to the Panchen Lama for his final ordination.

Back at Lhasa in time for the Monlam Chenmo, Lobsang Gyatso was faced with a crisis that threatened his own authority. During 1655, Gushri Khan died, precipitating renewed rebellion against the government. The Dalai Lama's position was further threatened when, less than a year later, Sonam Rabten, the great kingmaker and strongman of the Gelug hierarchy, also died. So concerned was he at the prospect of major unrest that Lobsang Gyatso ordered that the regent's death should not be made public. A whole year was to pass before an official announcement was made.

As ever during times of crisis, Lobsang Gyatso experienced several prophetic visions during which he received advice, mainly from Padmasambhava, on how to negotiate the difficulties he faced. The day before Sonam Rabten's long-delayed funeral, he experienced the last in a series of visions during a retreat he had undertaken on the express instructions of Pehar. Once again Padmasambhava gave him counsel concerning the conduct of the government during the year ahead, and, as usual, he wrote these down and stored his notes in a safe place. But being preoccupied with what was clearly a period of serious political instability, Lobsang Gyatso forgot about them almost immediately. By the time he read them again, they looked, he wrote, "like a dyke built after the flood has already passed by."[6]

Unfortunately, it is difficult to form a balanced view of precisely what form this flood took. But it was around this time that the crisis over Drakpa Gyaltsen, who came later to be identified with Dorje Shugden, came to a head.[*] Lobsang Gyatso's onetime rival for recognition as Dalai Lama was by now highly regarded

---

[*] Some Tibetan scholars have tried to show an earlier origin for the cult.

for his wisdom and learning. Moreover, he had won a great following among sections of the Mongol aristocracy. And although Drakpa Gyaltsen was always careful to identify himself as Lobsang Gyatso's disciple, it is evident that he had become the focus of opposition to the Dalai Lama's rule. How strong or credible this opposition really was is unclear, but there is little doubt that Drakpa Gyaltsen was detested by the Dalai Lama's court, and especially by Sonam Rabten. For this reason, his sudden death was—as it continues to be by some—immediately construed as an assassination. It seems reasonably likely he was murdered by an official we know only as Norbu, acting on the orders of the regent, but much is mere conjecture. The only certainty is that, in a move which causes deep unhappiness even today, the search for Drakpa Gyaltsen's reincarnation was banned immediately. Even the buildings of the Upper Chamber at Drepung which had been the home and headquarters of his lineage were destroyed.

According to one version of events, Drakpa Gyaltsen's demise followed his victory in a formal religious debate with the Dalai Lama. As remains customary, the Dalai Lama is said to have handed Drakpa Gyaltsen, the winner, a ceremonial silk scarf. The scarf was subsequently found to have been rammed down Drakpa Gyaltsen's throat. According to his followers, however, Drakpa Gyaltsen had become so disturbed at the degeneration in the purity of the Gelug teachings under the Fifth that he voluntarily submitted either to suffocation or strangulation in order to become the sect's protector.[7]

It is a common belief among Tibetans that, in such cases of violent death, victims are likely to transform themselves into *shi'dre*, wrathful spirits that seek to avenge the crime. Many believe this is precisely what happened in the case of Drakpa Gyaltsen. It is also said that when his body came to be cremated, a thick pall of black smoke rose from the pyre, briefly assuming the shape of an open hand, which hung suspended in the air before drifting away. Soon after, strange events began to be reported throughout central Tibet. The silver casket into which Drakpa Gyaltsen's ashes were placed began to emit a curious buzzing sound; the dishes on which the Dalai Lama's food was served upset themselves spontaneously; finally, the Dalai Lama began to hear noises, including the sound of stones crashing on to the roof of his palace. These eventually became so loud that he was unable to eat his meals without monks blowing huge *dung-chen*, or long horns, to drown out the sound. In desperation, the government ordered a special ritual to be performed by the abbot of Mindroling Monastery. The abbot duly trapped the spirit, but before he was able finally to dispatch it, his attention was distracted by the unexpected appearance of one of the great protector deities on whom the spirit called. Seizing its chance, the spirit escaped. Undaunted, the authorities ordered Drakpa Gyaltsen's casket packed into a wooden crate and pitched into Lhasa's Tsangpo River. This carried it to a remote place in southern Tibet, where finally it ended up in a small pool. When, however, news of its reappearance reached the Dalai Lama, he ordered a small temple built on the site. Thereafter, the spirit came to be propitiated as an emanation of the great protector, Gyalchen Dorje Shugden. In return for this fealty, he agreed to become protector of the Gelug tradition.[8]

Although it is tempting to read the whole Shugden controversy in purely political terms, this would be to impose modern, secular beliefs on to a culture with quite different parameters and beliefs. For whatever the truth of these legends, they are what underpin the hostility toward the rule of the Fifth of later Gelug hierarchs who resented the Dalai Lama's openness toward the other sects, and it is here that lie the origins of the bitterness that erupted in the slaughter of the monk Lobsang Gyatso on that cold winter's night in 1997.

Following these events, the new decade brought a great improvement in the fortunes of both the Dalai Lama and the

Ganden Phodrang. It was Lobsang Gyatso himself who emerged as the one who would fill the power vacuum created by the demise of Gushri Khan and Sonam Rabten. This was despite the fact that the former was succeeded in orderly fashion by his son, and the latter by another regent, Trinley Gyatso. But Lobsang Gyatso ensured that their authority was in name only. He was able to do so partly, of course, thanks to his powerful personality. Another key factor was the prestige that now attached to the office of Dalai Lama. Following Lobsang Gyatso's assiduous promotion of the cult of Chenrezig and, since his return to Lhasa, his renovation of many of the religious sites connected with the first diffusion of Buddhism in Tibet—all at the behest of his visionary interlocutors—what had been but one lineage among many, albeit an important one, had come to be identified with the Tibetan nation itself. Lobsang Gyatso's popularity was now such that not even a new setback in Bhutan could diminish his standing in the eyes of the people. Likewise, his authority among the Mongols was such that when, not long before the emperor died, the Manchu court, writing in the name of Shunzi, requested the Dalai Lama to bring some troublemakers on the border to heel, he showed he could successfully assert himself abroad as well. On the Dalai Lama's orders, the Mongols stood down.

The next incumbent of the Dragon Throne, Emperor Kangxi (r. 1661–1722), was one of the longest-reigning and most successful of all China's emperors. But thanks to the Dalai Lama's prestige among the Mongols, it was not long before he too was urging Lobsang Gyatso to use his influence over the Mongols. Following another successful intervention, Kangxi wrote an appreciative letter to the Dalai Lama during 1667, commending him for "the thought he had given to the good governance of the Chinese and the Mongols."[9]

Lobsang Gyatso was now at the height of his power. In the quarter-century since the unification of Tibet under the Ganden

Phodrang, he had presided over the emergence of a new—spiritual—empire. In some respects this outshone that founded by Songtsen Gampo. Not only did it hold sway over the whole of Tibet, and much of Mongolia besides, but its accumulation of wealth, particularly as a result of its relations with the Mongolians and, to a lesser extent, the Manchus, generated unprecedented economic power as well. Lhasa, besides being a destination for Buddhist pilgrims from all over Inner Asia, became a major trading center. By now home to a mercantile community of Muslims from Kashmir (who, as we have seen, monopolized the trade in meat), it also sustained a community of Nepalese* artisans. There was even a small number of Armenians who dealt in pearls, amber, textiles, and, most important, in musk, which they exported all the way back to Europe. Importantly, this new wealth enabled the religious community to commission great works, including the translation and printing of scripture, paintings on silk (*thangkas*), wall hangings, fine carpets, frescoes, reliquaries, robes, statues, and castings in silver, gold, and bronze.

It was unfortunate that this expansion of Tibetan power should have coincided with the swift ascendancy of the Qing Dynasty. And it was still more unfortunate that it was Kangxi who had ascended the Dragon throne. But given that in all he did the Dalai Lama's primary concern was always with spiritual matters, it is not surprising that the more worldly Kangxi should, in due course, outmaneuver him and, in so doing, expose the fatal flaw that lay at the heart of the concept of the spiritual and temporal rule of Tibet by the Dalai Lamas.

In the meantime, however, Lobsang Gyatso's position was further strengthened following the deaths, within a week of one another, of Dayan Khan, who was nominally king, and Trinley Gyatso, the regent. Neither had proved effective leaders and their successors, the Mongolian Tenzin Dalai Khan and the monk

---

* Or, strictly, Newari.

Lobsang Thuthop,* proved no more capable of asserting themselves, and Lobsang Gyatso retained full authority over the workings of the Ganden Phodrang. This he exercised in countless ways. One significant innovation was his introduction and assiduous promotion of an official administrative language. The Dalai Lama's interest in poetics and his study of Sanskrit grammar led him to evolve a complex—some say verbose and convoluted—style of writing. This, he insisted, should be standard among all government and monastic offices. He also introduced similarly complex regulations concerning court protocol. Besides reintroducing national dress for all members of the government and its growing civil service (supplied mainly by members of the aristocracy), the Dalai Lama also established a strict system of seating according to status. Henceforth, all government and monastic officials, all members of the aristocracy, all tribal chieftains, and all *dzongpön* and laymen in government service were precisely ranked in order of precedence.

Lobsang Gyatso's power even extended to the ability to dismiss the regent himself. In 1675, word reached the Dalai Lama's ears that Lobsang Thuthop was keeping a mistress. This meant that, technically at least, he was no longer a monk. Although the Dalai Lama took a lenient view of the matter, the regent was forced to choose between giving up his office or dropping his paramour. Unable to forsake her, Lobsang Thuthop and his lady retired to an estate at Langri, in the south, where they lived respectably ever after.

The Dalai Lama now offered the position to the nephew of an earlier regent. This was Sangye Gyatso, a young and brilliant scholar who had been brought up at court from an early age. Given that Lobsang Thuthop, the previous regent, had just been dismissed on the grounds of misconduct, it is astonishing that there is a well-established tradition that holds Sangye Gyatso to

* Pronounced "Too-top."

have been the Fifth Dalai Lama's natural son. The present Dalai Lama's brother, for example, recounts this allegation in his auto-biography, suggesting in mitigation that the Fifth may not have actually professed his final vows as a monk (although the official biography states otherwise). One other possibility is that he "gave back" these vows at some point. This is the relatively informal means by which, in the Tibetan tradition, monastics may be released from their commitments. The renouncer simply has to find a person who understands the full implications of what is being said—not necessarily a person of authority, or even another monk—and inform them that they are "giving back" their vows. At any rate, refusing the honor, Sangye Gyatso excused himself on the grounds of extreme youth. He was just twenty-two years old. The Dalai Lama therefore appointed another monk as regent. This was Lobsang Jinpa, an ineffectual leader who did nothing to avert the tragedy that gradually began to envelop the Tibetan government.

The origins of this tragedy have their roots in the rebellion of Wu San Quei against the Qing Dynasty back in 1659. Originally a general in the Ming army, it was Wu who had delivered Beijing to the Manchus in an act of blatant treachery. But twenty years later, he had managed to regain the support of many of the remaining Ming sympathizers, as well as the backing of huge numbers of ordinary people, on account of their hatred of the Manchus. Having expelled all Chinese from Manchuria, the Manchus had confiscated large tracts of land from the peasantry. In addition, the government forbade intermarriage between Manchus and Chinese, and compelled all males to shave the front of their heads and wear their hair in the hated Manchu *queue*, or plait, behind. For their part, Manchu women were forbid-den to practice the foot-binding then widely in vogue among the Chinese. The two peoples were thus kept strictly segregated. Capitalizing on the great resentment this caused, Wu had, within another ten years, succeeded in gaining control of much of south-ern and western China.

In 1674, Kangxi sent an urgent request to the Dalai Lama to send troops to assist the imperial forces in Gyal'thang, which the rebel forces had unexpectedly penetrated.[10] This put the Dalai Lama in a difficult position. Firstly, he was fearful that all-out war involving Tibetan, Chinese, Manchus, and Mongolians could erupt. Secondly, from afar, it must have seemed eminently feasible that the rebellion should succeed. If that was the case, he could find himself on the losing side. Fearing for the safety of the Tibetan clergy then residing in China, the Fifth agreed in the end to send a small detachment of troops. But no sooner had he done so than he received a deputation from Wu San Quei himself. This placed the Dalai Lama in a serious quandary: should he or should he not receive this embassy? His closest advisers all counselled against. It would be dangerous to be seen to be entering into diplomatic relations with an enemy of the Qing. But, presumably acting on supernatural advice, Lobsang Gyatso did accept Wu's gifts, justifying his decision on the grounds that it is "the particularity of the followers of [the Buddha] to love all human beings."

When the commander of the Tibeto-Mongol force subsequently wrote to the Dalai Lama to the effect that the route into the theater of war was too dangerous and pleaded to be relieved of his duty, Lobsang Gyatso in turn memorialized the emperor. Explaining that it was too risky for his troops to go any further, he expressed his dismay at Wu San Quei's rebellion. Nonetheless, he besought the emperor to spare the rebel's life, suggesting that, if necessary, some territory be ceded to him. Of course, to the emperor this was unacceptable, if not insolence itself. The Dalai Lama was an ally of the Qing. He must therefore undertake whatever the emperor requested of him or he would lose the rights the alliance conferred on him—not least the trading rights. From the Dalai Lama's perspective, however, matters were not so clear-cut and he demurred. Unfortunately, the very troops whom Lobsang Gyatso had absolved from their duty to pursue Wu San Quei are next heard of forming an alliance on the ground with the rebels. They proceeded to attack and seize two Chinese cities in what today is Yunnan province.[11] This unexpected development naturally aroused the emperor's suspicions. Was the Dalai Lama playing a double game?

Following eventual victory over Wu in 1681, Kangxi ordered that a search be made for any letters between the upstart and the Dalai Lama. And from that moment on, he sought direct relations with the Mongol chieftains, rather than rely on the Dalai Lama to mediate between them. This meant usurping established procedure, but since the Dalai Lama could no longer be trusted, the emperor must find his own way of dealing with the Mongols.

An extraordinary prophetic vision that Lobsang Gyatso had experienced some time earlier—remarkably, one of the first after a gap of almost ten years—may perhaps have influenced the Dalai Lama in his pursuit of what turned out to be a mistaken course of action. Clad in Gelug yellow and wearing a yellow hat, Padmasambhava (traditionally seen as the founding father of the Nyingmapa, let it be remembered) appeared to the Dalai Lama holding a vase in both hands. Lobsang Gyatso, having been anointed by the Lotus Born, felt that he traveled along a white path to a mansion shaped like the belly of a vase. There he met with the deity Lokesvara, bright-bodied and clad in antelope skin. The deity proceeded to give a prophetic discourse on the political situation in China, Mongolia, Nepal, and Bhutan. Thereafter, the Dalai Lama felt himself to have ascended with the deity to the summit of a high crystal stupa. From this vantage point, he could see, in the east, a large number of houses occupied by people with two heads and four arms dancing about. To the south, he could see a blazing fire in the middle of a forest, with flames that reached up to the heavens. To the west, he could see, rising at the foot of a high outcrop of rock, a torrential jet of water, at the top of which a turquoise-colored girl was bathing. To the north, he saw—most perplexing of all—a creature with a human body but a yak's head take out its own heart and weep as it looked at it. The Dalai Lama then saw Lhasa, among the golden roofs of which a monkey wearing a yellow hat now laughed, now cried, before making off in the direction of Drepung. The Dalai Lama asked Lokesvara the meaning of these extraordinary sights, but the deity did not reply. Instead they both returned instantly to the Potala.[12]

The Dalai Lama's strained relations with Kangxi were not the only foreign-policy problem of Lobsang Gyatso's last years. Closer to home, the Bhutanese launched attacks on the Sikkim and Chumbi valley areas that lay on the southern fringes of Gelug-controlled territory. And, during the same year, 1676, relations between Lhasa and the generally friendly autonomous kingdom of Ladakh broke down when the king moved against a number of Gelug monasteries in western Tibet. Lobsang Gyatso responded to both incursions by deploying troops. He did so without bothering to inform Tenzin Dalai Khan, still nominally king, showing thereby that at this point his hold on power was absolute. The Bhutanese were forced by this means to withdraw without too much difficulty, but the Ladakh insurgency proved more troublesome. At great cost in terms of tribute, the Ganden Phodrang's forces were compelled to obtain an alliance with the Muslim rajah of Bahadur. Fortunately, the end result was entirely satisfactory. The treaty subsequently achieved by the Ganden Phodrang held up until the twentieth century.

News of the successful outcome of the campaign against Ladakh reached Lhasa during the spring of 1680. It brought to a fitting close Lobsang Gyatso's quarter of a century at the helm of the Ganden Phodrang. During this time the Lhasa government had successfully extended its influence throughout Tibet so that, although there remained large areas that were more or less autonomous, especially in Kham, there is no question that the Ganden Phodrang was the single most powerful force in the land. And thanks to the Dalai Lama's own prestige, there is likewise no question that his authority cut across sectarian boundaries and united the country more fully than it had been since the days of empire. It was to be fully two hundred years before another Dalai Lama even approached such a position of personal power. Now, however, Lobsang Gyatso was determined to stand down and devote the remainder of his life to religion. The now twenty-six-year-old scholar-monk Sangye Gyatso was persuaded, at the second time of asking, to accept political office, taking the title of Desi. This was a step up from mere regency. In this capacity, he would act as viceroy, an appointment which, the young man remarked, was like "placing an ox's burden on a cow's back." But it was clear that Lobsang Gyatso intended that the Desi should be the one to identify and educate the next Dalai Lama.

From the time of Sangye Gyatso's appointment until the Dalai Lama's death just three years later, Lobsang Gyatso was as good as his word and devoted himself to the religious life. To be sure, he continued to preside over countless ceremonies, to confer countless initiations, and to bestow countless blessings, while he received an uninterrupted stream of visitors both of high rank and low, giving and receiving large quantities of gifts. He continued as well to experience prophetic dreams and visions, and to undertake numerous divinations. As ever, he ordained large numbers of monks and tonsured important novices. He likewise sponsored and directed the foundation of new monasteries and kept a close watch on the good order of the whole Gelug estate. Beyond this, he remained constantly involved with the redistribution of surpluses to those areas needing support, making any number of tea offerings (a form of economic subsidy), while also making grants for the ornamentation of religious buildings, for the repair of roads and bridges, and the digging of canals. He also attended all the important festivals of the liturgical calendar while keeping up his literary activities and, of course, spending several hours every day in meditation. It was not much of a retirement. The wonder is that his health did not break down sooner than it did, sometime during the winter of 1680.

When it did so, there began immediately an extraordinary nationwide effort, directed by the regent, to persuade the gods to relent. Starting in the early part of 1681, almost the entire monastic community was co-opted into a spiritual campaign, the like of which is unlikely ever to have been seen before or since. The opening salvoes were fired by the Doenye Ling [Don-g Nis] Monastery whose 150 monks recited the *MigTseMa** no less than 21,750,000 times. This was followed by a recitation, undertaken by thousands of novice monks, in accordance with divinations conducted by the Dalai Lama himself, of all one hundred and more volumes of the Kangyur an auspicious 108 times, the *Perfection of Wisdom in Eight Thousand Lines* three times, the *Bhadracari* 199,500 times, the *Namasangiti* 59,300 times, the *Sadhana of the Goddess of the White Umbrella* 105,500 times, the *Heart of the Perfection of Wisdom* 149,300 times, the *Hymn to Tara* 1,043,600 times and the *Life Dharani* 9,533,000 times. Even thirty Bonpo monks "recited sixteen considerable Bon books thirty times."[13]

On top of this, forty-five thousand ceremonies in honor of the god of medicine were performed, and on a hundred different peaks, one hundred blue flagpoles were erected and hung with prayer flags. Sacrificial cakes were offered to the serpent deities in a thousand separate ceremonies, while the Dalai Lama himself ransomed the lives of one hundred yaks and released ten prisoners. Lobsang Gyatso also ordered a general distribution of tea to every monastery within central Tibet, without distinction

---

* A verse in praise of Tsongkhapa recited as a mantra by Gelugpas.

of sect, and demon traps were set, bridges repaired, and animals destined for slaughter purchased and set free.*

Alas, although this astonishing effort began to be repeated the following year, the Dalai Lama's health continued gradually to deteriorate until, on the twenty-fifth day of the second month of the Water Dog year—1682—Lobsang Gyatso, having "bestowed many personal instructions and teachings" on his innermost circle, withdrew, for a period lasting a full five days, into a state of equipoise. Then, on April 7, reckoning by the Christian calendar, he "went to the light of the lotus to the accompaniment of many wonderful signs, including a tent of rainbow lights in the sky above."

---

* Setting free animals destined for slaughter is considered by Buddhists a particularly meritorious activity. It was enthusiastically practiced by the present Dalai Lama as a boy—to such an extent that his court began to be concerned at the numbers of protected, and therefore unproductive, animals he was accumulating.

19

The Tibetan God the Father Who Puts to Death Such as Refuse to Adore Him: An Interlude

On the sixth day of the eighth month in the year of the Earth Dragon—that is, on October 8, 1661—a party of travelers reached Lhasa. Among their number were two Jesuit missionaries: Father Johannes Grueber, thirty-eight years old, an Austrian of "affable temper and extremely civil," and Father Albert d'Orville, a Belgian of noble birth, also thirty-eight, who had spent two years at the court of the Duke of Lorraine before giving up the world to become a priest. The two men are credited with being the first Europeans ever to set foot in Tibet's holy city. Whether they remained in Lhasa for one month or two is unclear, but it was just long enough to misconstrue everything they saw.

Neither Grueber nor d'Orville left a proper account of their historic journey across the roof of the world. D'Orville was so exhausted when they reached the Jesuit community in Agra sometime during March the following year that he failed to rise from his bed the next day. There he remained until he died a few weeks later, on Easter eve 1662. Grueber lived another twenty years or so, but despite frequent promises, he never did get around to writing up his journal. A pity indeed, though perhaps we should not be too disappointed. As a later explorer of Tibet wrote, Grueber "had a bird's sense of the lie of the land, but he lacked the bird's blithe tongue." The short account of his adventures we do have is "arid as the Himalayan uplands."

Grueber did, however, correspond with Athanasius Kircher, another Jesuit and subsequently author of a celebrated study of China, popularly known as *China Illustrata*. This provides a fascinating insight of Christendom's first encounter with Tibet. In it, Kircher gives a brief and lurid account of Grueber and d'Orville's journey. He tells how the two men were "refreshed by the strange and wonderful sight" of the wildlife they encountered, the "tigers, lions, elephants, rhinoceri, leopards, sylvestran bulls, and unicorns," the last of which, he adds, "are a certain type of horned ass." He also mentions the thinness of the air they encountered, adding Grueber's opinion that it is impossible to cross one particular mountain in summer without mortal danger, due to "the noxious exhalations" of certain plants.

Kircher, following Grueber, states that there were two kings of Tibet. One of these is called the "Deva"—i.e., the then regent. The other is the "Great Lama," who resides in a citadel where he is "removed from the bother of all extraneous affairs and enjoys leisure in the secret solitudes of his palace." Grueber, rather charmingly, calls this building "the Pietala" instead of the Potala, and Kircher reproduces Grueber's sketch of the Dalai Lama's residence. It perplexes scholars to this day. In the foreground, there is shown a strange wheeled contraption. Yet, so far as we know, and indeed as far as they can remember, Tibetans have never used the wheel. Of course, they knew of it—they had seen it in both India and China for a start—but we have no evidence save Grueber's that it was used in Tibet to provide a means of transport prior to the Chinese invasion of 1949–50. Nevertheless, Heinrich Harrer, a fellow Austrian, who escaped internment by the British during the Second World War and famously spent seven years in Tibet, reported having seen, while working on a construction site, blocks of stone so large he was convinced they could only have been transported on wheels.

Grueber's account of the Tibetan religion, as recorded by Kircher, strikes a modern reader as hilarious. He looks as though he had no idea that Tibetans followed the teachings of the Buddha, but thought instead that they worshipped a nine-headed "idol" called Manipe. "The stupid people worship before this idol, making unusual gestures and performing their rites while repeating over and over, '*O Manipe mi hum, O Manipe mi hum,*' that is, 'Manipe save us.'"[1]

Grueber was full of bile toward the "ridiculous" and, in some cases, "even detestable" customs and institutions of Tibet. He was especially scandalized by his discovery that the most highly prized medicine in the Tibetan pharmacopeia was the Great Lama's excreta: "The man counts himself blessed who can obtain some . . . they quite stupidly think that they will remain perfectly healthy [by means of it]—what abominable filth!" Nevertheless, it seems that the two missionaries were kindly received by the people. It even appears they could have met with the Dalai Lama himself, save only that they were prevented by religious scruple. They were concerned that prostrating themselves before him would be unbecoming of their office as Catholic priests.

Grueber's lack of understanding is partly explained by the fact that the two priests' visit was merely by way of a stopover. They were attempting, for the first time in three centuries, the overland journey from Peking to the Holy See in Rome. (The last time this had been accomplished successfully was in 1330 when the Blessed Oderic of Pordenone, traveling via China and Mongolia, reached Avignon, where the Pope was then seated.) Both

Grueber and d'Orville had originally been appointed to the Jesuit mission in China, where they worked for two years, and it was intended that Grueber at least would return to Peking, should they be successful in their task. There was every chance that they might not be, but it was worth the risk of martyrdom to try for two pressing reasons. First, the sea journey was so dangerous that it is reckoned only one missionary in six actually made it all the way in either direction. Many of the ships sank. Sickness took the rest. Of his seventeen fellow missionaries who left Lisbon on the same vessel as d'Orville, two died, one went mad, and a fourth was paralyzed by the time they reached Goa, approximately the halfway point. The second, more urgent, reason for their journey was that Dutch privateers (Protestants all, and sworn enemies of the Jesuits) were blockading China's ports at the time. It was essential to establish some other means of communication with Rome.[2]

The original scheme was for the two priests to travel via Central Asia, as had Oderic during the time of the Mongol Empire. There was the hope that, in doing so, they might be able to establish an outpost at Samarkand on the way. This would serve as a resting-place and, perhaps, as another vantage point for the saving of heathen souls. In the event, and for reasons that are unclear, they forsook their original route, which was to have followed the northern branch of the old Silk Road. Their stay at Lhasa was thus entirely unplanned, and there was never any intention to attempt the conversion of Tibet. But had it been, Kircher noted, Grueber was certain they could have won thousands of souls for God since, as he explained—disregarding its outward form—the Tibetan religion "tallies in all essential points" with the Christian faith. To this unexpected claim, he is reported to have added, referring to the Dalai Lama, that he foresaw but one obstacle—"that devilish God the Father who puts to death such as refuse to adore him."[*]

---

[*] Actually, he said no such thing. This famous quotation is Astley's abridgement of Kircher and is completely without authority.

It is clear that Grueber had only the haziest grasp of everything he saw and experienced in Tibet—he probably lacked a
good interpreter. As a result, another sixty-five years were to
pass before the Holy Office in Rome received an accurate
account of Tibet. This was contained in the 643-page report
prepared by Father Ippolito Desideri, another Jesuit. The Society of Jesus (to give the Jesuits their full title) had originally
founded a mission in southern Tibet back in 1624, but it was
closed barely a decade later. The risks were considered too
great, and success too far from certain, to justify keeping it
open. It seems that the young Desideri was so struck with all
he had heard about Tibet that, while he was still a student in
Rome, he dreamed of reopening the mission. In the event, he
spent just less than seven years in Tibet, two of them in Lhasa,
between 1715 and 1722.[*]

During this time, Desideri made not a single convert. That
was to have come later. Instead he immersed himself first in
studying the Tibetan language, and then the scriptures. Astonishing as it will seem to anyone who has attempted the same,
he had mastered both of these sufficiently well to have been
able to compose, within just eighteen months of his arrival, the
first of what was eventually to be five volumes, written in classical Tibetan, refuting Buddhist doctrine.[†] As he explained
when he subsequently presented his work at the Tibetan court,
Desideri was motivated by his conviction that those who
subscribed to Buddhist beliefs were "in extreme error." He was
concerned, he said, to point out to them "the precipices down
which they were falling to their irreparable doom."

Yet Desideri, unlike Grueber before him, was profoundly
respectful of the culture he encountered. He abominated the

---

[*] Desideri crossed into Tibet on May 30, 1715 and left on December 17, 1721.
See Hosten, *A Missionary in Tibet*, p. 75, and de Filippi, *An Account of Tibet*, p. 312.
[†] The present Dalai Lama has read three of them. He described them to me
as being "very impressive."

Tibetan religion, but wrote frequently of his admiration both of the people and of their faith. For this reason, his *Breve e succinto ragguaglio,* describing his experiences in Tibet, remains a valuable document. For while others have written in greater detail, none can rival Desideri's firsthand experience.

Describing the Tibetan people, Desideri says that they are "by nature kindly and courteous." They have "a vivacious intellect and are ingenious and clever," as well as being both "virtuous and devout." With regard to Tibetans' religious practice of their faith, he can hardly contain himself:

> To begin with, not only are they well grounded in their belief, but they speak about it often with great affection and conscientiousness. Secondly, they have the greatest esteem, veneration, and respect for their lamas and monks; would to God that the Christian Catholics showed one-hundredth part of such sentiments to the Prelates, Ecclesiastics, and Religious of our holy Catholic Church! Thirdly, they are most diligent in learning long prayers by heart, and never neglect to pray in the morning when they rise, or at night when they go to bed. Fourthly, they are much given to reading and listening to religious and moral books. Fifthly, they are most attentive in . . . making pilgrimages to holy places, and are most respectful and devout in their behavior when they visit the temples. Sixthly, they often tell their beads, even when engaged in business, or out walking, or on journeys. Seventhly and finally . . . they show it in the liberal alms they give to the monks, the poor, and even to animals in the streets if they think they are starving, and in the care they take to bestow the first handful of their harvests on the poor, or to make offerings to their idols ere they eat or drink themselves.[3]

Regarding the scriptures, Desideri is again highly complimentary, while of Tibetan Buddhist ethical precepts, he is satisfied that in most respects they "agree with our moral laws." Speaking of prayer and meditation, Desideri notes that "the Thibettans not only have treatises and admirable rules about contemplation, but many follow them." He adds that "the rules prescribing that they are not to give way to indolence or to be alarmed at difficulties," or what he calls "dryness" in prayer, "are most excellent." It is only when Desideri describes Buddhist cosmology that he somewhat startles the modern reader: "I must tell you that this people believe the earth to be flat and circular." Yet Desideri does not scoff. He goes on to give an entirely respectful summary of *abhidharma* cosmology, the traditional Buddhist account of the nature and origins of the universe.

It is worth giving a brief overview of this cosmology, since, although modern Buddhist writers downplay its importance, traditionally it was this view of the universe to which every educated Tibetan subscribed, not to mention millions of others throughout the Far East. And while, like the Genesis story of Creation, it is not often taken literally these days, the *abhidharma* conception of the universe continues to exert an influence over ordinary Buddhists in traditional Buddhist societies. It also forms the heart of the mental landscape from which the Dalai Lamas emerged.

The relevant scriptures describe each universe, or "world system"—of which there are said to be no less than a thousand million—as an immense iron cylinder, the surface of which is roughly 2.7 million miles across. This contains, first, a layer of water that is likewise some 2.7 million miles deep. Then comes a layer of gold about 1.5 million miles deep, above which is another layer of water approximately 360,000 miles deep.* From the center of the cylinder rises a mountain, Sumeru,† to a height of 80,000 *yojanas*. This mountain has four slab sides and is somewhat wider

---

* The actual unit of measurement is a *yojana*, one unit of which is equivalent to something like four and a half miles, a distance that Desideri describes as a league.
† Literally, King of Mountains.

at its summit than at its base. Surrounding it are seven concentric mountain ranges, all made of gold, each of them half the height of the previous one, and separated from it by an ocean. The oceans are likewise half as far across as the previous one, and "vary in flavor and color, salt, sweet, like milk and so on."

Beyond the last, and lowest, mountain range lies the outer ocean in which are situated four groups of three island continents, one group at each of the four cardinal points of the compass. The earth as we know it is, in fact, the middle island of the group that lies to the south of Mount Sumeru. The reason we do not see this great world mountain is that it is far away and surrounded by clouds. Moreover, each of its four sides comprises one of the four precious elements—gold, silver, crystal, and lapis lazuli—and the southern continents look on to that face of Mount Sumeru which is of lapis, the color of the sky.

Of the four continental groups themselves, little is known. According to the sources used by Desideri, the northern continents are "without religion . . . only men of inferior merit are born there." They are happy throughout their lives—save for the last seven days, when the misery they endure far exceeds anything we humans know in a lifetime. It is also said that the northern continents are square in shape and that their inhabitants likewise have square faces.

As to the other continents, the western islands are circular in shape, like the sun. The people who inhabit them are giants, with round faces, who eat mostly butter and cheese, on account of the enormous number of cattle they have. The easternmost continents are crescent-shaped, like a half-moon, and the people who live there have—naturally—half-moon-shaped faces. These eat mainly rice and vegetables.

The southern continents are triangular in shape. Among them is our own world system. The island on which we humans live is called Dzambu Ling. It is unique in that beneath it are found the hell realms: eight of them hot, eight of them cold. Not that these hells are the only destiny of the damned. Those whose misdeeds are inspired principally by ignorance are reborn in the animal realm. There, in a mirror image of their human lives, they are ruled by the instincts for food and reproduction. Those who in their earthly existence are driven by greed are reborn as *yidags*, or "hungry ghosts." These strange creatures inhabit the underworld, perpetually tormented by their inability to satisfy their hunger. They are envisaged, Desideri tells us, as having mouths "the size of the eye of a needle. Their neck is large and many miles long, their eyes emit pestiferous and fiery gases which dry up everything, and their bellies are huge."

The hell realms themselves are the destiny of those whose lives are given over to anger and hate. Evidently impressed, Desideri gives a very detailed report of them, and of their various tortures. No doubt he has in the back of his mind Dante's Inferno with its nine circles; only Dante's hell is bloodless in comparison. The first of the Buddhist hells, which is situated 32,000 *yojanas*—around 145,000 miles—beneath the earth's surface, is a hell of perpetual return. The damned, armed with the ill deeds they committed in life, fight one another to the death, whereupon "a voice from heaven cries aloud, 'Arise!'" at which, somewhat in the manner of Sisyphus, they come to life again and continue fighting.

The second hell is the Hell of Black Lines (*T[h]ig nag*). It is so-called on account of its guardians, who draw black lines on the bodies of the damned before cutting them into pieces in accordance with their demonic draftsmanship. Naturally enough, the torments of each successively lower hell become more refined so that by the time we reach the sixth hell, the custodians "seize the damned, throw them into . . . large cauldrons [and] boil them like fish. They then impale them on red-hot iron stakes until their intestines obtrude and flames burst forth from their eyes, mouths, ears, and the pores of their skin." In the lowest realm, the sinners are having poured down their throats boiling copper, "which penetrates to their intestines and flows through the body."

So far as the freezing hells are concerned, the principal torments, Desideri tells us, are "intensely icy-cold winds, frozen pools, the rending of flesh, and"—somewhat prosaically—"the chattering of teeth."

Above ground, the great mountain Sumeru has four tiers, each corresponding to a different realm. These four realms are the abode of the *lha'ma'yin*, or "jealous gods"—themselves in fact more than one type of being. Not all authorities agree as to which type lives in which realm, but included among them are the *yakshas*, pot-bellied dwarves who guard celestial treasure; the *rakshas* and the *danavas*, both of which look more like oriental goblins; the *kumbhanas*, which again are dwarves, but with enormous testicles; and the *pishacas*, a kind of cannibalistic demon. Of each of these hideous creatures, there are countless legions—far outnumbering the human population of Dzambu Ling. They in turn are under the authority of the gods of the Four Directions. These, as their name implies, are the chiefs of each of the four sides of Sumeru. Among these, the god of the northern face, and thus of the northern continents, Kuru, is the god of wealth. According to the testimony of the Dalai Lama's eldest brother, it was this god to whom the monastery of which he was abbot would pray when in material need.

On the summit of Sumeru stands the city of Sudarsana, (Wondrous to Behold). Here reside the thirty-three chief gods of the world, each of them occupying one of the palaces arranged symmetrically around that of their leader, Indra. This palace is encircled by a hundred and one jeweled turrets and its grounds are encompassed by a golden wall. The earth on which it is built is described as being soft as cotton, and also made of gold. But although the thirty-three chief gods live splendidly, their condition is not to be envied. They spend their time fighting, both among themselves and with the *lha'ma'yin* of the lower realms. The fact that all these so-called jealous gods live on Sumeru means that their condition is, by definition, more exalted than that of human beings. But when they die, as all must eventually, they are often reborn in the hell realms.

The blissful gods, or *devas*, which occupy the heavens, of which there are twenty-four rising above Sumeru, enjoy a more enviable existence: their principal mental state is exultation. There are three groupings among the heavens. The first six are known as the heavens of the Desire Realm. They are so-called because the beings that reside there have, like us, a full complement of six senses (consciousness itself being considered a sense). They continue to know suffering, albeit that the higher the heaven, the more subtle its sufferings. Above the heavens of the Desire Realm come the sixteen heavens of the Form Realm, which are occupied by gods that, besides consciousness, have only sight, hearing, and touch. This want of the other senses is not a lack, however, but rather a mark of their spiritual perfection. The senses are the gateway of pleasure and pain, and thus of suffering.

Far, far above the great world mountain, above and beyond the realms of pure form, rise the four heavens of the Formless Realm. First comes that of infinite space. Then comes that of infinite consciousness. Then comes the heaven of nothingness. After nothingness comes the highest heaven of all, that of neither consciousness nor unconsciousness.* Yet although existence in this exalted realm is blissful to a degree we humans cannot even begin to imagine, it is still, according to Buddhist belief, unsatisfactory. It remains within Samsara. That is to say, it remains within cyclic existence, where the individual stays caught up within the dynamic of cause and effect. This means that even those beings which reside in the highest of the heavens are

---

* Or, in Sanskrit, *nevasannanasannayata*.

subject to the effects of their past actions. The gods occupying them can still be pitched to the lowest hell. Even they must, like the rest of us, age, die, and be reborn, though they may live for as long as eighty-four thousand eons.

But while it is theoretically possible for any being, whether human or god, to be reborn in any one of the so-called Six Realms—as hell-being, animal, hungry ghost, jealous god or blissful god—access to the Form and Formless Realms is open only to spiritual practitioners who have attained a high degree of progress.

The means by which beings attain any one of the thirty-one realms within Samsara, or for that matter life on any one of the twelve island continents, is, of course, through the mechanism of what Desideri called the "Pythagorean doctrine of metempsy-chosis," or rebirth. In Desideri's view, this was a scandalous notion. In common with his fellow missionaries, he was convinced that it was this belief which lay behind the high levels of infan-ticide they encountered in the East, especially in China. Very poor people would kill their children in the hope that they would be reborn to wealthier families, and if they were girls, that they might be reborn as boys.

The other problem with the doctrine so far as Desideri was concerned was what he took to be its irrationality. Surprising as it may seem to modern sensibilities, Buddhism has no answer to what in the Western tradition is arguably the most funda-mental question of all: why is there something rather than noth-ing? To this, the Buddhist will only answer that the world and all that is in it exists on account of the past actions of countless sentient beings. There was thus no beginning: no act of Creation and no Big Bang to inaugurate the absolute beginning of every-thing. Before this universe came into being, there existed another. Before that, another—and so on in infinite regression. The diffi-culty here, as the Jesuits saw it, is that if, as Buddhists believe, "I" come into being as the result of my past actions, it follows that my actions are antecedent to me—a proposition which, says Desideri, is "manifestly absurd."

In fact, Tibetans accept two types of rebirth. The first is the ordinary process whereby individual sentient beings from any one of the Six Realms are endlessly reborn until such time as they become fully enlightened Buddhas, thereby escaping Samsara. The other type is the means by which beings who are highly evolved spiritually are able to choose the circumstances of each successive birth in order to be able to serve all other sentient beings to the maximum extent possible. This is "reincarnation." The Dalai Lamas themselves are the preeminent examples of such beings. Thus when the present Dalai Lama departs this life (also, it is held, a matter of choice), he is able to decide where, when, and to whom he will be reborn.

Except that, in the case of the Sixth, there was considerable confusion as to what that choice was. There were in fact three "Sixth" Dalai Lamas.

20

The Scandalous Sixth

Among the instructions that the Great Fifth imparted on his
deathbed was one which was to have disastrous consequences.
He announced that his demise should be kept secret. According to the viceroy, or Desi, the Fifth set no time limit to this
subterfuge. Others maintained that he specified a limit of twelve
years. According to them, it was because this limit was exceeded
that misfortune befell both the Sixth Dalai Lama and the Desi
himself.

It is not difficult to see why Lobsang Gyatso might have
deemed it prudent that the Desi maintain the fiction that he
was still alive. The memory of the rebellion that broke out following the death of Gushri Khan was no doubt one good reason.
Another was of course the fact that, however soon the Sixth
might be found, it would be many years before he could be
expected to assume responsibility for affairs of state. And while
Desi Sangye Gyatso might be an effective leader in his own
right, he lacked the prestige that was attached to the Dalai Lama
himself. This was especially so thanks to the Fifth's lifelong
promotion of the cult of Chenrezig. Instead of making known

the mournful news of the Precious Protector's demise, the Desi therefore gave out that the Dalai Lama, having recovered from his illness, had withdrawn on indefinite retreat. To assist him in this ploy, he recruited a monk from Namgyal Monastery who bore a passing resemblance to the Fifth, whom effectively he imprisoned within the Dalai Lama's private quarters. On those occasions when there was no alternative to allowing important visitors to have audience of the Dalai Lama, this monk would take up position and perform the customary polite ceremonies of receiving and blessing supplicants. The rest of the time, the unfortunate impostor remained in almost total seclusion, chanting the scriptures, sounding drum and cymbal, and, at least ostensibly, meditating. From time to time, he threatened revolt and, we are told, was only kept at his post with a mixture of bribery and beatings.[1]

How well and for precisely how long the secret was kept is open to conjecture. The Fifth died in 1682, but Emperor Kangxi did not learn the truth until 1696, and even then it had not been officially announced. On the other hand, it is clear that many had their suspicions. The young reincarnation of one of the Fifth's Nyingma tutors who went in to receive a new name was asked to describe the Dalai Lama. The boy reported that he wore a hat of some sort, and an eyepatch. Lobsang Gyatso was well known to be almost completely bald and to have large protruding eyes. The inference is, of course, that the stand-in had neither of these attributes.

The Desi, meanwhile, took on his appointment as de facto head of state with great gusto. Already well established as an eminent scholar, he followed closely the example of his late master, commissioning public works and contributing extensively to the cultural life of his times. So far as affairs of state were concerned, he was so assiduous in the discharge of his duties that he would often turn up unannounced in different government offices. It soon became customary to keep a place for him at every meeting. He even went so far as to go out among the people in disguise in his quest to know all and everything that was being said and done in the capital.* Inevitably, it was not long before the Desi's incognito forays became notorious. People began to be wary of speaking their mind in public. On one occasion, however, the Desi is said to have fallen in with a drunkard whose opinion of the government he asked. "My business is drinking," replied the drunkard. "All other business is the Desi's."

The Desi, in addition to his scholarly, literary, and political activities, was also something of a man of action. Each year during the Monlam Chenmo, he would participate in the archery contests that took place alongside the feasting and merrymaking of the lay populace. It is reported that no one ever succeeded in shooting an arrow further than him. It is also said that Sangye Gyatso was something of a champion in the exercise of his one known weakness. At some indeterminate point, he "gave back" his monastic vows and took two official wives. But, in addition, of the "noble ladies of Lhasa and those who came there from the provinces, there was not a single one whom [he] did not take to bed."[2]

The Desi's principal task was, of course, to identify the new Dalai Lama. He was assisted in this by several detailed dreams he experienced, which were, in turn, corroborated by the oracles.† These all indicated strongly that the new incarnation should be sought in southern central Tibet. The Desi therefore appointed

* His disguise must have included some form of headgear, given that his nickname was Desi *Go'leb*, or Desi Flat Head, otherwise he would have been recognized easily.
† Here it is worth noting that the oracles are by no means straightforward communicators. To begin with, the actual mode of delivery presents its own difficulties. The Tenma oracle, for example, does not speak, but sings. The Gadong oracle is presently, and unaccountably, mute (though the medium certainly does go into trance). And Dorje Drakden's pronouncements issue in a sort of high-pitched whimper, delivered in short, sobbing bursts. And even when deciphered, the oracles' pronouncements then have to be interpreted.

two trusted monk officials to visit each of the major shrines of that area, explaining to them that they were looking for the reincarnations of two other recently deceased lamas, and telling them that they should investigate any promising leads.

The boy they were in fact looking for had been born on the first day of the third month of the year of the Water Pig—1683— a year and six days after the death of Lobsang Gyatso. His father was a married Nyingma lama belonging to the lineage of Pemalingpa (1450–1520), a great Nyingma saint who, like Ozer, was a celebrated treasure-revealer. The boy's mother was from a noble family, although she received no benefit from her patrimony. On the contrary, she was in litigation with various other members of her family over some land to which she had a claim. As a result, the family was poor, and, somewhat inconveniently, they lived right on the border with Bhutan, at Urgyen Ling.*

Initial indications that the child was exceptional included the fact that for three days after birth he did not suckle at his mother's breast. It was assumed that he was fasting. Also, and tellingly, his grandfather dreamed that the baby was constantly surrounded and protected by heavenly beings. Then, at a very early age, the boy fell ill with some unspecified malady. His face became so swollen that he could not open his eyes. His recovery, it was generally agreed, was thanks to the intervention of the protector deity Dorje Drakden. As a result of these remarkable phenomena, it was inevitable that people began to wonder whether the child might not be someone special. This was heightened when some Drukpa-Kagyu clergy began to take an interest in the boy— an unhealthy interest from the point of view of his father, it

*Tibetans note that the temple at which the Sixth's father officiated lay precisely on the route taken by the Fourteenth Dalai Lama on his flight into exile in 1959. Remarkably, Bhutan also had a corpse as its official head of state at the end of the seventeenth century. Shabdrung Nawang Namgyal's death had, like the Great Fifth's, gone unannounced, suggesting that this was not an uncommon practice. What is especially surprising in his case is the fact that he died in 1651 and was not officially succeeded until 1705.

seems. We are told that Nyingma black rites were performed in order to protect him from them. When, however, the boy came to the attention of the local Gelug clergy, they immediately took him into custody and placed him in a local government staging post at Sha'uk, right on the southernmost edge of the Ganden Phodrang's territory. These monks assumed he must be the reincarnation of an important local lama—despite the fact that the boy repeatedly denied that he was the lama in question.

As soon as the Desi came to hear of the child, he ordered him moved to the Ganden Phodrang's district headquarters at Tsona on the other (northern) side of the main Himalayan range. There, the future Dalai Lama began what turned out to be almost twelve years spent under what amounted to house arrest. His situation was rendered significantly worse by the fact that the two local governors responsible for him had, quite independently, taken sides against his mother in the litigation she had brought against her family. The young prodigy thus became a pawn in an ugly local power game. To add to his misery, Tsona itself was probably little different then from the "filthy, wind-swept . . . village of close on a hundred hovels scarcely fit for human habitation" described by a British botanist who passed that way during the late 1920s.[3] There was very little food for the boy and his family, and no fire—even though it was the height of winter. It was as if they were being kept in the "prison pit of the Lord of Death" himself.

To begin with, there was no suggestion that the boy was of especially high birth, because the two-man search party dispatched by the Desi had not yet arrived in the area. Not even the arrival of letters enquiring after the boy's health and bearing the seal of the Great Fifth himself shook the governors into treating him any better. Presumably they found it difficult to imagine that this down-at-heel household could produce even a minor *tulku*, let alone the reincarnation of a great saint.

This low opinion was actually confirmed by the visit of the

Desi's two-man search party, which finally reached Tsona during the early spring of 1686. Their meeting with the boy was a complete failure. Far from seeming to be anything out of the ordinary, he appeared confused and took no interest in the rosary belonging to the Great Fifth they showed him. Unsurprisingly, it was decided that he could not possibly be a serious candidate, and the two officials left to continue the search elsewhere. Unexpectedly, however, when they reached the great monastery of Samye, some divinations they performed suggested that the boy from Urgyen Ling had been the right one after all. This seemed to be confirmed when, on the return journey to Lhasa, the senior of the two lamas fell sick and dreamed that the investigations at Tsona had not been carried out correctly. All this they duly reported to the Desi. He, acting in accordance with his own personal investigations, therefore sent them back to Tsona—three weeks' hard travel to the southeast of the capital—where they were to undertake an exhaustive re-examination of the boy, this time telling them of his possible identity.

On the fifth day of the fifth month, the lamas arrived back at the *dzong* where, in spite of the scoffing and evident contempt of the two governors, they proceeded to propitiate the guardian deities. At the end of each day's ritual, they presented the boy with an item that had belonged to the Great Fifth, together with other, similar, objects. On each occasion, the boy responded faultlessly. By the end of the week he had correctly identified a ritual dagger, a figurine of Padmasambhava in union with his consort, a book (entitled *The Cow's Udder*), a crown, a knife, a horn used in magical rites, and a porcelain bowl. Finally, when shown a picture of the Great Fifth and asked who it was, the child pointed to himself with the word "me." There could no longer be any doubt that this was the boy they were looking for and "the two examiners shed tears involuntarily as happiness and sorrow vied with each other."

From that moment on, the family's situation improved considerably, although, on the Desi's instructions, the examiners kept to themselves the child's true identity. It was announced only that he was the reincarnation of an important lama. But if the family's material conditions improved somewhat, their lives were still full of anguish. They remained quartered at Tsona under the same two governors. And from now on, the little Dalai Lama lived separately from his parents—albeit within the same building—with the result that they saw very little of one another. This was a matter of enduring resentment on the part of his mother, who was forced to give up her son to two monk attendants left behind by the search party. He was still just three years old.

For the next ten years, therefore, the new Dalai Lama remained uncomfortably situated "halfway between the highest honors and remote oblivion," while the Desi took responsibility for his upbringing.[4] The boy's education began when a tutor was appointed to introduce him to the scriptures and to teach him how to read. A second tutor was appointed in 1690 to oversee his development as a scholar within the Gelug tradition, and twice a year the two lamas who had successfully identified him visited, in order to check up on the boy's progress and to report back directly to the Desi.

In the meantime, the discovery of the Great Fifth's successor was kept a momentous secret known only to the Desi and his most intimate circle. One important reason for continued secrecy was the construction of the Red Palace, a vast new complex being built alongside the original White Palace of the Potala. The Desi seems to have thought that this would be threatened if the truth of Lobsang Gyatso's demise were known, but perhaps a more compelling reason for secrecy lay in the foreign policy adventures in which, by this time, the Desi was deeply involved. While the Great Fifth (as he was now generally known) was still alive, another major threat to the Qing had emerged from within the Mongol heartlands. Galdan Khan was the latest in a long line of Mongol chieftains to lay claim to the legacy of the great Genghis. But whereas in the past, each pretender had contented himself with a vision of unifying the Mongol tribes, Galdan was more ambitious. Taking religion as his rallying point, he sought to create a pan-Buddhist alliance with which to confront the Qing. This was to include the whole of Tibet and her dependencies, alongside all those Mongol tribes that had converted to the faith. It was a vision to which the Great Fifth not only lent his support but in which he became intimately involved, for Galdan was in fact a *tulku*, a reincarnate lama whom he, Lobsang Gyatso, had personally recognized and tutored at Drepung Monastery.[5]

During 1671, Galdan's brother, Sangye—chieftain of the Dzungar tribe—was murdered by their two stepbrothers. With the Dalai Lama's approval, Galdan therefore abandoned his monastic vocation in order to avenge himself of this death in accordance with established Mongol procedure. Presumably the stepbrothers had assumed that the healing balm of the *buddhadharma* would, as it were, encourage Galdan to turn the other cheek and remain at his post in the monastery. They paid heavily for their miscalculation. One was himself murdered. The other was forced to flee into the arms of the Qing emperor.

Now although it fell to Galdan to avenge his brother's death, it did not follow that he would succeed to the leadership of the Dzungars. Instead, this honor went to the dead khan's nephew, who became, in turn, the third person to suffer Galdan's change of vocation. He was assassinated during 1676. Now khan himself, Galdan sought next to establish the Dzungars as the preeminent tribe among the Mongols. This he did firstly by annexing the land of various neighboring Mongol tribes and then by subduing the Uighurs, who had briefly been subjects of the Tibetan religious kings, and who were presently rulers of the culturally Islamic oases of western Sinkiang. By 1679, he was in a position to bid for the khanate of the western Mongols. In this he faced one major obstacle, however. Like Altan Khan before him, Galdan was not directly descended from Genghis Khan, and only those who were had a right to claim the succession. Galdan therefore applied to his mentor, the Dalai Lama, for help in achieving his lofty aim. Lobsang Gyatso responded by conferring on him the title Boshugtu Khan—Khan by Divine Grace. Thus equipped, Galdan declared himself khan of the western Mongols and continued to expand his empire as far afield as Siberia until, in 1688, he was ready to take on the might of the Mongols' eastern Khalka federation. Using a supposed slighting of the Dalai Lama's honor as a pretext, he inflicted such a heavy defeat on them that more than one hundred and forty thousand were forced to flee and seek the protection of the Qing.

Because Galdan kept up the fiction of his personal loyalty to Emperor Kangxi, the latter was reluctant to send troops against him, preferring instead to put pressure on the Dalai Lama to mediate. The greatest danger from the Qing perspective was the possibility that Galdan would forge a successful alliance with tsarist Russia and then take his troops into China proper. On the other hand, it was obvious to Kangxi that the Dzungars were bitterly divided among themselves. On more than one occasion, Galdan's troops fought with those of his own nephews. It was thus not until 1690 that Galdan clashed directly with the Qing army in an engagement that, although the official Chinese records claim victory for the emperor, was in reality at best a draw. Four years later still, when Galdan, impelled by a drought in the Dzungar pasturelands, attacked the Khalka remnant which had pledged loyalty to the Qing, Kangxi determined to deal with the upstart once and for all. Personally leading an army of some eighty thousand troops, the emperor set out in pursuit of the Mongolian chieftain, finally catching up with him at Jao Modo in 1696. Hopelessly outnumbered, Galdan was soundly beaten. He himself escaped with a handful of loyal soldiers, but his losses ran into thousands killed and wounded, with thousands more taken prisoner. And it was from these prisoners that the emperor learned, as he put it in a personal account of the affair, of "the strange story of how the Dalai Lama had in truth been dead for over nine* years, and how the Tripa† had covered this up and forced the Panchen Lama to go along with him, and how they had issued a false prophecy in the Dalai Lama's name: 'Galdan will be successful if he goes to the east.'"[6] Galdan committed suicide a year after his defeat.

No doubt the Desi judged that if the Great Fifth's death had become generally known, there was risk of harm to Tibet's favorable relationship with Galdan. Furthermore, had Galdan been successful in his aim to unite the Mongols under the spiritual leadership of the Dalai Lama, the potential benefit to the Ganden Phodrang must have seemed to outweigh the risk of the maneuver being detected. But it cannot have been any surprise to the Desi that, on discovering Sangye Gyatso's subterfuge, Kangxi should write reprimanding him in the strongest possible terms, threatening to order his armies in Yunnan, Sichuan, and Sha'anxi to march on Tibet.[7] In response, the Desi wrote a conciliatory, if still guarded and somewhat duplicitous, letter congratulating the emperor on his victory, adding that "to the misfortune of all his subjects, the Fifth Dalai Lama passed away in the Water Dog year. For fear of unrest among Tibetans, his death was not announced. His reincarnation is now fifteen years old and has been scheduled to be enthroned . . . in the Ox year. I beg Your Majesty to keep that a secret."[8] The emperor, though annoyed, seems at first to have agreed to this last request and to have been satisfied with the Desi's explanation. For reasons that are unclear, he subsequently changed his mind, made an official pronouncement on the subject and dispatched troops to Tibet.

---

* It was actually fifteen.
† It was actually the regent, of course.

On hearing this, the Desi was naturally perturbed. He began to fear that the emperor had decided after all to carry out his threat to invade. Accordingly, the Desi called for an enormous liturgical effort comprising both propitiatory rites to the guardian deities and the manufacture by Bonpo magicians of *btso*, or supernatural "bombs," to be thrown in the direction of the enemy. When eventually it transpired that the emperor had only sent a party of officials to congratulate the new Dalai Lama on his forthcoming installation, no doubt all agreed that this mystical campaign had been a complete success.

In the meantime, the Desi had finally broken the news of the death and rediscovery of the Dalai Lama to the government and people. This he did by composing, and causing to be read in public, a work entitled *A Feast for the Ears*.* There were three versions, each designed for a different audience: one, the complete, unabridged text, for lamas and high officials; a mid-length one for the generality of clergy; and a shortened version for the common people. It seems that the young Dalai Lama himself only learned of his true identity by reading the *Feast* some time during 1696. The two governors in whose care he remained were not shown it until the following summer, however. Predictably, they then made an ugly spectacle of themselves as, in a bid to "obliterate their faults," they scrambled to offer gifts to the boy and his family.[9] To no avail. The resentment that had built up over the years, particularly in the breast of the Gyalyum Chenmo, the Great Mother, was so great that, when the family finally took its rightful place as foremost in the land, she made it her business to pursue the two men. Eventually, both were reduced to the rank of common taxpayers and banished to their home districts.

Although *A Feast for the Ears* displeased some officials, who felt that they had been unreasonably misled, the majority of the

---

* Or *Na ba' bcud len* which, translated literally, means "the extraction of aural essences."

population was quite content to have been duped by the Desi and his popularity rose to an all-time high. He himself now began to prepare a spectacular homecoming for the Precious Protector. During the summer of 1697, the Sixth was moved with his family to Nankartse, where the Great Fifth had resided prior to his enthronement eighty years previously. At the same time, the Desi put in hand the construction of a new set of apartments for the Dalai Lama within the Potala. And, in preparation for the happy occasion of the Sixth's homecoming, the Desi ordered that a general tea offering should be granted to a hundred monasteries in the south of Tibet, that the war gods should be invoked in all ten districts, that prayer flags be hoisted on the peaks and flanks of three hundred sacred mountains, that ceremonial scarves be offered in all the major shrines in Lhasa, that a new set of statuettes be cast for the Dalai Lama's personal chapel and, for the benefit of the young man himself, that the rites of Pemalingpa, his great Nyingma ancestor, be performed by the monks of Namgyal Monastery.

Meanwhile, the young Dalai Lama was introduced to two of the Great Fifth's most important Nyingma teachers, by whom he was given the same secret name as his predecessor. And, most importantly, the Dalai Lama was at long last formally inducted as a novice monk by the Panchen Lama. It seems to have been at this ceremony that the young Dalai Lama set eyes on the Desi for the first time. It is reported that Tsangyang Gyatso, as he was now named, smiled and wept alternately. For his own part, the Desi was also quite overcome with emotion, crying unashamedly "in an inseparable mixture of joy and sorrow."

In many respects the hair-cutting ceremony, which marks the candidate's induction as a novice, is the most significant event in the life of a monk. It was therefore an auspice "difficult to understand," as the Desi put it, that, while the Dalai Lama was having his hair washed prior to the ceremony, he broke down in tears.

Shortly afterward, the Dalai Lama left Nankartse for the Nyethang Plain, just outside Lhasa, in the company of an awesome cavalcade. This comprised government officials, lamas high and low, ordinary monks and aristocrats, all accompanied by a vast retinue of servants and camp followers ranked strictly in order of precedence. For each of the seven nights of the journey, Tsangyang Gyatso's accommodation was pitched among one of 156 other tents arranged to the right and left of his. Yet this vast traveling pageant was as nothing to the tented city that was established at Nyethang. With prefabricated walls and gates at each cardinal point, its layout recalled the royal camps created for the Tibetan kings of the empire period. At night, it looked as though all "the stars of heaven [had] come down to earth."[10] And when, after a month during which the new Dalai Lama received the congratulations and obsequies of thousands of well-wishers, the mounted procession traveled the short remaining distance to the capital, it caused "such a thunder of hooves as had never been heard before in all China, India, or Mongolia."[11]

Tsangyang Gyatso now passed one final night under canvas, encamped right on the outskirts of Lhasa. On the morning of the twenty-fourth day of the tenth month*—a day that the Desi had selected after a minute and exhaustive astrological calculation—he bestowed his benediction on a crowd at least ten thousand strong before setting out on the final stage to the Potala. En route he was greeted successively by the Nechung and Gadong oracles in trance as well as by a hundred Chinese cavalrymen, the personal emissaries of Emperor Kangxi.

He now circumambulated the Potala twice, while the Desi, carrying lit incense, led the way. Tsangyang Gyatso was then seated on the throne last occupied by his illustrious predecessor. Immediately a young nobleman came forward and made

---

* It was by now September 1697, according to the Christian calendar.

an auspicious offering of a dish of curds. Next, the Desi made a long speech, reciting the whole sequence of events leading up to this momentous occasion. The seals of the Great Fifth were handed over, followed by splendid gifts offered on behalf of the Ganden Phodrang. Then came individual offerings from the highest dignitaries: the Panchen Lama first, followed by Mongolia's preeminent ecclesiastic, the Jangkya Hutuktu, who also presented letters patent and gifts from Kangxi. Next came the Ganden Tripa, the elected head of the Gelug sect, followed by the abbots of the Three Seats and other high lamas from those institutions. These were followed by the chiefs and nobles of the Khalka, Torgut, and Dzungar tribes. Altogether, the ceremony and its preceding pageantry created a spectacle of power and wealth unsurpassed before or since, at least not in Tibet. It is said that some of those present distinctly heard the delighted laughter of the deities in the sky above.

The day after his enthronement, the Sixth was presented with gifts from each of the provinces, and more still by the leaders of the non-Gelug traditions—the Sakya, the Drukpa-Kagyu, the Karma-Kagyu, the Nyingma, and the Bon schools, to name only those most familiar. Then for a further two days, there were private audiences for those visiting dignitaries, distinguished lamas, and nobles who had come to Lhasa from far away, followed in turn by the sons of the rulers of Sikkim, Ladakh, Zanskar, and the Kathmandu Valley. And all the while there was joyous feasting and dancing among the common people.

The excitement had barely died down when, just a month later, and again to the accompaniment of general merriment, the young Sixth, together with the Desi, consecrated the tomb of the Great Fifth. Known as the *dzam gling rgyan cig*—the Sole Ornament of the World—this vast sarcophagus [in Tibetan, *chöten* (*mchod rten*)] stands over fifty feet tall with gilding that is said to have consumed an astonishing 7,500 pounds of pure gold. Yet the jewels with which it is encrusted are said to have been more valuable still.

Thereafter, the newly anointed Sixth found himself thrown into a ceaseless round of audiences and liturgical events. At the same time, he now began in earnest his formal training under the direction of the Panchen Lama. We can only guess at the psychological and emotional impact that this extraordinary change of fortune can have had on him. Still only fourteen, just a year earlier he had been, so far as he knew, nothing more than a candidate for recognition as a relatively minor reincarnate lama. Today, he found himself the supreme religious figure, soon to be confirmed as head of state, of a spiritual and temporal empire that comprised much of Inner Asia.

It was not long before it became clear to the Desi, and to those closest to the person of the Dalai Lama, that this change of circumstances was not entirely to Tsangyang Gyatso's liking. For while the reports that had come from Tsona had all been entirely positive, it now began to seem as if these had been exaggerated to an unhealthy degree. The young Sixth showed little zeal in his religious studies, preferring archery to intellectual pursuits, and instead of the improvement in Tsangyang Gyatso's attitude for which the Desi hoped, it actually deteriorated. He began to keep company among the more louche young aristocrats of the day.

There is scant information concerning the Dalai Lama's progress over the next few years, but in 1701, the year in which he reached his majority, the Desi summoned the abbots of the Three Seats and explained that the Dalai Lama would listen to no one: not to himself, nor even to his mother. The next we hear is that, during the thanksgiving rituals conducted at the end of that year, the Sixth made only a brief appearance in the Great Hall of the Potala. When the Desi tried to persuade him to take his rightful place on the throne, Tsangyang Gyatso, in the sight of everyone present, refused to do so.

It was at this point that the Desi abandoned the diary that is our chief source of information on the period. As a result, all that we have are some brief glimpses of the young Sixth which emerge from, for example, the letters exchanged between the Desi and the Panchen Lama—the former begging the latter to intervene—and a subsequent exchange between the Panchen and Dalai Lama in which the Panchen asked Tsangyang Gyatso to visit him at Tashilhunpo, as was his due. To this request the Dalai Lama explained that, while he would be happy to see his senior tutor in due course, he was feeling a little unwell just at the moment. Under pressure, he agreed eventually to go, undertaking the journey to Shigatse during the summer of 1702. The Panchen Lama beseeched Tsangyang Gyatso to devote himself wholeheartedly to religion. Indeed, now that he had reached the age of twenty, the Dalai Lama should profess his final vows as a monk. Prostrating six times, the Dalai Lama recited the standard formula, "I confess to breaking my lama's commands," but he refused his teacher's entreaties. Instead, he announced that not only would he not accept ordination, but he desired to give back even his minor vows. We can only guess at the Panchen Lama's consternation. But Tsangyang Gyatso was not finished. He added that if his renunciation was not accepted, he would commit suicide while facing in the direction of Tashilhunpo itself. This was fighting talk. No greater calumny could be imagined than the Dalai Lama himself carrying out such a threat.

The Panchen Lama made one final bid to persuade the rebel to moderate his demands. Calling together the Dalai Lama's other teachers, along with the stewards of Drepung and Sera monasteries, several other high lamas, and members of both the local nobility and a number of Mongol chieftains (including, significantly as it would later turn out, a certain Lazang Khan of the Dzungars)—in short every man of rank that he could lay his hands on—the Panchen Lama urged the Dalai

Lama at least to accept ordination as a *gelong*. The whole assembly then pleaded with Tsangyang Gyatso, first singly, then as a body, to accept the Panchen Lama's petition, but "nothing happened except the Dalai Lama's replies became weaker and weaker." There was nothing the Panchen Lama could do but accept.

From Tashilhunpo, Tsangyang Gyatso returned to Lhasa, where, henceforth, though remaining in the Potala, he lived as a layman. One contemporary account describes the Dalai Lama as having long hair, dressing in the blue silk robes of a lay aristocrat, and wearing rings on his fingers.

For the Desi, the whole episode was a shattering and unmitigated disaster. To make matters worse, the young Dalai Lama now consorted openly with his various lay friends, accompanying them on visits outside Lhasa. He persisted in his love of archery and now added sensuality to his repertoire of questionable activities. By night, he would make forays into Shöl, the village that lies at the foot of the mound on which the Potala is built. It is said that the reason there came to be a considerable number of dwellings in Shöl that, instead of being painted white as usual, were painted yellow was that this was a sign that a daughter of the house had granted her favors to the amorous apostate. It is also said, to the Desi's further humiliation, that the Dalai Lama succeeded in bedding his daughter.

Yet for all this, and while nobody denies that the Dalai Lama was a controversial figure, today he is fondly remembered for his talent as a poet and lyricist. His gift to the Tibetan people of a body of some sixty-odd love songs, all of them enduringly popular, has ensured that, notwithstanding the scandal he caused, Tsangyang Gyatso is held in deep affection by his fellow countrymen and women.

Notoriously difficult to translate, many of the songs employ explicitly sexual imagery:

I wonder whether the soft-skinned girl in my bed—
Who seems so tender and loving—
Is not out to rob me of my treasure and my wealth
By means of her cunning

Though the meaning of this lyric seems at first glance straight-forward, an entirely spiritual reading of the texts is quite possible. From a religious perspective, for example, the word "treasure" may be construed in terms of good karma, while from a tantric perspective it may be seen as referring to the semen which a practitioner, at the point of orgasm, draws back into himself in order to experience the bliss of non-duality. For this reason, despite Tsangyang Gyatso's acknowledged licentious-ness, there was never any suggestion on the part of the people that he was not the true incarnation of the Great Fifth. Indeed, there is no evidence that the Sixth himself ever sought to deny his own authenticity. The present Dalai Lama's opinion is that the Sixth may in fact have intended the re-establishment of the Dalai Lama institution as one in which succession was by primo-geniture, though whether this justifies Tsangyang Gyatso's behav-ior still seems open to question.*

A folktale about the Sixth tells of how the Desi decided to make an example of one of the Dalai Lama's fast friends. This was a young noble by the name of Dargyeney. Judging him to be one of his main accomplices in the Dalai Lama's descent into vice, the Desi arranged to have Dargyeney assassinated. Unfortunately—so the story goes—the murderers attacked the wrong man. During a night of carousing and hilarity, Dargyeney and the Dalai Lama swapped clothes with their servants. Consequently, it was the servant who was stabbed in the back as he walked home in the early hours. Furious, the Dalai Lama

---

* Inevitably, many claim that Tsangyang Gyatso's antics were the outward sign of a practitioner of so-called crazy wisdom, but there does not seem to be contemporary evidence for this view.

determined to unmask the plotters and called in one of the oracles. The names of the plotters were duly revealed, where-upon, on the Dalai Lama's instructions, three were put to death. Only the Desi escaped retribution.

During 1703, the Desi stood down from office in favor of his eldest son, Ngawang Rinchen. This seems to have been in direct response to criticism that had begun to be voiced in connection with the Desi's role in the Dalai Lama's upbring-ing. Although there was no question that Tsangyang Gyatso was the authentic incarnation of Chenrezig, it was felt that the Desi had been insufficiently diligent in overseeing the young man's education. Furthermore, many felt that disobeying the Great Fifth in the matter of announcing his successor within twelve years was bound to bring misfortune on Tibet. Yet despite his growing unpopularity, this handover was in name only. The Desi, so long accustomed to power, was loath to relinquish it.

That same year, Tenzin Dalai Khan, still nominally king of Tibet, died. He was succeeded first by his eldest and then, almost immediately, by his younger son, the former having been poisoned by the latter. The new king was Lazang Khan, one of the Mongolian chieftains present at the Panchen Lama's unsuccessful attempt to persuade the Sixth to accept ordina-tion. From the first, Lazang Khan signaled that he had no intention of abiding by the gentlemanly principles of the *chö yon*, or priest-patron, relations between spiritual and secular heads of state. The Desi, for his part, nominally retired though he may have been, responded with an attempt to kill Lazang. He was almost successful. According to Father Desideri, the Italian Jesuit who first met the king some thirteen years later, Lazang Khan suffered the ill effects of poisoning until the end of his life.

Surprisingly, the king did not move immediately to exact his revenge, preferring to await further developments. His opportunity came immediately after the Monlam Chenmo of 1705. In a sitting of the grand council held before the Great Fifth's tomb (a council which, we are told, was not only presided over by the Dalai Lama himself but was also attended by the Panchen Lama and the abbots of the Three Seats), the Desi argued that Lazang Khan constituted an intolerable threat to the integrity of Tibet and needed to be dealt with once and for all. But the motion was not carried. In a sign that the Desi's own power was waning, a counterproposal merely decreed that Lazang Khan was to withdraw to the Kokonor region, while the Desi himself was also called on to retire completely from politics and to move to Gongkar.*

This edict was made known to Lazang Khan, who was by this time en route to central Tibet with his army. Feigning compliance, he withdrew eastward, halting, however, at Nagchu. There, he prepared for battle. By the fifth month, all was ready and he set out with the intention of seizing the capital. The only resistance came from the Desi, whose troops were, of course, completely routed. According to a story related by Desideri, despite this debacle, it took a forged order from the Dalai Lama, sealed by the hierarch himself while drunk, to bring about the Desi's final surrender. He now quit his post and left Lhasa. The Desi had not, however, gone far before he was intercepted by troops acting on behalf of Tsering Tashi, Lazang Khan's wife, who was bent on avenging the humiliation she had received at his hands. It is said that she had been the prize in a chess game played between the Desi and Lazang Khan some years previously. Hearing of the danger to the Desi, the Dalai Lama now attempted to intervene, sending a party to rescue him. Unfortunately, they were just too late: the Desi's decapitated remains were still warm when they arrived.

At once, Lazang Khan set out to deal with all who had opposed

---

* Gongkar was traditionally a place of exile for government ministers guilty of wrongdoing.

him. There were executions, floggings, and imprisonments in abundance, at the end of which only one obstacle remained between him and absolute mastery of Tibet: this was, of course, the person of the Dalai Lama himself.

We do not know how the Sixth reacted to the news of Lazang Khan's victory. The fact that he attempted to intervene on behalf of the Desi suggests that he was not an entirely passive bystander. We do know that he retained a vast reservoir of popular support, despite his wayward behavior. Lazang Khan therefore needed allies, both within the Gelug hierarchy and within the Qing court, who could be expected to protect the Dalai Lama if called on to do so. Lazang began sending extravagant gifts to the Panchen Lama at Tashilhunpo. He then wrote to the emperor pledging allegiance. Next, he began to put pressure on the abbots of the Three Seats to withdraw their recognition of Tsangyang Gyatso as the authentic incarnation of Chenrezig. At first they refused to do so, but when it became clear that Lazang's pledge of allegiance had had the desired effect of gaining the emperor's support, they reluctantly agreed that the *bodhi*, or Buddha-mind, "no longer dwelled" in the Dalai Lama. It was now but a short step to Lazang Khan's public declaration, during the summer of 1706, that Tsangyang Gyatso was not, after all, the reincarnation of the Great Fifth. On the first day of the fifth month (June 11), the Dalai Lama was brought under armed guard from the Potala to the Mongol military camp just outside Lhasa. There he was formally arraigned as an impostor by Lazang Khan, who read out a long list of his vices and failings. Tsangyang Gyatso was then informed that Kangxi had issued a summons that he appear before him in Beijing.

Inevitably, this provoked an extreme and hostile reaction from the populace, which had to be kept in check by Mongolian troops. Undaunted, stave-bearing monks from Drepung attacked the escort accompanying the Dalai Lama to China as they led him past Drepung Monastery the following day. Such was the ferocity of the mob's attack that they succeeded in carrying the Dalai Lama off in triumph to the palace of Ganden Phodrang. But as was only to be expected, Lazang Khan retaliated swiftly and ruthlessly. Supported by artillery, his troops surrounded Drepung, fired a hail of missiles into it and prepared to set the place ablaze. Seeing that a massacre was inevitable, Tsangyang Gyatso fled the monastery with just a handful of companions. When the last of these had fallen, he gave himself up to the Mongols. While the Dalai Lama was compelled to resume his journey to China, Drepung was stormed and sacked.

What finally became of Tsangyang Gyatso is open to conjecture. All our sources agree that the Dalai Lama fell ill when he arrived at Dam, the Mongols' summer pasturelands in Tibet. Despite this, he was forced to continue his journey. According to the Chinese, he perished just short of Kokonor on the tenth day of the tenth month—November 14, 1706. Father Desideri reports that his Tibetan sources were quite clear that the Dalai Lama was poisoned; but still others say that he simply disappeared.

21

A *Puppet and a Pretender*

Having rid himself of the only plausible obstacle to absolute rule, it was now incumbent on Lazang Khan to come up with a substitute for the Dalai Lama he had deposed. By this time the institution was so well established that it was as unthinkable that there should not be a Dalai Lama in Lhasa as that there should not be a Pope in Rome. That the man Lazang selected was rumored to be his natural son suggests that the khan may have had his identity in mind all along. A hitherto unknown member of the Gelug *sangha* who took the reign name of Nawang Yeshe Gyatso, he was three years younger than the deposed primate, and originally from Drepung Monastery. In order that this otherwise improbable candidate should have credibility in the eyes of the people, Lazang Khan prevailed on the Panchen Lama officially to recognize Yeshe Gyatso's authenticity. The Panchen Lama's willingness to do so was doubtless influenced by the substantial gifts and favors Lazang bestowed on the see of Tashilhunpo. At any rate, the Fifth Panchen having declared *nihil obstat*, the supposedly genuine reincarnation of the Great Fifth was duly installed at the Potala in 1707.

A wiser man than Lazang Khan would have guessed that his ill-treatment and peremptory replacement of the Sixth would cause untold resentment both among the Gelug clergy and the populace as a whole—including, indeed, many Mongols. Especially incensed were Lazang Khan's own kinsmen, who indignantly petitioned Emperor Kangxi. Diplomatically, Kangxi commissioned the Panchen Lama to reinvestigate Yeshe Gyatso's claim to the Lion Throne and unsurprisingly, the Panchen Lama confirmed his earlier finding and upheld the claim. However, concerned not to antagonize his Mongol neighbors, Kangxi wisely withheld formal recognition of the upstart for the present. Instead, he dispatched an imperial representative to "supervise" Lazang Khan.

Formally, the Qing envoy was instructed "to support Lazang Khan against the disaffected and to finish restoring order among the lamas [and] partisans of the [late] Desi." Informally, he was charged with upholding Qing interests in Tibet. But having limited resources available, the emperor's mission was of a diplomatic rather than military character. This meant that it was entirely dependent on Lazang Khan's goodwill for its success. As anyone less assured of his own prestige than Kangxi would have guessed, this was forthcoming only to a strictly limited degree, despite Lazang's professed allegiance to Qing. The emperor was soon forced to recognize that this attempt to extend his influence over Tibet was doomed to failure. Passing an order officially recognizing Yeshe Gyatso, Kangxi therefore withdrew his mission during the spring of 1710, leaving Lazang Khan as the de facto supreme political authority in Tibet.

For a total of ten years, Lazang ruled central Tibet as his personal fiefdom. It was, however, inevitable that the first signs of trouble for the khan should center on the appearance of a rival candidate for the office of Dalai Lama. To make matters worse, there were persistent reports of the survival of Tsangyang Gyatso himself.

In the autobiography of Thupten Jigme Norbu, the present Dalai Lama's eldest brother, we are told that when Tsangyang Gyatso arrived on the northern plateau, he was begged by local Tibetans not to continue his journey to Beijing. If he went, it would be sure to bring death to them and disaster to Tibet. While pondering this entreaty, Tsangyang Gyatso is said to have been visited in his tent by an old man. Questioned by the deposed Dalai Lama as to his name, he replied, "*Senge.*" To Tsangyang Gyatso's further question regarding the name of the lake near to which they were encamped, he replied, "*Kunga Nor.*" The two names in conjunction Tsangyang Gyatso took to be prophetic: "*Senge* means lion, a beast that stands for power; *kunga* means happiness. It is a sign that it is right for me to depart from here so that my people can be happy."[1] And with that, he stepped outside and vanished.

The following year, during the Monlam Chenmo, it is said that both the then regent and the Nechung oracle were seen to prostrate—in the manner reserved only for the Dalai Lama himself—toward a beggar in the crowd. This "beggar" was next heard of living as a simple shepherd, tending the flocks of a rich lady in Kham.

According to another legend, after leaving Lhasa, Tsangyang Gyatso manifested the *siddhi* of immortality and remains at large in the world to this day, not unlike the Wandering Jew of medieval Christian lore, disguised and dispensing spiritual succor where it is most needed and spiritual transformation to those who are ready.[*] The Thirteenth Dalai Lama seems to have been referring to a version of this legend when he told Sir Charles Bell, the British political officer resident in Lhasa during the 1920s, that Tsangyang Gyatso was known to appear in the Great Assem-

---

[*] It is said that, carrying his cross to Golgotha, Christ was chided by a young boy. "Go faster, Jesus, why dost thou linger?" Christ, turning, said, "I am indeed going, but thou shalt tarry till I come." The boy, though now vastly old and holy, cannot die before the Second Coming.

bly Hall at the Potala during the time of the Seventh Dalai Lama. He added that some had reported seeing him at different times during his own reign. The Thirteenth also suggested that the Sixth had practiced bi-location during his time as Dalai Lama. This, the Thirteenth explained, is frowned upon by all schools as it causes confusion among the faithful.

By far the most detailed account of the supposed survival of Tsangyang Gyatso is contained in a book called *A Tune from the Notes of the Divine Lute, [being] the Biography of the Omniscient Ngawang Chodrak Pelzangpo Containing a Melodious Discourse on His Most Excellent Acts of Virtue.*[2] Written in the first person, it begins in precisely the same way as the legend recounted by the present Dalai Lama's eldest brother. There is the omen connected with the names of the old man and the nearby lake, following which Tsangyang Gyatso leaves his tent. In this version, however, he sets out until he is caught up in a dust storm and disappears from sight. Completely blinded, he staggers about until he comes upon a nomad girl who leads him to safety. The storm subsides, the girl disappears, and Tsangyang Gyatso, wracked with thirst and hobbling with blisters, decides to become a wandering *yogin*. Subsequently, he joins a caravan of traders with whom he travels to Alashan.

He now embarks on a series of adventures. On one occasion,

I came to a household where there was a man with no head. I asked his wife and others for an explanation and was told that his head had been cut off . . . and that even after three years he had not died. With limitless pity I went to look. He was beating his chest with his hands and someone told me he did this because he was hungry. Where his neck had been were two holes. From a pot they poured into one of these holes a small quantity of warm and soft barley-flour [mixed with tea]. Bubbles rose up through this and in a little time the food went down to his stomach.[3]

Later, Tsangyang Gyatso visits Sera Monastery, where he is given teachings by the abbot. He then moves on to Drakshok, a monastery sanctified by a visit from Tsongkhapa. From Drakshok, our hero begins a pilgrimage to the holy sites of southeastern Tibet. On his way there, following rumors of his reappearance, he is arrested by troops acting on behalf of Lazang Khan. Making another miraculous escape, again shielded by a dust storm, the ex-Dalai Lama makes his way to India.

The journey takes him via his birthplace, on the way to which he is attacked, by a *mi'dre*, the fabled Abominable Snowman. Escaping without harm, he finally reaches northern India. But no sooner does he join up with some other Tibetan pilgrims than they are set upon again—this time by a pair of *rollang*, or zombies. Everyone else flees as the zombies strike out with "fists burning like fire," but Tsangyang Gyatso manages to knock them down and pulverize them to ash with rocks.[4] Finally reaching the monastery of Pulahari, the ex-Dalai Lama spends six months meditating on the Cakrasamvara Tantra.

The ex-Dalai Lama's final adventure in India concerns his meeting with the legendary six-tusked elephant of which the Buddha Shakyamuni's mother dreamed before giving birth. Appearing only once every hundred years, he describes it as looking "something like a mountain moving . . . [it was] so beautiful, one could not gaze at it long enough." Wonderstruck, he prostrates toward it three times as it "moved around me in a circle to the right." When it had completed "one round, it released before me a large dung"—a most auspicious occurrence.

By 1714, Tsangyang Gyatso is back in Tibet. A year later he visits Drepung, where he attends a public séance of the Nechung oracle. Unfortunately, Nechung again recognizes him and comes toward him, brandishing his sword in salutation. Given a stern look, the deity takes the hint and goes rushing off in every other direction so as to distract attention from his former master. From Lhasa, the ex-Dalai Lama returns, in 1716, to Amdo—exactly ten years since his disappearance. Establishing himself there, he enters into friendly relations with the local Mongolian ruler (an historical figure) and his wife. His reputation as a holy man now begins to grow and he starts to receive large numbers of visitors from among local Mongolian tribesmen. Before long, we find him accepting the abbacy of a monastery. At his investiture, a great tent is pitched for him which had earlier been used by the Great Fifth. But whereas his predecessor was made a gift of just thirty horses, the new abbot is given "three hundred white horses as large as camels, all well matched" and, we are assured, with "ears of different colors."[5]

Two years later, during a major revolt of the Mongols against the Chinese, his monastery is destroyed. It takes four years before work can begin on the restoration of the monastery, on a new site, and a further three before it is finally reoccupied. Several large bribes are required to be paid to the local Chinese governor, who obstructs the program throughout. When it is finally all but complete, the governor orders his soldiers to pull the building back down. Further bribes are paid, and the monastery is only saved when the governor dies suddenly, "blood pouring from his nine orifices."[6]

From now, life for the Dakpo Lama (as he was by now universally known) becomes more settled. In time, he is made the abbot of a total of fourteen monasteries. He has come to be the revered teacher of thousands of Mongols, including many nobles. Ironically, considering the young Sixth Dalai Lama's waywardness, he even corresponds with the Panchen Lama on the subject of the *vinaya*, the code of monastic discipline. He finally dies on the eighth day of the fourth month in 1748.

There remain many Tibetans who accept the identification of the Dakpo Lama with Tsangyang Gyatso. Indeed, it was until only recently the official position of the Tibetan government in exile that the secret biography is a genuine text, despite the fact that this would seem to undermine the claim to authenticity of the present Dalai Lama, not to mention all those of the intervening period. But for Tibetans, given that Chenrezig has the ability to manifest whenever and wherever he may be of most benefit to others, and to an infinite degree, it follows that he may choose to do so in a manner that, at first glance, seems paradoxical.

22

The Manchurian Candidate

His later adventures notwithstanding, the most famous of the Sixth Dalai Lama's love songs is said to have been written while detained in the Mongol military camp prior to his deportation to Beijing:

> *Lend me your wings, white crane;*
> *I shall go no further than Lithang,*
> *And thence, return again.*

Although clearly prophetic, it is said that the lady friend to whom the lyric was smuggled did not see its significance until many years later, after the new Dalai Lama had been discovered. Be that as it may, Kelsang Gyatso, the child subsequently recognized as the Seventh Dalai Lama, was indeed born in Lithang, on September 3, 1708. He first came to notice when his mother took him into a chapel at the local monastery. Seeing him, a monk present went into spontaneous trance.* Channeling the

---

* I myself once witnessed an example of spontaneous trance midway through the New Year's Day prayer ceremony conducted on the roof of the Tsug Lakhang temple in 1988. On this occasion, the deity channeled was unable to

wrathful protector Pehar, he announced that the infant was the "unmistakable reincarnation of the master Thongwa Donden" (literally, "Meaningful to Behold," the name by which all the Dalai Lamas are addressed by Pehar) adding that it was essential to "be careful with him. It is not appropriate for Thongwa Donden to remain in a household. Bring him to the monastery." Then the monk, still in trance, took the child on his lap and inquired whether he wanted to become a monk. Kelsang Gyatso nodded in assent. "And am I Pehar Gyalpo?" Again, he nodded.

The boy's parents were stunned and fearful. Was not the authentic Sixth Dalai Lama seated on the Lion Throne in Lhasa?* Afraid of what might happen if the monk's prophetic words became generally known, they begged the monastic authorities to keep the incident secret; but the news spread like brushfire. By the time the boy was four, Lazang Khan himself had heard the rumor and dispatched a party to investigate the claims being made on his behalf. It was immediately apparent that Kelsang Gyatso was a highly unusual child. Nonetheless, it was officially concluded that he was not Tsangyang Gyatso's reincarnation. Besides, "even if he was," the Tibetan official leading the delegation announced, "it would be of no special significance. Tsangyang Gyatso was, as we all know, incorrectly identified as the reincarnation of the Great Fifth." In secret, however, the same official told senior members of the Lithang hierarchy that the boy should be taken in and given protection.

Thus it was not long before the boy was back at Lithang, where he came under the care of Chuzang Nomohan, one of the greatest Gelug lamas of his day. The "intensity of the boy's spiritual growth was like the growth of a water lotus . . ." At the age of five, he experienced visions of the Buddha Shakyamuni accompanied by the Sixteen Arhats. And so eloquent and

---

make itself understood and all that issued was a noise something like the hoarse, staccato bark of a fox.
* That is to say, Yeshe Gyatso, the khan's puppet Dalai Lama.

profound were the words he spoke that he moved to tears all who heard him.

In the meantime, the Kangxi Emperor came to hear of this new pretender to the see of Lhasa. Although he had formally recognized Yeshe Gyatso, Lazang Khan's Dalai Lama, the emperor was aware that this was nothing but a political appointment. When it became clear that all of eastern Tibet was convinced of Kelsang Gyatso's authenticity, the emperor accordingly requested that he be allowed to sponsor his formal induction as a novice at Kumbum Monastery, scheduled for 1715. How far Kangxi's motives were political and how far spiritual it is impossible to decide. But there is little doubt that he saw himself as a Buddhist, even though he was devoted to hunting. Indeed, the picture we have of the emperor is of a man who combined Buddhism with Confucian ideas in such a way as to lead a life of exemplary rectitude. He rose daily at 5 a.m., washed, consumed nothing during the morning but milk, tea, and bird's-nest soup, prior to spending a short period of time in meditation in front of a Buddhist shrine. Thereafter, he would read from the Chinese classics, before being carried to the Palace of Heavenly Purity, where he conducted state business and received his subjects in audience. After a frugal meal at 2 p.m., he relaxd either by reading, painting, practicing calligraphy, or by going out hunting. In the evening, he returned to his state papers, often working until late. Monk-fashion, he ate nothing after lunch. And on those occasions when he traveled outside the capital, he liked nothing better than to sleep rough under the stars. When his intended successor, the only son among his fifty-six children actually born to an empress, grew up to be "dissolute, lawless, and mentally unstable"[1] with an open predilection for immorality with young boys, the horrified Kangxi did not hesitate to have the young man demoted and his associates exterminated.

Whatever Kangxi's motives, the effect on Lazang Khan of his sponsorship of Kelsang Gyatso's induction was disastrous.

Attended by pilgrims from all over Tibet, the ceremony was the grandest that had been seen at Kumbum for two generations. And when the monastery's oracle solemnly pronounced in favor of the boy, a clash with the Lhasa authorities was inevitable. Unexpectedly, however, it turned out that there was a third leader with an interest in the child. This was Tsewang Arabten [Tshe-dtsan Rab-br Tan], the chief of the Dzungars of the western Mongol federation. Following the demise of Galdan, Tsewang Arabten was the latest to bid for the mantle of Genghis Khan. Seeing in Kelsang Gyatso a means to obtaining legitimacy throughout Mongolia, the khan also recognized a way to outwit the Qing and obtain power over Tibet. If, at the same time as attacking Lazang Khan, he could wrest the boy from the hands of the small Qing force stationed at Kumbum, he would be sure to have the support of all Tibet. Tsewang Arabten therefore sent envoys to Lazang proposing a new marriage alliance between their two families (they were already brothers-in-law). He would give his daughter to Lazang's son, together with a dowry of one hundred thousand taels of silver. The only proviso was that the wedding should take place on Tibetan soil. Lazang Khan was immediately suspicious. Unfortunately his son, presumably motivated more by the riches on offer than anything that he can have known about the girl in question, threatened suicide if his father did not permit the union. And Lazang Khan, being, at least according to Desideri's account, an easygoing character, gave in to his son's pleading.* The stipulation of a wedding in Tibet gave the Dzungars the cover they needed for troop movements into Tibet. But whereas they were expected to approach Lhasa via the Kokonor region, they made instead an audacious forced

---

* The marriage did eventually take place, and the boy moved with his bride back to Dzungaria. He came to a bad end, however. Charged with black magic against his father-in-law, he met his end pressed between two red-hot cauldrons.

march over the Kunlun Mountains direct to Dam. There they found Lazang Khan midway through celebrating another family wedding and completely unprepared for battle. He was moreover an old man now and, like most elderly Mongol men of his day, it seems, completely dissipated in drink. So even .though the troops he faced were exhausted, Lazang could do no more than hold them off for a month before retreating back to Lhasa at the end of November 1717.

In the meantime, a second Dzungar force attacked the Qing militia at Kumbum with the intention of carrying off Kelsang Gyatso. Disastrously for them, they were repulsed. In order to keep the population on side for as long as possible, the Dzungars nonetheless let it be known that they had successfully liberated the Dalai Lama in waiting. The Dzungars then attacked Lhasa at the beginning of December. Having secretly recruited batches of monks from among the Three Seats, the Mongols were helped by placemen in the capital who let down ladders, enabling them swiftly to breach the city's strongholds. A massacre ensued, leaving many hundreds dead. For the next two days, the invaders, assisted by their monastic allies, who proved both greedy and cruel, systematically looted the town.[2] Desideri and his fellow missionaries were also targeted. Although their lives were spared, they were stripped and flogged in an effort to make them reveal where their (nonexistent) treasures lay. Lazang Khan himself was soon run to ground and killed. Thereafter, the Dzungars proceeded also to sack the Potala in a most thorough manner—even to the extent of desecrating the Great Fifth's reliquary stupa.

With the Dzungars now firmly in control of Lhasa, Tsering Donduk, their leader in Tibet, set about imposing a new government. The post of Desi was given to an elderly aristocrat, Lha'gyal Rabten, described in a contemporary (if clearly partisan) account as "heavy with a skull-like white face, toothless with hanging jowls, a staggering gait, and unclear and stammering speech."[3]

At the same time, the spurious Sixth was deposed and Kelsang Gyatso acknowledged as the rightful Dalai Lama.*

But there was general dismay when it became clear that he remained at Kumbum. This failure on the part of the Dzungars meant that the only hope they now had of ruling Tibet was through terror and intimidation. They began with a wholesale destruction of the Nyingma sect, burning books, destroying every image of Padmasambhava they could find, sacking monasteries, and murdering the leading figures within the ancient tradition. It was just as well that the Dzungars did not control the whole of Tibet. Since the death of the Great Fifth, the power of the Ganden Phodrang had declined to the point where Lhasa's influence did not extend outside the Gelug monasteries, except in central Tibet. Kham was thus largely independent. Amdo was more or less directly under the control of the eastern Mongols (themselves subjects of the Qing), southern Tibet was only partially under Dzungarian control, and western Tibet was politically something of a no-man's land. As a result, the extent of their power was limited.

The revolt against the Dzungars, when it came, arose in southern and western Tibet. During the spring of 1720, two aristocrats, Polhané (in the south) and Kanchenna (in the west), began to gather troops around them with a view to restoring Tibetan power under the leadership of the young Dalai Lama (himself still in Kumbum under Qing protection). But before these two could put their plan into action, the Dzungars were overcome in a stunning raid on Lhasa executed by Qing forces. This followed a forced march over mountains such as the Dzungars had themselves used against Lazang Khan. The capital was taken with very little fighting. It was left to the other wing of the Qing army to deal with the Dzungars' principal concentration of troops at

* Thanks to the intervention of the Panchen Lama, Yeshe Gyatso was permitted to return to his former position as an ordinary monk at Chakpori Medical College.

Dam. After frenzied fighting, Qing prevailed. Only about five hundred Mongols survived to return to Ili, the Dzungarian capital. And, happily for the Tibetans, even the caravan carrying Lhasa's looted treasures was intercepted, with the result that most were returned to their rightful owners.

Most widely appreciated of all was the fact that, traveling in the rear of this battle-bloodied mixed Chinese and Manchurian army was Kelsang Gyatso himself. Amid the rejoicing of the entire population, he reached Lhasa during the second week of October 1720. It was thus Kangxi who was seen as responsible for delivering the Precious Protector to his people, and Kangxi, who now became, effectively, Tibet's kingmaker.

The longed-for new Dalai Lama's first public engagement was at the Jokhang, where he gave a public teaching to many thousands of monks and laypeople, all of whom "gained a breath of fresh air and experienced profound serenity."[4] From the Jokhang, Kelsang Gyatso was escorted, under the watchful eye of his ambitious father, by a cohort of Manchu, Chinese, and Mongolian princes to the Potala, of which desolate palace he now took possession. It was there that, a month later, he was officially installed as Dalai Lama, in a ceremony over which the Panchen Lama presided. A provisional government consisting of two Tibetan nobles, two Khalka, and two Qoshot chieftains was now inaugurated under the leadership of the victorious (Chinese) general, Yansin. At once Tibet's new masters began to move against the old. Among those put to death was the unfortunate Lha'gyal Rabten, an event greatly resented by the people. The old man had never been more than a figurehead used by the Dzungars in a lame attempt to confer legitimacy on their own regime.

In an important edict, Kangxi now abolished the post of Desi on the grounds that it concentrated too much power in the hands of one man. In its place, he created a council of ministers (the Kashag), under the nominal leadership of the Dalai Lama. This institution remains active today, though at that time all its decisions were subject to the approval of the commander of the Qing garrison. In this way, by a combination of astute military and political maneuvering, the emperor transformed Tibet from the dominion of a Mongolian strongman into a protectorate of the Qing Dynasty.

So far as Kelsang Gyatso himself was concerned, these new arrangements left him replete with all the privileges that went with the exalted spiritual status of the Dalai Lama, but bereft of any political power. His intelligence, his eloquence, and his increasing mastery of the whole vast corpus of Buddhist teaching and practice ensured that he himself enjoyed the utmost respect among Tibetans generally. The emperor's representatives treated Kelsang Gyatso with punctilious deference, and he maintained a frequent and cordial correspondence with Beijing. Similarly, his relations with the Mongol chieftains were excellent and he received tribute from the rulers of Sikkim, Bhutan, Gu'ge, and from the Nepalese kingdoms of Kathmandu, Bhaktapur, and Patan, but he did not exercise secular power in his own right.

Although Tibet's new status as a protectorate of the Qing began well enough, it was not long before the garrison at Lhasa began to cause serious problems for the local people. Food costs rose by a factor of three. The people became increasingly bitter: "Even if the Dzungars were to come back, what distress heavier than this could befall us?" The Kashag accordingly memorialized the emperor, requesting that he withdraw his troops. This provoked a furious reaction from Beijing. Kangxi ordered at once the replacement of the local Qing officials and sent a new governor to examine the situation in Tibet. This new appointee found, however, that the new garrison could indeed be smaller in size and duly petitioned the emperor. The emperor finally agreed to a reduction in the size of the force from 3,500 to 1,900 men. It was almost his last act. On December 22, after a reign lasting some sixty-one years, Kangxi died and was succeeded by Emperor Yongzhen.*

The Dalai Lama was much grieved at the news. He felt gratitude toward Kangxi for his role in establishing him in his position as Dalai Lama. In addition to organizing commemorative services, he himself therefore offered prayers and oblations to the late emperor's memory for the full forty-nine days prescribed by Tibetan tradition.

Yongzhen, the new emperor, took a very different view of empire from that of his father. In particular, he felt that Tibet was a backwater that did not justify the drain on resources of a permanent garrison. He was content, therefore, to rely on the relationship between himself and the Dalai Lama to guarantee the position of the Qing authorities in Lhasa and the loyalty of the Tibetan people to the Qing. Accordingly, he gave orders in council for his staff to submit proposals for the complete withdrawal of troops from central Tibet. This elicited protests on the grounds that the Dzungars remained a threat and that, while the Panchen Lama was old, the Dalai Lama was young and fickle. But the garrison was withdrawn nonetheless, leaving in place only a handful of officials and their staff. It was a grave miscalculation. Almost at once the Tibetan administration split into two factions. On one side, in favor of alliance with the Qing, were the chief minister, Kanchenna and Polhané (the two men who had mobilized against the Dzungars). On the other were the remaining members of the Kashag—men who were strongly nationalistic, even to the extent of retaining sympathy for the

---

* Kangxi has claim to being the greatest of all the Chinese emperors. During his rule, corruption was greatly reduced, the economy prospered, the arts flourished, and the empire was extended to a size not seen since the glory of T'ang. But while this expansion into Central Asia has in the past generally been interpreted as the expansion of the Chinese Empire, modern scholarship emphasizes the fact that this empire was a Qing (and therefore Manchu) creation, of which China was the most important part, but a part that was nevertheless subservient. China's great weight of history and culture were put to the service of Manchu ideals and policies, and not the other way round.

Dzungars, whom they saw as potential allies against Qing. The Dalai Lama's father, though not a minister, was a key supporter of this faction.

Matters came to a head when, later that year, a mission from Yongzhen arrived, carrying with it an edict ordering a general suppression of the Nyingma sect. Only two monasteries were permitted to remain, and the traditional Nyingma practices of exorcism, fire offering, and the manufacture of *btso*, or mystical "bombs," were proscribed. The arrival of the edict caused surprise and dismay in equal measure. Not only was it totally unexpected, but the reasons behind it were unclear, as they remain today, though it is a fact that the Seventh Dalai Lama himself showed no great enthusiasm for the sect.

The consternation the edict caused was largely due to the fact that, although as we have seen, Tibetans of different religious affiliation often came to blows with one another, on the whole, Tibetan Buddhism was tolerant of diversity. Yongzhen's edict was therefore construed as a completely unjustified interference in Tibetan affairs. But there were some, including Kanchenna, who were prepared to obey the emperor's directive. This caused a further split in the Kashag. Polhané for one, coming as he did from a traditionally Nyingma family, could not accept the new policy. Although his offer to resign was not accepted, he used the excuse of a sick wife to absent himself from Lhasa.

It was left to the Dalai Lama's father to petition the emperor to reconsider his orders. But when news came, during the summer of 1727, of a new imperial mission carrying with it confirmation of the original order, the nationalists opposed to Kanchenna— who had meanwhile begun to carry out the suppression—decided to take matters into their own hands. On August 5, the Kashag convened in the treasury office adjoining the Jokhang. A confident and relaxed Kanchenna smiled and jested with his *kalons*, or ministers, as they sat down to business. Suddenly, one of the *kalons* seized his hair ornaments from behind, while the others drew their knives and attacked him. Joined by their retainers from outside the room, the assassination was so violent—so impassioned—that several of the perpetrators were themselves wounded. Not content with what they had done, the following day, the rebels butchered, in cold blood, the chief minister's wife and sister.

We know very little of what happened during the course of the next year. The faction that included the Dalai Lama's father now assumed power, while Kelsang Gyatso himself remained mainly at Sera Monastery. But in the meantime, Polhané began to raise an army in the west and south of Tibet.

Polhané is a remarkable figure in the history of Tibet. Although fiercely opposed to the emperor's policy toward the Nyingma, he realized that the Manchus would move swiftly to reassert their authority over Tibet. If, however, he could take Lhasa before the imperial army arrived, he would be in a strong position to have himself appointed chief minister. He could then use his power to mitigate the emperor's anti-Nyingma stance—if indeed this genuinely reflected Yongzhen's personal view. He therefore issued a general call to arms, to which, because of resentment against Lhasa for its role in the suppression of the Nyingma, many were receptive. One exception was the abbot of Thöling Monastery. But we are told, without further amplification, that he was done to death by black magic.

Within a month of Kanchenna's assassination, Polhané was on the march toward Lhasa. It was left to the Dalai Lama and the Panchen Lama to try to intervene and persuade the two sides to negotiate, but their efforts went unrewarded.

The main threat to the success of Polhané's campaign were the various Mongol groups still present in and around the capital. Having no particular interest in the outcome of the conflict, they could only be made to fight through the payment of extravagant bribes. Toward the end of 1727, the government succeeded by this means in persuading a mixed Mongol force to take to

the field to stop Polhané advancing any further. He was soundly
beaten; but his opponents did not reckon on Polhané's tenacity. Presuming that he would now have to retreat and raise fresh
troops in the New Year, they paid off the Mongols. But by sheer
force of personality, Polhané succeeded in regrouping his forces
and capturing Gyantse unopposed.* First accepting but then
repudiating a truce negotiated by the Panchen Lama, Polhané
now marched east to Dam. There he secured an alliance with
the Mongol tribe at that time occupying the valley, and began
preparations for a final assault on the capital. A committee of
ecclesiastics made one final attempt to persuade Polhané to
re-enter dialogue with the Kashag, but he refused to listen. At
the end of June, his final advance began. But while the monastic authorities feared great bloodshed, Polhané's occupation of
Lhasa went largely unopposed. The Kashag's defenses simply
melted away, leaving only a handful of men, who did not surrender, occupying the Potala. Among these were three members
of the Kashag, together with the Dalai Lama's father and the
Dalai Lama himself.

Polhané at once demanded that the triumvirate of ministers
be handed over to him or, failing that, that Kelsang Gyatso should
leave the building under escort and retire to Drepung. In the
event, the Dalai Lama persuaded Polhané to allow the *kalons* to
return to their homes, where they would remain until the arrival
of the emperor's mission, which was by now on its way. When
the Qing forces finally reached Lhasa two months later, Polhané
was firmly in control and it remained for them only to see that
the emperor's justice was done. Unfortunately for the triumvirate, this meant death for them and their leading supporters,
though not the Dalai Lama's father. Following a trial that lasted
seven days, the condemned men were led to a public place where

---

* This personality included a streak of ruthlessness. Faced with the prevari-
cation of one of the Tsang chieftains, Polhané had the man thrown down the
battlements of the fortress in which they had met.

the three ministers were dispatched by what is known euphemistically as the "slicing method":

> The criminal is fastened to a rough cross, and the executioner, armed with a sharp knife, begins by grasping handfuls from the fleshy parts of the body, such as the thighs and the breasts, and slicing them off. After this he removes the joints and the excrescences of the body one by one—the nose and ears, fingers and toes. Then the limbs are cut off piecemeal at the wrists and the ankles, the elbows and knees, the shoulders and hips. Finally, the victim is stabbed to the heart and his head cut off.*5

The two lamas who had provided the chief ecclesiastical support were slowly strangled, and the remainder were decapitated with three sword strokes. The families of two of the ministers were also executed, while that of the third was deported into slavery. As intended, this loathsome and disgusting exhibition had a profound impact on the Tibetans. However cavalier they themselves could on occasion be in their attitude toward the Buddha's injunction against killing, they were appalled at the exquisite cruelty of the Manchus and their Chinese officials.

But in some ways even more devastating to the people was the punishment meted out to the Dalai Lama. Kelsang Gyatso himself was condemned to internal exile for what turned out to be a full seven years. Monks and layfolk thronged the precincts of the Potala in tears and sorrow as they watched him leave, once again under the armed escort of the Qing army.

With Kelsang Gyatso now banished, the emperor decreed a

---

* This account was recorded by my great-grandfather Henry Norman (later Sir Henry Norman, Bt.) in his book *The Peoples and Politics of the Far East*, evidently following a local authority. Although he did not personally witness an execution by slicing, Henry Norman was present on one occasion when fifteen men were decapitated. Thoroughly revolted, he bought the executioner's sword as a "valuable antidote to much that I read about the advancing civilization of China." It remains in family possession.

new system of government whereby two Qing officials, known by Tibetans as *ambans*, were established as joint heads of a permanent imperial mission. This was to be supported by a standing army of some two thousand soldiers, or bannermen. Another permanent garrison of a thousand bannermen was established simultaneously at Chamdo. The function of the *ambans* was to oversee the Kashag, now reconstituted with four members under Polhané.

Kelsang Gyatso himself was meanwhile escorted as far as Lithang, while his father, Sonam Dargye, proceeded to Beijing. There, chained between his two wives, Sonam Dargye was presented to the emperor. Having been formally chastised for his role in the recent disturbances, he was made to swear on pain of death henceforth never again to seek to interfere in the governance of Tibet. He was then freed to join his son in internal exile.

In political terms, the Dalai Lama's exile was of course a humiliation, but insofar as it enabled Kelsang Gyatso now to focus wholeheartedly on his spiritual studies, this period of his life was by no means sterile. As well as being enlivened by what seems to have been a genuine bond of friendship with the emperor's brother, who acted as imperial envoy, it is to this time that belong some of Kelsang Gyatso's most important writings. Like the Great Fifth, he was a prolific author. Had he lived as long, it is likely he would have exceeded his predecessor's immense output. As it was, he left behind some two hundred works of various lengths, and he remains the most widely read of all the Dalai Lamas. Though much of what he wrote is beyond the scope of the uninitiated, a number of his compositions have an attractive immediacy both of style and content, while he could on occasion display an engaging earthiness:

> *What is like a smelly fart*
> *Which, although invisible is obvious?*
> *One's own faults, which are precisely*
> *As obvious as the effort made to hide them.*[6]

Back in Lhasa, Polhané, nicknamed by Tibetans Mipham, the Invincible One, by making clear his unswerving loyalty to Qing, was able gradually to render superfluous the two *ambans* appointed by the emperor. Indeed, so confident in his own position did he become that, in due course, he signaled his willingness to allow Kelsang Gyatso to return to the capital. Accordingly, during 1736, the Dalai Lama, with the emperor's approval and yet again under a Qing escort, progressed slowly back to central Tibet. Stopping frequently to give teachings and to grant audiences along the way, he arrived in Lhasa to the customarily tumultuous welcome, but his homecoming was hardly a triumph. The clergy was broadly favorable to the alliance with Qing. So while Polhané stayed in control, Kelsang Gyatso remained a negligible figure on the political scene.

Four years later, the new Qing emperor, Qianlong (whose reign from 1736 to 1795 spanned almost sixty years), awarded Polhané the title of Fou, or Duke, the second highest dignity in the empire. This marked the high point of the Invincible One's career. He was now in complete control of Tibet, while the Ganden Phodrang was essentially defunct, the Dalai Lama in abeyance, and Qing supervision of Tibetan affairs only nominal. Even their garrison had largely been replaced by a Tibetan standing army.

The first major threat to the stability of the relationship between Tibet and the Qing Dynasty occurred in 1747, when Polhané died—presumably from blood poisoning—following the growth of a suppurating boil on his neck. He was succeeded, in accordance with his own wishes, by his younger son, Gyurmé Namgyal. But it was a bad choice. Gyurmé Namgyal was, if not Tibet's Caligula, clearly unhinged. On one occasion he hurled a spear at one of his ministers. It missed and instead wounded a horse standing outside. So he threw another. Again he missed his intended target, this time fatally wounding an attendant.[7]

By all accounts, Kelsang Gyatso could hardly stand the sight of the new leader, and apparently supported Gyurmé Namgyal's passed-over elder brother, but it was not long before the latter died in unexplained circumstances. Thereafter, Gyurmé Namgyal began secretly to approach the Dzungars, seeking an alliance with them as a prelude to sundering relations with Qing. In a meeting with the two *ambans*, he subsequently announced that the Tibetan army could perfectly well protect the Dalai Lama and safeguard the security of the country. Neither the *ambans* nor their remaining escort were either welcome or necessary.

Correctly deducing that he intended military action, the two *ambans* decided to take immediate action. It cost them their lives, though it gained them a memorial in the Hall of Zealots of the Qing Dynasty. On November 11, 1750, they invited Gyurmé Namgyal to their residence on the pretext of wanting to hand over gifts from the emperor. Arriving with just two attendants, he was swiftly disarmed and run through with his own sword.[8] But as soon as news of the assassination became known, a riot broke out among the local populace. At once, the Dalai Lama sent his secretaries to speak to the mob and try to dissuade them from violence. At the same time, notices were hurriedly put up announcing that Gyurmé Namgyal had been justly executed for his crimes. The people should not therefore do harm either to the *ambans* or to their property. But this only provoked the fury of the mob. Surrounding the Qing officials' residence, they soon broke in. One of the *ambans* was killed immediately, the other, after defending himself valiantly, committed suicide. A further 128 men, mainly Chinese soldiers and civilians, were killed in the fighting or were burned to death when the building was set ablaze. The mob then turned its attention to the imperial treasury, which it looted to the tune of eighty-five thousand measures of silver. That night, confusion and panic reigned as the remaining two hundred imperial staff made their way to the Potala, where they took refuge under the personal protection of the Dalai Lama.

Unfortunately for the leaders of this uprising, while the storming of the Qing Embassy was accomplished with little difficulty, they had no idea what to do next. The Kashag remained in place, and both the clergy and the Dalai Lama were committed to the relationship with Qing. With no prospect in sight other than punishment, they therefore packed up hastily and fled with as much booty as they could carry, bound for Dzungaria. The main beneficiary of the whole affair was Kelsang Gyatso. By feeding, clothing, and protecting the surviving members of the Qing Embassy, by appointing an interim chief minister to take control of the government in Gyurmé Namgyal's place, and by posting a proclamation ordering that no Tibetan should give refuge or succor to the fugitive leaders, he quickly filled the political vacuum. By the time the Qing expeditionary force—dispatched by an angry Emperor Qianlong as soon as he received word of the affair—arrived in Lhasa, not only had order been restored but the government was running smoothly. By this time, too, the fugitives had been arrested and about half the booty returned (the emperor was content to write off the balance), so it was just a matter of the now familiar ritual of slicing, slow strangulation, and decapitation of the criminals.

This done, it remained only for the Qing commander to make known the emperor's plans for yet another reorganization of the governance of Tibet. These were contained in a thirteen-point document, the "Program for the New Administration of Tibet." From now on, the Dalai Lama himself would appoint the Kashag, which was to comprise three laymen and one member of the *sangha*. The Dalai Lama was also to appoint all district, provincial, and military commanders, acting on the advice of the Kashag. The only restraint on the Dalai Lama's authority was the need for his office to clear all decisions with the two *ambans* first. By this means, the emperor's power over

Tibet was in no way diminished, but that of the Dalai Lama
was substantially increased. Finally, at the age of forty-two,
Kelsang Gyatso attained to a modicum of secular as well as
spiritual authority over his countrymen. Of course, it was a
power much diminished in comparison with that of the Great
Fifth, but this seems not to have been particularly uncongenial to him. From Kelsang Gyatso's perspective, the emperor
was the guarantor of the peace and stability necessary for the
propagation and practice of the *buddhadharma*:

> *Of all activities, the supreme*
> *Is that of transmitting the Dharma.*

It is this devotion to the faith for which Kelsang Gyatso is
chiefly remembered. Doctrinally, much of his effort was dedicated to a revival of interest in the teachings of Tsongkhapa, the
founder of the Gelug sect. Scholastically, he was instrumental in
revising the system of examinations within the monastic universities. Liturgically, he was responsible for the restoration of the
Kalachakra Tantra to a central place within the Tibetan tradition. Kelsang Gyatso was also responsible for establishing an
academy for lay officials that taught the three main subjects relevant to government: calligraphy, the literary arts, and astrology.
Finally, Kelsang Gyatso is particularly commemorated as a
teacher, most notably of the Third Panchen Lama, but also of
many other lamas within the Gelug tradition. He is reported to
have ordained no less than 16,993 monks. Yet his most attractive quality was his modesty. It is said that from time to time
during his period of exile, he would disguise himself as an ordinary monk and live for weeks at a time among the ordinary
people. A charming story is told of how, on one of these forays,
he was engaged by a peasant to perform a ritual. So impressed
was this layman that he begged the young mendicant to stay
another day—then another, and another. In the end, the anony-

mous monk stayed several weeks, chanting prayers and dispensing wisdom to the peasant's family. Finally, Kelsang Gyatso prevailed on the man to let him go. On his departure, the peasant offered the disguised Dalai Lama a small plate of solid gold in gratitude for his service. Neither desiring this nor wishing to offend his host, Kelsang Gyatso hid the plate behind some other items on the household altar. Then, as he left, he told the peasant that if ever he visited Lhasa, he should seek him out. The next day, the peasant found the plate. Not wishing to keep what he had given in offering to a member of the *sangha*, he took it outside and hurled it into the sky. To his amazement, it disappeared in mid-flight. Some years later, the peasant made a pilgrimage to Lhasa, where he duly made inquiries after his young friend. This was reported to the Dalai Lama, who summoned the man to the Potala where, to his great astonishment, the peasant found himself installed as the personal guest of the Precious Protector. On being reintroduced to Kelsang Gyatso, what should he see but the gold plate set in a prominent position on the Dalai Lama's altar.

23

The Reluctant Eighth

The last we hear of the saintly Seventh is in a letter he wrote to the Panchen Lama explaining that he was ill. Although he had received all available treatments, his condition had not improved. The Panchen Lama responded by dispatching a celebrated physician from Tashilhunpo, but it was to no avail. On the third day of the second month of the Fire Ox year—March 22, 1757—Kelsang Gyatso "saw that his work for his disciples was complete." Sitting in meditation, he "absorbed his mind in the clear light of death and, arising from it, went to the Tushita Paradise, from there to send out emanations in accordance with the needs of the world."[1]

At once, a conference was held among the leading Gelug ecclesiastics of the day to discuss the search for the Eighth Dalai Lama. There was considerable doubt as to whether or not this should be undertaken. A number of prophecies seemed to suggest that the institution would end with the passing of the Seventh. Most explicit was one in the *Book of Kadam*:

> *An incarnation of Chenrezig will work for seven lifetimes*
> *To benefit the black-haired peoples of Tibet.*

Eventually, a decision was taken that the search for a new Dalai Lama should indeed go ahead, but almost immediately, the hierarchy ran into difficulties. Three equally strong candidates emerged, and each had their supporters. Worse was to come. Before an assembly which included the Panchen Lama, the Kashag, the *ambans*, and other senior officials, the five most important oracles were called on to identify which of the three was the authentic candidate; but the oracles could not agree. Instead, all behaved strangely: one of them seizing the throne of another, still another apparently changing its mind. With farce threatening, the deadlock was broken only when the Panchen Lama declared for Jamphel Gyatso, a boy from Tsang—his own province.[2] Thus it was that in August 1762, the Eighth Dalai Lama was solemnly enthroned at the Potala Palace.

A remarkable scholar-saint by the name of Yeshe Gyaltsen was appointed tutor to the young Dalai Lama. The scion of an illegitimate branch of the Tsang aristocracy, Yeshe Gyaltsen is proof of the generally meritocratic nature of the Gelug tradition. Unrecognized by his legitimate cousins, Yeshe Gyaltsen's father had adopted the religious life soon after the birth of his son. By no means uncommon, such changes of direction were generally seen as conferring honor on a family. They certainly did not entitle the wife to take up with another man. Yet this is what Yeshe Gyaltsen's mother now did. When he heard of what had happened, the newly professed hermit abandoned his cave, vowing revenge. Fortunately, the six-year-old Yeshe Gyaltsen, showing early signs of the eloquence for which he was to become famous, managed to dissuade his father from taking his mother's life.[3] Entered soon afterward on a monastic career at Tashilhunpo, the young Yeshe Gyaltsen proved himself an exceptional scholar. Even before he had completed his studies, he began to attract a personal following. Although unknown outside Tsang when the Panchen Lama appointed him tutor to the Dalai Lama, his reputation began to grow exponentially. When he died, the lineage he founded became one of the four that were eligible to provide regents during the minority of future Dalai Lamas. So close and so devoted was the young Eighth to his tutor that not only did he build the older man a monastery for his retirement, but he also wrote his biography. This, according to one Western scholar of Tibetan literature, is "a work of great charm and spontaneity written in [the] simple flowing style that represents literary Tibet at its best"—albeit that there must be some question over its authenticity.[4] The present Dalai Lama is by no means the first to have had books ghosted for him.

At the age of nineteen, Jamphel Gyatso was called on to assume (the limited) power that was his due as nominal head of the Tibetan government. He declined, citing his youth as an impediment. This was plausible enough, but there may also have been a degree of self-awareness in his refusal. It had by now become apparent that, though unquestionably sincere in his devotion to the religious life, Jamphel Gyatso was a much lesser figure than had been either the Seventh or the Great Fifth. Two popular sayings about him reflect this. One described the Eighth as a Buddha but not a king. The other took the contrary view that he was a king but not a Buddha. In reality, he was neither—that is, he was neither a great spiritual nor a great secular leader.

In both respects, he was overshadowed by the Panchen Lama who, born in 1738, had a well-established reputation for his learning, his saintliness, and for his qualities as a leader. These qualities are confirmed by an unlikely source. In 1774, Warren Hastings, governor general of the British East India Company, desirous of entering into trade relations with Tibet, sent an envoy to Tashilhunpo. Its leader was one George Bogle. An engaging Scot, Bogle wrote a highly readable account of his stay at Tashilhunpo. His personal liking for the Panchen Lama is emphasized in several passages and corroborated in his private correspondence as well:

The . . . Lama is about forty years old.* He is of cheerful and affable temper, of great curiosity and very intelligent . . . His views are liberal . . . [he is] naturally gentle and humane . . . averse to war and bloodshed, and in all quarrels endeavors by his mediation to bring about a reconciliation. In conversation he is plain and candid, using no flattery or compliments himself, and receiving them but badly if made to him. He is generous and charitable and is universally beloved and venerated by the Tibetans, by the Kalmuks [Mongols], and by a great part of the Chinese.†

Bogle rounds off his encomium with warm tribute: "I will confess, I never knew a man whose manners pleased me so much, or for whom upon so short acquaintance I had half the heart's liking."‡5

Emperor Qianlong's repeated requests for the Panchen Lama to visit him cannot therefore have been motivated solely by a desire to make life difficult for the Dalai Lama, as some Tibetan writers suggest. The emperor took a keen interest in Buddhism, having as a teacher his friend since childhood Changkya Rinpoché, the most respected lama at the Qing court. It seems that he now wanted instruction from the highest authority available—and in the general view, this was the Panchen and not the Dalai Lama. So it was that, as usual protesting Tibetans' traditional fear of smallpox, the Panchen Lama, ignoring the advice of Jamphel Gyatso, eventually acquiesced in the emperor's entreaties and accepted. Traveling first to Jehol, the Manchu's summer residence,** he met with the

---

* He was actually thirty-six.
† Of whom there were plenty in evidence. The reader of Bogle's travelogue is left in no doubt of the significant extent to which Tibet was now subject to the emperor.
‡ According to family legend, Bogle fell in love with a female relative of the Panchen Lama and took her back to Calcutta, where she bore him two daughters. These two girls were subsequently sent home to Scotland, where eventually they both married and raised families of their own.
** At which the emperor had erected a replica of the Potala Palace as a birthday present for his mother, herself a devout Buddhist.

emperor, later following him to Beijing. There, in 1780, he duly contracted smallpox and died.

Following Jamphel Gyatso's repudiation of temporal leadership, a new regent was confirmed in office by the *ambans*. This was Nawang Tsultim, a brilliant scholar-diplomat. When, earlier, the emperor had sent to Tibet for a personal guru, it was Nawang Tsultim who was unanimously recommended by the abbots of the Three Seats. For fifteen years he served as imperial preceptor, during which time he became an intimate of the emperor, whose full confidence he enjoyed. He later became the Ganden Throne-holder and was universally acknowledged to be one of the outstanding figures of his time. Appointed regent during the summer of 1777, he remained in that capacity until 1781, when Jamphel Gyatso, now in his twenty-fourth year, could no longer delay his assumption of temporal power, though he insisted that the (now ex-) regent remain at his side.

This state of affairs continued until 1786, when Nawang Tsultim was recalled to Beijing. For just less than three unhappy years Jamphel Gyatso took the reins of government alone. Unfortunately for him, it was precisely at this time that Tibet's relations with Nepal deteriorated to the point where war broke out. There were three principal factors at work in this. The Tibetans, for their part, accused the Nepalese of debasing the silver currency which, by tradition, they minted on behalf of the Tibetan government. The Nepalese countered that the Tibetans were adulterating with sand the salt they sold to Nepal. The third factor was the attack by Nepal on Tibet's traditional allies in Sikkim, the small Buddhist kingdom that had a border with both countries. An additional factor was a letter received by the Kashag from the young king of Nepal announcing that he had taken the Sharmapa—an important lineage-holder within the Karma-Kagyu sect—as hostage until such time as the dispute was resolved. To this, the Kashag responded coolly. The truth was that the Tibetan government was immediately suspicious of the Sharmapa's sudden appearance in this context. He was well known to be furious that, following the death of his brother, the Panchen Lama, he had not received the share of that hierarch's estate to which he believed himself entitled.

The fact that, remarkably enough, the two brothers were each leaders of different and, in political terms, traditionally hostile sects of course had a bearing on this. Ordinarily, a younger brother could expect to receive a portion of his deceased elder brother's estate, even if both parties were monks; but on this occasion the guardians of Tashilhunpo, citing the fact that the Sharmapa already had extensive estates of his own, refused to hand over what he claimed. It was thus clear to all that he had sought the assistance of the Nepalese king in pursuit of his aims. At the same time as refusing to meet the Nepalese demands, the Kashag therefore gave orders for the borders with Nepal to be strengthened. Unfortunately, these measures were soon found wanting. In 1788, the Nepalese Gurkha army invaded three strategic valleys in southern Tibet. By summer, it had advanced to within a short distance of Shigatse, where Tashilhunpo itself stood. The Tibetan government responded by sending troops, which, though they succeeded in retaking the two towns in question, failed to expel the Gurkhas from Tibet. In the meantime, Emperor Qianlong, alerted by the *ambans*, dispatched an imperial army under the overall command of a certain Bazhong, one of his most trusted officials. When eventually this force arrived, though the Tibetans urged an all-out attack on the Nepalese, Bazhong took a more cautious approach, ordering the army to remain stationary during the winter months.

The following spring, the Sharmapa (a hostage no more) wrote offering to negotiate between the opposing parties, a proposal which Bazhong was quick to accept. Of course, this infuriated the Tibetans. From their perspective, if they were to enter discussions without fighting, they would be cast in the role of pleaders rather than negotiators. But the emperor's man would not listen. Accordingly, the two sides—including, among the Nepalese team, a gloating Sharmapa—met at Kyirong, where the Tibetans were compelled to accept a humiliating treaty that bound Lhasa to payment of yearly tribute to the Gurkha king. It was an arrangement that suited Bazhong particularly well: he himself benefited to the tune of large sums taken in bribes and backhanders.

Meanwhile, Jamphel Gyatso was faring none too well in his capacity as head of the government during the crisis. His first reaction was to request that the emperor permit Nawang Tsultim to return to Tibet. At first, the emperor refused, giving in only when the *ambans*, alarmed at the Nepalese crisis, added their voices in support. No sooner was he back in Lhasa than Nawang Tsultim—famous for his directness—flew into a rage at the Kashag. Emptying a bowl of *tsampa* over the heads of the four men, he lambasted them for their weakness. He immediately demoted the Tibetan army's senior general. And notwithstanding their connections, he sent two of the Dalai Lama's brothers, together with several others guilty of financial malpractice, into internal exile. When Nawang Tsultim came subsequently to know the full terms of the treaty with Nepal, he announced that if the Nepalese wanted their tribute, they would have to come and get it themselves. The Tibetan militia was to be put at readiness at once, and he himself, though an old man now, and notwithstanding that for seven years he had sat on the Ganden Throne, would take position as their commander. As to the Kashag's suggestion that they send to Nepal a proposal to reduce the amount to be paid, they were to do no such thing. Unfortunately, Nawang Tsultim died shortly after delivering this blistering rebuke.

The ex-regent was immediately replaced by another high-ranking monk official, Kundeling Rinpoché, despite the fact that

Kundeling himself had earlier been under suspicion of being in league with the Eighth's nefarious siblings. The Nepalese, meanwhile, began to demand their money: three hundred ingots of silver. The Kashag decided at this point to sue for a renegotiation of its treaty with the Gurkha king. A team of officials was duly dispatched to the fort at Nyalam, in the south. On arrival, the Nepalese demanded that some of the negotiators proceed to a preliminary conference closer to Nepal. Thus divided, the Tibetans were easy prey. At Nyalam, some Nepalese who had already arrived requested permission to hold a religious festival within the grounds of the fort. Granted this, Gurkha soldiers disguised as traders and their porters were able to enter the fort, which they took that night after a brief but fierce fight. The Tibetan negotiators were led away in chains, as were those of the advance party, which was likewise attacked and overwhelmed.

When news of the debacle reached Lhasa, it was obvious to all that a fresh Nepalese invasion was imminent. Already the Panchen Lama had fled Tashilhunpo and now several high-ranking members of the government, together with the *ambans*, began to make preparations for a general retreat to Chamdo. Soon after, reports (entirely accurate) began to circulate that not only was Shigatse being looted by the Nepalese, but that Tashilhunpo itself had been desecrated. Fear gripped the people. The Gurkha army was surely bound for Lhasa.

At last, and for the only time in his life, Jamphel Gyatso bestirred himself in defense of his country and of the faith. Addressing a tumultuous crowd from the balcony of the Jokhang, he told the people that there was no cause for alarm, that the Nepalese would not reach Lhasa, and that he himself had no intention of abandoning the city. In view of this, all government officials should carry out their normal duties without undue excitement. His oration was sufficiently persuasive that the majority remained at their posts. A few, including the *ambans*, were still determined to leave. But now the abbots of the Three Seats added their voices in support of the Dalai Lama's. In an interview with the wavering members of the Kashag they guaranteed to send monks to protect the Potala and the Jokhang, adding that "if people of high rank and extensive estates could not stay and serve their country at that crucial hour, when would they ever serve it?"[6] It was no use listening to the emperor's men. There was nothing to choose between them and the Nepalese. The latter killed and looted because they came as enemies. The former did the same thing, though they came as friends.[7]

As a result of these protestations of resolve, morale among the Tibetan militia was greatly strengthened, and attacks were launched both on the Gurkhas occupying Shigatse and their supply lines back to Nepal. Victory was assured when news came of a fresh contingent of Qing troops en route to the area—at which point Bazhong, leader of the first contingent, realizing that the emperor was now fully aware of the bribed peace he had earlier negotiated, drowned himself.

In Nepal, the Sharmapa, hearing that the combined forces of the Tibetan and Qing armies were heading for Kathmandu, bent on extracting tribute from the Nepalese king, followed suit, only in his case by means of poison.* Subsequently, and to the scandal of his followers, the Sharmapa's ritual hat was solemnly carried back to Lhasa and, so it is said, buried at the very entrance to the Jokhang. No greater insult could be imagined. This meant that for all time every visitor to Tibet's holiest shrine would be compelled symbolically to tread on it. To add further injury to this outrage, the Kashag decreed that no further incarnations of the Sharma lineage should be sought. This ban was only lifted

---

* Though it is fair to add that no mention of this is made by historians of the Sharma lineage.

during the 1960s by the present Dalai Lama—and with disastrous consequences.*

In the aftermath of this successful defeat of the Nepalese, the king sent reparations to Tibet. This included all the booty looted from Tashilhunpo and an elephant for the Dalai Lama. The *ambans* meanwhile erected a pillar at the foot of the Potala bearing an inscription celebrating the victory in Tibetan, Manchu, and Chinese. Far from showing gratitude to the imperial forces, however, the Tibetan people claimed (perhaps somewhat optimistically) that they could have managed quite well without them and were quick to make plain their hostility to Qing. Posters were put up and seditious pamphlets circulated, accusing the *ambans* and an ex-minister of financial misconduct.

Overall, however, the whole episode added to the detriment both of Tibet and of the Dalai Lama institution. Emperor Qianlong issued a new decree concerning the governance of Tibet. This stripped the right of the Dalai Lama and of the Panchen Lama to "memorialize the Throne"—that is, to petition the emperor personally. Instead, they were authorized only to "report [to the *ambans*] and ask their orders."[8] But most hateful and humiliating of all, the emperor decreed that, henceforth, the selection procedure for both lineages was to be by means of lots drawn from a golden urn, which he sent to Tibet for that purpose. As to the general management of Tibetan affairs, from now on these were entrusted to the Li Fan Huan, the Ministry for Administering Dependencies, in Beijing. All this was in clear abrogation of the original priest-patron relationship which, for Tibetans, was the only possible justification for relations with Qing in the first place.

This clear appropriation of power by Qing reflects poorly

* The fact that there are presently two claimants to the Karmapa lineage is largely due to the intervention of the current Sharmapa.

on Jamphel Gyatso. As one official wrote, the Eighth was "very pious and well read in the sacred texts, but too credulous in front of others and without authority and wisdom."[9] When he died, in November 1804, there were no doubt some members of the Gelug hierarchy who regretted not having called time on the Dalai Lama institution half a century ago. The outcome could hardly have been worse.

24

Rule by Regent

Following the demise of the Eighth, two candidates emerged as possible successors, one from Amdo, the other from Lithang, in Kham. Both were investigated by Gelug officials, and, having convinced the two search parties of their worth, both were brought back to Lhasa. There they were examined in front of a gathering of the leading figures of the day, including the regent, the Panchen Lama, the new *ambans*, several important *tulkus*, the four members of the Kashag, and the secretaries and chief attendants of the Eighth. Such an ordeal might be thought to be too much for a two-year-old child, yet the Lithang candidate "entered the room walking slowly and elegantly, like a lion among ordinary beings, as though long familiar with receiving such respect."[1] When shown by the *ambans* (it seems to have been them and not the regent) articles belonging to the Eighth mixed up with others, he unerringly chose the correct ones.

On the strength of this public success, the regent was able to persuade the *amban* officials to memorialize the emperor, requesting that he permit the successful candidate to be recognized without recourse to the golden urn, or *bumba*, that the Qianlong Emperor had stipulated should be used as the final stage of the selection procedure. Granting special dispensation, the emperor was adamant that this was "a unique matter and should not be taken as a precedent."

The boy, named Lungtok Gyatso, was duly enthroned as Ninth Dalai Lama at the end of 1808. In 1810, the regent died and was replaced in office by Demo Rinpoché. Despite a reputation for eccentricity bordering on insanity, this was a popular choice. During Demo Rinpoché's tenure of office, there was no popular unrest and, always a reliable indicator of a leader's virtue, there was a succession of good harvests. The one major blemish on the regent's career was the death of Lungtok Gyatso, in March 1815, at just nine years of age.

The Ninth would have vanished entirely from history, save among the pages of the improbably lengthy biography of him written by Demo Rinpoché, had it not been for his meetings with the remarkable, and also eccentric, Thomas Manning, the first Englishman to visit Lhasa.

Born in 1772, the son of a Norfolk clergyman, young Thomas was a sickly child. On account of this, he was educated at home, where he developed a precocious interest in Plato. On recovering his health, he was admitted to Clare College, Cambridge, where he conceived a passion for the East and became obsessed with the idea of visiting China. To that end, the young Manning began a ferocious study of the language and culture of a country that was then all but unknown in Europe. This took him, at the turn of the century, to Paris, where he became the student of a certain Dr. Hagar. When, on the eve of the Battle of Trafalgar (1805), Manning was arrested with all other known English travelers in France, he was the only one to whom Napoleon (whose "Godlike face" he was able to study on a visit to the Tuileries Palace) granted a passport to leave the country.* Returned to England, Manning decided that he must visit the East, to the consternation of his friend Charles Lamb, the great essayist. Lamb good-humoredly tried to dissuade him of his ambition. "For God's sake, don't think any more of Independent Tartary . . . depend upon it they'll never make you their king . . . I tremble for your Christianity. They'll certainly circumcise you . . . Pray try and cure yourself."[2] But his plea fell on deaf ears. Manning succeeded in obtaining passage in an East India Company ship bound for Canton, where he spent the next three years living in the English trading outpost on China's southern coast. There, unable to find a way into China proper, Manning subsequently conceived the idea of traveling to Beijing via Bengal and Tibet. Accordingly, he took a ship bound for Calcutta, where he seems to have created an unfavorable impression among Company officials. According to one, Manning had taken to wearing fancy dress, though according to Manning it was the costume of "Tartar gentlemen"; but "with his broad English face and full-flowing beard, [he looked] as little like a Tartar as any son of Adam one might meet in London."[3]

Traveling only with an interpreter for company, Manning arrived at Lhasa during the winter of 1811. Writing in his journal, which fortunately survives, Manning wrote that if the Potala exceeded his expectations, "the town as far fell short of them." It was, he wrote, "a miserable place to live. There is nothing striking, nothing pleasing in its appearance."

Manning's "first care" on taking up residence in the capital was to provide himself with a proper hat. Thus equipped, he was soon granted an audience with the young Dalai Lama. The five-year-old hierarch had, he wrote, the "simple and unaffected manners of a well-educated princely child," adding that "his

---

* On his way back from China in 1817, Manning obtained a private interview with the by-then deposed emperor on the island of St. Helena, during which he reminded Napoleon of this favor. History does not record whether Bonaparte was grateful for the souvenir.

face, was, I thought, poetically and affectingly beautiful." The boy himself was "of a gay and cheerful disposition; his beautiful mouth perpetually unbending into a graceful smile." It seems that little Lungtok Gyatso took considerable interest in this strange visitor: "He inquired whether I had not met with molestations and difficulties on the road; to which I promptly returned the proper answer. I said I had had troubles, but now that I had the happiness of being in his presence, they were amply compensated. I thought of them no more. I could see that this answer pleased both the Lama and his household people." Immediately after the interview, Manning told the regent that he would like some books about the Tibetan religion, though this elicited only a vague response. Nonetheless, he was "extremely affected" by the whole experience: "I could have wept through strangeness of sensation."[4] Later, he made two drawings of the Dalai Lama from memory, though regrettably these seem not to have survived.

Maddeningly, Manning's journal tails off soon after his first audience with the Dalai Lama, becoming little more than epigrammatic thereafter. He records that he saw the Ninth for a second time after the Dalai Lama had completed the—generally three-week-long—retreat which, even at this young age, he was compelled by tradition to undertake prior to the Monlam Chenmo. The boy was "pale and in worse health, I thought, for his seclusion." On Tibetan New Year's Day he visited Lungtok Gyatso once again, this time presenting the boy with a telescope. Finally, on April 6, 1812, he "took leave of the Grand Lama with a sorrowful heart."

Manning was in due course sent back to India by the *ambans*. He finally made it to Beijing as a member of Lord Amherst's embassy in 1816. But on his return to England, resentful at what he saw as his maltreatment by the East India Company, Manning never wrote, or even, it seems, spoke about his adventures.

Instead, he lived more or less as a recluse. And though, to the end, he kept up his Chinese studies, his knowledge died with him, in the genteel city of Bath in 1840.

Manning's appearance in Lhasa foreshadowed the long history of British relations with Tibet. A year after his departure from Lhasa, British troops went to war with Nepal, a development that marked a new departure in Asian history. For the next century and more, the British Empire was to play a dominant role not only in India, but also in the Himalayan region and in South-East Asia. Despite Nepal's relatively recent conflict with Tibet, the Nepalese king appealed to Lhasa for support against the British. Unsurprisingly, this was not forthcoming. But it does seem that the regent circulated a letter to all the monasteries in the land requesting prayers for a Nepalese victory over the invaders. To no avail, however: the British duly defeated the Gurkhas and forced a treaty on the king. Annexing Darjeeling in 1835, the British went on to take Ladakh, Sikkim, and, eventually, the Spiti Valley, which lay on the southern fringes of Tibetan cultural influence. Although the Qing emperor quickly became aware of the threat to his own empire, he was powerless to divert resources outside China itself. Already Qing had been weakened by the rebellion of a millenarian sect, the White Lotus Society, which united poor and landless peasants against the Manchu government. This was put down only with difficulty. There followed, later in the century, the two Opium Wars (1840–2 and 1858–60) and the Taiping Rebellion (1850–64). As a result, Tibet was less and less effectively governed from Beijing. Unfortunately, however, none of the Dalai Lamas between the Eighth and the Thirteenth succeeded in taking effective control.

The Ninth, who had so charmed Thomas Manning, died when a cold contracted prior to the Monlam Chenmo of 1815 progressed to pneumonia, only two months past his ninth birthday. It was, nonetheless, a "good death," according to Demo Rinpoché who recorded, with what embellishment, if any, we can only guess, that the young Dalai Lama passed away soon after dictating a letter to the emperor, sitting up on his bed and reciting tantric mantras.

> Like this he continued the three-cycle tantric breathing, until he gradually induced the experience of clear light consciousness. He then allowed the subtle elements of his body to dissolve. First the sign of the mirage came; then an appearance like wispy smoke; then sparks, like fireflies at night; then an awareness like the light of an undisturbed butter lamp. After this came the four emptiness experiences, beginning with the appearance like a cloudless sky, until the fourth emptiness arose, the great radiance of the primordial clear light mind . . . Thus he passed away without experiencing the slightest fear or discomfort.[5]

When the emperor received news of Lungtok Gyatso's death, he was furious. "If the testimonies were as alleged [that Lungtok Gyatso was the authentic incarnation of Chenrezig], he should have lived a long life . . . instead of dying a premature death. This shows that what [the *amban*] reported was mainly exaggerated, and I regret even now that I should have been so easily prevailed upon [to dispense with the golden urn]."[6] He would brook no such break with the command of the illustrious Qianlong in the case of the Tenth.

In the meantime, Demo Rinpoché began the task of identifying the new incarnation. A total of five candidates emerged. This was quickly narrowed to three. The regent finally found in favor of a candidate from Lithang, Tsultrim Gyatso. Both unaware of the emperor's feelings on the subject, Demo Rinpoché persuaded the *amban* to write to the emperor requesting permission once again to dispense with the ceremony of the golden urn. This drew an angry response from Beijing. In April 1819, a letter to the regent arrived rebuking him sharply and warning that, should he dare to go to Beijing to present his petition personally, "let him be arrested and punished."[7] But by then the regent himself was dead of smallpox.

This unfortunate development threw the question of who was to be the next Dalai Lama into abeyance for a full three years. The new regent was the twenty-eight-year-old Tsemonling Rinpoché. Unsurprisingly, his youth and inexperience enabled the *ambans* to outmaneuver him over the selection procedure. They began to encourage supporters of the other candidates to press their claims, desisting only when the regent struck a deal with the *ambans*. The Lithang candidate would be officially confirmed in office without recourse to the golden urn but, for form's sake, they would give out that it had in fact been used. By this means, the *ambans* secured a crucial victory. True or not, it was officially acknowledged that the golden urn had been used. The emperor could henceforth claim a precedent.

Once Tsultrim Gyatso's identification as the authentic incarnation had been confirmed and ratified by the Qing emperor, he was duly enthroned in the Potala Palace. As usual, the young Dalai Lama entered his novitiate under the direction of the then Panchen Lama, who performed the hair-cutting ritual that signified the beginning of his monastic career. The Tenth Dalai Lama was a sickly child, however, and it is said that his tutor spent almost as much time praying for his well-being as he did instructing him. It is further reported that the young hierarch much preferred the company of the common people to that of his court officials. During the brighter months, he was often to be found sunning himself on the verandah in the company of his office clerks. The government meanwhile sent him the best physicians and frequently ordained special prayers and rituals to win the young Dalai Lama better health. But when, on one occasion, the regent and members of the Kashag paid him a visit, he rebuked them, saying that the trouble they were taking on his behalf was really for their own prestige. Referring to recent disturbances in the districts of Powo and Kokonor, he bewailed the suffering of the people in these places. Despite the ministers' claims to have settled the grievances of the local inhabitants, the country was actually worse off than before: "Whether you are making these improvements as you claim or not, the condition of my subjects has deteriorated."[8] Although Tsultrim Gyatso received full ordination from the Panchen Lama in 1834, following the completion of his studies at Drepung Monastery, and although this was when he might have been expected to assume temporal power, this seems never to have occurred. He died three years later, aged just twenty-one.

There has been much speculation as to whether Tsultrim Gyatso might have been slowly poisoned. A Chinese source hints at a more violent end.[9] "The Dalai Lama was wounded in the neck and blood was running down. [The regent] knew this but did not try to help him. The case was very suspicious. The emperor ordered the *amban* and the Panchen Lama and other officials to interrogate all the suspects to get their confession."[10] But if an inquiry was indeed carried out, nothing came of it. Meanwhile, the regent, Tsemonling Rinpoché, was tasked with identifying the Eleventh Dalai Lama. For the third time in succession, one of the most promising candidates was born in Kham, this time in the small town of Gartar.* Among the evidence for the authenticity of the Gartar candidate was the appearance of a rainbow which seemed to enclose the local monastery like a tent on the day he was born. It was also noted that wherever the boy went, a large crow, which had first been spotted in the vicinity of the family home, seemed to follow

---

* This preponderance of candidates (and indeed of Dalai Lamas) from Kham arguably reflects the efforts on behalf of the Gelug sect to extend its influence in a region with traditional links to the Kagyu sect.

him. And not only that, but the bird seemed fearless, accepting with dignity whenever anyone took it food. It was surely an emanation of Mahakala.

At the final interview of candidates, just two remained. The boy from Gartar chose unerringly the items that had belonged to the Tenth Dalai Lama. But then the detested *bumba* was brought out and the names of both boys were inscribed on tallies and placed inside. Fortunately, the *amban* drew out the one bearing the name of the Gartar candidate. At precisely that moment, the boy himself, who was not in the room for this part of the procedure, is said to have announced to his mother that his name had just been drawn. In 1842, at the age of four, the Eleventh Dalai Lama was enthroned at the Potala and tonsured by the Panchen Lama who gave him his religious name, Khedrup Gyatso.

It is somewhat surprising that, on this occasion, the *ambans* succeeded in obtaining complete control over the confirmation of Khedrup Gyatso as Dalai Lama, given that it must have been clear to Tibetan officials that the Qing Dynasty was at this moment under intense pressure both at home and abroad. The regent's acceptance of the golden-urn procedure almost certainly reflects his desire to obtain Qing favor as a means to shoring up his own position against the Kashag, which was agitating for his impeachment on the grounds of corruption. When, after the Dalai Lama's enthronement, two ministers went to the regent's house in order to arraign him, they were met by a contingent of monks from Sera Mey, the monastic college to which he belonged, who beat the two *kalons* so badly that one of them died a few months later without recovering. Outraged, the Kashag, together with the Panchen Lama, confounded the regent by appealing directly to the Daoguang Emperor. The Emperor in turn sent a special envoy to investigate the claims against the regent, as a result of which Tsemonling Rinpoché was duly stripped of office and exiled to Manchuria in disgrace. His allies at Sera Mey intervened on his behalf again, however, causing the deaths of several people and briefly freeing the regent. But realizing his position was hopeless, Tsemonling Rinpoché gave himself up, and he was led away in chains. Devastatingly, the emperor now decreed that the Tsemonling reincarnation should no longer be sought, on the grounds that he had brought shame on the Gelug sect.

As to the Dalai Lama, we know little about the Eleventh, other than that he spent the next decade undergoing his monastic education in the manner befitting an incarnation of Chenrezig. It is clear that he was considered promising. He was offered the position of head of state at the unusually early age of seventeen. Accepting, he was invested with full authority during the Monlam Chenmo of 1855. Yet barely eleven months later, he too was dead. Some Tibetans said that the *ambans* were responsible this time. Others alleged that the new regent, Reting Rinpoché, was implicated. But again, nothing was proven.

If the Qing Dynasty was weak at this time, a third succession crisis in forty years meant that Tibet was also poorly placed to withstand the external pressures that now began to mount. A year after the death of the Eleventh Dalai Lama, a newly resurgent Nepal invaded southern Tibet once again. As usual, trade violations were the pretext. Monks from the Three Seats vowed to expel the Gurkhas and large numbers made for the battle zone. But before there was any fighting, the Tibetan government was forced to accept a humiliating treaty. It was an inauspicious prelude to the life of the new incarnation of the Precious Protector.

The Twelfth Dalai Lama was the first to come from central Tibet for four generations. The imposing stone mansion at Olkha where he was born still stands. But although his family owned property, it had fallen into debt some time before his miraculous birth. His parents were on the point of moving when they both experienced a number of auspicious portents. His father dreamed that the sky filled with celestial beings. These told him that the "sun of his happiness" was about to rise. And after the birth of the child, further signs occurred in Lhasa, including the spectacle of clouds gathering above the capital which took clearly the form of the Tibetan syllable *ol*. Naturally, this was taken to be an indication that the search should take place in and around Olkha. When, in due course, he and two other candidates were examined by the usual high dignitaries—including the regent, but not the Panchen Lama, who was, at this time, himself just an infant—he was the only one correctly to identify the *vajra*, bell, and rosary of the Eleventh. Surviving trial by golden vase and given the religious name of Trinley Gyatso, the boy was enthroned a few months short of his third birthday.

In 1862, when the Dalai Lama was six years old, a minister by the name of Shatra began to plot against the regent. Unfortunately for him, Reting Rinpoché became aware of his plans and succeeded in having Shatra banished from Lhasa. It seems indeed that the regent intended to have Shatra killed. He failed in this probably only because he could not, as a monk, be seen to order a political assassination. This enabled Shatra, though confined now to a monastery, to make contact with his old friend and ally, the thuggish Palden Dondhup, monk-treasurer of Ganden Monastery. By playing on the fact that the regent had been interfering with revenues due to Drepung, Palden Dondhup won over not only his own but also Drepung Monastery to Shatra's cause. Subsequently liberated by a party of monks drawn from both communities, Shatra returned to the vicinity of Lhasa. On arrival, he received greetings in the form of a *khatag*, or silk scarf, sent with the blessings of the Dalai Lama. This indicated that Trinley Gyatso's court had taken Shatra's side. Thus emboldened, Shatra announced that he intended to attack the regent the next day. In response, a force from Sera, the only one of the Three Seats to oppose Shatra, deployed troops to protect Reting Rinpoché in his palace. Meanwhile Shatra's forces published a list of errors committed by the regent—not the least of which was his acquiescence in the use of the golden urn in the selection of the Dalai Lama—and asked for the support of the people.

Next day, as good as his word, Shatra gave the requisite order and supporters attacked those guarding the regent. Outmaneuverd and outnumbered, the regent fled, making his way finally to China, there to put his case to the emperor in person. No sooner had Reting gone than the government granted full temporal authority to the Dalai Lama. As he was then only six years old, this was just a machination necessitated by the tradition that no one save a monk of the Gelug could rule in the name of the Dalai Lama. Shatra, a layman, was then immediately confirmed in the dignity of Desi, the post being revived especially for him. All this took place while the *ambans*, with no troops of their own, looked on helplessly. The emperor was at that time fighting for survival. The fury of the Taiping Rebellion required all his resources to be deployed in China.

We have a unique description of Shatra from the French Catholic missionary Père Evariste Régis Huc, who visited Lhasa with a priest companion back in 1845. Shatra had, he wrote, a "broad, smiling face [and] a dignity that was truly regal; his black eyes, under long lashes, were intelligent and full of kindness." Recounting several interviews with Shatra, Huc portrayed the Tibetan as a wise and accomplished politician with a great interest in the doctrines of the missionaries. "Your religion is the same as ours; the principles are the same, we differ only in the explanations," he said, though from Huc's perspective, Shatra's views led in the end only to "vague pantheistic conceptions" of the nature of created reality.[11]

For the two years of life that remained to him after his seizure of power, much of Shatra's time was taken up with hunting down a rebel chieftain. This was Gonpo Namgyal, who had, over the course of the past two decades, come to dominate a large part of Kham. Gonpo Namgyal's cruelty was legendary. It is reported that on one occasion at least, he succeeded in causing an outbreak of plague by firing arrows attached to which were small bags of snuff blended with the dried pustules of smallpox sufferers and the excreta of cholera victims. It is also said that he would force-feed the captured children of his enemies with milk and curd and then, hurling them from the battlements of his fortress, take pleasure when their stomachs burst as they hit the ground.

Remarkably, despite his abject immorality, Gonpo Namgyal still has his apologists among some Tibetans.[12] These regard him as a patriot who, in addition to fighting the central government, also took on the Chinese. Appropriately enough, Gonpo Namgyal died, probably at his own hand, in the flames which burned his stronghold a few months after the death of Shatra in 1865.

Shatra's own death caused yet another power vacuum. Trinley Gyatso, being at the time still only eight years old, could not, of course, be expected to assume the duties which technically his office demanded. Instead, the Ganden Throneholder was appointed regent in his stead, while Palden Dondhup, Shatra's old ally, held the post of Lord Chamberlain to the Dalai Lama, a position which carried great influence. During the course of the next six years, Palden Dondhup built up a reputation as a harsh and unforgiving official known particularly for the zeal with which he pursued those dilatory in paying their taxes. It is said that he always kept a fresh animal skin hanging outside the door of his office as a warning to any who fell foul of him. Though completely unlearned, there is no doubt that Palden Dondhup was quick-witted. On one occasion, it was pointed out to him that he was holding some documents upside down while handing down judgment in a case brought before him. "I am deliberately holding them upside-down," he replied, "because it is an upside-down man we are dealing with here."[13]

During the spring of 1871, Palden Dondhup convened a meeting of the Kashag at his residence. When the four ministers failed to emerge even after two days had passed, it was clear that mischief was afoot. It turned out that one had been sewn inside one of Palden Dondhup's animal skins and tossed into the river, while the other three remained under arrest. The old rascal was mounting his own coup. On this occasion, the *ambans* appear to have moved swiftly to escort the Dalai Lama from the Potala to the Norbulingka Palace.* Meanwhile, another leading member of the Dalai Lama's staff was called on to ensure that the monasteries of Drepung and Sera did not support the rebel. No doubt seeing an opportunity to advance their own interests at the expense of Ganden, they agreed, a development which Palden Dondhup seems not to have anticipated. He fled his house, in the direction of his old monastery at Ganden. Under attack from government troops reinforced by a contingent of monks from Sera, Ganden was eventually forced to capitulate after a vigorous defense. According to Chinese records, Palden Dondhup was then taken away, tried and shot.[14] According to Tibetan accounts, he committed suicide.

A year later, the Dalai Lama was finally confirmed in office, as head of state, a position he had held nominally for more than ten years now. He survived just two years and fifteen days before himself "retiring to the Tushita Paradise." Yet again, there were accusations of foul play. Two of the Dalai Lama's monk attendants, both of whom had used his friendship to gain honors and titles for their friends, were accused of having a hand in his demise. Accordingly, they were arrested, tortured, and finally

---

* The Jewel Path, the Dalai Lama's summer residence.

exiled. That same year, 1875, the Kashag nominated as regent the new Kundeling Rinpoché. It was he who successfully led the search for the incarnation destined to stamp the full authority of Chenrezig on the government of Tibet for the first time in more than two centuries.

25

The Great Thirteenth

The Great Thirteenth, as he came to be known, was born of humble stock at Dakpo, two days' journey to the southeast of Lhasa. On the night of his conception, an earthquake shook the region, and, during his mother's pregnancy, it is said that a great many other miracles occurred. On one occasion, while the family was preparing the winter store of dairy produce, they returned from lunch to find previously half-empty churns spilling over with the richest butter they had ever seen. And, significantly, a large white bird settled in a walnut tree close to the family home. Each morning it flew off in the direction of Lhasa; each evening it would return, circling the house three times before alighting. Then, on the day of his birth, the fifth day of the fifth month in the year of the Fire Mouse (June 26, 1876), a brilliant rainbow appeared over the house.

By the time he was two years old, the infant prodigy was one of three candidates wanted for questioning by the authorities in Lhasa. Having successfully identified the previous Dalai Lama's belongings, the boy from Dakpo was the only one left. It just remained for the *ambans* to inform the emperor. On this occasion, there was no question of using the golden urn. The Qing Dynasty, now in terminal decline, was not in any position to enforce its use. The child was duly taken from its family and installed with all ceremony at Gungthang Monastery, just to the south of Lhasa, remaining there several weeks. During this time the boy was tonsured by the Panchen Lama, who gave him his religious name, Thupten Gyatso. He was then taken to a temple just to the east of the capital where he remained a year "to rest and prepare himself for his future role."[1] The actual enthronement ceremony took place in the Potala during the summer of 1879.

At the age of nineteen, Thupten Gyatso was elevated to full temporal and spiritual authority over his fellow Tibetans, though of course this authority had been largely nominal since the time of the Great Fifth. According to one account, a Qing official of the time remarked that "affairs had been managed very badly."[2] Thupten Gyatso was a strong, healthy, vigorous, and energetic young man who, the *ambans* should have realized, would make life extremely difficult for them. The official felt they would have been well advised to prepare a fate similar to that of the previous four Dalai Lamas.

In fact, there was one attempt to murder Thupten Gyatso. Remarkably, though, it came not from the Qing side but from within the Dalai Lama's own closest circle. When the newly empowered hierarch began to experience bouts of illness, he naturally consulted the Nechung oracle as to the cause. Shockingly, the oracle revealed that the ex-regent, Demo Rinpoché, had prepared a spell, which he had secreted in a pair of boots he had given to Terton Sogyal. The latter was a close associate of the Thirteenth and a man widely acknowledged for his high spiritual attainments, especially in relation to Shinje, the Lord of Death. Terton Sogyal was duly summoned for cross-examination. Yes, he had received a pair of boots as a gift from the ex-regent; and yes, he had noticed something strange about them. Every time he wore them, he suffered a nosebleed. The boots themselves were then examined. To the amazement of all, in one of the soles a scrap of paper was found on which was inscribed the Dalai Lama's name alongside an occult symbol: this was black magic. At once, the ex-regent, his brother the chief minister, and their associates were arrested. The National Assembly, convening an emergency session, called for the imposition of the death penalty on each of the accused. This included the chief minister's wife, along with sixteen Bonpo priests. The Dalai Lama was, however, against capital punishment, so bamboo was driven under the nails of those chiefly responsible (though not those of the regent) and each received a hundred lashes.[3] Demo Rinpoché himself died in custody, drowned, it would seem, in a vast copper vat of water.[4] Even the chief minister's wife was flogged and compelled to sit for a week, manacled, and wearing the *cangue*, in Lhasa's main thoroughfare before being sent into exile with her husband. And Tengyeling, the regent's monastery, was punished with the appropriation of his estates and withdrawal of official recognition of the Demo lineage. No further incarnations were to be sought for—an edict which caused great resentment within Tengyeling's monastic community. It was a humiliation for which they were to exact a terrible revenge.

A man of great moral courage, Thupten Gyatso immediately sought a reform of the *sangha*. In one of his earliest public sermons, the young Dalai Lama made known his concerns about lax monastic discipline. "Some rough men* . . . drink, smoke, and gamble. They roam about the countryside in various dresses and they wander into the villages and oppress the poor villagers." Henceforth, good order was to be observed and the *sangha* was to dedicate itself to propagating the *buddhadharma*. Cats and dogs were banned from monastic precincts, and there were to be strict limits on the amount of interest

---

* Meaning, of course, monks.

that monasteries could charge on any loans they made to their lay tenants. If a member of the *sangha* was found guilty of crime, no favor was to be shown him. To emphasize his authority over even the abbots of the great monasteries, Thupten Gyatso once kept those of Sera standing for two days in his anteroom before calling them in and fining them for overburdening their peasants.

The twenty-five years or so that spanned the close of the nineteenth century and the opening of the twentieth saw momentous changes in Tibet's relationship with the rest of the world. While the Qing Dynasty tottered to extinction, Tibet became the focus of the so-called Great Game, the quest for power in Central Asia played between the competing superpowers of Great Britain and Russia. By the time of the Thirteenth's accession, the Qing Dynasty's role in Tibetan affairs was, as we have seen, largely symbolic. What remained of its garrison in Lhasa was reduced almost to a laughing stock. Its soldiery consisted largely of the offspring of mixed Chinese and Tibetan unions, and its chief occupation was performing dragon dances in return for alms. The central government had long since ceased to pay regular wages. And, according at least to popular opinion, many of its members suffered the effects of *rgya nad,** or syphilis.[5]

The greatest threat to Tibet itself came from the great trading empire founded by the British. By now, India, the jewel in Queen Victoria's crown, was formally governed by a viceroy answerable directly to the British Parliament in Whitehall. Whereas the East India Company, which had previously looked after British interests, was content to confine itself to trade alone, the British Mandarins who ran the empire were quick to extend British government wherever it could be shown to be in Her Majesty's interest. Already, Ladakh, Sikkim, and

---

* Literally, the "Chinese disease."

Bhutan had been taken into the orbit of Britain's Indian Empire. This the British justified on the grounds of wanting to secure India's northern borders, particularly against encroachment by Russia, then seen as the chief external threat. Up until 1887, there was no direct confrontation between the British and Sikkim's Tibet; but when Tibetan troops occupied a fort, Khamba Dzong, in Chumbi Valley, an area that the British considered to fall within their territory, a direct confrontation was certain. If the Tibetans did not withdraw, British troops would expel them by force. The maharajah of Sikkim earnestly counselled dialogue: for the Tibetan army to challenge the British would be "like throwing an egg against a rock." But the authorities in Lhasa refused to back down, with the result that their troops were soundly defeated.

Two years later, the British called a convention in order to define the boundary between Sikkim and Tibet, and to secure formal recognition of Sikkim's status as a protectorate of the British Empire. Assuming that Tibet was governed from Beijing, only the *ambans* were called to the conference. No Tibetan officials attended. In 1893, a further meeting was held to append trade regulations to what was effectively a treaty concerning Tibet between Britain and Qing. Again, no Tibetans attended. But soon after, rumors began to reach British ears suggesting that Tibet, unknown to its Qing overlords, was receiving military aid from Russia. And then Claude White, the political officer in Sikkim, concluded that the emperor of China had "no authority whatever" in Tibet. These disquieting developments began to raise the question in British minds as to whether they ought not to be speaking directly to the Dalai Lama.

Whispers about Russian aid to Tibet continued to circulate, taking on greater credibility when it became clear that one of the Dalai Lama's closest advisers was a Russian national. This was a monk originally from the Buryat Republic, a Russian dependency, who went under the thrillingly sinister name of Agvan Dorjieff. He must be a spy. During 1901, questions were put before the British Parliament: Was Her Majesty's government aware of Russian involvement in Tibet?* Gradually a climate of suspicion developed in India and Whitehall, which helped to lay the foundations of one of Britain's last great imperial adventures.

Thupten Gyatso himself was of course completely unaware of mounting British concern about Tibet. Still less was he aware of burgeoning interest in his homeland as the dwelling place of the improbably named (and certainly fictitious) Koot Hoomi, one of the enlightened spiritual masters who would lead the world to a higher spiritual plane. This was the "mahatma" with whom another shadowy Russian émigré, Madame Blavatsky, founder of the Theosophical Society, claimed to be in touch telepathically. Tibet was just beginning to become identified as a land of magic and mystery. The Dalai Lama, for his own part, was preoccupied with stamping his authority on the government and with fulfilling his own, rather more onerous, vocation. From the first, he seems to have distrusted most of his high officials. Even when their loyalty was not in question, he was frustrated by their lack of energy and often complained of their lack of drive and guts.[6]

Meanwhile, the British were edging ever closer to a general confrontation with Tibet. The new viceroy, George Nathaniel, Lord Curzon, was quick to recognize the emptiness of Qing claims to authority over Tibet. Nervous at the eastern expansion of the Russian empire—its steady progress by means of railway, telegraph line, and local administrators toward the Indian border— his first move in relation to Tibet was an attempt to initiate a correspondence with the Dalai Lama. His first letter was returned, unopened, several months later. Curzon tried again in 1901 and

* The first of these was put by my paternal great-grandfather, Henry Norman.

in 1902, with the same result on each occasion. His interest, piqued at first, turned to ire when he learned that the mysterious Dorjieff had in the meantime visited the Russian capital not once but twice. It was even rumored that the feckless—if thoughtful—young tsar, whom Dorjieff had certainly met, had converted to Buddhism.

By 1903, Curzon was convinced that the Tibetans had signed a secret treaty with the Russians. Though quite untrue, the fear was a reasonable one. Russia's eastern push was real enough. It is also true that Dorjieff, though not a spy, was doing his best to encourage the Dalai Lama to turn to Russia for support. By linking Russia with the mythical kingdom of Shambala, he had convinced a number of influential Tibetans to identify the tsar with White Tara, another form of Chenrezig. He even persuaded an initially skeptical Thupten Gyatso that the tsar was indeed on the point of conversion to the faith. When that happened, he would take all Russia with him. But Dorjieff's motives were not what Curzon thought. He did not seek straightforward Russian dominance of Tibet. Instead, he seems to have dreamed of a pan-Mongol–Tibetan Buddhist confederation at the heart of Central Asia under the spiritual leadership of the Dalai Lama and under the material protection of the tsar.

In July 1903, Curzon met a young, ambitious and impetuous imperial adventurer, Lieutenant-Colonel (later Colonel Sir) Francis Younghusband. He seemed the ideal man to lead an exploratory mission to Tibet. Backed by seven hundred troops, Younghusband was duly dispatched to Khamba Dzong, from which Tibetan troops had recently been ejected. Ostensibly this was in order to open talks with the Lhasa government over trade with India. Curzon's ulterior motive was, of course, to find out more about the workings of this mysterious country. The Tibetans responded by hastily convening the Tsongdu.* This quickly concluded that the British

* The National Assembly.

were enemies of Buddhism and must be rebuffed. Any negotiations must take place outside Tibetan territory. The Kashag, however, took a more cautious line, advising the Dalai Lama to accede to British requests. Unfortunately for his cabinet, this was not the answer Thupten Gyatso wanted to hear. No less impetuous than Younghusband himself, the Dalai Lama immediately had the four ministers placed under house arrest. One subsequently died, or committed suicide—it is not clear which. In their place, the Thirteenth appointed four new ministers, men who shared his opinion that the British should be sent back, encouraged by main force if necessary. Meanwhile, the British continued to occupy Khamba Dzong, conducting, as one Tibetan historian observes, "impressive military exercises, taking photographs, botanizing, and geologizing"—and, he might have added, hunting.[7]

In due course, two officials arrived from Lhasa to insist that the British had to return to India before the Tibetan government could consider their requests. Dissatisfied, Younghusband demanded that the Tibetan government send more senior officials with whom he could hold meaningful talks. None was forthcoming. Meanwhile, the two men tasked with persuading the British to leave procrastinated and evaded the British as far as possible, hoping that with the onset of winter, the *inji* (as all Europeans continue to be known) would go away. They finally did. But early in the new year, the British were back. This time, Younghusband had with him a force comprising some five thousand mixed Sikh and Gurkha troops. At the behest of the new Kashag, the Tibetan government now responded by sending an army of its own to block Younghusband's path. Thupten Gyatso and his ministers were convinced that, with the full resources of the *sangha* mobilized to invoke the protection of the wrathful deities, the Tibetan troops could not fail to drive these lowlanders back. Just how mistaken this was became clear in the first major clash, which took place on March 31,

1904 at Chumi Sengbo. Using fifty shrapnel shells, 1,400 machine-gun rounds, 14,351 rounds of rifle ammunition, and without loss of life to themselves, the British killed 628 Tibetans. Among the dead were two Tibetan generals and two monk officials.

The battle of Chumi Sengbo must surely rank as one of the least glorious feats of arms in the history of the British Empire. Younghusband himself admitted that the action was a massacre, though he claimed that it was brought about by the Tibetans themselves. But nothing could now stop the imperial advance on Lhasa. Several more engagements ensued, each with a crushing victory to the British. There was a degree of surprise and admiration on both sides, however. The British were greatly impressed with the Tibetans' calmness and tenacity under fire, and the Tibetans were astonished to find their wounded treated at the enemy's field hospitals, while those taken prisoner were merely disarmed and given money and cigarettes before being set free.[8]

On April 12, Younghusband reached Gyantse. Again finding no one with whom he could conduct meaningful negotiations, he wrote to the Dalai Lama, informing him that he had until June 12 to send competent negotiators. His letter, sealed and beribboned in best imperial fashion, was dispatched to Lhasa in the care of a prisoner recently released. Several days later, the man reappeared, bearing no reply but only the very same package, unopened. To the British, this was as insulting as it was frustrating, and it did not take much argument on the part of Younghusband to persuade his political masters to sanction a final push to the capital. At once, he attacked the main Tibetan stronghold in Gyantse. Victory secured, Younghusband ordered his men to Lhasa. At last, the Dalai Lama accepted that he must agree to Britain's demands or risk the capital. But it was now too late. The British were just days away. Hastily appointing the Ganden Tripa as regent, Thupten Gyatso left Lhasa at dawn on July 30 leaving Younghusband to his prize, the unveiling of the sacred city.

Taking a small party of officials with him, the Dalai Lama struck northward in the direction of Mongolia. His one reliable ally was the Jetsundamba Lama, or Hutuktu, the senior incarnation within the Gelug tradition in Mongolia. Reaching Urgya after several weeks' travel, Thupten Gyatso was dismayed to find himself less than generously welcomed by the Mongolian hierarch. According to the Dalai Lama's official biography, there was a dispute over the proper height of the Hutuktu's throne in relation to that of Thupten Gyatso. But according to another account, the Dalai Lama was aghast to find that his Mongolian counterpart had taken a wife, was given to drink, and addicted to tobacco.[9] He even had the temerity to smoke in the Dalai Lama's presence. In Thupten Gyatso's eyes, smoking tobacco was a greater vice even than drinking alcohol.[*] For the time being, however, he was compelled to remain in Urgya while the Ganden Throne-holder dealt with Younghusband back in Lhasa. Principally, the British required the Lhasa government to recognize their claim to the protectorate over Sikkim; the Tibetan government must also accept the establishment of regulated trade markets at Gyantse, Phari, and Dromo (there was to be a garrison of troops in support, quartered at Gyantse), while Lhasa must not enter into separate agreements with other foreign powers. This granted, the British withdrew in September, leaving the Tibetans as stunned as they were relieved to see the back of them. But with relief came a sense of bereavement too, as the British made clear that they did not wish to see the Dalai Lama back in Lhasa for the time being.

A member of the Russian Geographical Society, P. K. Kozlov, who met the Dalai Lama in Urgya, described how, during their conversation his "expression was one of great calmness . . . He

---

[*] Not only is tobacco considered an intoxicant within the Tibetan tradition, some hold that it can actually kill deities.

Secret Lives of the Dalai Lama

often looked me straight in the eye, and each time our glances met, he smiled slightly and with great dignity." However, "as soon as the matter of the English and their military expedition to Tibet was touched upon, his expression changed. His face clouded with sorrow, his gaze fell, and his voice broke with nervousness."[10] The invasion had clearly dealt the still-young hierarch a confidence-shattering blow. To make matters worse, the overtures he now made to the tsar were firmly, if politely, rebuffed. Thupten Gyatso found himself entirely without friends.

From Urgya, the Dalai Lama traveled, in 1906, to the Kokonor region, and thence to Kumbum Monastery. But lest it should seem that in these "wanderings" (as the Chinese spoke disparagingly of his years in the wilderness) the Dalai Lama was less than fully occupied, it should be remembered that wherever he went he received thousands in audience, bestowed countless blessings, gave frequent public sermons, initiating and ordaining a constant stream of monastics even as he continued his scholastic study of the *buddhadharma*. He also began to take a keen interest in world affairs. And while at Kumbum, Tsongkhapa's birthplace, finding monastic discipline poorly maintained, he used his religious authority—undamaged by his political troubles— to re-impose good order.

From Kumbum, Thupten Gyatso traveled to Wutaishan, the holy mountain in China, where again he remained several months. While there, the Dalai Lama received a formal invitation to visit Emperor Guangxu in Beijing. Although extremely dubious of Qing motives, Thupten Gyatso had come to the conclusion that he must at least try to influence the emperor and his court with respect to Tibet. The response of the government in Beijing to the British invasion had been to use the debacle as a means to strengthen its own position in Tibet. Realizing that China itself was now vulnerable to invasion from the West, the Qing ordered a program of rapid Sinocization in Kham. The mandarin charged with implementing this policy began by criticizing the *sangha* and calling for a ban on monastic recruitment for the next twenty years. This, together with other acts of sacrilege, provoked a rebellion during which the official himself was murdered, apparently by a gang of monks.[11] In retaliation, Qing troops attacked several monasteries, slaughtering many hundred ecclesiastics. The Dalai Lama thus felt he must do all he could to shame the authorities into abandoning their assault on the *sangha*. Besides, a visit to Beijing might also permit the Dalai Lama opportunities to meet with officials from other countries having diplomatic relations with the Qing.

Thupten Gyatso arrived in Beijing during September 1908. Reminding court officials that Emperor Kangxi had stood up and advanced to greet the Great Fifth on foot, the Dalai Lama signaled his refusal to kowtow to the emperor and was eventually granted permission merely to genuflect. But even having to touch one knee to the ground, on being admitted to the presence of Emperor Guangxu, was a powerful reminder of the Dalai Lama's diminished prestige. This was further emphasized when Thupten Gyatso was granted, as tradition demanded, a new title by the emperor. Humiliatingly, it referred to him as the "Subservient . . . Buddha of the West." Never before had the Manchus claimed the relationship between the emperor and the Dalai Lama to be anything less than one of personal equality. Yet the emperor's addiction to opium was not lost on the Tibetans. He was unable so much as to feed himself at the banquet he gave in the Dalai Lama's honor. It was in fact his aunt, Cixi, the dowager empress, who really ruled.

That winter, the Tibetan hierarch was called on to perform long-life rituals for both the emperor and his all-powerful aunt. The Dalai Lama did as he was told, but the rituals were of no avail: remarkably, both were dead a matter of days later, the emperor himself widely believed to have been murdered at Cixi's command on the eve of her own death.

The political upheaval that accompanied the accession of the child destined to be China's last emperor gave Thupten Gyatso the opportunity he needed. Having already indicated to Sir John Jordan, the British minister in China, that His Holiness now desired friendly relations with British India and "thoroughly under[stood] the position . . . whereas [formerly it had been] concealed from him by his subordinates," the viceroy [Now Lord Minto. Curzon had been maneuvered into resigning by his archenemy Lord Kitchener in 1905.] signaled that he would be content to see the Dalai Lama return to Lhasa. Thus, after an absence of just over five years, Thupten Gyatso made his way back to the Tibetan capital, arriving in December 1909. While he remained in exile, the Qing *ambans* had done as much as they could to undermine the Dalai Lama. They had overseen the establishment of a telegraph link between Beijing and Lhasa. They had founded a Chinese military academy in the capital, along with a Chinese school for the children of the noble and merchant classes. They had laid plans for a road link to China, and they had drawn up a scheme for the exploitation of Tibet's mineral resources. They had also succeeded in flattering the young Panchen Lama, whom they had entertained in Lhasa. Nonetheless, great was the rejoicing of the people at the return of the Precious Protector.

Proportionately extravagant was Tibetan dismay at reports that began almost immediately to reach the Tibetan capital of a Chinese-led army, under the generalship of the brutal Chao-Ehrfeng, storming its way through Kham and clearly headed for Lhasa. According to the Thirteenth's official biography, Chao not only caused the deaths of thousands of monks who sought to bar his way but also, in his contumely, caused religious images to be melted down and used in the manufacture of ammunition, while also ordering that sacred scripture should be torn up and used for soling soldiers' boots.

Thupten Gyatso was completely confounded. He had no

inkling of the intentions of the new emperor's court actually to invade central Tibet. But there was nothing he could do. Less than two months after his triumphant return, he was forced to flee the capital once more, this time running for his life: General Chao put a price on his head and a crack cavalry unit on his tail. Taking into account the advice of the protectors, the Dalai Lama fled not north but south in the direction of India, via Phari, where he occupied the British *dak*, or postal relay, bungalow at Dromo, the village at which the Fourteenth Dalai Lama was later to stop en route to his exile in India. Still in fear of his pursuers, the Dalai Lama remained only a day before pushing on into Sikkim, where again he sought refuge with the British, this time in the telegraph office. Its resident NCO, astonished to receive so distinguished a visitor at what was considered to be one of the dreariest postings in the whole of the British Empire, described the Tibetan leader as "absolutely worn out by fatigue and mental strain." But still the Dalai Lama did not feel safe. Though it was the middle of winter and snow lay deep on the ground, the Tibetans left almost immediately, forging their way over the high passes to Darjeeling. It took them just nine days to cover the 270 miles in between—a remarkable feat. Fortunately, Thupten Gyatso had inherited all the strength and physical endurance of his peasant forebears.

In Darjeeling, the Dalai Lama came into contact with the British political officer for Sikkim and Bhutan, Mr. (later Sir) Charles Bell, with whom he was to establish a lifelong personal friendship. A fluent Tibetan speaker, Bell later recalled his first meeting with the Precious Protector. He was, he wrote, rather squat with a somewhat pock-marked face adorned by a "full mustache with the ends well waxed," adding that his "small, neat hands" belied the rest of his features, which clearly showed "the plebeian origins of the farmer's son." After putting him up in the government rest house for some time, the British, who were not entirely displeased to have the Tibetan leader

as their guest, rented him a house nearby, the prosaically named
"Hillside."

It is clear that in seeking refuge in India and offering assurances
of his desire now to establish cordial relations with Great Britain,
Thupten Gyatso fully expected a reciprocal gesture of support.
When, therefore, Bell announced that His Majesty's government
(Edward VII having succeeded Victoria) would in no way intervene over Tibet in any dispute with the Qing, "he was so surprised
that for a minute or two, he lost the power of speech. That depre-
cating look in his eyes became for an instant the look of a man
being hunted to his doom." Yet Thupten Gyatso was nothing if
not resilient. He turned now to the old enemy, Nepal, and again
to the tsar, though in both cases without success. The interview
the Dalai Lama obtained with the viceroy of India in March 1910
was also disappointing. But still he did not give up hope, instead
using his time to learn all he could about British methods. And
during the winter of 1910 he made a pilgrimage to Lumbini, Bodh
Gaya, Saranath, and Kushinaga, the sites where respectively the
Buddha was born, achieved enlightenment, delivered his first
sermon, and entered into *parinirvana.**

Nine months later, rebellion against the Qing broke out across
China. Almost immediately, the garrison at Lhasa mutinied, though
it took almost a year to regain the capital, largely because both
Drepung's Loseling College and Tengyeling—the Demo Regent's
monastery—sided with China. Eventually, all that remained of
Qing officialdom in Tibet took up residence at Tengyeling, where
they held out for still another six months against sporadic attacks
by Tibetan government militia. The Dalai Lama meanwhile moved
to Kalimpong before finally setting out for home during the summer
of 1912. En route, he stopped at Chokhor Gyal, the monastery
dedicated to the Dalai Lamas' personal protector deity, Palden

*Or died.
† With whom Queen Victoria had been identified by many Tibetans, according to Sir Charles Bell.

Lhamo.[†12] While the Dalai Lama prayed there, the remnants of Qing officialdom were finally expelled from Lhasa, its leaders granted safe passage back to China via India. Thus it was that Thupten Gyatso returned to the Potala in January 1913, almost exactly five years since he had last seen the place, and more than eight since he had first fled on the eve of the British invasion. The city lay in ruins, its temples, monasteries, and palaces systematically looted by the Qing forces.

Seated on the Lion Throne once more, Thupten Gyatso was determined to ensure that never again would Tibetans be compelled to endure foreign domination. To this end, he began by issuing a proclamation which amounted to a declaration of independence. From his perspective, with the Manchus gone, Beijing had no valid claim to Tibet. The relationship with Qing was based purely on the *chö yon* dispensation that existed between the emperor and the Dalai Lama. Since there was no longer a Qing emperor, the relationship no longer obtained. Next, realizing that Tibet urgently needed the means to defend itself properly, Thupten Gyatso began to enact a series of political reforms, among which were the establishment of a police force in Lhasa and, for the first time since Tibet's own empire period, of a standing army. The Dalai Lama also implemented a series of religious initiatives. He began by reminding his people that "peace and happiness can only be obtained by preserving the Buddhist faith." Buddhism should therefore be "taught, learned, and meditated upon properly." Hence, "except for [authorized persons], the administrators of the monasteries [were] forbidden to trade, loan money, deal in any kind of livestock" or to subjugate another's tenants.[13] In 1914, he bestowed Tsongkhapa's *lam rim* ("Stages to the Path") cycle of teachings on a congregation of monks and officials gathered in the courtyard of the Norbulingka Palace, and he began personally to superintend the examinations of the *lharampa* candidates— those vying for recognition as scholars of the highest degree.

At the same time, from his own resources, he began the work of restoring the capital's many damaged buildings, and he commissioned the publication of new editions of numerous religious texts, including one of the Kangyur. Nor was his role in these enterprises restricted to paying for them. An accomplished painter himself, he often visited the workshops of the craftsmen he had engaged, and each page of the 108-volume Kangyur was brought to him for scrutiny.

Thupten Gyatso also took a close interest in affairs of state. When, at his command, the telegraph line linking Gyantse to India was extended to Lhasa, he had it routed via his own personal quarters in the Norbulingka so that he could tap it at will.[14] He also involved himself personally in the establishment of the army. Through Charles Bell (with whom he kept in close touch) he hoped to persuade the British government to grant military aid to Tibet—a desire which was eventually fulfilled in 1921, when Bell organized for delivery of a small arsenal.* No doubt the Dalai Lama's offer of one thousand Tibetan soldiers to the British on the outbreak of World War I had some bearing on the matter.[†] But lest this offer seem a purely political gesture, it is worth noting that Thupten Gyatso had also mobilized the monasteries, at considerable expense, to obtain supernatural assistance for the British.

Not that the Thirteenth's warm feelings toward Great Britain went unopposed, nor that there was no resistance to his plans for a regular army. In both spheres, he aroused the hostility of the *sangha*. It was generally feared by senior monk officials that fostering relations with the British must lead to harm to the

---

* This comprised ten mountain guns, twenty Lewis guns, and ten thousand rifles with ammunition. Bell also organized for four officers and three hundred NCOs to be trained at the British garrison at Gyantse, and for a further four officers and twenty NCOs to be trained in the use of mountain guns at Quetta. Still others were trained as armorers and in cavalry tactics.

† The offer was graciously refused, although, according to Bell, many Tibetans joined up as medics and in other noncombatant roles.

buddhadharma. As to the establishment of a strong standing army, it was readily apparent to the monasteries that they themselves might easily be its target. Thus it was the *sangha* that, though it had the most to gain from the Dalai Lama's plans to protect his country, was paradoxically his fiercest opponent in the matter. The majority of lay Tibetans were likewise suspicious of the idea of a permanent standing army. For them, the monasteries were the chief guardians of the land, but curbing the power of the monasteries themselves was one of Thupten Gyatso's chief concerns.

An example of the Dalai Lama's use of the army in precisely the way they feared occurred during 1921, when he moved against Loseling College to punish it for supporting the Chinese following the collapse of the Qing Dynasty.* Having caused the arrest of the three college principals, he had two of them flogged and their property confiscated (the third was released). In retaliation, the principals' monastic brethren, knowing him to be on retreat there, stormed the Dalai Lama's compound at the Norbulingka and, shouting and chanting at the tops of their voices, trampled the flowers, broke his vases, and defecated all over the Precious Protector's garden. Thupten Gyatso pretended, however, to know nothing of the men's fate and refused to come out. Eventually, the monks dispersed. That evening, the Dalai Lama ordered the army to deploy. Government troops surrounded Loseling and a standoff ensued. When, as he had calculated, neither Ganden nor Sera, nor even Drepung's other colleges, answered Loseling's call for support, it was forced into a humiliating withdrawal, and to give up the sixty or so ringleaders of this act of insubordination. Having won the argument, Thupten Gyatso responded by ordering lenient treatment for the offenders.[†]

---

* He had already disbanded Tengyeling.
[†] Although he permitted flogging and the use of the stocks and the *cangue*, the Thirteenth reserved execution for the most heinous crimes against religion and the state. He also forbade amputation save in exceptional circumstances. He much preferred punishments to serve some useful purpose, such as road-mending. In at least one instance, he ordered an offender to plant a thousand willow trees.

The successful confrontation with the monks of Loseling, coupled with Bell's shipment of arms to Tibet, represent the high-water mark of Thupten Gyatso's military program. Thereafter, he was forced, partly by events and partly by the continued opposition of the *sangha* and its allies within official circles, to retreat from his plans to increase the size of the army still further. One such event was the summary mutilation of a Lhasa policeman by the Commander-in-Chief of the army.* This provoked widespread dismay among the people: the army was becoming as arrogant as it was becoming increasingly and dangerously powerful. Intriguingly, however, another cause of Thupten Gyatso's about-face may be that he had become aware of a plot by the military, masterminded by the British, to unseat him and install a purely secular government. But although there are some tantalizing clues to the existence of such a plot, the relevant British government documents remain embargoed.[15]

By the late 1920s, the Tibetan army was again in an extremely poor condition. The old Commander-in-Chief having been sacked, his successor (a nephew of the Dalai Lama) was an opium addict.† Although the soldiery continued to drill every day, their weaponry was in many cases useless. Their uniforms were in rags, and many had either bare feet or wore a single boot.[16] Thus when, right at the end of his life, Chinese troops again threatened Tibet and Thupten Gyatso again began to agitate in favor of a strong army, it was too late. By now exhausted, Thupten Gyatso was no longer capable of bringing about the resurgence he desired.

In the end, the monasteries succeeded in derailing the Dalai Lama's quest to build an army that would enable Tibet to be

---

* The policeman's arm was cut off.
† As were considerable numbers of the Tibetan aristocracy during the first few decades of the twentieth century, according to one senior member of the present Dalai Lama's administration.

self-sufficient militarily. And while it is clear that the *sangha*'s resistance rested on the popular view that any embrace of modern methods would harm religion, it is clear that this view was considerably bolstered by the emergence of a new religious practice. During the early years of the twentieth century, a brilliant scholar-monk named Phabongkha began to popularize the worship of Dorje Shugden, the wrathful protector associated with Drakpa Gyaltsen, the lama assassinated during the time of the Great Fifth, and implicated in the murder of Lobsang Gyatso in 1997. An important characteristic of this practice was, as it remains, a determined resistance on the part of many enthusiasts to any "pollution" of the Gelug tradition either through contact with other sects or with modern ideas. In turn, this fed into the intransigent and narrowly formed conservatism of the monasteries, which, in general, were constitutionally unable to tolerate innovation either in the religious or secular sphere. It was in no small part due to the success of the Dorje Shugden movement that the Thirteenth ultimately failed in his attempt not only to build a capable army but also to modernize Tibet. And although some say that Thupten Gyatso personally upbraided Phabonghka for his advocacy of the cult, extracting a promise that he would desist from honoring the deity, it continued to grow and spread.

Further resistance to the Thirteenth came from Tashilhunpo, the monastery founded by Gendun Drub, the First Dalai Lama. Although the Thirteenth was the young Panchen Lama's spiritual director, and although personal relations between the two men were cordial enough, the same could not be said of their respective officials. The southern region was by now thoroughly Gelug, but the historic animosity between U (the central province) and Tsang (the western) had found its way into the relationship between Tashilhunpo and the central government. This tension was aggravated by the Chinese leadership, which, in its various forms, had long had independent relations with

Tashilhunpo. A catastrophic rift developed in 1923, when the Lhasa government sought significant increases in the revenues due to it from Tashilhunpo. The Panchen Lama refused to pay. When the Dalai Lama began to pressure him, the Panchen Lama responded by abandoning his monastery and seeking refuge in China. Deeply grieved at this development, Thupten Gyatso ordered the dispatch of troops to intercept his young protégé, but, uncertain of where he was headed, they failed. Writing to him later, the Dalai Lama was blunt in his condemnation of the Panchen's actions. "It is not understood why you have left your monastery in which you should now be sitting in meditation . . ."[17] "You seem to have forgotten the sacred history of your predecessors and wandered away to a desert . . . like a moth attracted by lamplight."[18] To Thupten Gyatso's lasting regret, the rift between the two hierarchs persisted until the Dalai Lama's death.*

By the time he was in his early fifties, Thupten Gyatso was, according to Charles Bell, an old man. Partly this reflects the adversity he had had to face, but partly it reflects the astonishing degree to which he drove himself. Living frugally and eating plainly, the Dalai Lama was a glutton only for hard work. He invariably rose early and retired late—sometimes going to bed after midnight and beginning his devotions less than three hours later. Thupten Gyatso started his day with two hours of prayer. Thereafter, he was occupied with both private and public ceremonials, as well as audiences not only for government officials and members of the *sangha* but for ordinary laypeople too. He was by no means a remote figure and anyone undertaking a long journey could seek his personal blessing. He was also fully engaged in matters of civil law. If anyone wrote the Dalai Lama's name on a petition, it must by right be laid before him, though

---

* Though the Panchen Lama subsequently declared his intention to return home, he died in 1937, still in exile.

because the applicant himself would be punished if the case were thought unworthy of the Dalai Lama's attention, this was a privilege that was rarely abused. In addition, so long as he was able, Thupten Gyatso remained closely involved in every aspect of government, from the allocation of funds to the minutiae of everyday administration. He was also intimately involved with the search for, identification, naming, and education of important incarnations, and he rarely delegated authority to anyone, if only because he distrusted the competence of the majority of his ministers. As he once remarked to Bell, "Parliament will talk and talk, but this matter cannot wait."

Throughout his life, Thupten Gyatso remained courageous, strong-willed and quick-tempered, although he also had a well-developed sense of humor. For relaxation, he would sometimes fly kites, play *shata*—a Mongolian form of chess—or take a short drive in one of the three cars he had imported into Tibet: a U.S.-built Dodge and two British-built Baby Austins. But his greatest love was nature. He loved beautiful surroundings, the open air, animals, birds, and flowers. Besides establishing, with the help of two gardeners trained in British horticultural methods, a flourishing garden in the grounds of the Norbulingka, he also kept a menagerie within its adjacent parkland. This included several leopards, two elephants, and even a tiger from Nepal.

Shortly before he died, during December 1933, Thupten Gyatso drew up his final testament—a remarkable and prophetic document—exhorting his people to be faithful and diligent in the discharge of their duties. Failing that, he warned,

. . . it may happen that here in Tibet, religion and government will be attacked both from without and within. Unless we guard our own country, it will now happen that the Dalai and Panchen Lamas, the Father and the Son, and all the revered holders of the Faith, will disappear and become name-

less. Monks and their monasteries will be destroyed. The rule
of law will be weakened. The lands and property of government officials will be seized. They themselves will be forced
to serve their enemies or wander the country like beggars. All
beings will be sunk in hardship and overwhelming fear; the
days and nights will drag on slowly in suffering.[19]

The end itself came quickly. For about twelve days, the Dalai
Lama was sick with what appeared to be a bad cold. His appetite
diminished and he complained of shortness of breath. It was with
great difficulty that his attendants finally persuaded Thupten
Gyatso to miss a ceremony at the Upper Tantric College, but
over the next five days, his condition worsened. At that point,
Nechung was sent for. The oracle prepared medicine for the
Dalai Lama, which, it seems, the Dalai Lama tried to refuse.
Nechung, still in trance, forced it on him. Almost immediately,
the Precious Protector's condition worsened, and by noon of the
same day he was unconscious. That afternoon, Nechung was
summoned once more, together with various high lamas and
government officials, all of whom beseeched the Dalai Lama to
recover and live long, but although he opened his eyes once, he
did not speak again. He died the following evening, when, it is
said, he withdrew his spirit to the Tushita Paradise. All Tibet
was plunged in mourning. The golden roofs of the Jokhang and
other buildings were draped in black, the citizenry was forbidden to wear new clothes, government officials took the pendants
signifying their rank from their ears, and women wore their hair
down. Great was their desolation, and rightly so. Even though
he did not fully succeed in his ambitions, Thupten Gyatso's
legacy was indeed extraordinary. Following the humiliation of
the British invasion and his subsequent exile, he had secured a
period of genuine independence for his country. He had greatly
improved both discipline and academic standards within the
sangha. The army, though at the time of his death not what it

had been, was still greatly superior to the force he had inherited, and he had successfully checked the greed, laziness, and corruption of the government. Had it united under strong leadership after his demise, and had Thupten Gyatso's final testament been taken with the seriousness it demanded, it is plausible to imagine that, even if the forthcoming struggle with China could not have been won, at least there would have been no return to the catastrophic infighting of the last regency period. Alas, no such leadership emerged, and his words were not heeded. The result was as predictable as it was unedifying.

26

Tenzin Gyatso

The death of the Thirteenth, known among Tibetans today as the Great Thirteenth, precipitated an immediate power struggle. Kumbela, the Dalai Lama's last great favorite, seemed certain to be the one who would dictate events, but to everyone's surprise, he failed to capitalize on his position.

This allowed his rival, Lungshar, to make a bid for supremacy. Lungshar's power base was a secret movement, the Reform Party, which he had founded and which was dedicated to making Tibet an independent democratic republic. It was an audacious platform, too audacious for the majority of aristocrats and monk officials whose support he needed. Lungshar therefore cloaked his aims with patriotic rhetoric. To begin with, the Reform Party showed every sign of winning over majority support within the government; but, unfortunately for him, Lungshar had too many enemies. When one potential ally switched sides in a fit of resentment, he publicly accused Lungshar of planning to assassinate several key officials. This gave Trimön, the arch-conservative chief minister of the Kashag, the opportunity he needed. If he could somehow publicly expose Lungshar, the

Reform movement must collapse. Lungshar was duly arrested. On being taken into custody, as was customary, the top-knot of Lungshar's hair was undone, his charmbox and his government robes removed. When his boots were also removed, pieces of paper fell from each. One of these Lungshar managed to grab and swallow. The other proved to have Trimön's name on it, together with an occult symbol. This was all the evidence needed. Not only was Lungshar engaged in dangerous politics, he was also using black magic. The Kashag called for the death penalty, though eventually the lesser punishment of mutilation—by blinding—was settled on.

Lungshar's punishment was carried out in his prison cell at the Potala during the spring of 1934. Involving the application of yak knuckles to each temple with a tourniquet, the operation was successful on one side, but not on the other. The recalcitrant eyeball was therefore gouged out with a knife. The sockets were then cauterized with boiling oil—despite which horrific treatment, Lungshar survived and lived another year.

A particular feature of Lungshar's Reform movement was its resolutely anti-Chinese stance. Immediately following the demise of the Thirteenth, the Nationalist government in Peiping (as the Nationalists renamed Beijing) had proposed sending a condolence mission to Tibet. Realizing that such a mission would surely be used as a pretext to re-establish a permanent presence at Lhasa, Lungshar had been vehemently opposed to the proposal. Now, however, the government, with Trimön as its most important member, and backed by the monastic interest (which no doubt looked forward to the largesse the Chinese could be expected to distribute), granted its permission. Headed by General Huang Mu Sung, the Chinese delegation reached the capital during August 1934. Immediately, it became clear that Chinese intentions far exceeded that of merely paying respect to the deceased Dalai Lama. The general immediately began trying to persuade the government to accept political

subordination on the basis that Tibet was a member of China's
"family of races." Although this was rejected out of hand, as
Lungshar had foreseen, the Chinese left in place a permanent
staff, equipped with Tibet's first radio transmitter, when the
general departed.

Despite the power struggle between Kumbela, Lungshar, and
Trimön, a regent was appointed soon after the death of the Thirteenth. This was the young, inexperienced, but mystically
talented Reting Rinpoché. It was now Reting who gradually came
to prominence. Having successfully completed the first of the
tasks incumbent on a regent—the construction of the mausoleum
of the departed Dalai Lama—Reting Rinpoché formally initiated the search for the Fourteenth during the summer of 1935.
He began with a pilgrimage to the sacred lake, Lhamo Lhatso,
in the hope of receiving a vision. He was amply rewarded. Not
only did he see three letters, corresponding, he later deduced,
to a district within the Amdo region, but also a three-storied
monastery with its second floor painted turquoise and a "thread-
like path leading . . . east from the monastery reaching up to the
foot of a hill where there was a one-storied house with a blue
roof."[1] But while this was the main purpose of the visit to the
lake, Reting had another motive. Informing Trimön, who had
accompanied him, that he intended to resign the regency (we
do not know what reasons he gave) on his return to Lhasa, Reting
persuaded Trimön that it would be appropriate for him to do the
same thing. As good as his word, Trimön duly wrote a letter of
resignation to the Kashag. Reting, however, did not. Trimön could
thus only watch helplessly as Reting Rinpoché maneuverd
himself into a position of absolute power.

The British, who maintained an official presence in Lhasa,
described Reting as "gauche" and lacking in "poise," but he was
at least open-minded enough not to oppose diplomatic initiatives by other countries. His years as regent saw a succession of

foreign missions arrive in Lhasa, including one sent by Himmler, who fancied that the Tibetans were a lost Aryan tribe.[*] In the meantime, of three search parties that the regent had dispatched to eastern Tibet, the one sent to Amdo identified a most promising candidate.[†] This was a little boy by the name of Lhamo Dhondup, the youngest of several brothers of Taktser Rinpoché, an important incarnation based at Kumbum Monastery. Of particular interest to the search party was the favorable report of the Panchen Lama, who had seen the boy shortly before his own death in 1937. Following an initial interview with the leader of the search party, Lhamo Dhondup was put through the standard selection procedure, during which he correctly identified his predecessor's belongings from among duplicates. It was considered particularly auspicious that when asked to choose from several walking sticks, he picked up one in particular before putting it down in favor of another. The first stick was one that the Great Thirteenth had owned but then given away.

On hearing this news, Reting Rinpoché consulted the relevant oracles, each of which confirmed that this was the authentic rebirth of the Precious Protector. Unfortunately, there were several obstacles to be surmounted before the new Dalai Lama could be brought to the capital.

Not only did the Lhasa government have the Chinese Nationalists to contend with, but also Ma-Pufeng, the (Muslim) warlord who, in the chaos of China's recent civil war, had made a large swathe of the Sino-Tibetan borderland his own personal fiefdom. As soon as he heard that a contender for the position of Dalai Lama had been identified within his territory, Ma-Pufeng

[*] Another delegation, from the United States, arrived in 1942, soon after Reting's resignation.
[†] Apart from the clues given in Reting's vision, it was also noted that twice during the time that the Great Thirteenth's embalmed body had sat in state the head had turned slightly to the east.

began to assert himself. He began by refusing to grant a travel permit to the boy—even though the Tibetans advanced the fiction that he was but one of several candidates.* Pressed by the Tibetan authorities, Ma indicated that he might be persuaded to relent in return for a generous donation. But though this was paid, he continued to stall. In view of the tremendous difficulties the boy's move would entail, a further three hundred thousand silver coins should be remitted to him. This was of course intolerable to the Ganden Phodrang. Quite apart from the sum involved, what was to say that, if paid, Ma-Pufeng might not demand more? The impasse was only broken when the Lhasa government struck a deal with some local merchants whereby Ma-Pufeng would receive his money when the child was safely in central Tibet. There remained, however, the problem of the Chinese official who now attached himself to the new Dalai Lama's escort. In order to forestall the possibility of the Chinese claiming that they needed to be on hand in order officially to approve the boy as the authentic incarnation, the Ganden Phodrang decided to dispense with tradition (and with it any question of the use of the dreaded golden urn), proclaiming Lhamo Dhondup the authentic incarnation while he was still en route to Lhasa. The enthronement ceremony itself was scheduled for February 1940, at the end of the New Year Festival.

This was the customarily extravagant pageant, recalling not only the glories of past Dalai Lamas, but also the imperial splendor of Tibet's ancient history. The whole of Lhasa turned out to celebrate, and there was an unbridled outpouring of emotion on the part of the populace. Present were the usual delegations from the remotest corners of the Tibetan cultural world as well as

---

* In fact there had been one other serious contender, a boy born into the family of the Great Thirteenth, but though many were nervous of the regent's insistence that the authentic incarnation was to be found in the Chinese-dominated east, this other child was quickly sidelined.

dignitaries from China, Nepal, and Great Britain. All who saw the little boy were impressed with the child Dalai Lama's dignity, his self-assurance and with his obvious intelligence.

Having now tonsured and renamed the new Dalai Lama*— henceforth he would be known as Tenzin Gyatso—Reting Rinpoché had completed the second of the regent's two essential tasks. His popularity among the people was immense. Yet rumors now began to surface concerning his personal conduct. It was well known that the regent enjoyed the picnic parties and theatricals that were the habitual entertainment of the Lhasa upper class. He was famously fond of dogs and horses— the latter endearing him to the new Dalai Lama's father, the Yapshi Kung.† He was also said to be delighted with the ciné films brought out to Tibet by the British delegation. But to the horror of his monastic confrères, the regent learned to ride a bicycle, enjoyed pistol shooting (he once persuaded a young *tulku* to let him shoot an egg from the palm of his outstretched hand) and took pleasure in kicking a soccer ball. Perhaps because it reminded people of Chinese troops sporting with broken religious statuary, the game of soccer was known among the *sangha* as "kicking the Buddha's head."‡ Yet that was not all. It was widely believed that the regent drank alcohol and had taken lovers of both sexes. Alcohol is forbidden to monks, and though, remarkably, homosexual relations between monks were a tacitly accepted practice, provided that its expression did not involve penetrative sex, taking a female lover was considered a serious infraction of the monastic code.** To compound the

* The Panchen Lama having recently died.
† Or *yab zhis gung*. This is the formal title by which the Dalai Lamas' fathers were known.
‡ The sport itself was introduced to Tibet by the British. It is reported that by 1936 there were more than a dozen teams playing in Lhasa, from a population of around ten thousand.
** The key Buddhist precept governing sexual misconduct specifies the mouth and anus as "inappropriate orifices." It is on these grounds that sexually expressive homosexuality is both wrong and unnatural according to Tibetan tradition.

crime, Reting Rinpoché had fathered a child—on his half-brother's wife.

Toward the end of 1940 it became apparent that Reting was contemplating resigning the regency. Given that this was not the first time he had hinted at the possibility, many assumed that this was brinkmanship. But then, on the first day of the first month of the Iron Snake year—February 1941—Reting's resignation was formally announced. In his place emerged the elderly Taktra Rinpoché. The exact circumstances behind this event have never been satisfactorily explained. The official story was that Reting had received a supernatural warning that if he did not enter a prolonged spiritual retreat, he was in danger of his life. But there was also the fact that the regent was to preside over the young Dalai Lama's profession of his *getsul* vows.* It seems likely that he dare not risk the opprobrium of conducting a ceremony which would be rendered invalid on account of his having broken his own vows. The reasons behind Reting's choice of Taktra to replace him have also not been satisfactorily explained. It was later said that the two men had a private agreement whereby, when the time came, Taktra would yield the regency back to Reting. Whatever the truth, if Reting had ever imagined that he would be able to influence Taktra from behind the scenes, he was quickly disabused of the idea. Famously conservative, Taktra moved at once to restore the high standards of probity and devotion to duty that had obtained during the lifetime of the Great Thirteenth. This was signaled particularly in the way the new regent dealt with the Dalai Lama's father.

Although ennobled and granted two large estates by the Ganden Phodrang, the Yapshi Kung had complained that these were insufficient. Reluctantly, the National Assembly consented to give him three more estates, but he continued to court unpopularity with

---

* Novice vows.

his unruly behavior. On one occasion, he became involved in an altercation with the abbot of Drepung's Loseling College and threatened to shoot him. And he insisted that everyone he met in the street dismount to show respect, his servants beating anyone who failed to do so. Eventually, Taktra ordered the Yapshi Kung's behavior to be debated in the National Assembly. This resulted in an official proclamation, bearing the seal of the Kashag, ordering the Dalai Lama's father "henceforth to behave himself." Despite this rebuke, it seems not to have satisfied his enemies. When the Yapshi Kung died in 1947, the British doctor then resident in Lhasa was certain, after seeing his corpse, that the cause of death was certainly poison.[2]

But if Taktra was successful in restoring a measure of probity to public life at least in Lhasa, he failed entirely to grasp, let alone deal with, the need to engage with the modern world. This was the time when Tibet might have applied to join the United Nations, but no such approach was made. And although originally he supported the founding of a new English-language school in Lhasa, Taktra did nothing to intervene when the *sangha* demanded its closure on the familiar grounds that foreign concepts were likely to harm the *buddhadharma*.

In 1947, however, Taktra himself was forced to challenge the might of the *sangha* when some Sera monks beat to death a government official, in a dispute over their right to collect interest on a loan that the monastery had made to a small farming community near Lhundrup Dzong. When the Ganden Phodrang made clear that it intended to punish those responsible, there was a moment when it looked as if the whole college—several thousand strong—would rebel. It had access to some two thousand rifles and, what was more, the ex-regent indicated his support. Only when it became clear that the government had quietly moved in troop reinforcements of its own did sense prevail. In the meantime, however, Reting Rinpoché was emboldened to come to Lhasa in order to try to regain the regency from

Taktra. In this he failed entirely, but from that moment on, Reting and his court began to plot against the regent.

Treacherously, the conspirators, seeking outside support, made contact with the Chinese. Reting seems even to have written personally to Chiang Kai Shek. This elicited an invitation to the ex-Regent to attend a meeting in Nanking. But when it became clear that the Nationalists were committed to negotiating with Taktra's government, the conspirators decided on direct action. Since Taktra rarely went out in public, this would not be easy. Eventually, they decided to make an attempt on his life on the eve of the Butter Sculpture Festival of February 1947. The assassins were a monk from Drepung and a lay Khampa. But Taktra apparently received a warning and failed to appear. Reting's party then decided to make another attempt, but by indirect means. This involved delivering a parcel bomb to a government official, together with a message that the package contained a letter together with an offering for the regent from a leading aristocrat. Unfortunately for the conspirators, the package was set aside by a clerk who did not consider it urgent. After several weeks had passed without an explosion, the plotters spread a rumor that an important document was being deliberately withheld from the regent. Still nothing happened. Eventually, a servant suspicious of the parcel's disproportionate weight began secretly and carefully to unwrap it. As he began to slide the box's cover open, the grenade inside began to hiss, at which point the young man dropped the package and ran from the room, only just escaping serious injury.

Taktra did not react immediately. He suspected that Reting and his supporters were behind the plot, but he needed evidence. He did not have to wait long. On April 14, 1947, a top secret coded telegram was received in Lhasa from the Ganden Phodrang's office in Nanking. This revealed that Reting had recently sent a message to the Chinese urging troops, arms, and air support to assist in the overthrow of the regent. The telegram further showed that Reting had requested a response within five days. Seeing that he must act now, Taktra immediately ordered Reting's arrest.

Reting was apprehended on April 16. Hearing of this, the monks of Sera Jé (his old college) rose immediately in support of the ex-regent. The most militant of them demanded that their abbot, a Mongolian forced on the college by the government following the Lhundrup Dzong incident, intercede directly with the government. He refused. That evening, a mob of angry *dob dob* monks [monastic ruffians who acted as a sort of ecclesiastical police force] made its way toward the abbot's quarters. Realizing the monks' intentions, the monastery manager took up a gun and killed their leader and wounded another. His weapon then jammed, and he was immediately killed, along with two of his servants. The abbot, who lived upstairs, meanwhile climbed out on to the roof, only to be caught when he hesitated to jump the gap between the next building. Struck down with knives, an ax, and a sword, he too was killed.

The mob, under the new leadership of a young lama—an incarnation of Tamdrin, principal protector deity of the college, and thus presumed to have great supernatural powers—now headed for Reting's Lhasa headquarters, knowing arms to be stored there. Unfortunately for them, the house had already been sealed and was being guarded by government troops. The Sera Jé monks then decided they must rescue Reting Rinpoché when he and his escort passed in front of their monastery en route to the Potala. When, however, they mounted their rescue bid, the government's troops were waiting for them and they were met with relentless gunfire. They were forced back. The next day, still determined to preserve the honor of their college and to force Taktra to release Reting, the Sera Jé monks raided another house they knew to have weapons stored inside. Five of their number were killed during the break-in, as were two government guards, but they managed to carry off a number of rifles.

When the government announced its terms for a ceasefire, the monks answered that they would fight to the last man. On April 26, therefore, the government ordered an assault on Sera Jé itself. After three more days of fighting—during which anywhere between two and three hundred monks were killed—the soldiers stormed the building. Seeing that defeat was upon them, the monks put their weapons down and returned to their rooms, chanting prayers as they waited for the soldiers to arrive.

In the meantime, back at Reting monastery, the monks there rose against the small number of soldiers left behind to guard the monastery following Reting Rinpoché's arrest. As there were only sixteen, it was a relatively easy task to overpower them. Not content with taking prisoners, however, the monks cold-bloodedly murdered them all. Several days passed before the monks themselves were forced to flee. Having occupied the monastery, troops from Lhasa first looted and then destroyed Reting's private residence, while desecrating and plundering several other buildings.[3]

The investigation into Reting Rinpoché's misdemeanors began as soon as he was arrested. The government quickly amassed irrefutable evidence of treachery, including a cache of incriminating letters written by the ex-regent and his closest circle. Yet even today, Reting has his advocates,* who argue that he was the victim of unscrupulous advisers, in particular of his manager, Nyungne Lama, who subsequently shot himself. The government of the day had no such misgivings. For them, the problem was what punishment to exact. Some argued that, in accordance with Songtsen Gampo's ancient code, the traitor should be pushed

---

* The present Dalai Lama appears to be one of them. When he was tonsured by Reting, he received two of the regent's names as his own, Jamphel Yeshe. Following Reting's downfall, these were dropped from all official documents, but Tenzin Gyatso has since reinstated them.

from a high cliff. Others called for leniency. But before they could agree, Reting was dead.

All Lhasa was aghast at the news. Most suspected murder, while rumors abounded. One that was taken seriously by many suggested that Reting died from having his testicles crushed. This was presumed to be punishment for having broken his vow of celibacy. It would also account for the screams that some reported to have heard issuing from the prison at the foot of the Potala on May 7. Most likely, however, and still consistent with the screams, is that the cause of death was poison.

Taktra was now secure in his position. With Reting dead, there would be no figurehead for any general rebellion. But a majority of the people was scandalized at what was generally seen as his heavy-handed treatment of a highly accomplished spiritual master. As a result, the regent's authority was severely compromised and he now found himself head of a country thoroughly hostile to him.

At the time of Reting Rinpoché's death, the present Dalai Lama was two months short of his thirteenth birthday. Although he had occasional contact with Taktra, he had little to do with the turmoil of Tibetan politics. Instead, Tenzin Gyatso was deeply immersed in his formation as a monk under the direction of his two tutors, Ling Rinpoché and Trijang Rinpoché. In his bestselling autobiography, *Freedom in Exile*, the Fourteenth Dalai Lama paints an engaging picture of a childhood which, if somewhat lonely, was made reasonably happy by the companionship of his immediate elder brother and by that of the sweepers—the lowly room attendants—who were his daily familiars. He was a lively and intelligent boy who showed an early interest in all things mechanical. A famous escapade involved one of his predecessor's cars, which the young Tenzin Gyatso took for a drive around the garden of the Norbulingka Palace. In later life, he has spoken of his laziness as a child, more interested in the workings of the ciné-projector on which he would watch newsreels and other films supplied by the British Mission now established in Lhasa. It is clear that, even as a youngster, the Dalai Lama was acutely conscious of Tibet's material backwardness. A reformist by temperament, he seems to have been frustrated with the innate conservatism of the system at the head of which he found himself. But if these were hopeful qualities, he was in no position at this stage to exercise them, nor to influence the momentous events that were about to engulf his country.

In October 1949, Mao Zedong's Communist Party swept to power in China. One of Mao's first announcements made clear that the "peaceful liberation" of Tibet would be a priority for the new regime. Taktra's government for its part, sensing that a Communist victory was likely, had earlier ordered a large consignment of arms from India, together with a wholesale reform of Tibet's dilapidated army. But even though the *sangha*, all too well aware of the destruction that Communism had already wrought on religion in Mongolia, did not oppose these moves, it was of course far too little, far too late.

By July 1950, the People's Liberation Army (PLA) had advanced to within a hundred miles of Chamdo, the capital of Kham. The first serious engagement between the two sides, at Dengo, was technically a victory for the Tibetans. But if the Chinese army in the area was only twenty thousand strong— against the Tibetans' five thousand—a further five million men under arms stood behind them. The eventual result was a foregone conclusion. On October 5, the PLA launched a full-scale attack on Chamdo itself, deploying its troops in a pincer movement. Ngabo, the ineffectual aristocrat governor of Kham, sent several urgent telegrams to Lhasa telling of impending disaster and requesting instructions. There was no reply. On October 15, one of his aides de camp succeeded in contacting Lhasa by radio. He was told that, although his telegrams had been received, they had yet to be decoded as the Kashag was currently engaged in its annual weeklong series of picnic parties. This brought the justly celebrated rejoinder "Shit on their picnic."[4] But at least it was now clear that Ngabo faced the might of the PLA alone. Two days later he was given permission to retreat. On October 19 he was captured and with him all Kham fell into Chinese hands.

There now began a period of intense uncertainty for the Tibetans. The Chinese were in a position to launch an assault on Lhasa, which it was clear must succeed. For their part, however, the Communists were committed to taking over Tibet peacefully. This was a "liberation," after all. In Lhasa, after the initial shock had subsided, the government was divided between those who believed that Tibet should find some way to resist the invader and those who sought a negotiated settlement. Taktra himself seems to have had it in mind to send the Dalai Lama into exile while talks were held. This idea was greatly disliked, however: the thought of being without the Precious Protector filled most Tibetans with dread. It was dropped altogether when the state oracles of Gadong and Nechung made clear that now was the time for the young Dalai Lama to be invested with temporal authority. Though still only sixteen years old and quite unprepared, Tenzin Gyatso had no option but to accept and allow the reviled Taktra to retire.

Having announced the Dalai Lama's accession, the Ganden Phodrang hurriedly petitioned Britain, the United States, and India to intervene with China on Tibet's behalf. It also appealed to the United Nations for support. All four initiatives came to nothing. In the face of international indifference, the government made preparations to remove the Dalai Lama to southern Tibet, close to the Sikkimese border. He arrived at Dromo, together with senior members of his staff and government, in early January 1951. There now began further intense debate over the wisdom of the Dalai Lama seeking political asylum abroad. Backed by El Salvador, which took an unlikely interest in Tibet, the government made a second attempt to raise the Tibetan crisis with the United Nations. This initiative also failed, but it did prompt the United States to review its stance toward Tibet. Having made initial contact with the Dalai Lama back in 1943, when two American officers had visited Lhasa en route to China, the U.S. Department of State began to think that if the Tibetan leader could be persuaded to refuse to negotiate with China, it might be worth backing him and supporting Tibetan resistance as a means to halting the dangerous spread of Communism. The U.S. Embassy in India began to make overtures to Tenzin Gyatso via his brother Taktser Rinpoché. This was the same brother who had until recently been abbot of Kumbum Monastery. Having sought out the U.S. ambassador on his own initiative, Taktser Rinpoché was a leading advocate of asylum and resistance.

To begin with, Tenzin Gyatso was minded to take his brother's advice. The majority of his officials were, however, against this course of action. The Protectors were likewise against. For several months, therefore, the Tibetans prevaricated. Eventually Ngabo, the ex-governor of Kham, since released from captivity, was instructed to proceed to Beijing (the capital having been recently renamed) in order to conduct negotiations with the Communist government.

The talks centered on a document now generally referred to as the Seventeen-Point Agreement. Its first paragraph stated that the "Tibetan people shall unite and drive out imperialist aggressive forces in Tibet: the Tibetan people shall return to the big family of the Motherland—the People's Republic of China." Surprisingly, while this clearly signaled the subjugation of Tibet to China, Ngabo was satisfied that the rest of the document provided for the continued existence of the Ganden Phodrang, the monasteries, and the landed aristocracy. He therefore agreed to China's terms. He did not, however, have authority actually to sign the agreement, nor did he have with him the relevant seals of state. In assenting to the Seventeen-Point Agreement, it seems likely that Ngabo was merely following the line of least resistance in the expectation that the Kashag would subsequently reject it. But the Chinese overcame the lack of seals by manufacturing new ones, to which Ngabo and his fellow delegates were invited to attach their signatures. They did not refuse. So it was that Tibet formally became a part of the People's Republic of China. The Dalai Lama himself heard the news three days later, over a crackly radio broadcast.

It was at this point that the United States began seriously to woo the Dalai Lama. If he would repudiate the agreement, the United States would supply both military and financial assistance. It would also facilitate the young hierarch's exile. But deciding against the offer, the Tibetan government agreed that the Dalai Lama would meet with Chinese officials in Dromo. He would then return to Lhasa. On October 24, 1951, Tenzin Gyatso formally assented to the capitulation of Tibet by sending a telegram accepting the terms of the Seventeen-Point Agreement directly to Chairman Mao.[5]

There now began a seven-and-a-half-year period during which the young Dalai Lama sought to find a workable compromise with the Chinese. At first, there seemed grounds for optimism. The Chinese troops, which arrived in the capital with great fanfare, proved well disciplined and respectful toward Tibetans, and especially toward the *sangha*. Moreover, they took nothing without overpaying for it. This financial largess was quickly exploited by the aristocracy, in whose hands lay most of the country's trade. Nonetheless, popular feeling, although at first muted in its opposition to the Chinese presence out of respect for the Dalai Lama, gradually began to harden. Inflation, previously unknown, caused the price of basic commodities to spiral, prompting the Indian representative in Lhasa to remark that "while most officials live smugly in their ivory towers, leading much the same life of idle dissipation, the common people find the heavy burdens imposed on them insupportable."[6]

During the height of this honeymoon period, the Chinese central government issued an invitation to the Dalai Lama, his family, and some four hundred officials to visit China. Greatly to the consternation of the people, who feared that he would be detained there, Tenzin Gyatso accepted. He felt that if he could meet the Chinese leadership, he might be able to influence their thinking on Tibet. Traveling part of the way along the road that the Communists were building, with extraordinary rapidity, between China and Tibet, the Dalai Lama arrived in Beijing during 1954. His optimism seemed vindicated when he had the first of several interviews with Chairman Mao. The Chinese leader seemed both sincere and sympathetic toward Tibet. He also showed knowledge of Tibet's ancient imperial greatness.

The Dalai Lama and his countrymen were then taken on a propaganda tour of China and shown the full extent of the technological revolution instigated by the Communists. At the same time, Tenzin Gyatso received private instruction in Marxist ideology. Enthused, the young leader began to think in terms of a possible alliance between Communism and Buddhism. The former would look to supplying people's material needs, the latter to its spiritual needs. That this was naively optimistic was made clear when he had his final interview with Mao. Apparently mistaking the young man's enthusiasm for modernity as a sign that he was less than fully committed to his faith, the Great Helmsman began to give Tenzin Gyatso some friendly advice. His concluding remarks were to the effect that "religion is poison."

Back in Tibet, to which he returned during the summer of 1955, events began to confirm that the Dalai Lama's enthusiasm had been misplaced. It became clear that Chinese Communism entailed attacking the very foundations of the Tibetan way of life. At first, the evidence was anecdotal. Then, in 1956, the PLA launched an aerial bombardment of Lithang, the monastery founded by the Third Dalai Lama and also associated with the Seventh. When news of this reached Tenzin Gyatso, he was devastated. The

Chinese justified the attack on the grounds that the monastery was supporting the attempts of local tribesmen to resist them. In retaliation, the Communists not only bombed Lithang, but they also conducted horrific public exhibitions of their might, forcing monks and nuns to break their vows of celibacy and even to kill people.[7] Although Tenzin Gyatso protested by writing directly to Chairman Mao, successive letters went unanswered.

The Dalai Lama now began actively to consider repudiating the Seventeen-Point Agreement and seeking asylum abroad, preferably in India. An opportunity presented itself the following year when he was unexpectedly given permission by the Chinese to accept an invitation to travel to India to attend the Buddhajayanti celebrations marking the 2,500-year anniversary of the birth of the Buddha. This enabled him to meet with Pandit Nehru, the Indian prime minister, and to see for himself whether there was any hope of support from India. But while making clear that he would not refuse a request for asylum, Nehru was adamant the Dalai Lama should return to Tibet and try to salvage the situation from within. The Americans again made contact with offers of support—having already begun secretly to arm and train a Tibetan resistance movement. But given that India was evidently pursuing a policy of appeasement toward China, it was clear that unless the Americans would commit themselves to all-out military support, there was no real alternative to the Dalai Lama returning to Tibet. A meeting with Chou En Lai, the Chinese vice-premier, who called in to India en route to Europe, did nothing to reassure him.

Outwardly, Tenzin Gyatso's relations with Chinese officialdom improved somewhat after his return to Lhasa in March 1957, but by the end of the year it was clear to all that a crisis was in the offing. The whole of Kham and Amdo were now in open rebellion. Thousands of refugees began to flood into central Tibet. The resistance fighters started to cause serious problems for the Chinese, blowing up roads and bridges and harassing troop movements. Yet the Ganden Phodrang refused to lend its support. On the one hand, it would be politically reckless to do so; on the other was central Tibet's traditional hostility to the Khampas. They were considered wayward, untrustworthy, and dangerously belligerent. Yet the more the Chinese took their revenge on innocent people, the more easily the resistance recruited men to its cause.

By the beginning of 1959, there were an estimated fifty thousand refugees camped in and around Lhasa. The atmosphere fizzed with excitement and fear. The Monlam Chenmo of that year was a particularly important one. Tenzin Gyatso was to appear before the abbots of the Three Seats and other high monk officials for his final examinations. Throughout the turmoil, he had diligently pursued his religious studies and was now deemed ready to submit to the public debates that would qualify him as a *lharam geshe*. Some remarkable ciné film of the event survives to give an inkling of the atmosphere. Amidst a vast audience of monks and lay officials, the young scholar is seen debating triumphantly with some of the leading ecclesiastics of the day. Many of those in the picture would be dead or imprisoned before the year was out.

Ostensibly to honor the Dalai Lama following his successful graduation, the Chinese invited him to attend a dance performance by a Hungarian dance troupe newly arrived from China. But as word leaked out that the Precious Protector was due to visit the enemy in his lair, thousands of monks, lay pilgrims, and refugees gathered around the Norbulingka Palace. It was clear to them that this was a ploy to kidnap the Dalai Lama. They would therefore see to it that he did not leave. The next day, March 10, 1959, thousands more gathered outside the Potala to denounce the Chinese presence. More public protests occurred during the following week, including one staged by women. The Chinese looked to the government to control the people. It could not. Meanwhile, the strength and intensity of the protests grew. It became apparent that the protesters' target was as much the Ganden Phodrang itself, together with the ruling classes, which had continued to prosper under the Chinese while doing nothing to oppose them. Paralysis ensued. The Kashag, fearful of Chinese military intervention, was apologetic for the disturbances, but impotent. The one authority capable of defusing the crisis was clearly the Dalai Lama himself. Either he must support what was rapidly turning into a general uprising, or he must support the Chinese and call on the protesters to disperse. Declining the latter option, but judging confrontation to be suicidal, he acquiesced in plans being laid to engineer his flight from the palace into exile in India. On March 17, in a consultation with the oracle, he was instructed to go: "Go tonight!" Paradoxically, the oracle in question seems to have been none other than that of Dorje Shugden.* The medium then snatched up some paper and a pen and "wrote down, quite clearly and explicitly, the route I should take out of the Norbulingka, down to the last Tibetan town on the Indian border."[8] That night, dressed as an ordinary soldier, he stepped outside and made his way nervously through the crowds to a prearranged rendezvous with his younger brother and sister and a select number of his closest circle of advisers. Together, they headed south, over the river and past the unsuspecting garrison of PLA troops, en route to an uncertain future.

Escorted by Khampa fighters, Tenzin Gyatso's flight to freedom in exile took twelve days. At Lhuntse Dzong, the party paused just long enough for the Dalai Lama officially to repudiate the Seventeen-Point Agreement. But no sooner had he done so than news began to reach them that the PLA had destroyed both the Potala and the Norbulingka palaces and were even now in fevered pursuit. They hurried on, arriving at the border on March 30. The Dalai Lama was at this point ill with dysentery and unable to ride a horse as befit his dignity. Instead he was borne on the back of a *dzo*, the cross between a yak and a cow, which is considered by Tibetans the humblest form of transport.

---

* This is the claim made by Zémé Rinpoché in his *Yellow Book*.

27

Freedom in Exile

Over the next few months Tenzin Gyatso was followed by a further eighty thousand and more refugees. Most arrived destitute, creating serious logistical problems for the Indian government. Yet Nehru, abashed at his misreading of the Tibetan crisis, rose generously to the challenge. At once, the Indian government set up refugee camps and plans were laid for permanent settlements, mainly in southern India. Within a remarkably short time, the Tibetans were functioning together as a semi-autonomous community, with a reconstituted government in exile, under the energetic leadership of the now twenty-five-year-old Dalai Lama.

Back in Tibet, the Chinese were quick to crush what had quickly become a general uprising in Lhasa. When he heard of the Dalai Lama's escape, Mao is reported to have exclaimed, "In that case, we have lost the battle." And although early rumors that the PLA had destroyed both the Potala and the Norbulingka turned out to be unfounded, there was major loss of life. A Chinese report, captured some years later by Khampa resistance fighters, suggested eighty-seven thousand killed as a result of military action in central Tibet between March 1959 and September 1960.[1] Given the timescale, this figure must reflect not only the suppression of the revolt in Lhasa but also resistance to so-called democratic reform, which the Chinese introduced immediately. These reforms brought about a wholesale assault on the cultural and historical fabric of Tibetan life. Officially, China claims that the major destruction in Tibet occurred later, during the Chinese Revolution, but in fact Tibet began to be laid waste during the immediate aftermath of the Dalai Lama's flight. All but a handful of some six thousand monasteries and temples were severely damaged, if not destroyed entirely. Many were turned into warehouses or into accommodation for troops and Communist Party workers. The precious artifacts that were the glory of Tibet were burned, melted down, gratuitously smashed, or shipped back to China destined either for state art collections or smuggled out for sale on the international market. And of course the people suffered proportionately. Tens of thousands were incarcerated in forced labor camps, many of them never to be seen again. And, just as in China itself, farm collectivization resulted in food shortages and starvation such as had never been known before in Tibet. Added to this physical hardship was the immense mental strain created by the Chinese effort to convert the people to the new religion of Communism. Entailing re-education on a massive scale, this was accompanied by the notorious "struggle sessions" during which those deemed to show signs of resistance were compelled, generally at gunpoint, to condemn themselves to beatings, torture, and even death.

While the figure claimed by the Dalai Lama's government in exile of 1.2 million Tibetan dead as a direct result of the Chinese invasion and occupation has been questioned, there is no doubt that in the Sinocization of Tibet, great numbers of innocent people of all ages and of both sexes died, whether from execution, torture, starvation, or neglect. Nor, from what we know of

what occurred in China itself, is there reason to doubt the pitiful stories of children compelled to denounce and kill their
parents, of hunger so acute that people would tease the worms
from their own excrement to eat, of prisoners forced to dance
on the graves of fellow inmates they had been forced to murder,
of people deemed to have offended with their tongues having
them torn out with meat hooks, of widespread torture using elec-
tric cattle prods inserted into the mouth and anus. The catalog
is as grotesque as it is long.

Although he escaped with his life, the story of the Seventh
Panchen Lama during the Mao years is emblematic of what befell
Tibet. A few years younger than the Dalai Lama, the Panchen
Lama was now pushed forward as acting chairman of the so-
called Preparatory Committee for the Autonomous Region of
Tibet, by means of which "democratic reform" was to be introduced. In this position, he was expected to promote the party's
policies. Instead, and showing great courage, he wrote a lengthy
indictment of Chinese failings in Tibet known as the Seventy-
Thousand-Character Petition. In this, he put forward a minute
justification for a remark he famously made after a visit to eastern Tibet, that "in the socialist paradise, unlike in feudal times,
beggars do not even have a bowl with which to beg."[2] Mao was
apoplectic. The Panchen Lama's petition, which he sent directly
to the leadership, was "a poisoned arrow aimed at the heart of
the party." For the next two years, the Panchen Lama was held
in isolation in Shigatse. At the end of this period, he was subjected
to fifty days of interrogation, during which he was verbally abused
and physically degraded, and following which he was deemed
to wear the "Three Hats": the hat of an enemy of the party; the
hat of an enemy of the people; the hat of an enemy of socialism.
Thereafter, the Panchen Lama spent almost ten of the next fourteen years in prison in China, the balance under house arrest. From
time to time he was taken out for carefully choreographed struggle
sessions conducted before large audiences at sports stadiums

in Beijing where he was ritually humiliated. In 1966, his sister-in-law was brought on stage, where she accused him of raping her. His younger brother then beat him for the alleged offense. The Panchen Lama was finally released after the death of Mao in 1976, after which he continued, to the extent that he was able, to combine his restored political position with advocacy of human rights in Tibet. He died in 1989—many say in suspicious circumstances—on a rare visit to his monastery at Tashilhunpo, where again he spoke out against Chinese misrule in Tibet.*

While the Panchen Lama endured fourteen years of deprivation, Tenzin Gyatso himself was likewise compelled to adapt to a mode of living quite different from the one for which he was educated. In his case, however, the change was not entirely uncongenial. Exile gave Tenzin Gyatso the freedom drastically to curtail the courtly etiquette which had hitherto largely defined his relationship with others. From now on, for example, visitors would be seated on chairs of equal height. He would sit on a throne only in religious settings, and from the outset he made clear his eagerness to meet with non-Tibetans from all walks of life and from every cultural and religious background. Nevertheless, he remained heavily constrained in his movements. Although Nehru welcomed Tenzin Gyatso to India, he did not admit the Tibetan leader as a fellow head of state. Nor had he any intention of changing India's policy toward China. Instead the Dalai Lama and his government in exile were encouraged to make their headquarters a full day's journey from the Indian capital in what was, before the days of instant global communication via satellite, a remote corner of Himachal Pradesh.

---

* The Panchen Lama's woes continued even after the Seventh's death. When the Dalai Lama, acting on the advice of the Nechung oracle, preempted the Chinese by naming the new incarnation, Beijing retaliated by officially recognizing another candidate. As a result, there are presently two Panchen Lamas, one being educated at Tashilhunpo, the other under house arrest, probably somewhere in China.

Besides resettling his fellow refugees—and there has been a
steady flow of new ones over the past quarter century, averag-
ing perhaps three thousand a year*—Tenzin Gyatso's main priority since going into exile has been the preservation of Tibetan
culture. From the beginning, he encouraged the re-founding of
the principal monasteries in India.† He also recognized the need
for institutions both to preserve cultural forms, such as traditional opera and dance, and to archive material brought out of
Tibet, and these he helped set up. Then, toward the end of the
1960s, the Dalai Lama inaugurated a written constitution for a
future free Tibet. This was the first in a series of moves which
clearly show that Tenzin Gyatso is aiming to decouple the institution of the Dalai Lama from secular affairs. In its place, he
would like to see a democratically elected political leadership.
To that end, and controversially, this constitution provided a
mechanism for his impeachment and removal from office. But
while most Tibetans regarded the possibility as unthinkable—
if not actually blasphemous—Tenzin Gyatso saw that it was
precisely such measures which would win credibility in the wider
world, and particularly the West.

For the decade prior to Chairman Mao's death in 1976, very
little news of what was happening in Tibet reached even the
hundred miles or so to Dharamsala where the Dalai Lama now
lived. Having the leisure to do so, Tenzin Gyatso therefore began
at this time a series of lengthy retreats, during which he seems
to have had a number of deep spiritual experiences. It is to this
period that his repudiation of Dorje Shugden belongs. Having
originally been initiated into the cult by his junior tutor, Trijang
Rinpoché, he now began to speak out against what he termed
its dangerous practices. On the secular plane, it emerged that

* The still-growing Tibetan diaspora was thought in 2006 to number around a
quarter of a million or more.
† So successful has this been that, at the time of writing, the Three Seats in exile
have a combined population of around seven thousand monks.

the CIA was continuing, albeit somewhat haphazardly, to equip the Tibetan resistance movement, which had its headquarters in Mustang, a remote Tibetan province just inside the Nepalese border. This ceased only in 1973, when the United States finally recognized the People's Republic of China. In 1969, there had been another widespread uprising in Tibet, which resulted, according to some reports, in even greater numbers killed in the reprisals that followed than in those a decade earlier. But for many years, there was little concrete information. Occasionally, foreign journalists with Communist sympathies were admitted for carefully controlled visits to Lhasa, but their reports were of little value. After an initial flurry of interest in the immediate aftermath of the Dalai Lama's escape, Tibet vanished from the world's consciousness. Not even when the Dalai Lama himself began to travel, first through South-East Asia in 1967, then to the West during the early 1970s, did people pay much attention. In those days, Tenzin Gyatso was little more than a curiosity, the exiled "God King."

During 1980, however, Beijing, confident in the progress that had been made in Tibet, unexpectedly made contact. Using the Dalai Lama's second-eldest brother, Gyalo Thondup, as a conduit, the Chinese leadership invited the Tibetan hierarch to send a series of fact-finding missions to his homeland.* Their thinking seems to have been that, when he fully understood the situation, the Dalai Lama would have no grounds for opposing Chinese rule.

It was an extraordinary misjudgment on the part of the Chinese. The fact-finding missions did indeed visit Tibet. They found, however, that support for the Dalai Lama had not diminished in the least. Everywhere they went, they were mobbed by thousands of tearful Tibetans clamoring for news

---

* Besides Gyalo Thondup and Taktser Rinpoché, whom we have already met, there were two more brothers, as well as two sisters.

of the Precious Protector. So far as material progress was concerned, while they found it was true that much had changed, the main beneficiaries were not Tibetans, but those Chinese who had migrated to Tibet to take advantage of special concessions offered by the government. Furthermore, it became clear that China was committed to a policy of mass inward migration to Tibet, a policy suggested to Mao by the Russian tyrant Joseph Stalin.* There could be no question of the Dalai Lama returning to Tibet in these circumstances.

But if the picture of Tibet obtained by the delegations was dismal, abroad matters were about to change dramatically. The steady growth of interest in Buddhism throughout the West gradually began to have the effect of kindling interest in Tibet itself. Tenzin Gyatso made several successful trips to the United States, culminating, in 1987, with an invitation to address Congress. He used the occasion to put forward his Five-Point Peace Plan for the future of Tibet. According to this, Tibet would be demilitarized and turned into the world's largest natural park, a place of "peace and harmony." It was a bold, if idealistic, proposal to which the Chinese government reacted furiously. Tibet was an inalienable part of the People's Republic of China and the Dalai Lama nothing more than a troublemaker. As to his proposals, they were simply a ruse to facilitate a split in the fabric of the country. In turn, however, this denunciation by the Chinese sparked off several days of well-reported rioting in Lhasa, which gained the Tibetan leader and his people vastly more publicity and sympathy than they had received since 1959.

China's response to the riots was, first, drastically to restrict access to Tibet and, secondly, to introduce "re-education" on a scale unknown since the Mao era. When subsequently the Dalai Lama was awarded the Nobel Prize for Peace, in 1989,

* This has since resulted in the outnumbering of Tibetans by Chinese, even in central Tibet.

China reacted by imposing martial law on Tibet. But while the Chinese leadership has since continued to imprison and often torture those it deems guilty of activities designed to split the Motherland, and although it has instigated successive campaigns to root out resistance and to re-orientate the thinking of the Tibetan masses, the Dalai Lama himself has gone on to acquire iconic status as an advocate of peace and of religious harmony.* Now a multi-million-selling author, he sells out sports venues from Sydney to San Francisco, from Jerusalem to Johannesburg. His books are in translation in more than forty languages. His face adorns T-shirts, wristwatches, screensavers, and shrine rooms from secular Europe to Catholic South America. The toast of Hollywood, he is the subject of two major feature films, not to mention scores of documentaries. Feted by presidents and pop stars alike, he creates headlines wherever he goes. In 2007, he was awarded the United States' most prestigious civil award, the Congressional Gold Medal.

It would be pleasant to recount that the emergence of Tenzin Gyatso as a major world figure has had the effect of unifying Tibetans themselves and completely extirpating the factionalism that is such a feature of Tibetan history, but the murder of Lobsang Gyatso and the bitterness surrounding the Dalai Lama's proscription of Shugden worship suggests that, although his resolutely nonsectarian approach has gone a long way to encourage openness in others, it has not succeeded entirely. On reflection, however, this is hardly surprising. If there is such a place as the Tibetan universe, it is one where deities both compassionate and wrathful are every bit as real as the market forces which are said to govern life in the modern world. It follows, then, that if Tibetan religion and culture are to remain vital, this traditional conception of the universe must likewise remain vital.

* A Chinese government report on the suppression of Tibetan opposition, issued during the mid-1990s, was picturesquely, if chillingly, entitled *Cutting Off the Serpent's Head*. More than ten years on and Chinese repression in Tibet has lessened little, if at all.

It is nevertheless a paradox of the Western world's enthusiasm for Buddhism and for Tibet that the one is perceived as being a uniquely peaceful religion and the other as a uniquely peaceful place. As we have seen, these perceptions entail gross over-simplifications. Yet this realization should not be allowed to rob us of all perspective. Whatever we may feel about Buddhism and about religion in general, there can be no doubt that its eleva-tion of and emphasis (however frequently ignored) on compas-sion before all else places it among humanity's noblest and finest achievements. So if the collective history of the Dalai Lamas startles us with its passion and its bloodiness, we should also recognize some of the contrasts between traditional Tibetan society and that of the modern world. Theirs was not a perfect society, but it was a society in which, generally speaking, the ideals of reli-gion flourished and selfishness was scorned. It was a society in which few amassed great wealth, but in which few went hungry, and it was a society in which, on the whole, families stayed together and looked after one another. Old people were cher-ished for their wisdom and not regarded as an encumbrance to be put away, while large families were considered a blessing and not a burden. Conversely, although people's sexual habits were relatively free—British officials noted an unusually high incidence of sexually transmitted disease—abortion was looked on with horror. One has, too, the sense that most Tibetans, for all the drawbacks they faced living in a feudal society, nevertheless lived lives that were in many ways freer than is the case for the major-ity of people caught up in the struggle of modern industrial capi-talist society. By most accounts they were certainly happier.[3]

It is arguably a failing of the way in which history is done today that, because it focuses largely on secular events, and espe-cially on those which are merely striking and unusual, we read much more about individuals' shortcomings than about their virtues. No doubt this book is in many respects an example of such a tendency. Worse still, modern history tends to ignore the mass of lives, decently lived, often under trying circumstances, which is probably how most people do in fact live. When, however, we look at Tibetan history in broad perspective, we see that the institution of the Dalai Lamas, far from being something remote and mysterious, is in fact a living link with a type of society that, if not entirely unique, is fast vanishing from view: a society in which kindness—not material wealth—is seen as the highest attainment of humanity. Looking at the Tibetan tradition from this wide perspective, it is clear that the answer to the question posed at the beginning of this book—whether the tragedy of Lobsang Gyatso is not symptomatic of a malaise lying at the heart of Tibetan religion and culture—is that it reflects something deeper: a wound in the human spirit itself. As the event itself declares, and as the Dalai Lama readily admits, Tibet never was Shangri-La. Unquestionably, Tibetan Buddhism is as prone to sectarian rivalry as any other religion, if only because all religions are practiced by human beings. Nor is it so surprising that religious believers sometimes resort to violence. People are naturally passionate when what they hold dearest seems threatened. The problem is rather that it is we human beings who are flawed. This is precisely why, as Tenzin Gyatso puts it, we need the "medicine" of religion. So while it would be easy enough to make a case for saying that in reality, Tibet was a backward, monk-ridden society where religion was used by the powerful to exploit the powerless—China has long made just such a claim—it is worth recalling that the three great attempts of the twentieth century to found avowedly atheistic societies, those led by Hitler, Mao, and Stalin, ended in unspeakable suffering for countless millions.

It is also worth comparing the personal example of the present Dalai Lama with each of those leaders, all of whom spent the latter part of their lives subsumed in an ecstasy of paranoia—like crows afraid of their own shadow, as the Tibetan proverb says. We saw earlier that whatever his doctrinal commitments may be, Tenzin Gyatso is, to paraphrase St. Paul, very clearly someone who would sooner bless than curse his enemies, who, to the utmost of his ability, seeks to be at peace with everyone; someone who is patient; who is kind; who is neither boastful nor conceited; who is neither rude nor seeks his own advantage; who is always ready to make allowances, to trust, to hope, and, in adversity, to endure whatever trials may come his way. He is, we may say, an exemplary achievement of traditional Tibetan culture, someone who strives every moment to conform his life to the pattern of Chenrezig, Bodhisattva of Compassion.

Yet for all his remarkable personal qualities, it is a fact that there are some for whom these are not enough. This is true not only of a minority of his own people. It is also true of some who see in him a champion of causes more parochial than universal responsibility and compassion. The animal and gay rights lobbies, the Christian syncretists, and others who draw inspiration from the Dalai Lama for their projects have mostly been confounded by his reluctance to endorse their campaigns. And many would-be Buddhists are perplexed when he tells them to look first to the resources of their own religion and culture. It is only when we place Tenzin Gyatso within the context of the institution of the Dalai Lamas, and the religious, cultural, and political forces which shaped it, that we begin to see that the Dalai Lama of popular imagination—the Dalai Lama as friend to everyone (and most notably to a clutch of enter-tainment-world royalty), offering comfort to the victim in us all, a spiritual teacher who reassures without requiring repentance, who consoles without demanding contrition, a politically correct god for a godless world—is an imaginative construct.

Similarly, when we set him in the context of his own culture, we see that Tenzin Gyatso is as remarkable as his most ardent admirers assert, though perhaps not quite in the way they assert. Refusing every inducement to a life of ease, he has almost single-handedly kept alive the issue of justice for his people, despite the apathy of politicians and the hostility of vested inter-est. He has pricked the conscience of millions. Yet he himself is no romantic. The Dalai Lama's unswerving dedication to non-violence in the face of extreme provocation both challenges and expands conventional notions of what compassion entails: not passivity but rather engagement and resolve; not meekness but rather tenacity and fortitude. In this, the Dalai Lama bears prophetic, yet also pragmatic, witness to the possibility of peace in the world. These achievements are all the greater for the contrast between his personal integrity and the tumultuous background from which he has emerged. They are greater still for being the achievements of an ordinary man.

As to the future of the institution of the Dalai Lamas, clearly its one great weakness is its unique system of succession. Of necessity there must be a gap of two decades between the passing of one Dalai Lama and the maturity of the next. And if we add to this some years of diminished power at the end of one life and a few more in order to acquire a working knowledge of statecraft in the next, inevitably this means a hiatus of a generation between effective rulers, even if ill health or misfortune do not intervene. Humanity being the same the world over, it is also inevitable that in the interim there should be a struggle for power. In many ways, it is remarkable that the manifest corruption and self-seeking that have tended to characterize these struggles have not actually destroyed the institution of the Dalai Lamas. One is reminded of the cardinal's retort when Napoleon announced that he intended to destroy the Catholic Church: "Not even we have managed that."

Whether, and for how long, the institution survives, will clearly depend to a great extent on the strength of the religious tradition on which it relies. As yet, there is no evidence that the faith of Tibetans generally is declining; besides, not just in the West but particularly in China itself, increasing numbers of people are developing an interest in Tibetan Buddhism. If, then, as is clearly his wish, Tenzin Gyatso is successful in decoupling the institution from secular affairs and returning it to something like the purely religious office it was before the time of the Great Fifth, there is reason to hope that it will cease to be an object of sectarian rivalry. And if that happens, we may expect the Dalai Lamas to continue to play an increasingly important role in the spiritual leadership of the world.

Notes

Introduction

1. For "wisdom tradition," see, for example, Goleman, Dan, "Universal Responsibility and the Seeds of Empathy" in Mehrotra, Rajiv (ed.), *Understanding the Dalai Lama*, 131. For Buddhism as "inner science," see Sogyal, Rinpoché, *Tibetan Book of Living and Dying*, 352. See also Thurman, Robert, *Inner Revolution*, e.g. 31–6, 39, and 247.

Chapter 1

1. In June 2007, an international warrant was issued via Interpol, calling for the arrest of two named Tibetans. At the time of writing, however, nothing has come of this development.
2. I can personally testify that the Dalai Lama does not own a pair of Gucci loafers, though he does have at least one pair of Hush Puppies.

Chapter 2

1. See Conze, Edward, *Perfection of Wisdom in Eight Thousand Lines*.
2. Wood, Frances, *The Silk Road*, 23.

3. Adapted from Conze, Edward, *Perfection of Wisdom in Eight Thousand Lines*, 36.
4. The historical Buddha who lived, probably, during the fifth century BCE. This timescale is implied in the *Mani Kanbum*. See Dharma Publishing, *Ancient Tibet*, 104–5.
5. Gyaltsen, Sakyapa Sonam, *The Clear Mirror*, 78.
6. Ahmad, Zahiruddin (trans.), *Sans-rgyas rgya-mtsho*, 47.
7. Ibid., 118.
8. Ibid., 115.
9. Edwardes, Michael (ed.), *A Life of the Buddha*, 108.

Chapter 3

1. Narain, A. K., "Indo-Europeans in Inner Asia," in Sinor, Denis (ed.), *The Cambridge History of Early Inner Asia*.
2. Foltz, Richard C., *Religions of the Silk Road*, 46.
3. See Uray, Géza, "Tibet's Connections with Nestorianism and Manicheism in the 8th–10th Centuries," in *Contributions on Tibetan Language, History and Culture." Proceedings of the Csoma de Körös Symposium*, vol. 1, 1983. See also Hunter, Erica C. D., "The Church of the East in Central Asia," *Bulletin of the John Rylands University Library of Manchester*, vol. 78, no. 3, Autumn 1996.
4. St Augustine, *Confessions*, 49.

Chapter 4

1. Adapted from Gyaltsen, Sakyapa Sonam, *The Clear Mirror*, 96.
2. Here I follow Matthew T. Kapstein, whose essay "The Imagined Persistence of Empire," which provides the background to this observation, appears in his outstanding contribution to Tibetan scholarship, *The Tibetan Assimilation of Buddhism*.
3. See Wangdu, Passang and Hildegard Diemberger, *dBa'bzhed*.
4. Richardson, Hugh, *High Peaks, Pure Earth*, 130.
5. Ibid., 134.
6. Ibid., 136.
7. Ibid., 156.

8. From the *T'ung-tien*, quoted in Haarh, Erik, *The Yar-lun Dynasty*, 345.

9. For a discussion of Songtsen Gampo's likely dates, see "How Old Was Srong-brtsan Sgam-po?" in Richardson, Hugh, *High Peaks, Pure Earth*, 3.

10. Paludan, Ann, *Chronicle of the Chinese Emperors*, 89.

11. Schafer, Edward H., *The Golden Peaches of Samarkand*, 254.

12. Richardson, Hugh, *High Peaks, Pure Earth*, 134.

13. Hoffmann, Helmut, *Tibet: A Handbook*, 42.

14. Norbu, Thupten Jigme and Colin M. Turnbull, *Tibet*, 136.

15. Beckwith, Christopher I., *The Tibetan Empire in Central Asia*, 25.

Chapter 5

1. Richardson, Hugh, *High Peaks, Pure Earth*, 118.

2. Schafer, Edward H., *The Golden Peaches of Samarkand*, 254.

3. Ibid., 253–54.

4. Quoted in Beckwith, Christopher I., *The Tibetan Empire in Central Asia*, 45.

5. Richardson, Hugh, *High Peaks, Pure Earth*, 198.

6. Ibid., 211.

7. Quoted in Beckwith, Christopher I., *The Tibetan Empire in Central Asia*, 76.

8. Ibid., 101.

9. Ibid., 116.

10. Ibid., 128.

11. Ahmad, Zahiruddin (trans.), *Sans-rgyas rgya-mtsho*, 143.

12. Wangdu, Passang and Hildegard Diemberger, *dBa'bzhed*, 36.

13. Hoffmann, Helmut, "Early and Medieval Tibet," in Sinor, Denis (ed.), *The Cambridge History of Early Inner Asia*, 383.

14. See Whitfield, Susan, *Life Along the Silk Road*, 71.

15. Thomas, F. W., *Tibetan Texts and Documents*, vol. 2, 251.

16. Ibid., 437.

17. Ibid., 197.

18. Beckwith, Christopher I., *The Tibetan Empire in Central Asia*, 109–10.
19. Norbu, Thupten Jingme and Colin M. Turnbull, *Tibet*, 35.
20. See, for example, Wangdu, Passang and Hildegard Diemberger, *dBa'bzhed*, 52.
21. Ibid., 57.
22. Ibid., 59.
23. Ibid., 73.
24. Ibid., 76.
25. Rin-Chen-Gru Bu-Ston, *The History of Buddhism in India and Tibet*, 197.
26. Schafer, Edward H., *The Golden Peaches of Samarkand*, 254.

Chapter 6

1. See Hoffmann, Helmut, *Tibet: A Handbook*, 46.
2. Norbu, Thupten Jingme and Colin M. Turnbull, *Tibet*, 170.
3. Rin-Chen-Gru Bu-Ston, *The History of Buddhism in India and Tibet*, 197.
4. Gyaltsen, Sakyapa Sonam, *The Clear Mirror*, 261.
5. Smith, Warren W., Jr., *Tibetan Nation*, 74.
6. Hoffmann, Helmut, "Early and Medieval Tibet," in Sinor, Denis (ed.), *The Cambridge History of Early Inner Asia*, 389.
7. See Petech, Luciano, "The Disintegration of the Tibetan Kingdom," in Kvaerne, Per (ed.), *Tibetan Studies*, 649–59.
8. See Karmay, Samten Gyaltsen, *The Arrow and the Spindle*, 307.
9. Ch'en, Kenneth, *Buddhism in China*, 228.
10. Karmay, Samten Gyaltsen, *The Arrow and the Spindle*, 11.
11. Tucci, Giuseppe, *The Religions of Tibet*, 24.

Chapter 7

1. Hoffmann, Helmut, *The Religions of Tibet*, 118.
2. Watson, Francis, *A Concise History of India*, 89.
3. Ibid., 66.
4. Bu Ston, *The History of Buddhism in India and Tibet*, 213.
5. For a complete list, see Dowman, Keith, *Masters of Mahamudra*.

6. Ibid., 334, quoting Atisha's biography.

7. Ibid., 357.

8. Ibid., 359.

9. Shakabpa, Tsepon W. D., *Tibet: A Political History*, 57.

10. Chattopadhyaya, Alaka, *Atisha and Tibet*, 429.

11. Ibid., 430.

12. Ibid., 352.

13. Here I follow Chattopadhyaya, Alaka, *Atisha and Tibet* despite Hugh Richardson's caustic review in *High Peaks, Pure Earth*.

14. For a full discussion, see van der Kuijp, Leonard W. J., "The Dalai Lamas and the Origins of Reincarnate Lamas," in Brauen, Martin (ed.), *The Dalai Lamas: A Visual History*.

15. Dorje, Gyurme (ed.), *Tibet Handbook*, 146.

16. Ahmad, Zahiruddin (trans.), *Sans-rgyas rgya-mtsho*, 155.

17. 'Gos Lo-tsa-ba Gzon-nu-dpal, *The Blue Annals*, 844.

18. Ibid., 455.

Chapter 8

1. See Taylor, Charles, "Closed World Systems," in Wrathall, Mark (ed.), *Religion after Metaphysics*.

2. Dudjom Rinpoché, Jikdrel Yeshe Dorje, *The Nyingma School of Tibetan Buddhism*, 755.

3. Ibid.

4. Tsogyal, Yeshe, *The Lotus-Born*, 64.

5. Ibid., 72.

6. Ibid., 185.

7. Ibid., 195.

Chapter 9

1. For a full discussion, see Samuel, Geoffrey, *Civilized Shamans*, 186–88.

2. Ekvall, Robert B., *Tents Against the Sky*, quoted in ibid., 188.

3. Tucci, Giuseppe, *The Religions of Tibet*, 172–73.

4. Karmay, Samten Gyaltsen, *The Arrow and the Spindle*, 255.

Chapter 10

1. Tucci, Giuseppe, *Tibetan Painted Scrolls*, vol. 1, 85–6.
2. 'Gos Lo-tsa-ba Gzon-nu-dpal, *The Blue Annals*, 589.
3. Ahmad, Zahiruddin (trans.), *Sans-rgyas rgya-mtsho*, 179.
4. Dawson, Christopher (ed.), *The Mongol Mission*. See introduction.
5. Ibid., 16.
6. Ruysbroeck, Willem von, *The Mission of Friar William of Rubruck*, 192.
7. Petech, Luciano, "Tibetan Relations with Sung China and with the Mongols," in Rossabi, Morris (ed.), *China among Equals*, 182.
8. Paludan, Ann, *Chronicle of the Chinese Emperors*, 78.
9. Ahmad, Zahiruddin (trans.), *A History of Tibet by the Fifth Dalai Lama of Tibet*, 96–7.
10. Shuwen, Yang et al., *The Biographical Paintings of "Phags-pa*, 50.
11. See Rossabi, Morris, *Khubilai Khan*.
12. Shuwen, Yang et al., *The Biographical Paintings of "Phags-Pa*, 58–9.
13. Rossabi, Morris, *Khubilai Khan*, 141.
14. Davidson, Ronald M., *Indian Esoteric Buddhism*, 330. Thupten Jinpa qualifies this by suggesting "a powerful king" in place of Davidson's "Universal Ruler."
15. See Seyfort-Ruegg, D. S., "The Preceptor-Donor (YON MCHOD) Relation in Thirteenth-Century Tibetan Society," in Krasser et al., *Tibetan Studies*.
16. Tucci, Giuseppe, *Tibetan Painted Scrolls*, vol. 1, 102–3.
17. Petech, Luciano, *Central Tibet and the Mongols*, 21.
18. Ibid., 37.
19. Franke, Herbert, *China Under Mongol Rule*, 301.
20. Shuwen, Yang et al., *The Biographical Paintings of "Phags-pa*, 142.
21. Petech, Luciano, *Central Tibet and the Mongols*, 24.
22. Ibid., 25.

Chapter 11

1. For a full account, see Lhalungpa, Lobsang P., *The Life of Milarepa*.
2. See Benson, Herbert, *Your Maximum Mind*, 16–22.
3. Lhalungpa, Lobsang P., *The Life of Milarepa*, 166.
4. See Dorje, Rinjing, *Tales of Uncle Tompa*.
5. See, however, van der Kuijp, Leonard W. J., "The Dalai Lamas and the Origins of Reincarnate Lamas," in op. cit., for a full discussion.
6. See Li, Tieh-Tseng, *Tibet, Today and Yesterday*, 21.
7. Here I follow Shakabpa's account. It may be less precise than Petech's, but it gives a much better picture of the man.
8. See Petech, Luciano, *Central Tibet and the Mongols*, 107.
9. Ahmad, Zahiruddin (trans.), *A History of Tibet by the Fifth Dalai Lama of Tibet*, 137.
10. Tucci, Giuseppe, *Tibetan Painted Scrolls*, vol. 1, 23.

Chapter 12

1. Ahmad, Zahiruddin (trans.), *A History of Tibet by the Fifth Dalai Lama of Tibet*, 193.
2. Huc, Evariste Régis, *Lamas of the Western Heavens*, 108.
3. Douglas, Nik and Meryl White, *Karmapa*, 57.
4. Hanzhang, Ya, *Biographies of the Tibetan Spiritual Leaders Panchen Erdenis*, 5.
5. Dreyfus, Georges B. J., *The Sound of Two Hands Clapping*, 314.

Chapter 13

1. Adapted from Tucci, Giuseppe, *Tibetan Painted Scrolls*, vol. 2, 591.
2. Mullin, Glenn H., *The Fourteen Dalai Lamas*, 64.
3. Sperling, Elliot, "The Fifth Karma-pa and Some Aspects of the Relationship between Tibet and the Early Ming," in Aris, Michael and Aung San Suu Kyi (eds.), *Tibetan Studies in Honor of Hugh Richardson*.

4. Richardson, Hugh, *High Peaks, Pure Earth*, 345.

5. Douglas, Nik and Meryl White, *Karmapa*, 62.

6. Sperling, Elliot, "The Fifth Karma-pa and Some Aspects of the Relationship between Tibet and the Early Ming," in op. cit.

7. Norbu, Dawa, *China's Tibet Policy*, 64.

Chapter 14

1. See Mullin, Glenn H., *The Fourteen Dalai Lamas*.

2. See Mullin, Glenn H., *Mystical Verses of a Mad Dalai Lama*, 83.

3. Tucci, Giuseppe, *Tibetan Painted Scrolls*, vol. 2, 654.

Chapter 15

1. See Paludan, Ann, *Chronicle of the Chinese Emperors*, 179.

2. Tucci, Giuseppe, *Tibetan Painted Scrolls*, vol. 1, 46.

3. Mullin, Glenn H., *The Fourteen Dalai Lamas*, 144.

4. See Li, Chi-ch'ang, *The Travels of an Alchemist*.

5. Ahmad, Zahiruddin (trans.), *Sans-rgyas rgya-mtsho*, 220.

Chapter 16

1. Some authorities question whether the father was really Sechen. See Smith, Warren W., Jr., *Tibetan Nation*, 303, note 392. It is certain, however, that he was one of Altan's line.

2. Tucci, Giuseppe, *Tibetan Painted Scrolls*, vol. 1, 54.

Chapter 17

1. Ahmad, Zahiruddin (trans.), *Sans-rgyas rgya-mtsho*, 248.

2. Ibid., 249.

3. *Dukula*, vol. 1, 55, quoted in Pommaret, Françoise (ed.), *Lhasa in the Seventeenth Century*, 69.

4. Published in abridged form as *The Secret Visions of the Fifth Dalai Lama*.

5. See Dreyfus, Georges B. J., *The Sound of Two Hands Clapping*, 120–23.

6. Douglas, Nik and Meryl White, *Karmapa*, 147.

7. Shakabpa, Tsepon W. D., *Tibet: A Political History*, 106.

8. Ahmad, Zahiruddin, *Sino-Tibetan Relations in the Seventeenth Century*, 128.

9. Gos-bzang, quoted in Shakabpa, Tsepon W. D., *Tibet: A Political History*, 109–10.

10. Karmay, Samten Gyaltsen, *Secret Visions of the Fifth Dalai Lama*, 29.

Chapter 18

1. Shakabpa, Tsepon W. D., *Tibet: A Political History*, 123.

2. There are several variations of this story, but their theme remains constant. See Nebesky-Wojkowitz, René de, *Oracles and Demons of Tibet*, 104.

3. Smith, Warren W., Jr., *Tibetan Nation*, 120.

4. Ahmad, Zahiruddin, *Sino-Tibetan Relations in the Seventeenth Century*, 175.

5. Ibid., 173.

6. Karmay, Samten Gyaltsen, *Secret Visions of the Fifth Dalai Lama*, 47.

7. For further accounts see Dreyfus, Georges B. J., "The Shugs Idan Affair: History and the Nature of a Quarrel," *Journal of the International Association of Buddhist Studies*, and also his *The Sound of Two Hands Clapping*, 300–3; Karmay, Samten Gyaltsen, "The Fifth Dalai Lama and the Reunification of Tibet," in Pommaret, Françoise (ed.), *Lhasa in the Seventeenth Century*; Religion and Culture, Dept of, *The Worship of Shugden*.

8. For accounts of Dorje Shugden and the related controversy, see Dreyfus, Georges B. J., *The Sound of One Hand Clapping*. Also Karmay, Samten G., "The Fifth Dalai Lama and His Reunification of Tibet," in Pommaret, Françoise (ed.), *Lhasa in the Seventeenth Century*.

9. Ahmad, Zahiruddin, *Sino-Tibetan Relations in the Seventeenth Century*, 197.

10. Ibid., 208.

11. Hanzhang, Ya, *The Biographies of the Dalai Lamas*, 63.
12. Karmay, Samten Gyaltsen, *Secret Visions of the Fifth Dalai Lama*, 63.
13. Ahmed, Zahiruddin (trans.), *Sans-rgyas rgya-mtsho*, 281–82.

Chapter 19

1. Nonetheless, his translation of the six-syllable mantra is arguably accurate, and certainly more so than the usual translation: "Hail jewel in the lotus." See Lopez, Donald S., *Prisoners of Shangri-La*, Chapter 4.
2. For details see Wessels, C., *Early Jesuit Travelers in Central Asia*.
3. De Filippi, *An Account of Tibet*, 191.

Chapter 20

1. Shakabpa, Tsepon W. D., *Tibet: A Political History*, 126.
2. Aris, Michael, *Hidden Treasures and Secret Lives*, 123.
3. Fletcher, Harold R., *A Quest of Flowers*, quoted in ibid., 134.
4. Here I paraphrase Aris in ibid., 135–37, in much of the foregoing passage.
5. Ahmad, Zahiruddin, *Sino-Tibetan Relations in the Seventeenth Century*, 232.
6. Spence, Jonathan, *Emperor of China*, 21.
7. Hanzhang, Ya, *The Biographies of the Dalai Lamas*, 43.
8. Ibid., 43.
9. Aris, Michael, *Hidden Treasures and Secret Lives*, 143.
10. Ibid., 149.
11. Ibid. op. cit. paraphrase.

Chapter 21

1. Norbu, Thupten Jingme and Colin M. Turnbull, *Tibet*, 291.
2. Aris, Michael, *Hidden Treasures and Secret Lives*, 167.
3. Ibid., 186.
4. See ibid., 193. Aris's translation describes him knocking them unconscious, but this hardly seems right.

5. Ibid., 203.
6. Ibid., 206.

Chapter 22

1. Paludan, Ann, *Chronicle of the Chinese Emperors*, 194.
2. Petech, Luciano, *China and Tibet in the Early XVIIIth Century*, 46–7.
3. Ibid., 53.
4. Mullin, Glenn H., *Gems of Wisdom from the Seventh Dalai Lama*, 53.
5. For a full, if gruesome, account, see Norman, Henry, *The Peoples and Politics of the Far East*, 226–29.
6. Adapted from Mullin, Glenn H., *Gems of Wisdom from the Seventh Dalai Lama*, 88.
7. Petech, Luciano, *China and Tibet in the Early XVIIIth Century*, 212.
8. See Shakabpa, Tsepon W. D., *Tibet: A Political History*, 149.

Chapter 23

1. Adapted from Kachen Geshe Gyaltsen, quoted in Mullin, Glenn H., *The Fourteen Dalai Lamas*, 307.
2. See Smith, E. Gene, *Among Tibetan Texts*, 141, for this account.
3. Ibid., 173.
4. Ibid.
5. Markham, C. R. (ed.), *Narratives of the Mission of George Bogle to Tibet*, 132.
6. Shakabpa, Tsepon W. D., *Tibet: A Political History*, 165.
7. Ibid., 162.
8. Kolmăs, Josef, *Tibet and Imperial China*, 48.
9. See Petech, Luciano, *Selected Papers on Asian History*, 139.

Chapter 24

1. Mullin, Glenn H., *The Fourteen Dalai Lamas*, 347.
2. Letter dated February 19, 1807. See Marrs, Edwin W., Jr.. (ed.), *The Letters of Charles and Mary Lamb*, vol. 2, 96.

3. Markham, C. R. (ed.), *Narratives of the Mission of George Bogle to Tibet.*
4. Ibid., 265–66.
5. Mullin, Glenn H., *The Fourteen Dalai Lamas*, 352–53.
6. Hanzhang, Ya, *Biographies of the Tibetan Spiritual Leaders Panchen Erdenis*, 179.
7. Rockhill, William Woodville, *The Dalai Lamas of Lhasa*, 54.
8. Shakabpa, Tsepon W. D., *Tibet: A Political History*, 176.
9. The official records of the Qing Dynasty, quoted in Hanzhang, Ya, *Biographies of the Tibetan Spiritual Leaders Panchen Erdenis*, 183–84.
10. Quoted in ibid., 181.
11. Huc, Evariste Régis, *Lamas of the Western Heavens*, 218–41.
12. See Tsering, Tashi, *"Nag-ron mGon-po rNam-rGyal*: A 19th Century *Khams-pa* warrior," in Aziz, Barbara Nimri and Matthew Kapstein (eds.), *Soundings in Tibetan Civilization.*
13. Shakabpa, Tsepon W. D., *Tibet: A Political History*, 188.
14. Petech, Luciano, *Selected Papers on Asian History*, 144.

Chapter 25

1. Tada, Tokan, *The Thirteenth Dalai Lama*, 12.
2. Bell, Sir Charles, *Portrait of the Dalai Lama*, 42.
3. Ibid., 62.
4. Goldstein, Melvyn, *A History of Modern Tibet*, 43.
5. See accounts in Das, Sarat Chandra, *Journey to Lhasa and Central Tibet*, and Shakabpa, Tsepon W. D., *Tibet: A Political History.*
6. Bell, Sir Charles, *Portrait of the Dalai Lama*, 183.
7. Shakabpa, Tsepon W. D., *Tibet: A Political History.*
8. Ibid., 214.
9. Bell, Sir Charles. See his *Portrait of the Dalai Lama.*
10. Kozlov, Petr Kuz'mich, *Tibet I Dalai-Lama*, 70.
11. See accounts in Goldstein, Melvyn, *A History of Modern Tibet*, and Dhondup, K., *The Water-Bird and Other Years.*
12. See Bell, Sir Charles, *Portrait of the Dalai Lama*, 58.
13. Goldstein, Melvyn, *A History of Modern Tibet*, 60.

14. Tada, Tokan, *The Thirteenth Dalai Lama*, 72.

15. Alex McKay, who first came across evidence pointing to this possibility, provides a full account in his excellent *Tibet and the British Raj*.

16. Goldstein, Melvyn, *A History of Modern Tibet*, 136.

17. Ibid., 117.

18. Mehra, Parshotam, *Tibetan Polity 1904–37*, 45.

19. HH XIV Dalai Lama, *Freedom in Exile*, 36.

Chapter 26

1. Wangdu, Khemey Sonam, et al., *Discovery, Recognition and Enthronement of the XIVth Dalai Lama*, 11.

2. Personal communication of Dr. Morgan to Tsering Shakya, author of *The Dragon in the Land of Snows*.

3. Goldstein, Melvyn, *A History of Modern Tibet*, 519–20.

4. Ibid., 692.

5. Ibid., 812–13.

6. Shakya, Tsering, *The Dragon in the Land of Snows*, 105.

7. HH XIV Dalai Lama, *Freedom in Exile*, 121.

8. Ibid., 149.

Chapter 27

1. HH XIV Dalai Lama, *Freedom in Exile*, 162

2. Adapted from Nyima, Chokey, HH Xth Panchen Lama, *A Poisoned Arrow*, xvii.

3. See, for example, the accounts of Desideri, Bogle, Huc, Harrer.

A *Note on Sources*

This book does not pretend to any great originality. For this reason, I have sought not to overburden the text with notes, generally limiting myself to citing authorities only where my claims seem controversial. My main historical sources have been Tibetan works in translation which I have used together with some of the many excellent studies and papers produced by mainly European academics during the past century or so. For readers wishing to deepen their knowledge of Tibetan history, the works of three great Italian scholars are indispensable: those of Ippolito Desideri, Giuseppe Tucci, and Luciano Petech. For foundational studies of Tibetan culture, the key figures are Helmut Hoffmann (though his work on Bon religion has been superseded), R. A. Stein, H. E. Richardson, and David Snellgrove. On the history of the Tibetan Empire, the work of Géza Uray, Erik Haarh, and, latterly, Christopher Beckwith is unmissable. And on the folk-religious culture of Tibet, the works of René de Nebesky-Wojkowitz and Robert Ekvall are essential reading.

Lately there has been an increasing flow of first-rate work originating in the U.S. academy, among the best being that of

Melvyn C. Goldstein, Janet Gyatso, Matthew T. Kapstein, Leonard van der Kuijp, and Donald Lopez. Tibetan studies continue to flourish in Europe and Scandinavia under excellent scholars such as Per Sørensen in Leipzig, Charles Ramble at Oxford, and Per Kvaerne in Oslo, while in Japan notable work has been published by Ishihama Yumiko. Mention should also be made of the contribution of the world's first non-Tibetan *geshe*, Georges Dreyfus, as also of the pioneering work of Zahiruddin Ahmad and E. Gene Smith. I have drawn freely from the work of each of these fine scholars. Besides these, I have also drawn extensively from the outstanding work of a small number of native Tibetan scholars working in English, especially that of Samten Karmay and Thupten Jinpa. Mention should also be made of the modern histories of Tsering Shakya and Dawa Norbu.

In the bibliography that follows I have cited those works which have been most helpful to me, though there are sure to be others that I could have profited from reading. I have almost completely neglected the work, much of it evidently of very high quality, of modern Tibetan scholars publishing in Tibetan. This could be construed as a major failing. On the other hand, this book is unashamedly an outsider's view. Finally, so far as my use of primary sources is concerned, generally this has been limited to what I have gathered with my eyes and my ears.

Bibliography

Ahmad, Zahiruddin (trans.). *A History of Tibet by the Fifth Dalai Lama of Tibet*. Bloomington: Indiana University Research Institute for Inner Asian Studies, 1995.

Ahmad, Zahiruddin (trans.). *Sans-rgyas rgya-mtsho: Life of the Fifth Dalai Lama*. Vol. 4, part 1. New Delhi: International Academy of Indian Culture and Aditya Prakashan, 1999.

Ahmad, Zahiruddin. *Sino-Tibetan Relations in the Seventeenth Century*. Rome: Instituto Italiano per il Medio ed Estramo Oriente, 1970.

Alai (trans. Howard Goldblatt and Sylvia Li-chun Lin). *Red Poppies*. London: Methuen, 2002.

Ancient Tibet: Research Materials from the Yeshe de Project. Berkeley: Dharma Publishing, 1986.

Anderson, G. A. (ed.). *The Letters of Thomas Manning to Charles Lamb*. New York: Harper and Brothers, 1926.

Aris, Michael. *Bhutan: The Early History of a Himalayan Kingdom*. Warminster: Aris & Phillips, 1979.

———. *Hidden Treasures and Secret Lives: A Study of Pemalingpa (1450–1521) and the Sixth Dalai Lama (1683–1706)*. London: Kegan Paul International, 1989.

————. *Lamas, Princes and Brigands: Joseph Rock's Photographs of the Tibetan Borderlands of China.* New York: China Institute in America, 1992.

————. *Views of Medieval Bhutan: The Diary and Drawings of Samuel Davis, 1783.* London: Serindia, 1982.

Aris, Michael and Aung San Suu Kyi (eds.). *Tibetan Studies in Honor of Hugh Richardson: Proceedings of the International Seminar on Tibetan Studies, Oxford 1979.* Warminster: Aris & Phillips, 1980.

Attwater, Rachel. *Adam Schall: A Jesuit at the Court of China, 1592–1666.* London: Geoffrey Chapman, 1963.

St Augustine (trans. H. Chadwick). *Confessions.* Oxford: Oxford University Press, 1992.

Aziz, Barbara Nimri and Matthew Kapstein (eds.). *Soundings in Tibetan Civilization.* New Delhi: Manohar, 1985.

Bacot, Jacques and Charles Toussaint. *Documents de Touen-Houang— Relatifs à l'Histoire du Tibet.* Paris: Guenther, 1946.

Baker, Ian. *The Dalai Lama's Secret Temple: Tantric Wall Paintings from Tibet.* London: Thames & Hudson, 2000.

Barfield, Thomas J. *The Perilous Frontier: Nomadic Empires and China.* Oxford: Basil Blackwell, 1989.

Batchelor, Stephen. *The Tibet Guide.* London: Wisdom, 1987.

Bechert, Heinz and Richard Gombrich (eds.). *The World of Buddhism: Buddhist Monks and Nuns in Society and Culture.* London: Thames & Hudson, 1984.

Beckwith, Christopher I. *The Tibetan Empire in Central Asia: A History of the Struggle for Great Power among Tibetans, Turks, Arabs and Chinese during the Early Middle Ages.* Princeton: Princeton University Press, 1987.

Beer, Robert. *The Encyclopedia of Tibetan Symbols and Motifs.* London: Serindia, 2003.

Bell, Sir Charles. *Portrait of the Dalai Lama.* London: Collins, 1946.

Benson, Herbert. *Beyond the Relaxation Response: How to Harness the Healing Power of Your Personal Beliefs.* New York: Times Books, 1984.

————. *Your Maximum Mind*. New York: Random House, 1987.

Berzin, Alexander. *Taking the Kalachakra Initiation*. Ithaca, NY: Snow Lion, 1997.

Beyer, Stephan V. *The Cult of Tara: Magic and Ritual in Tibet*. Berkeley: University of California Press, 1973.

Bishop, Peter. *The Myth of Shangri La: Tibet, Travel Writing and the Western Creation of Sacred Landscape*. Berkeley: University of California Press, 1989.

Bkra-sis-rgyal-mtshan, Sar-rdza (trans. and ed. Samten Gyaltsen Karmay). *The Treasury of Good Sayings: A Tibetan History of Bon*. London: Oxford University Press, 1972.

Blunt, Wilfred. *The Golden Road to Samarkand*. London: Hamish Hamilton, 1973.

Bokar, Rinpoché. *Chenrezig: Lord of Love*. San Francisco: Clearpoint Press, 1991.

Boulnois, Luce (trans. Dennis Chamberlin). *The Silk Road*. London: Allen and Unwin, 1966.

Brauen, Martin (trans. Martin Willson). *The Mandala: Sacred Circle in Tibetan Buddhism*. London: Serindia, 1997.

Brauen, Martin (ed.). *The Dalai Lamas: A Visual History*. Zurich and Chicago: Ethnographic Museum of the University of Zurich and Serindia, 2005.

Briggs, George Weston. *Gorakhnath and the Kanphata Yogis*. Calcutta: np., 1938.

Brown, Mick. *The Dance of Seventeen Lives*. London: Bloomsbury, 2004.

Butterfield, Stephen T. *The Double Mirror*. Berkeley: North Atlantic Books, 1994.

Caraman SJ, Philip. *Tibet: The Jesuit Century*. Tiverton: Halsgrove, 1998.

Chandra, Lokesh. *The Thousand-Armed Avalokitesvara*. New Delhi: Abhinav Publications, 1988.

Chattopadhyaya, Alaka. *Atīsha and Tibet: Life and Works of D pamkara Sr jñ na in Relation to the History and Sources of Tibet*. Calcutta: Motilal Banarsidass, 1967.

Ch'en, Kenneth. *Buddhism in China: A Historical Survey.* Princeton: Princeton University Press, 1964.

Chophel, Norbu. *Folk Culture of Tibet.* Dharamsala: Library of Tibetan Works and Archives, 1983.

Chos-'phel, Gendun (trans. Samten Norbu). *The White Annals.* Dharamsala: Library of Tibetan Works and Archives, 1978.

Coleman, Graham (ed.). *A Handbook of Tibetan Culture: A Guide to Tibetan Centers and Resources Throughout the World.* London: Rider, 1993.

Compiling Committee. *A Survey of Tibet.* Lhasa: The Tibet People's Publishing House, 1987.

Conze, Edward. *Perfection of Wisdom in Eight Thousand Lines.* Oxford: Oxford University Press, 1973.

Conze, Edward (trans.). *The Buddha's Law Among the Birds.* Oxford: Bruno Cassirer, 1955.

Cornu, Philippe. *Tibetan Astrology.* Boston: Shambhala, 1997.

Cutler, Howard C. and HH XIV Dalai Lama. *The Art of Happiness.* New York: Riverhead Books, 1998.

Dargyay, Eva M. *The Rise of Esoteric Buddhism in Tibet.* Delhi: Motilal Banarsidass, 1977.

Das, Sarat Chandra (ed. W. W. Rockhill). *Journey to Lhasa and Central Tibet.* London: np., 1904.

David-Neel, Alexandra. *Magic and Mystery in Tibet.* London: Souvenir Press, 1967.

Davidson, Ronald M. *Indian Esoteric Buddhism: A Social History of the Tantric Movement.* New York: Columbia University Press, 2002.

Dawchyuan, Yu and Dr. Jaw Yuanrenn. *Lovesongs of the Sixth Dalai Lama.* Peiping: Accademia Sinica, 1930.

Dawson, Christopher (ed.). *The Mongol Mission: Narratives and Letters of the Franciscan Missionaries in Mongolia and China in the Thirteenth and Fourteenth Centuries.* London: Sheed and Ward, 1955.

Dawson, Raymond (ed.). *The Legacy of China.* Oxford: Clarendon Pre 1964.

De Filippi, Filippo (ed.). *An Account of Tibet, The Travels of Ippolito Desideri of Pistoia, SJ, 1712–1727*. London: G. Routledge, rev. ed., 1937.

de Lubac SJ, Henri (trans. George Lamb). *Aspects of Buddhism*. London: Sheed and Ward, 1953.

Demiéville, Paul. *Le Concile de Lhasa*. Paris: Bibliothèque de L'Institut des Hautes Études Chinoises, 1952.

Dhondup, K. *The Water-Bird and Other Years: A History of the Thirteenth Dalai Lama and After*. New Delhi: Rangwang Publishers, 1986.

———. *The Water-Horse and Other Years: A History of 17th and 18th Century Tibet*. Dharamsala: Library of Tibetan Works and Archives, 1984.

Dorje, Gyurme (ed.). *Tibet Handbook: With Bhutan*. Bath: Footprint, second edn., 1999.

Dorje, Rinjing. *Tales of Uncle Tompa*. New York: Station Hill Arts, 1997.

Douglas, Nik and Meryl White. *Karmapa: The Black Hat Lama of Tibet*. London: Luzac, 1976.

Dowman, Keith. *The Divine Madman*. Middletown, CA: Dawn Horse Press, 1980.

———. *Masters of Mahāmudrā: Songs and Histories of the Eighty-Four Buddhist Siddhas*. Albany, NY: State University of New York Press, 1985.

———. *The Sacred Life of Tibet*. London: Thorsons, 1997.

Dreyfus, Georges B. J. *The Sound of Two Hands Clapping: The Education of a Tibetan Buddhist Monk*. Berkeley: University of California Press, 2002.

Dudjom Rinpoché, Jikdrel Yeshe Dorje. *The Nyingma School of Tibetan Buddhism, Its Fundamentals and History*. Boston: Wisdom, 1991.

Dunne SJ, George H. *Generation of Giants: The Story of the Jesuits in China in the Last Decades of the Ming Dynasty*. Notre Dame, IN: University of Notre Dame Press, 1962.

Eberhard, Wolfram. *Conquerors and Rulers*. Leiden: E. J. Brill, 1970.

Ebrey, Patricia Buckley. *The Cambridge Illustrated History of China*. Cambridge: Cambridge University Press, 1996.

Edwardes, Michael (ed.). *A Life of the Buddha from a Burmese Manuscript*. London: Folio Society, 1959.

Ekvall, Robert B. *The Lama Knows: A Tibetan Legend is Born.* Oxford and New Delhi: IBH Publishing Co., 1979.

―――. *Tents Against the Sky.* London: Gollancz, 1954.

Elisseeff, Vadime (ed.). *The Silk Roads: Highways of Culture and Commerce.* Paris: UNESCO Publishing, 2000.

Ferguson, W. N. *Adventure, Sport and Travel on the Tibetan Steppes.* London: Constable, 1911.

Foltz, Richard C. *Religions of the Silk Road.* New York: St. Martin's Press, 1999.

Forêt, Philippe. *Mapping Chengde: The Qing Landscape Enterprise.* Honolulu: University of Hawaii Press, 2000.

Fox, Edward. *The Hungarian Who Walked to Heaven: Alexander Csoma de Koros.* London: Short Books, 2001.

Francke, Rev. August Hermann. *A History of Western Tibet, One of the Unknown Empires.* London: Partridge, 1906.

Franke, Herbert. *China under Mongol Rule.* Princeton: Princeton University Press, 1981.

French, Patrick. *The Life of Henry Norman.* Privately printed, 1995.

―――. *Tibet, Tibet: A Personal History of a Lost Land.* London: Harper-Collins, 2004.

―――. *Younghusband: The Last Great Imperial Adventurer.* London: HarperCollins, 1994.

Frye, Richard N. *The Heritage of Central Asia: From Antiquity to Turkish Expansion.* Princeton: Markus Viener Publishers, 1996.

Fu, Lo-shu. *A Documentary Chronicle of Sino-Western Relations, 1644–1820.* Tucson, AZ: Rainbow Bridge Book Co., 1966.

Furen, Wang and Wenging, Suo. *Highlights of Tibetan History.* Beijing: New World Press, 1984.

Geoffroy-Schneiter, Bérénice (trans. David Wharry). *Gandhara: The Memory of Afghanistan.* New York: Assouline, 2001.

Gernet, Jacques. *Chine et Christianisme.* Paris: Gallimard, 1982.

―――. *Daily Life in China on the Eve of the Mongol Invasion 1250–1276.* New York: Macmillan, 1962.

————. *Le Monde chinois*. Paris: Librairie Armand Colin, 1972.

Gethin, Rupert. *The Foundations of Buddhism*. Oxford: Oxford University Press, 1998.

Gillman, Ian and Klimkeit, Hans-Joachim. *Christians in Asia before 1500*. Richmond: Curzon, 1999.

Goldstein, Melvyn. *A History of Modern Tibet, 1913–1951: The Demise of the Lamaist State*. Berkeley: University of California Press, 1989.

Goldstein, Mervyn and Cynthia M. Beall. *Nomads of Western Tibet*. Hong Kong: Odyssey, 1990.

Goldstein, Mervyn, William Siebenschuh and Tashi Tsering. *The Struggle for Modern Tibet: The Autobiography of Tashi Tsering*. Armonk, NY: M. E. Sharpe, 1997.

'Gos Lo-tsa-ba Gzon-nu-dpal (trans. George N. Roerich). *The Blue Annals*. Calcutta: Royal Asiatic Society of Bengal, 1949.

Gould, B. J. *The Jewel in the Lotus: Recollections of an Indian Political*. London: Chatto & Windus, 1957.

Grousset, René (trans. Naomi Walford). *The Empire of the Steppes: A History of Central Asia*. New Brunswick, NJ: Rutgers University Press, 1970.

Gyaltsen, Khenpo Könchog. *The Great Kagyu Masters*. Ithaca, NY: Snow Lion, 1990.

Gyaltsen, Sakyapa Sonam. *The Clear Mirror*. Ithaca, NY: Snow Lion, 1996.

Gyatso, Janet. *Apparitions of the Self: The Secret Autobiographies of a Tibetan Visionary*. Princeton: Princeton University Press, 1998.

Gyatso, Lobsang. *Memoirs of a Tibetan Lama*. Ithaca, NY: Snow Lion, 1998.

Haarh, Erik. *The Yar-lun Dynasty: A Study with Particular Regard to the Contribution by Myths and Legends to the History of Ancient Tibet and the Origin and Nature of its Kings*. København: Gad, 1969.

Haig, Sir Wolseley (ed.). *Cambridge History of India*. Vol. 3. Cambridge: Cambridge University Press, 1928.

Hanzhang, Ya (trans. Wang Wenjiong). *The Biographies of the Dalai Lamas*. Beijing: Foreign Languages Press, 1991.

Hanzhang, Ya (trans. Chen Guagsheng and Li Peizhu). *Biographies of the Tibetan Spiritual Leaders Panchen Erdenis.* Beijing: Foreign Languages Press, 1994.

Harrer, Heinrich (trans. Richard Graves). *Seven Years in Tibet.* London: Rupert Hart-Davis, 1953.

Harris, Clare and Tsering Shakya (eds.). *Seeing Lhasa: British Depictions of the Tibetan Capital 1936–1947.* Chicago: Serindia, 2003.

Heller, Amy. *Tibetan Art: Tracing the Development of Spiritual Ideals and Art in Tibet, 600–2000 AD.* Woodbridge: Antique Collectors' Club, 1999.

Hergé. *Tintin in Tibet.* London: Reed International Books, 1962.

Herrmann, Albert. *An Historical Atlas of China.* Chicago: Aldine, new ed. 1966.

HH XIV Dalai Lama. *Ethics for the New Millennium.* New York: Riverhead Books, 1999.

———. *Five Point Peace Plan for Tibet.* Dharamsala: Information Office, Central Tibetan Secretariat, 1987.

———. *Freedom in Exile.* London: Hodder & Stoughton, 1990.

———. *My Land and My People.* London: Weidenfeld & Nicolson, 1962.

Hoffmann, Helmut (trans. Edward Fitzgerald). *The Religions of Tibet.* London: Allen and Unwin, 1961.

Hoffmann, Helmut. *Tibet: A Handbook.* Bloomington: Indiana University Research Institute for Inner Asian Studies, 1975.

Hopkirk, Peter. *Foreign Devils on the Silk Road: The Search for the Lost Cities and Treasures of Chinese Central Asia.* London: John Murray, 1980.

Hosten, H. (ed. and trans.). *A Missionary in Tibet: Letters and Other Papers of Fr. Ippolito Desideri, S. J. (1713–21).* New Delhi: Cosmo Publications, 1998.

Huc, Evariste Régis (trans. Charles de Salis). *Lamas of the Western Heavens.* London: Folio Society, 1982.

Huc, Evariste Régis and Joseph Gabet (trans. William Hazlitt). *Travels in Tartary, Thibet and China 1844–1846.* London: G. Routledge, 1928.

Illion, Theodore. *In Secret Tibet: In Disguise among Lamas, Robbers and Wise Men—A Key to the Mysteries of Tibet.* London: Rider & Co., 1937.

Juliano, Annette L. and Judith A. Lerner. *Monks and Merchants: Silk Road Treasures from Northwest China, Gansu and Ningxia 4th–7th Century.* New York: Harry N. Abrams, 2001.

Jinpa, Thupten. *Self Reality and Reason in Tibetan Philosophy: Tsongkhapa's Quest for the Middle Way.* London, RoutledgeCurzon, 2002.

Kapstein, Matthew T. *The Tibetan Assimilation of Buddhism: Conversion, Contestation and Memory.* Oxford: Oxford University Press, 2000.

Karmay, Samten Gyaltsen. *The Arrow and the Spindle: Studies in History, Myths, Rituals and Beliefs.* Kathmandu, Mandala Book Point, 1998.

———. *The Great Perfection: A Philosophical and Meditative Teaching in Tibetan Buddhism.* Leiden: E. J. Brill, 1988.

———. *Secret Visions of the Fifth Dalai Lama: The Gold Manuscript in the Fournier Collection.* London: Serindia, 1988.

Khedrup, Tashi. *Tibetan Fighting Monk.* Bangkok: Orchid Press Books, 1988.

Kingdon-Ward, Frank (ed. John Whitehead). *Himalayan Enchantment: An Anthology.* London: Serindia, 1990.

Kircher SJ, Athanasius. *China Illustrata.* Bloomington: Indiana University Press, 1987.

Klafkowski, Piotr (trans.). *The Secret Deliverance of the Sixth Dalai Lama: As Narrated by Dharmatala.* Vienna: Arbeitskreis für Tibetische und Buddhistische Studien Universität Wien, 1979.

Kolmăs, Josef. *Tibet and Imperial China: A Survey of Sino-Tibetan Relations up to the End of the Manchu Dynasty in 1912.* Canberra: Center of Oriental Studies Australian National University, 1967.

Kozlov, Petr Kuz'mich. *Tibet I Dalai-Lama.* St. Petersburg: np., 1920.

Kunsang, Erik Pema. *Yeshe Tsogal, The Lotus Born.* Boston: Shambhala, 1993.

Kvaerne, Per. *The Bon Religion of Tibet.* Boston: Shambhala, 1995.

Kvaerne, Per. *Tibetan Studies: Proceedings of the 6th Seminar of the International Association for Tibetan Studies, Fagernes, 1992.* Oslo: Institute for Comparative Research in Human Culture, 1994.

Larsen, Knud and Amund Sinding-Larsen. *The Lhasa Atlas: Traditional Tibetan Architecture and Townscape.* London: Serindia, 2001.

Latham, Ronald (trans.). *Travels of Marco Polo.* London: Penguin, 1958.

Lattimore, Owen. *Inner Asian Frontiers of China.* New York: American Geographical Society, 1940.

Lhalungpa, Lobsang P. *The Life of Milarepa.* San Francisco: Far West Editions, 1979.

Li, Chih-ch'ang (trans. Arthur Waley). *The Travels of an Alchemist: The Journey of the Taoist, Ch'ang-ch'un, from China to the Hindukush at the Summons of Chingiz Khan, Recorded by his Disciple, Li Chih-ch'ang.* London: Routledge, 1931.

Li, Tieh-Tseng. *Tibet, Today and Yesterday.* New York: Bookman Associates, 1960.

Linrothe, Rob. *Ruthless Compassion: Wrathful Deities in Early Indo-Tibetan Esoteric Buddhist Art.* London: Serindia, 1999.

Liu, Xinru. *Ancient India and Ancient China: Trade and Religious Exchanges, AD 1–600.* Oxford: Oxford University Press, 1988.

———. *Silk and Religion: An Exploration of Material Life and the Thought of People, AD 600–1200.* Delhi: Oxford University Press, 1996.

Lopez, Donald S. *Prisoners of Shangri-La: Tibetan Buddhism and the West.* Chicago: University of Chicago Press, 1998.

Lopez, Donald S., Jr. (ed.). *Religions of Tibet in Practice.* Princeton: Princeton University Press, 1997.

Loup, Robert. *Martyr in Tibet.* New York: David McKay, 1956.

McCrindle, J. W. *Ancient India as Described in Classical Literature.* London: Archibald Constable, 1901.

McKay, Alex (ed.). *The History of Tibet.* 3 vol. London: Routledge Curzon, 2003.

McKay, Alex. *Tibet and the British Raj: The Frontier Cadre, 1904–1947.* Richmond: Curzon, 1997.

———. *Tibet and Her Neighbors: A History.* London: Edition Hansjörg Meyer, 2003.

Maraini, Fosco (trans. Eric Mosbacher). *Secret Tibet.* London: Hutchinson, 1952.

Markham, C. R. (ed.). *Narratives of the Mission of George Bogle to Tibet and of the Journey of Thomas Manning to Lhasa.* London: Trubner, 1876.

Marrs, Edwin W., Jr. (ed.). *The Letters of Charles and Mary Lamb.* 3 vols. Ithaca, NY: Cornell University Press, 1975.

Mayer, Karl Ernest and Shareen Blair Brysac. *Tournament of Shadows: The Great Game and the Race for Empire in Central Asia.* London: Little, Brown, 1999.

Mehra, Parshotam. *Tibetan Polity 1904–37: The Conflict between the 13th Dalai Lama and the 9th Panchen—A Case Study.* Wiesbaden: O. Harrassowitz, 1976.

Mehrotra, Rajiv (ed.). *Understanding the Dalai Lama.* New Delhi: Penguin/Viking, 2004).

Mengele, Irmgard. *dGe-'dun-chos-'phel—A Biography of the 20th Century Tibetan Scholar.* Dharamsala: Library of Tibetan Works and Archives, 1999.

Meyer, Fernand and Gyurme Dorje (eds.). *Tibetan Medical Paintings: Illustrations to the Blue Beryl Treatise of Sangye Gyamtso (1653–1705).* London: Serindia, 1992.

Michael, Franz H. *Rule by Incarnation: Tibetan Buddhism and its Role in Society and State.* Boulder, CO: Westview, 1982.

Millward, James A., Ruth W. Dunnell, Mark C. Elliott and Philippe Forêt (eds.). *New Qing Imperial History: The Making of Inner Asian Empire at Qing Chengde.* London: RoutledgeCurzon, 2004.

Morgan, David. *The Mongols.* Oxford: Basil Blackwell, 1986.

Morris, James. *Farewell the Trumpets: An Imperial Retreat.* London: Faber and Faber, 1978.

Morris, Jan. *Conundrum.* London: Faber, 1974.

Moses, Larry William. *The Political Role of Mongol Buddhism*. Bloomington: Indiana University Research Institute for Inner Asian Studies, 1977.

Mullin, Glenn H. *The Fourteen Dalai Lamas*. Santa Fe: Clear Light, 2001.

———. *Gems of Wisdom from the Seventh Dalai Lama*. Ithaca, NY: Snow Lion, 1999.

———. *Mystical Verses of a Mad Dalai Lama*. Wheaton, IL: Theosophical Publishing House, 1994.

———. *Path of the Bodhisattva Warrior, Life and Teachings of the Thirteenth Dalai Lama*. Ithaca, NY: Snow Lion, 1988.

———. *Selected Works of the Dalai Lama III*. Ithaca, NY: Snow Lion, 1983.

Namgyal, Acarya Ngawang (trans.). *Two Classic Tibetan Fables*. Dharamsala: Library of Tibetan Works and Archives, 1996.

Nebesky-Wojkowitz, René de. *Oracles and Demons of Tibet: The Cult and Iconography of the Tibetan Protective Deities*. The Hague: Mouton, 1956.

Nebesky-Wojkowitz, René de (trans. Michael Bullock). *Where the Gods are Mountains: Three Years among the People of the Himalayas*. London: Weidenfeld & Nicolson, 1956.

Nikam, N. A. and Richard McKeon (trans. and eds.). *The Edicts of Asoka*. Chicago: Chicago University Press, 1959.

Norbu, Dawa. *China's Tibet Policy*. Richmond: Curzon, 2001.

———. *Khache Phalu's Advice on the Art of Living*. Dharamsala: Library of Tibetan Works and Archives, 1987.

———. *Red Star Over Tibet*. London: Collins, 1974.

———. *Tibet: The Road Ahead*. New Delhi: HarperCollins, 1997.

Norbu, Jamyang. *Illusion and Reality*. Dharamsala: Tibetan Youth Congress, 1989.

Norbu, Namkhai (trans. Adriano Clemente and Andrew Lukianowicz). *Drung, Deu and Bön: Narrations, Symbolic Languages and the Bön Tradition in Ancient Tibet*. Dharamsala: Library of Tibetan Works and Archives, 1995.

Norbu, Namkhai (trans. Maria Simmons). *Journey among the Tibetan Nomads: An Account of a Remote Civilization.* Dharmasala: Library of Tibetan Works and Archives, 1997.

Norbu, Namkhai. *The Necklace of gZi.* Dharamsala: Office of Information and International Relations, 1981.

Norbu, Thubten (trans. Edward Fitzgerald). *Tibet is My Country, As Told to Heinrich Harrar.* London: Hart-Davis, 1960.

Norbu, Thupten Jigme and Colin M. Turnbull. *Tibet: Its History, Religion and People.* London: Chatto & Windus, 1969.

Norman, Henry. *The Peoples and Politics of the Far East: Travels and Studies in the British, French, Spanish and Portuguese Colonies, Siberia, China, Japan, Korea, Siam and Malaya.* London: T. Fisher Unwin, 1895.

Nyima, Choekyi, HH Xth Panchen Lama. *A Poisoned Arrow.* London: TIN, 1997.

Onon, Urgunge (trans.). *Chinggis Khan: The Golden History of the Mongols.* London: Folio Society, 1993.

Paludan, Ann. *Chronicle of the Chinese Emperors: The Reign-by-Reign Record of the Rulers of Imperial China.* London: Thames & Hudson, 1998.

Peacock, John. *The Tibetan Way of Life, Death and Rebirth: An Illustrated Guide to Tibetan Wisdom.* London: Duncan Baird, 2003.

Pearlman, Ellen. *Tibetan Sacred Dance.* Vermont: Inner Traditions, 2002.

Pemba, Lhamo. *Tibetan Proverbs.* Dharamsala: Library of Tibetan Works and Archives, 1996.

Pemba, Tsewang Y. *Young Days in Tibet.* London: Jonathan Cape, 1957.

Petech, Luciano. *Aristocracy and Government in Tibet: 1728–1959.* Rome: Instituto Italiano per il Medio ed Estremo Oriente, 1973.

———. *Central Tibet and the Mongols: The Yüan-Sa-skya Period of Tibetan History.* Rome: Instituto Italiano per il Medio ed Estremo Oriente, 1990.

———. *China and Tibet in the Early XVIIIth Century: History of the Establishment of Chinese Protectorate in Tibet.* Leiden: Brill, 2nd ed., 1972.

————. *The Kingdom of Ladakh: c. 950–1842 AD.* Rome: Instituto Italiano per il Medio ed Estremo Oriente, 1977.

————. *Mediaeval History of Nepal (c. 750–1482).* Rome: Instituto Italiano per il Medio ed Estremo Oriente, 1984.

————. *Selected Papers on Asian History.* Rome: Instituto Italiano per il Medio ed Estremo Oriente, 1988.

Pommaret, Françoise (ed.). Trans. Howard Solverson. *Lhasa in the Seventeenth Century: The Capital of the Dalai Lamas.* Leiden: Brill, 2003.

Powers, John. *Introduction to Tibetan Buddhism.* Ithaca, NY: Snow Lion, 1995.

Rahul, Ram. *The Dalai Lama: The Institution.* New Delhi: Vikas Publishing House, 1995.

————. *The Government and Politics of Tibet.* New Delhi: Vikas Publishing House, 1969.

Rawski, Evelyn Sakakida. *The Last Emperors: A Social History of the Qing Imperial Dynasty.* Berkeley: University of California Press, 1998.

Religion and Culture, Dept of. *The Worship of Shugden.* Dharamsala: Central Tibetan Administration, 1998.

Richardson, Hugh. *Ceremonies of the Lhasa Year.* London: Serindia, 1993.

————. *High Peaks, Pure Earth: Collected Writings on Tibetan History and Culture.* London: Serindia, 1998.

————. *Tibet and its History.* Boulder, CO: Shambhala, rev. ed., 1984.

Rigzin, Tsepak. *Festivals of Tibet.* Dharamsala: Library of Tibetan Works and Archives, 1993.

Rin-Chen-Gru Bu-Ston, Bu-Ston (trans. Eugene Obermiller). *The History of Buddhism in India and Tibet.* Heidelberg: Otto Harrassowitz, 1932.

Rockhill, W. W. *The Dalai Lamas of Lhasa and Their Relations with the Manchu Emperors of China 1644–1908.* Dharamsala: Library of Tibetan Works and Archives, 1998.

Rossabi, Morris. *Central and Inner Asia*. London: Thames & Hudson, 1975.

————. *Khubilai Khan: His Life and Times*. Berkeley: University of California Press, 1988.

Rossabi, Morris (ed.). *China among Equals: The Middle Kingdom and its Neighbors, 10ᵗʰ–14ᵗʰ Centuries*. Berkeley: University of California Press, 1983.

Ruysbroek, Willem von (trans. and ed. Peter Jackson). *The Mission of Friar William of Rubruck: His Journey to the Court of Great Khan Möngke, 1253–1255*. London: Hakluyt Society, 1990.

Samuel, Geoffrey. *Civilized Shamans: Buddhism in Tibetan Societies*. Washington, DC: Smithsonian Institution Press, 1993.

Samuel, Geoffrey, Hamish Grego and Elisabeth Stutchbury (eds.). *Tantra and Popular Religion in Tibet*. New Delhi: International Academy of Indian Culture, 1994.

Schafer, Edward H. *The Golden Peaches of Samarkand: A Study of T'ang Exotics*. Berkeley: University of California Press, 1963.

Sekino, Tadashi. *Summer Palace and Lama Temples in Jehol*. Tokyo: Society for International Relations, 1935.

Shakabpa, Tsepon W. D. *Tibet: A Political History*. New Haven: Yale University Press, 1967.

Shakya, Tsering. *The Dragon in the Land of Snows*. New York: Columbia University Press, 1999.

Shuwen, Yang, Zhang Jiayan, Xu An and Dan Luo. *The Biographical Paintings of 'Phags-pa*. Beijing: New World Press, 1987.

Singer, Jane Casey and Philip Denwood (eds.). *Tibetan Art: Toward a Definition of Style*. London: Laurence King, 1997.

Sinor, Denis (ed.). *The Cambridge History of Early Inner Asia*. Cambridge: Cambridge University Press, 1990.

Skilton, Andrew. *A Concise History of Buddhism*. Birmingham: Windhorse, 1994.

Smith, E. Gene. *Among Tibetan Texts: History and Literature of the Himalayan Plateau*. Boston: Wisdom, 2001.

Smith, Warren W., Jr. *Tibetan Nation: A History of Tibetan Nationalism and Sino-Tibetan Relations*. Boulder, CO: Westview, 1996.

Snellgrove, David. *The Hevajra Tantra: A Critical Study*. Oxford: Oxford University Press, 1959.

———. *Indo-Tibetan Buddhism: Indian Buddhists and their Tibetan Successors*. London: Serindia, 1987.

———. *The Nine Ways of Bon: Excerpts from gZi-brjid*. Oxford: Oxford University Press, 1967.

Snellgrove, David and Hugh Richardson. *A Cultural History of Tibet*. London: Weidenfeld & Nicolson, 1968.

Sogyal Rinpoché. *The Tibetan Book of Living and Dying*. London: Rider Books, 1992.

Sopa, Geshe Lhundub, Roger Jackson and John Newman. *The Wheel of Time: The Kalachakra in Context*. Ithaca, NY: Deer Park Books, 1985.

Spence, Jonathan. *Emperor of China*. New York: Knopf, 1974.

Spence, Jonathan D. *The Memory Palace of Matteo Ricci*. New York: Viking Penguin, 1984.

Stein, R. A. (trans. J. E. Stapleton Driver). *Tibetan Civilization*. London: Faber & Faber, 1972.

Studholme, Alexander. *The Origins of OM MANIPADME HUM: A Study of Kāraṇḍavyūha Sūtra*. Albany, NY: State University of New York Press, 2002.

Su, Wenming (ed.). *Tibet: Today and Yesterday*. Beijing: Beijing Review, 1983.

Tada, Tokan. *The Thirteenth Dalai Lama*. Tokyo: Center for East Asian Cultural Studies, 1965.

Tayé, Jamgön Kontrul Lodrö. *Myriad Worlds: Buddhist Cosmology in Abhidharma, Kālacakra and Dzong-chen*. Ithaca, NY: Snow Lion, 1995.

Temple, Robert. *The Genius of China: 3000 Years of Science, Discovery and Invention*. London: Prion, 1998.

Thomas, Edward J. *The History of Buddhist Thought*. London: Routledge & Kegan Paul, 2nd ed., 1951.

————. *The Perfection of Wisdom*. London: John Murray, 1952.

Thomas, Edward J. (trans. and ed.). *Early Buddhist Scriptures: A Selection*. London: Kegan Paul, Trench, Trubner & Co., 1935.

Thomas, Frederick W. *Tibetan Texts and Documents*, 4 vols. London: Royal Asiatic Society, 1951.

Thondup, Khedroop. *Tibet in Turmoil, 1950–1959*. Tokyo: Nihon Kogyo Shimbun, 1983.

Thurlow, Clifford. *Stories from Beyond the Clouds: An Anthology of Tibetan Folk Tales*. Dharamsala: Library of Tibetan Works and Archives, 1975.

Thurman, Robert. *Inner Revolution*. London: Riverhead Books, 1998.

Trungpa, Chogyam. *Shambhala: The Sacred Path of the Warrior*. Boulder, CO: Shambhala, 1984.

Tsarong, Dundul Namgyal. *In the Service of His Country*. Ithaca, NY: Snow Lion, 2000.

Tucci, Giuseppe. *Opera Minora*. Rome: University of Rome, 1971.

————. *Tibetan Folk Songs from Gyantse and Western Tibet*. Ascona: Artibus Asiae, rev. ed. 1966.

————. *Tibetan Painted Scrolls*. 3 vols. Rome: Libreria dello Stato, 1949.

————. *To Lhasa and Beyond*. Rome: Libreria dello Stato, 1956.

————. *The Tombs of the Tibetan Kings*. Rome: Instituto Italiano per il Medio ed Estremo Oriente, 1950.

Tucci, Giuseppe (trans. Geoffrey Samuel). *The Religions of Tibet*. London: Routledge & Kegan Paul, 1980.

Victoria, Brian. *Zen at War*. New York: Weatherhill, 1997.

Vitali, Roberto. *Early Temples of Central Tibet*. London: Serindia, 1990.

————. *Records of Tho.ling: A Literary and Visual Reconstruction of the "Mother" Monastery in Gu'ge*. Dharamsala: Amnye Machen Institute, 1999.

Waddell, Laurence Austine. *The Buddhism of Tibet or Lamaism.* London: np., 1895.

Wangdu, Khemey Sonam, Sir Basil J. Gould and H. E. Richardson. *Discovery, Recognition and Enthronement of the XIVth Dalai Lama: A Collection of Accounts.* Dharamsala: Library of Tibetan Works and Archives, 2000.

Wangdu, Passang and Hildegard Diemberger (trans.). *dBa'bzhed: The Royal Narrative Concerning the Bringing of the Buddha's Doctrine to Tibet.* Vienna: Verlag der Österreichische Akademie der Wissenschaften, 2000.

Wessels SJ, C. *Early Jesuit Travelers in Central Asia, 1603–1720.* The Hague: Nijhoff, 1924.

Watson, Francis. *A Concise History of India.* London: Thames & Hudson, 1974.

Whitfield, Susan. *Life Along the Silk Road.* London: John Murray, 1999.

———. *The Silk Road: Trade, Travel, War and Faith.* London: British Library, 2004.

Williams, Paul. *Mahayana Buddhism: The Doctrinal Foundation.* London: Routledge, 1989.

———. *Songs of Love, Poems of Sadness: The Erotic Verse of the VIth Dalai Lama.* London: I. B. Tauris, 2004.

Wood, Frances. *The Silk Road: Two Thousand Years in the Heart of Asia.* London: British Library, 2003.

Wrathall, Mark (ed.). *Religion after Metaphysics.* Cambridge: Cambridge University Press, 2003.

Xuanzang (trans. Samuel Beal). *Si-yu-ki: Buddhist Records of the Western World.* London: Trubner, 1884.

Zeitlin, Ida. *Gessar Khan: A Legend of Tibet.* New York: George H. Doran, 1927.

Zürcher, E. *The Buddhist Conquest of China: The Spread and Adaptation of Buddhism in Early Medieval China.* Leiden: Brill, 1972.

Papers and Book Chapters

Ardussi, John and Lawrence Epstein. "The Saintly Madman in Tibet." In James F. Fisher (ed.), *Himalayan Anthropology: The Indo-Tibetan Interface*. 327. The Hague: Mouton, 1978.

Ball, Warwick, "How Far did Buddhism Spread West? Buddhism in the Middle East in Ancient and Medieval Times." *Al-Rafidan, Journal of Western Asiatic Studies*, vol. X, 1989, 1–11.

Beckwith, Christopher I. "The Introduction of Greek Medicine into Tibet in the Seventh and Eighth Centuries." *Journal of the American Oriental Society*, 99.2, 1979, 297–313.

———. "The Plan of the City of Peace." *Acta Orientalia Academia Scientiarum Hung*, tomus XXXVIII (1–2), 1984, 148 and 160.

———. "Tibet and the Early Medieval Florissance in Eurasia: A Preliminary Note on the Economic History of the Tibetan Empire." *Central Asiatic Journal*, 21, 1977, 89–103.

Brown, Peter. "The Rise and Function of the Holy Man in Late Antiquity." *Journal of Roman Studies*, 61, 1971, 80–101.

Dabringhaus, Sabine. "Chinese Emperors and Tibetan Monks: Religion as an Instrument of Rule." *China and her Neighbors, South China and Maritime Asia*, vol. 6, 1997, 119–34.

Dargyay, Eva K. "Srong-btsan sgan-po of Tibet: Bodhisattva and King." In Phyllis Granoff and Shinohara Koichi (eds), *Monks and Magicians: Religious Biographies in Asia*. Oakville, Ontario: Mosaic Press, 1988.

Dhondup, Tsering. "Tibetan Personal Names and their Meanings." *Tibet Foundation Newsletter*, 31, February 2001, 4–5.

Dreyfus, Georges B. J. "The Shugs Idan Affair: History and the Nature of a Quarrel." *Journal of the International Association of Buddhist Studies*, vol. 2, November 1998.

Goleman, Dan. "Universal Responsibility and the Seeds of Empathy." In Rajur Mehrota (ed.), *Understanding the Dalai Lama*.

Goldstein, Melvyn C. "A Study of the *LDAB LDOB*." Paper for Inner Asia Research Project Colloquium of the Far East Institute at the University of Washington.

Grupper, Samuel M. "Manchu Patronage and Tibetan Buddhism during the first half of the Ch'ing Dynasty." *Journal of The Tibet Society.*

Gruschke, Andreas. "The Jonangpa Order: Causes for the downfall, conditions of the survival and current situation of a presumably extinct Tibetan-Buddhist School." Paper presented at the Ninth Seminar of the International Association for Tibetan Studies, Leiden University, 24, June 30, 2000.

Hoffmann, Helmut. "Early and Medieval Tibet." In Denis Sinor (ed.), *The Cambridge History of Early Inner Asia.*

Hunter, Erica C. D. "The Church of the East in Central Asia." *Bulletin of the John Rylands University Library of Manchester*, vol. 78, no. 3, Autumn 1996.

Kapstein, Matthew. "Remarks on the *Mani bKa'-'bum* and the Cult of Avalokitesvara in Tibet." In Ronald Davidson and Steven Goodman (eds.), *Tibetan Buddhism: Reason and Revelation*. Albany, NY: SUNY Press, 1992.

Katz, Nathan. "Contacts between Jewish and Indo-Tibetan Civilizations through the ages: Some Explorations." *Tibet Journal*, 16(4), 1991, 90–109.

Klieger, P. Christiaan. "The Institution of the Dalai Lama as a Symbolic Matrix." *Tibet Journal*, 16(1), 1991, 96–107.

Logan, Pamela. "Tulkus in Tibet." *Harvard Asia Quarterly*, Winter 2004.

Martin, Dan. "Bonpo Canons and Jesuit Cannons: On Sectarian Factors involved in the Ch'en-lung Emperor's Second Goldstream Expedition of 1771–1776 Based Primarily on Some Tibetan Sources." *Tibet Journal*, 15(2), 1990, 3–27.

Orofino, Giacomella. "Apropos of some foreign elements in the Kalacakratantra." *Tibetan Studies*, 1997, 717–24.

Petech, Luciano. "The Disintegration of the Tibetan Kingdom." In Per Kvaerne (ed.), *Tibetan Studies*. Oslo: Institute for Comparative Research in Human Culture, 1994.

———. "Turfan and Tun-Huang in the First Millennium AD: Encounters on the Silk Road." *Orientalia Venetiana IV*, 1992.

Phuntsok, Chabpel Tseten (trans. Tsepak Rigzin). "A Historical Interpretation of the Songs of Tsangyang Gyatso." *Tibet Journal*, vol. 5, no. 3, 1990.

Seyfort-Ruegg, D. S. "The Jo Nan Pas: A School of Buddhist Ontologists According to the GRUB MTHA' SEL GYI ME LON." *Journal of the American Oriental Society*, vol. 83, 1963.

———. "The Preceptor-Donor (YON MCHOD) Relation in Thirteenth-Century Tibetan Society and Polity, its Inner Asian Precursors and Indian Models." in Krasser et al. (eds.), *Tibetan Studies*.

Sheikh, Abdul Ghani. "Tibetan Muslims." *Tibet Journal*, 16(4), 1991, 86–9.

Smith, E. Gene. "Persistent Themes in the Cultural History of Lamaist Polities: Two Attempts at re-writing the Early Life of the Fifth Dalai Lama." (abstract), from the History of Tibet New Resources and Perspectives workshop, St. Antony's College, Oxford, 23, May 4, 1997.

Taylor, Charles. "Closed World Systems." In Mark Wrathall (ed.), *Religion after Metaphysics*.

Topgyal, Tsering. "The *shou* and *fan* of China's Tibet policies." *Tibetan Review*, April 2001, 19–22.

Tsering, Tashi. "*Nag-ron mGon-po rNam-rGyal*: A 19th Century *Khamspa* Warrior, Dharamsala, India." In B. Aziz and M. Kapstein, *Leadership in Tibetan Civilization*.

Uray, Géza. "Tibet's Connections with Nestorianism and Manicheism in the 8th–10th Centuries." In Ernst Steinkeller and Helmut Tauscher (eds.), *Contributions on Tibetan Language, History and Culture. Proceedings of the Csoma de Körös Symposium*. Vienna: Arbeitskreis für Tibetische und Buddhistische Studien, 1983.

van der Kuijp, Leonard W. J. "On the Life and Political Career of Ta'I-si-tu Byang-Chub rGyal mTshan (1302–?1364)." Paper, Seattle.
———. "Ta'I-sit-tu Byang-chub rGyal-mTshan as a Man of Religion." *Fourteenth Century Tibetan Cultural History 1*, paper, University of Washington, 140–9.

Walter, Michael and Christopher I. Beckwith. "Some Indo-European Elements in Early Tibetan Culture." In Helmut Krasser (ed.), *Proceedings of the International Association for Tibetan Studies*. Vienna, 1997.
White, Lynn Jr. "Tibet, India and Malaya as Sources of Western Medieval Technology." *American Historical Review*, vol. 65, issue 3, April 1960, 515–26.
Wylie, Turrell V. "Reincarnation: A Political Innovation in Tibetan Buddhism." In Louis Ligeti (ed.), *Proceedings of the Csoma de Körös Memorial Symposium*. Budapest, 1978.

Yumiko, Ishihama. "On the Dissemination of the Belief in the Dalai Lama as a Manifestation of the Bodhisattva Avalokitesvara." *Acta Asiatica: Bulletin of the Institute of Eastern Culture*, no. 64, 1993.

Index

Tsurphu, 169
Tsybikov, Gombojab, 200
Tucci, Giuseppe, 102

U province, 87, 351
United Nations (UN), 369–70
United States (US), 369–70, 371,
 381, 382
Urgya, 341–2
Urgyen, *see* Padmasambhava
Urgyen Ling, 261, 263

Vajrapani, 66
Victoria, queen of Great Britain,
 335, 346n
Vikramasila, 81, 85
vinaya (canon of monastic
 discipline), 90, 148, 153, 164,
 207, 285
Vishnu the Preserver, 83

Wang Tao-Shih, 431
Wengchen, Princess, 39–40, 41,
 49–50
White, Claude, 336
White Lotus Society, 321
White Lotus sutra, 18
William of Rubruck, 114n
Wu San Quei, 238–40
Wu Zeitan, empress, 56–7
Wutaishan, 342
Wuzong, emperor, 74

Xuanzang, 17, 43
Xuanzong, emperor, 60

Yansin, 293
Yapshi Kung, 361, 362–3
Yarlha Shampo, 34
Yarlung (Pugyal) Dynasty, 44, 78, 79
Yarlung Valley, 197
Yazang, 146
Yeshe Gyaltsen, 307–8
Yeshe Gyatso, Nawang, *see* Dalai
 Lama (Sixth)
Yeshe Ö, 78, 79–83
Yeshe Tsogyal, 95, 225
Yogi of the Burning Ground, 21, 77
Yongzhen, Qing emperor, 295–6
Yonten Gyatso, *see* Dalai Lama
 (Fourth)
Younghusband Francis, 338–41
Yuan Dynasty: collapse, 169, 184;
 decline, 145; replaced by Ming,
 150n, 168; Tibetan rule, 147,
 149, 215

Zanskar, 271
Zémé Rinpoché, 375n
Zhang Zhang script, 35–6
Zhang Zhung, 47
Zhongzong, emperor, 56, 57
Zoroastrianism, 29–30, 31
Zurchen, 221, 222, 224
Zutse, 45